The Institutionalization of the International Criminal Court

Salla Huikuri

The Institutionalization of the International Criminal Court

palgrave
macmillan

Salla Huikuri
University of Helsinki
Helsinki, Finland

ISBN 978-3-030-07064-9 ISBN 978-3-319-95585-8 (eBook)
https://doi.org/10.1007/978-3-319-95585-8

Cover credit: Zen Rial/Getty Images

This Palgrave Macmillan imprint is published by the registered company
Springer Nature Switzerland AG
The registered company address is: Gewerbestrasse 11, 6330 Cham, Switzerland

Dedicated to Ville, Elia, and Amos

Acknowledgements

First and foremost, I am indebted to Kim Lane Scheppele, my doctoral advisor and mentor. I am grateful for having had the possibility to learn from her. Alison Brysk and Henri Vogt pre-examined my dissertation, on which this book builds, and Professor Beth Simmons acted as the opponent at my unforgettable public defense in 2014. I am thankful for their helpful comments. I also feel privileged for having had the opportunity to gain from the advice of John Ikenberry, Andrew Moravcsik, and Robert Keohane. Timo Kivimäki discussed numerous drafts of this project and has been encouraging over the years. Tero Erkkilä pushed me to revise the dissertation into a book and I am very thankful for that.

Over the years, many professors and colleagues have commented on different drafts of this project or helped me in other ways. In particular, I wish to thank Juhana Aunesluoma, Olivier Costa, Tuomas Forsberg, Helen Hartnell, Anne Holli, Mareike Kleine, Juri Mykkänen, Kari Möttölä, Hanna Ojanen, Heikki Patomäki, Antti Ripatti, Brad Simpson, Teivo Teivainen, Rainer Tetzlaff, Teija Tiilikainen, and Raimo Väyrynen. I am also thankful for Mariko Kawano, who invited me to the Waseda University School of Law. Professor Wolfgang Danspeckgruber introduced me to many diplomats who work on the ICC, including the Permanent Mission of Liechtenstein to the United Nations. From the Ministry of Foreign Affairs of Finland, I am obliged to Sari Mäkelä, Marja Lehto, and the Embassy of Finland in Tokyo. I also wish to thank all diplomats, NGO workers, parliamentarians, and professors whom I interviewed in Brussels, Helsinki, Hiroshima, Mexico City, New York City, Osaka, and Tokyo.

The research on this book clearly would not have been possible without funding and I am appreciative for the generosity of the Jenny and Antti Wihuri Foundation, the Alfred Kordelin Foundation, the University of Helsinki Ryoichi Sasakawa Young Leaders Fellowship Fund, and the Finnish Cultural Foundation. The ASLA-Fulbright Graduate Grant, a tuition fellowship of Princeton University, and Academy of Finland made my American dream come true and the Tokyo Foundation Sylff Research Abroad Award allowed my stay at the Waseda University in Tokyo. Moreover, travel grants from the Finnish Graduate School in Political Studies, the Chancellor's Fund of the University of Helsinki, and the International Studies Association have enabled me to present papers at international conferences. This book was finalized as part of the Academy of Finland project "Policy Instruments and Global Governance: Concepts and Numbers" (grant number 268181).

My peers at the University of Helsinki and from Princeton University are clearly to be thanked also. As they are quite numerous, I thank them collectively. Some of them have become good friends and I particularly wish to thank Marina Henke, Lotta Lounasmeri, Leena Malkki, Veera Mitzner, Ossi Piironen, Pia Ranna, Maria Svanström, and Hanna Wass. My friends from the outside of the academic world have helped me in their own, wonderful ways. Thank you for everything, Rodrigo Feliciano, Zbyněk Garský, Katja Hepting, Juha Hopia, Kirsi Kouhi, Tiina Laukkonen, Jenny Lindfors, Riikka Rantala, Mari Sairanen, Heidi Seppä, Riikka Tolvanen, and Laura Vehkanen.

Last comes my lovely family. I wish to acknowledge my dear aunts, uncles, godmother, and my cousins, especially Tuomas Ouni. Moreover, I value my sister Suvi Huikuri's backing and friendship. My late father Kauko Huikuri rarely challenged my undertakings, and here I am not saying that all of them were smart, while my mother Sinikka Huikuri tends to advise me quite frequently. Yet, her unconditional care is incomparable—even when I deviate from her advice.

Finalizing this manuscript wouldn't have been possible without the backing of my wonderful and caring husband Ville Erkkilä. Ville and our sweet sons Elia and Amos make me feel loved and happy every day.

In Helsinki on July 22, 2018.

Contents

Abbreviations

A/...	Document of the United Nations General Assembly
ACP	African, Caribbean, and Pacific Group of States
AG	Attorney General
AGO	Attorney General's Office
AHRC	Asian Human Rights Commission
AJIL	American Journal of International Law
AMM	Monitoring Mission
ASEAN	Association of Southeast Asian Nations
ASP	Assembly of States Parties of the International Criminal Court
ASPA	American Service-Members' Protection Act
AU	African Union
BGBl	Bundesgesetzblatt (Federal Law Gazette), Germany
BIA	Bilateral Immunity Agreement
BRD	Bundesrepublik Deutschland (German Federal Republic)
BT	Bundestag (House of Representatives), Germany
BT-Drs	Bundestag Drucksache (Printed Document of the German Bundestag)
BVerfG	Bundesverfassungsgericht (Federal Constitutional Court), Germany
BVerfGE	BVerfG-Entscheidung (Decision of the Federal Constitutional Court)
CAR	Central African Republic
CARICOM	Caribbean Community
CAT	Convention against Torture and Other Cruel, Inhuman or Degrading Treatment or Punishment

CAT/...	Document of the United Nations Committee Against Torture
CEDAW	Convention on the Elimination of All Forms of Discrimination against Women
CIA	Central Intelligence Agency, United States of America
CICC	Coalition for the International Criminal Court
COCIS	Cabinet Oversight Committee on Internal Security
COJUR	EU Council Working Group on Public International Law
COM...	Document of the European Commission
CONFEO	Conference of New Emerging Powers
CRC	Convention on the Rights of the Child
DDR	Deutsche Demokratische Republik (German Democratic Republic)
DFA	Department of Foreign Affairs
DOD	Department of Defense
DPR	Dewan Perwakilan Rakyat (House of Representatives), Indonesia
Draft Code	Draft Code of Offences Against the Peace and Security of Mankind
DRC	Democratic Republic of Congo
E/...	Document of the United Nations Economic and Social Council
EC	European Community
ECHR	European Convention on Human Rights
ECJ	European Court of Justice
EEAS	European External Action Service
EIDHR	European Initiative for Democracy and Human Rights, since 2006 European Instrument for Democracy and Human Rights
ELSAM	Institute for Policy Research and Advocacy, Indonesian Human Rights NGO
EOC	Elements of Crimes
ESDP	European Security and Defence Policy
ESS	European Security Strategy
EU	European Union
G20	Group of Twenty
GA/...	Press Release of the United Nations General Assembly
GDP	Gross Domestic Product
Gestapo	Geheime Staatspolizei (Secret State Police)
GG	Grundgesetz Für Die Bundesrepublik Deutschland (Basic Law of the BRD)
GOI	Government of Indonesia

G.R. ...	Decision of the Supreme Court of the Philippines
H	Hypothesis
H. CON.	Document of the United States Congress
H.R. ...	Document of House of Representatives, United States Congress
HR0...	Resolution of House of Representatives, Congress of the Philippines
HRWG	Human Rights Working Group
ICC	International Criminal Court
ICC-...	Document of the International Criminal Court
ICCPR	International Covenant on Civil and Political Rights
ICESCR	International Covenant on Economic, Social and Cultural Rights
ICG	International Crisis Group
ICICC	Indonesian Civil Society Coalition for the International Criminal Court
ICJ	International Court of Justice
ICMRW	International Convention on Protection of the Rights of All Migrant Workers and Members of Their Families
ICRC	International Committee of the Red Cross
ICTJ	International Center for Transitional Justice
ICTR	International Criminal Tribunal for Rwanda
ICTY	International Criminal Tribunal for the Former Yugoslavia
IKOHI	Ikatan Keluarga Orang Hilang Indonesia (Indonesian Association of Families of the Disappeared)
ILC	International Law Commission
IMF	International Monetary Fund
Imparsial	Indonesian Human Rights Monitor
IMT	International Military Tribunal (Nuremberg)
IMTFE	International Military Tribunal for the Far East (in Tokyo)
INTERFET	International Force for East Timor
IO	International Organization
IR	International Relations
IV	Independent Variable
Komnas-HAM	National Human Rights Commission, Indonesia
KontraS	Komisi Untuk Orang Hilang dan Korban Tindak Kekerasan (Commission for the Disappeared and Victims of Violence), Indonesia
L/...	Press Release of the Preparations Considering the Establishment of the ICC
LCICC	Law on Cooperation with the ICC, Germany
LMS	Like-Minded States

LRA	Lord's Resistance Army
MEP	Member of the European Parliament
MERCOSUR	El Mercado Común del Sur (Common Market of the South)
MFA	Ministry of Foreign Affairs
MLHR	Ministry of Law and Human Rights, Indonesia
NAM	Non-Aligned Movement
NATO	North Atlantic Treaty Organization
NGO	Non-Governmental Organization
NKVD	Народный комиссариат внутренних дел (Law Enforcement Agency of the USSR)
NS	Nazi/nationalsozialistisch (national socialist)
NSA	Non-Surrender Agreement
OAS	Organization of American States
OECD	Organisation for Economic Co-operation and Development
OIC	Organization of Islamic Cooperation
P.S. …	Resolution of the Senate, Congress of the Philippines
P-5	Permanent Members of the United Nations Security Council
PCA	Partnership and Cooperation Agreement
PCICC	Philippine Coalition for the International Criminal Court
PCNICC/…	Document of the Preparatory Commission for the International Criminal Court
PGA	Parliamentarians for Global Action
PH	The Republic of the Philippines
PKI	Partai Komunis Indonesia (Communist Party of Indonesia)
PrepCom	Preparatory Committee on the Establishment of an International Criminal Court
PrepCommission	Preparatory Commission for the International Criminal Court
PRES0…	Press Release of the European Union at the United Nations
RAF	Rote Armee Fraktion
RANHAM	National Action Plan on Human Rights, Indonesia
RPE	Rules of Procedure and Evidence
S. …	Document of the Senate of the United States of America
S/…	Document of the United Nations Security Council
SC/…	Press Release of the United Nations Security Council
SD	Sicherheitsdienst (Security Service)
Sixth Committee	United Nations General Assembly Legal—Sixth Committee
SOFA	Status of Forces Agreement
SS	Schutzstaffel (Protection Squadron)
SS-Oberführer	Senior leader of a SS-division
TAC	Treaty of Amity and Cooperation
TFC	Truth and Friendship Commission

TNI	Tentara Nasional Indonesia (Indonesian National Armed Forces)
TRC	Truth and Reconciliation Commission
UDHR	Universal Declaration of Human Rights
UK	United Kingdom of Great Britain and Northern Ireland
UN	United Nations
UNAMID	African Union/United Nations Hybrid Operation in Darfur
UNCTAD	United Nations Conference on Trade and Development
UNGA	United Nations General Assembly
UNMIBH	United Nations Peacekeeping Mission in Bosnia and Herzegovina
UNSC	United Nations Security Council
UNSTATS	United Nations Statistics Division
UNTAET	United Nations Transitional Administration in East Timor
UNTC	United Nations Treaty Collection
UP	University of The Philippines
UPR	Universal Periodic Review of the United Nations Human Rights Council
USA	United States of America
USAID	United States Agency for International Development
USD	United States Dollar
Waffen-SS	Armed, military division of the SS (see SS)
WTO	World Trade Organization
WWI	First World War
WWII	Second World War

List of Tables

PART I

Understanding the Institutionalization of the ICC

CHAPTER 1

Introduction

This book engages with the International Criminal Court (ICC), one of the most important new institutions of the post-Cold War era. The emergence of the ICC, like almost all international institutions, is a two-act play. The first act occurs mainly in the international arena as states negotiate a treaty that forms the features of a prospective institution and then vote or agree on its adoption. The second act is performed in the domestic realm, where the executive, the legislative, and other domestic stakeholders contemplate whether the respective state should accede to the institution through treaty ratification. Both acts are equally important, because the institution will not materialize without a founding treaty that in most cases requires a certain number of ratifications before the institution can become operational. This book addresses the institutionalization of the ICC from multilateral negotiations on the Rome Statute to state commitment to the ICC through treaty ratification.

With the adoption of the Rome Statute in July 1998, states conclusively codified norms of international criminal law, established a permanent institution to punish the gravest crimes, and eliminated retroactive and selective prosecution of most horrendous atrocities. However, the negotiations on the ICC were not straightforward as international jurisdiction touches delicate issues, such as state sovereignty and territorial integrity. In fact, considering traditional theoretical explanations for international cooperation, the institutionalization of the ICC was quite exceptional. Realist theories of international relations explain the design of international institutions by the preferences of superpowers and

S. Huikuri, *The Institutionalization of the International Criminal Court*,
https://doi.org/10.1007/978-3-319-95585-8_1

institutionalization with hegemonic preponderance or hard power capabilities, which coerce smaller states into cooperation. The ICC flies in the face of such theories for two reasons. First, European countries and not the USA were the *primus motor* behind the ICC and, second, while the USA wanted to secure control over the ICC through the United Nations Security Council (UNSC), European states succeeded in realizing their agenda of an ICC, independent from the direct control of powerful states. Hence, the most powerful state of the system neither initiated nor controlled the establishment of the ICC. While realist theories emphasize hard power capabilities, institutionalist theories explain the emergence of a new institution by states' own or mutual interests that serve as engines of cooperation. However, the ICC does not generate direct benefits and significantly restricts state sovereignty and, therefore, it does not directly respond to such rationalist preferences. From these theoretical perspectives, it is puzzling why the ICC emerged against the will of the USA and why the European Union defied the USA in the case of the ICC.

After the Rome Statute was adopted, a number of states were eager to institutionalize the ICC and the Rome Statute swiftly received the required number of ratifications for the court to become operational. When the ICC was about to materialize in July 2002, the Bush Administration started to challenge its jurisdiction at all levels of foreign policymaking: in the multilateral framework of the United Nations (UN), through bilateral diplomatic relations, and at the national legislative level. A significant part of the ICC's demotion was a global drive for bilateral agreements, aimed at securing immunity for all Americans from the court. The Bush Administration wanted to conclude these agreements with all states and used economic threats and sanctions to coerce its way through. The European Union responded to the US actions by launching a universal campaign in support of the ICC. As a result, third states that contemplated joining the ICC faced two most powerful actors in terms of economic and development aid that exercised pressure in order to realize their respective agendas. During the heyday of the Bush Administration's campaign against the ICC, the ratification rate drastically declined, but after the Obama Administration took over and adopted a friendlier approach to the ICC, the Rome Statute intriguingly received ten new ratifications in less than two years. From these developments follows the second puzzle of this book, namely which factors explain states' desire to ratify the Rome Statute after more than ten years?

The juxtaposition of the Bush Administration and the European Union campaigns on the ICC, the shift in the US policy after Obama took over, and third states' responses to these events create a framework that allows the analysis of the role of external actors and incentives on states' decision to commit to the ICC. Regarding this second act of the emergence of institutions, legal scholars and political scientists have traditionally maintained the ratification of international treaties as a domestic matter and the sovereign right of a nation-state. Accordingly, the ratification of the Rome Statute has so far been explained with domestic preferences, constituted by rational calculations of political players, or common identities, created through a socialization process that results in commitment to common values, such as the ICC. I demonstrate that the accession to international treaties is not solely an endogenous decision of a nation-state but is also influenced by interests and actions of external actors. Accordingly, the process leading to a state's commitment to the ICC proceeds simultaneously at multiple levels, domestic, bilateral, and international ones, and cannot be explained with one single variable.

To summarize, this book addresses two intertwined events: the materialization of the ICC through multilateral negotiations and their aftermath that influenced state commitment to the Rome Statute. It offers an alternative theoretical account for the emergence of international institutions by developing a novel concept of normative binding. Normative binding is a strategy that provides middle powers means to tie down unilateral policies of powerful actors that do not prefer to cooperate. The idea is to promote new multilateral norms and deposit them in institutions, which have the prospect to become binding even on unilateralist actors, if the majority of states adhere to them. Thus, normative binding provides grounds to explicate why international institutions may emerge against the will of powerful states and how norms can become binding on states that reject them.

1.1 Negotiations on the Rome Statute of the International Criminal Court

After the Nuremberg and Tokyo war crimes trials and the adoption of the Genocide Convention, it was not unexpected that in its first meeting the International Law Commission (ILC) of the UN started to consider the "desirability and possibility" of establishing an ICC to try persons accused of genocide and other international crimes (A/RES/260 (III) B 1948).

However, the ILC's work on this topic was disrupted in the year 1954, first because of the failing definition of the crime of aggression and later because of the power politics of the Cold War and the resulting lack of political will to proceed with the matter. The ILC resumed its work on an ICC in the beginning of the 1980s and when Trinidad and Tobago requested the United Nations General Assembly (UNGA) to address the question in 1989 because of drug trafficking and transnational crime, a process that resulted in a permanent ICC was triggered (A/44/195 1989; A/44/770 1989; A/C.6/44/L.18 1989; A/RES/44/39 1989).

In addition to the UNGA's reawakening on the matter of an ICC, the ethno-religious conflict in Bosnia-Herzegovina contributed to the development of international criminal law. Since 1991, the UNSC (UNSC) repeatedly called for the cessation of violations of international humanitarian law in Yugoslavia, imposed sanctions on the Federal Republic of Yugoslavia, and received reports of widespread violations of international humanitarian law. As the calls proved ineffectual, in May 1993 the UNSC, acting under Chapter VII of the UN Charter, established an International Criminal Tribunal for the Former Yugoslavia (ICTY) to prosecute persons responsible for the atrocities and to restore peace (S/RES/827 1993; S/RES/808 1993; S/RES/757 1992; S/RES/713 1991). One year after the creation of the ICTY, uncontrollable violence broke out in Rwanda and the UNSC established another ad hoc court, the International Criminal Tribunal for Rwanda (ICTR) (S/RES/955 1994). The ICTY and the ICTR are *ad hoc* tribunals, because their mandate and personal jurisdiction is limited to a certain territory and a certain period of time. The tribunals are part of the UN organization and all UN member states are obligated to cooperate with them (S/RES/827 1993; S/RES/955 1994).

In the year 1994, the ILC presented a draft proposal for the organization and establishment of procedures for an ICC to the UNGA and two years later it adopted a draft Code of Crimes, which provided legal grounds for the preparation of the Rome Statute (A/RES/47/33 1992; A/49/10 1994; A/51/332 1996). In the meantime, the UNGA established an Ad Hoc Committee in 1995 (A/RES/49/53 1995; A/50/22 1995) that was hoped to provide the basis for an international conference. However, "[d]ebates within the Ad Hoc Committee revealed rather profound differences among states about the complexion of the future court, and some delegations continued to contest the overall feasibility of the project" (Schabas 2007, 16). Thus, negotiations continued in a Preparatory Committee on the establishment of an ICC (PrepCom), which held six sessions during the years 1996 and 1998 (A/RES/50/46 1995; Hall 1998). The Ad Hoc Committee and the PrepCom were well attended: more than one hundred governments, numerous NGOs, and representatives of the UN prepared a draft text for a diplomatic conference, which, in April 1996, it was decided should be held in Rome in 1998. The PrepCom was organized by the UNGA and, unlike with the ICTY and the ICTR, the "permanent members of the Security Council had to get used to dealing on a more equal footing with other countries on the substance of a peace and security issue" (Benedetti and Washburn 1999, 4; A/RES/51/207 1997). Not least because of this, many political issues—including the jurisdiction of the court, the role of the Prosecutor and the UNSC, and the definitions of crimes—remained unsettled when the PrepCom concluded its work in April 1998.

After almost a decade of preparations, the Diplomatic Conference of Plenipotentiaries on the Establishment of an ICC (Rome conference) convened on July 15, 1998, in Rome. In contrast to the founding of the ad hoc trials that relied on the power of the UNSC, the establishment of the ICC was a highly complex diplomatic undertaking from many perspectives. First, the Rome conference was the largest UN codification conference ever held, with participants from 160 states, 17 intergovernmental organizations, 14 UN-agencies and funds, and 124 Non-Governmental Organizations (NGOs). Moreover, the matter at hand, namely what would be the best way to prosecute individuals for grave human rights abuses, was not just politically challenging, but also a complicated legal matter. Lastly, the negotiations in Rome were held in simultaneously organized, formal, and informal working groups that discussed different parts of the Rome Statute. As a result, many small delegations with only few delegates were not able to participate in the drafting of all parts of the treaty (Benedetti and Washburn 1999; Lee 1999, 21). The working groups adopted pieces of the treaty through consensual decisions and forwarded the articles to the Conference's Committee of the Whole, chaired by a Canadian diplomat Kirsch (Schabas 2007, 20).

Despite the complexity of the matter at hand, in terms of coalitions of states the Rome conference was not characterized by a multitude of competing regional and political caucuses, which usually complicate negotiations in the UN framework, but by three main groupings. The biggest and most organized group was the coalition of Like-Minded

States (LMS), which members were committed to negotiate a strong, independent, and effective ICC. According to the LMS, the potency of the ICC would arise from its jurisdiction over all core crimes; it should be autonomous from the UNSC and have an independent Prosecutor. Lastly, its effectiveness should emerge from a universal obligation of states to cooperate with the court and its discretion to decide when it intervenes. The LMS increased its power by expanding the coalition with new member states and by allying with NGOs. The coalition, comprised 60 middle powers and developing countries, was steered among others by Germany, Netherlands, Canada, Australia, Argentina, and South Africa and had all European Union (EU) member states, except France on board (Benedetti and Washburn 1999, 20ff.; Washburn 1999, 368; Schabas 2011, 19).

The permanent members of the UNSC (P-5), without the UK, formed the heaviest counterweight to the LMS. Their core policy was to secure UNSC control over the ICC, which would enable them to veto all undesired actions of the ICC. The P-5 opposed, among others, independent Prosecutor and the ICC's jurisdiction over the crime of aggression. In general,

> Permanent members of the Security Council [...] feared that the proposed court would impede their collective duty to take action to maintain world peace and order. The permanent members' initial vision of the institution was indeed closer to a permanent ad hoc tribunal of the Security Council than to an independent international judicial institution. (Benedetti and Washburn 1999, 18)

The Non-Aligned Movement (NAM) formed the third strongest group. The NAM did not want the UNSC to exercise control over the ICC, but preferred a much weaker court than the LMS (Washburn 1999, 367). It supported the principle of complementarity and emphasized that the ICC should respect state sovereignty. In addition, the NAM wanted to include the crime of aggression in the Rome Statute, which was strongly opposed by the P-5 (CB/MM-Doc.6 1998; A/CONF.183/13 (Vol. II) 1998, 73; Kirsch and Holmes 1999, 4–5). However, during the negotiations, the NAM coalition started to fracture and many states joined either the LMS or regional coalitions (Benedetti and Washburn 1999, 31).

The positions of the caucuses did not significantly change during the negotiations (Schabas 2007, 20). The USA, arguably the sole superpower of the 1990s, participated in the Rome conference with the largest delegation that had the goal to negotiate a "fair and efficient" court, which would accommodate the US national interests (A/CN.4/L.488 1993; Borek 1995; Richardson 1997; United States Delegation 1998). When the conference drew to its close, the majority of the envoys voiced their support for a final package prepared by the Committee of the Whole, but the American delegation opposed it. The USA had unsuccessfully tried to extend the conference and, as a last attempt to hinder the materialization of the ICC, it acted against the prevailing wish to adopt the final package with a consensus and called for non-recorded voting. Quite unprecedented for international negotiations establishing a new institution, the LMS were able to force through their vision of an independent ICC against the will of the most powerful state in the system and the Rome Statute was adopted with 120 votes to 7, with 21 abstentions (A/CONF.183/C.1/SR.42 1998; A/CONF.183/SR.9 1998; Arsanjani 1999, 22–23; Lee 1999, 26).

This was a "diplomatic defeat of epic proportions" (Brown 2000, 66) for the USA, which joined China, Cuba, Iraq, Israel, Yemen, and Qatar in voting against the ICC. The members of the US delegation felt isolated by the LMS, whose leadership was perceived to be exclusive:

> The process launched in the final forty-eight hours of the Rome Conference minimized the chances that these proposals and amendments to the text that the U.S. delegation had submitted in good faith could be seriously considered by delegations. The treaty was subjected to a mysterious, closed-door and exclusionary process of revision by a small number of delegates, mostly from the like-minded group, who cut deals to attract certain wavering governments into supporting a text that was produced at 2:00 A.M. on the final day of the conference. (Scheffer 1999, 20, see also Scheffer 2012, 220)

The goal of the LMS was not to trump the USA: its support was perceived to be crucial and throughout the conference the LMS had made a series of compromises to accommodate US demands (United States Senate 1998, 12, 38). However, the European states did not want to sacrifice the independence of the ICC and therefore left the USA behind (Kinkel 1998; Kaul 1998, 129–30) (Table 1.1).

The main US concerns remained the ICC's potential jurisdiction over its citizens, the powers of the Prosecutor to initiate investigations, and

Table 1.1 Adoption of the Rome Statute, vote

	Like-Minded States (LMS)[a]	*Others*	*Small delegations*[b]
Yes	Andorra, Argentina, Australia, Austria, Belgium, Benin, Bosnia and Herzegovina, Brunei, Bulgaria, Burkina Faso, Burundi, Canada, Chile, Republic of the Congo, Costa Rica, Croatia, Czech Republic, Denmark, Egypt, Estonia, Finland, Gabon, Georgia, Germany, Ghana, Greece, Hungary, Ireland, Italy, Jordan, Latvia, Lesotho, Liechtenstein, Lithuania, Luxembourg, Malawi, Malta, Namibia, Netherlands, New Zealand, Norway, Philippines, Poland, Portugal, Republic of Korea, Romania, Samoa, Senegal, Sierra Leone, Slovakia, Slovenia, Solomon Islands, South Africa, Spain, Swaziland, Sweden, Switzerland, UK, Venezuela, Zambia (60)	Afghanistan, Albania, Angola, Armenia, Azerbaijan, Bangladesh, Belarus, Bolivia, Botswana, Brazil, Cameroon, Colombia, Comoros, (Cuba?), Cyprus, Democratic Republic of Congo, Dominican Republic, Ecuador, El Salvador, France, Guatemala, Guinea, Guinea-Bissau, Haiti, Japan, Kazakhstan, Kenya, Macedonia, Madagascar, Mali, Mauritania, Mozambique, Nicaragua, Niger, Nigeria, Pakistan, Paraguay, Peru, Republic of Moldova, Russia, Rwanda, Sudan, Tanzania, Thailand, Tunisia, Uganda, Ukraine, United Arab Emirates, Uruguay (48)	Bahamas, Barbados, Belize, Cape Verde, Central African Republic, Chad, Djibouti, Dominica, Eritrea, Honduras, Iceland, Jamaica, Kyrgyzstan, Lebanon, Liberia, Mauritius, Monaco, Panama, Saint Lucia, Sao Tome and Principe, Tajikistan, Togo (22)
Abstain[c]	Singapore, Trinidad, and Tobago (2)	Algeria, Bahrain, Ethiopia, India, Indonesia (?), Iran, Kuwait, Libya (?), Mexico, Morocco, Oman, Saudi Arabia, Sri Lanka, Syria, Turkey, Vietnam (16)	Laos, Malaysia, Nepal, Uzbekistan (4)
No[d]		China, Indonesia (?), Iraq, Israel, Cuba, (Libya?) Qatar, USA, Yemen (7)	
Did not participate to the Conference	Antigua and Barbuda, Bhutan, Cambodia, Cook Islands, Democratic People's Republic of Korea, Equatorial Guinea, Fiji, Gambia, Grenada, Guyana, Kiribati, Maldives, Marshall Islands, Micronesia, Mongolia, Montenegro, Myanmar, Nauru, Palau, Papua New Guinea, Saint Kitts and Nevis, Saint Vincent and the Grenadines, Serbia, Seychelles, Somalia, Suriname, Tonga, Turkmenistan, Tuvalu, Vanuatu (30)		

Note 160 states participated to the conference, 120 voted for the adoption of the Rome Statute, 21 abstained, and 7 voted against, meaning that 12 participating states did not participate to the voting. Since the vote was unrecorded, there is no certainty about which states abstained and opposed the adoption. Only China, USA, and Israel announced that they voted against, Mexico declared it did not take part to the vote, and Sri Lanka, Singapore, and Trinidad and Tobago said they abstained in the voting. Accordingly, the table lists 130 votes in favor. For participating states and their delegations to the conference, see A/CONF.183/13 (Vol. II) 1998

[a]Schabas (2011), 18–19; Amnesty International 2003, 17

[b]States that sent one to three delegates to the Rome conference, see A/CONF.183/13 (Vol. II) 1998

[c]Van Schaak (2007), 50

[d]Scheffer (2012), 224; A/CONF.183/13 (Vol. II) 1998, 123, 143–44

the faltering nexus between the UNSC and the ICC. Overall, the USA was not able to control the ICC (Scheffer 1999, 18; Grossman 2002; A/C.6/53/SR.9 1998; A/C.6/59/SR.27 2004). After the inauguration of Bush, the USA started coercing governments into signing Bilateral Immunity Agreements (BIA) that provide formal immunity for all US citizens from the ICC (Bush 2002, 1618). The coercion was economic in nature as states that did not sign into a BIA were threatened with the loss of millions of US-dollars of military and economic aid. As the USA started to carry out its threats, many developing states faced vast economic losses and eventually signed BIAs.

Despite the US opposition, states were eager to join the ICC. The Rome Statute opened for signatures on the day of its adoption, July 17, 1998, and states had the possibility to sign the treaty up to December 31, 2000. During that time, 139 states signed the Rome Statute and by so doing indicated their objective to refrain *bona fide* from acts that would violate the treaty obligations. A signature, however, does not establish legal obligations. To join the ICC, states need to submit an instrument of ratification, signed by the head of state, head of government, or the minister of foreign affairs, to the UN Secretary-General, who is the depositary of the Rome Statute (UN Office of Legal Affairs 2006, 9–10). States that did not sign the Rome Statute can accept, approve, or accede the treaty, which serves the same purpose of becoming bound by a treaty. For the ICC to become operational, the Rome Statute required 60 ratifications. This number was achieved on April 11, 2002, and the ICC launched its operations on July 1, 2002.

1.2 The International Criminal Court

The result of the Rome conference was historical: a treaty establishing a permanent ICC. Conventional human rights treaties and international humanitarian law obligate states to protect and enforce human rights on their own territory and in their activities abroad, however, without prescribing direct sanctions, legal consequences, or personal responsibility. These treaties create obligations and formal "hard law," but since they do not contain enforcement mechanisms, they embody "soft law" characteristics. By contrast, the ICC is provided with enforcement mechanisms, albeit limited ones, and creates hard law (Abbott and Snidal 2000, 421). The Rome Statute establishes a legal framework that imposes individual responsibility for the gravest crimes—genocide, crimes against humanity, war crimes, and the crime of aggression—and by so doing challenges traditional understanding of state sovereignty as the ICC under certain circumstances has supremacy over the national jurisprudence (for an introduction to the ICC, see Schabas 2011).

The main aim of the ICC, as proscribed in the Preamble of the Rome Statute, is to put an end to impunity for the gravest crimes. These offences are erga omnes, concern of the whole world, and they violate ius cogens, the absolute rules of international law (Aust 2010, 10). They are large-scale and systematic crimes, executed with intent, knowledge, and as part of a wider plan or politics. They are international delinquencies, not only because of the scale of their horror, but also because they are usually perpetrated by governments or with their complicity (Mayerfeld 2003, 25; Crawford 2003). The ICC has personal jurisdiction for these crimes and the Rome Statute does not recognize immunities or amnesties, meaning that all persons over the age 18 fall under its jurisdiction regardless of their official capacities or domestic immunities. Furthermore, military commanders are responsible for violations conducted under their command and superior orders do not relieve inferiors from personal responsibility. Such personal jurisdiction has the implication that those individuals who are responsible for the ratification—heads of states and members of governments and parliaments—will also fall under the ICC's jurisdiction.

The ICC has neither retroactive nor universal jurisdiction. In principle, its temporal jurisdiction starts after the entry into force of the Rome Statute in July 2002. In practice, however, the ICC's jurisdiction over its States Parties commences roughly two months after the ratification date.[1] This means that jurisdiction as of July 2002 applies only to states that had joined the ICC by the end of April 2002 and on cases referred by the UNSC. After a state has ratified the Rome Statute, the ICC's jurisdiction covers genocide, crimes against humanity, and war crimes committed in the territory or by citizens of that country. The jurisdiction of the ICC can be triggered by a States Party, the ICC Prosecutor acting on her own initiative, *proprio motu*, a non-States Party recognizing the jurisdiction ad hoc, or by the UNSC. The UNSC also has powers

[1] States joining the ICC have the possibility to opt out from jurisdiction for war crimes for seven years and can ratify amendments on the crime of aggression and of Art. 8 and Art. 124 of the Rome Statute.

to defer prosecutions and investigations of a specific case for one year at a time. However, to refer or defer cases, the UNSC must act under Chapter VII of the UN Charter and determine that the case to be referred or deferred poses a threat to international peace and security. Under the principle of complementarity, one of the central principles of the Rome Statute,[2] the ICC takes over the prosecution only when the state of primary jurisdiction is unable or unwilling to act. It is, however, up to the ICC's Pre-Trial Chamber to decide whether the state in question is unable or unwilling to investigate and/or prosecute the crime in question. The virtue of this principle is that one may expect that states, wanting to avoid the ICC's intervention, will work harder to prosecute and prevent the gravest human rights violations domestically.

When it comes to an investigation, States Parties shall cooperate with, and provide assistance to, the court. Wider obligations are imposed by the UNSC referrals, which (so far) have urged all states and international as well as regional organizations to fully cooperate with the ICC and its Prosecutor (S/RES/1593 2005; S/RES/1970 2011). The Prosecutor's activities are controlled by the Pre-Trial Chamber that issues arrest warrants and summons and decides whether the evidence suffices for a prosecution and whether the case will proceed to trial. During trial, the Trial Chamber shall ensure fair and efficient proceedings and, among other things, determines whether the accused is guilty and decides on appropriate sentences, the maximum sentence being life imprisonment. So far, the ICC has opened investigations in eleven situations. Uganda (referral in 2004), Democratic Republic of Congo (2004), Central African Republic (2005 and 2014), and Mali (2013) are States Parties to the Rome Statute and their governments referred the cases to the ICC. The UNSC has referred two cases, Darfur (2005) and Libya (2011), and the Prosecutor has opened investigations *proprio motu* in Kenya (2010), Côte d'Ivoire (2011), Georgia (2016), and Burundi (2017). Georgia ratified the Rome Statute in 2003, Burundi in 2004, Kenya in 2005, and Côte d'Ivoire in February 2013, but Côte d'Ivoire had accepted the ICC's jurisdiction ad hoc already in 2003. Following the authorization

[2] The Rome Statute also includes, among others, the following central principles of international criminal law: *ne bis in idem* (the prohibition of double jeopardy, Art. 20 of the Rome Statute); *nullum crimen sine lege, nulla poena sine lege* (no crime and no punishment without encoded law at the time of the offence, Art. 22–23 of the Rome Statute); and *aut dedere aut judicare* (either extradite or prosecute, Schabas 2011, 131)

of the ICC Prosecutor to investigate potential state violence against opponents of the ruling party, Burundi withdrew from the Rome Statute (ICC 2017).

The loudest criticism focuses on the ICC's case selection and prosecutorial strategies. The ICC is often accused of being a colonial institution through which European countries dominate and discipline weak African states. Moreover, it is argued that the cases are selected not only by legal criteria and the gravity of each case, but also in consideration of the political interests of powerful actors. For instance, the case of Uganda was first accused of serving the purposes of the Ugandan President and later of stalling the peace process in the country. Furthermore, the decision of the Prosecutor to issue an arrest warrant for Sudan's President Al-Bashir was accused of compromising the peace, security, and humanitarian situation in Darfur. Al-Bashir's indictment also resulted in growing opposition to the ICC among the Arab League and African Union and contributed significantly to the debate about the timing of justice during peace processes (Ainley 2011, 310, 319, 325–26; Schabas 2010, 544–45; Hoile 2010; Roach 2011; Mills 2012; Rodman and Booth 2013). Further points of criticism have been over the ICC's slowness to bring cases to the courtroom, the power of the UNSC to refer and defer its proceedings and decide about the occurrence of the crime of aggression, and the fact that more than half of the world's population remains outside the ICC's jurisdiction—among others the most populous countries, China, India, the USA, Indonesia, and Russia have not joined the ICC. Last, the P-5 powers can paralyze the ICC through the UNSC, if they so wished.

While due to its international mandate, the ICC investigations and Prosecutor will probably always be subject to criticism, the integrity of its chambers has proved to be fairly high. For instance, the Prosecutor's proceedings against Lubanga (DRC) have been stalled twice: first by the Trial Chamber, because the Prosecutor was not able to disclose certain evidence and for a second time by the Appeals Chamber, because the defense brought various challenges to the proceedings. However, Lubanga was the first person to be convicted by the ICC and he was sentenced to 14 years imprisonment for enlisting and using child soldiers (ICC-01/04-01/06 2012). The Prosecutor was also challenged in the Darfur case as the Pre-Trial Chamber first refused to include genocide counts to al-Bashir's arrest warrant because of "an erroneous standard of proof." Nevertheless, after receiving supporting materials, it issued a second arrest warrant, which included genocide charges in addition to five counts of crimes against humanity and two counts of war crimes (ICC-02/05-01/09 2010).

In addition to the abolition of impunity through the jurisdiction of the Rome Statute, the deterrence of future atrocities is often mentioned as one of the most important aspirations behind the establishment of the ICC. The idea is that the threat of legal consequences increases the costs of human rights violations, and governments thus opt for not engaging in such acts. Whereas there is so far no sound evidence in support of the deterrence effect (Rudolph 2001; Akhavan 2001; Gilligan 2006; Roach 2009, 226ff.), the ICC seems to have positive influence on domestic laws. Because of the principle of complementarity, many states have adopted implementing legislations, providing legal grounds for domestic prosecution of the core crimes. As Ainley points out, also the stimulus for domestic proceedings is already evident. When Moreno-Ocampo took office as the first Prosecutor of the ICC, he considered the cases of Colombia and the DRC his main concerns. Instead of inviting Ocampo to launch investigations in the country, Colombia

> reacted to ICC pressure (and pressure from the United States) by establishing the Justice and Peace laws, and has recently claimed impressive results: 'i) around 50,000 demobilized individuals; ii) over 18,000 weapons given up and destroyed; iii) the main leaders of the self-defense groups and their accomplices behind bars awaiting trials; iv) more than 280,000 people recognized and registered as victims; v) more than 36,000 criminal actions, previously unknown, being investigated.' (Ainley 2011, 317)

Such cases highlight the fact that the ICC's authority not only operates in the international domain, but also impacts domestic protection of human rights and responses to atrocities.

1.3 Normative Binding and the Institutionalization of the ICC

Simmons and Danner puzzle about the establishment of the ICC, because "it is not clearly in any given government's interest" (Simmons and Danner 2010, 226). This book points out that the ICC was indeed in the interests of the EU and the puzzling question about its emergence is how was the EU able to realize its agenda against the will of arguably the most powerful state in the system? As the case studies will elaborate, during the negotiations on the Rome Statute, the EU member states made efforts to get their way and when the USA started to challenge the jurisdiction of the ICC the EU launched a global campaign in support of the court. In the year 2001, the EU adopted a common policy on the ICC with the aim

> to support the effective functioning of the Court and to advance universal support for it by promoting the widest possible participation in the Rome Statute. [...] the European Union and its Member States shall make every effort to further this process by raising the issue of the widest possible ratification, acceptance, approval or accession to the Statute and the implementation of the Statute in negotiations or political dialogues with third States, groups of States or relevant regional organisations, whenever appropriate. [...] In furtherance [...] the Union shall cooperate as necessary with other interested States, international institutions, non-governmental organisations and other representatives of civil society. (2003/444/CFSP 2003)

The campaign to promote the ICC in non-EU states constituted an antipode to US policy and encompassed diplomatic *démarches*, issue-linkages through bi- and multilateral agreements on development aid and economic cooperation, and economic support for NGOs, working on the universalization of the ICC.

According to Art. 2 of the Treaty on European Union, the EU "is founded on the values of respect for human dignity, freedom, democracy, equality, the rule of law and respect for human rights [...]." These values and strong emphasis on multilateralism guided the EU's agenda in the negotiations on the Rome Statute and led the European countries into a collision course with the USA. The Bush Administration's efforts against the ICC provide another juncture for normative binding to enter the stage, as it is triggered by unilateral policies of the leading state and power disparity between the leader and other actors. When secondary powers cannot balance the leader with hard power without risking their security or economies, normative binding offers an alternative to check the behavior of the leader. Normative binding means that states initiate new norms and institutions that, once institutionalized, can limit the scope of maneuver of also reluctant states. Moreover, successful institutionalization of norms potentially increases the legitimacy of the norm entrepreneur—the binder—as it succeeds in shaping the standards of international behavior and in offering an alternative multilateral order.

Normative binding presumes that the binder forms a coalition of states in support of institutionalization. When most states accept the validity of new norms and adapt their behavior within the scope of the norms, the norms start shaping state policies in the international domain and eventually become binding also on those who do not officially adapt to them. Institutions are convenient instruments to accommodate desired norms as they have the potential to be perceived as rational, legitimate, and legal. Actors aiming at utilizing normative binding policies need to be perceived as persuasive, legitimate, and credible by others. Lastly, since institutions become binding only if enough states maintain them, normative binding's success depends on the binder's ability to form a supporting coalition. Here, persuasion and issue-linkages are successful tactics to build such coalition. This book demonstrates that the EU employed the strategy of normative binding during the Rome conference and continues to do so with its attempt to universalize the ICC's jurisdiction.

1.4 Ratification of the Rome Statute and the Obama Effect

From a moral point of view, the decision to join the ICC is not particularly puzzling: It is indeed hard to find state representatives of either a ratifying or non-ratifying country, who would openly share the idea that genocidaires should go unpunished. In addition to ending impunity, further contributions of the ICC for international peace and order are as follows. First, it is the first permanent international instance to punish masterminds and material authors behind most horrendous human rights abuses. Second, having established a permanent institution, states now have a financially and politically "cheaper" alternative for addressing grave crimes than the financially more expensive ad hoc courts, which also bear heavier political burden due to their direct connection to the UNSC. Third, the ICC overcomes the problems of selectivity and retroactivity, problems with which ad hoc tribunals inevitably battle. Fourth, due to its specificity, the Rome Statute is a remarkable document that codifies and clarifies international criminal law. Although it is disputable whether the ICC will ever have deterring effect, its contribution to national legislations and prosecutions is significant. Lastly, if the ICC would deter genocide from occurring, or more modestly crimes against humanity or war crimes, then all attempts to strengthen its institution are worthwhile. This is the answer to the "so what?" question regarding the relevance of the ICC: once people's lives are at immediate danger, the financial crisis is not their first priority. Instead, they want to deter the threat. And if crimes are committed, most people desire justice and reparations for victims. This is something the ICC can deliver.

The following aspects are arguably subject to political and legal considerations, when a state contemplates the commitment. First, the ICC has supremacy over national jurisprudence, as it can exercise jurisdiction over the territory and citizens of a State Party. While the principle of complementarity guards national proceedings, it does not provide certainty that the ICC would not interfere. Second, states can neither control the court proceedings nor the Prosecutor and if they refer a case to the ICC, all participating sides of a conflict, including the referring government, fall under its jurisdiction. Lastly, the enforcement of the ICC's mission largely rests on the shoulders of the States Parties, as they are the financers of the court and obligated to cooperate with it. This means that while states have no assurances of their citizens being protected from ICC prosecutions, they must carry the enforcement costs, which, for instance, in the case of arrest warrants can be politically high (Kirsch 2008).

One could presume that despite the costs of ratification, most states support the principles and values of the ICC and join it because the probability of getting prosecuted by the ICC is low. Accordingly, only two types of states have reasons to be worried about the ICC: those that engage in military activities at home or abroad and those, whose likelihood of becoming involved in grave human rights abuses is high. In both cases, an ICC investigation is possible only if the respective state is judicially incapable or unwilling to prosecute the crimes. However, the ICC poses significant limits to state sovereignty, as it can interfere in a state's domestic concerns and prosecute individuals regardless of their official capacity.

Due to the ICC's jurisdiction and powers, one may expect that states' fundamental preferences and policy strategies play a more significant role when they consider joining the ICC than when they ratify human rights treaties, whose unenforceable nature gives them cheap talk characteristics. Considering the principle of *pacta sunt servanda*, the States Parties' obligation to cooperate with the ICC, and the fact that acceding to a treaty is voluntary, the ratification of the Rome Statute is a commitment to cooperation. Although cooperation rarely implies full compliance, one may expect that the commitment and the limits it creates for state behavior are taken seriously (Henkin 1979, 47; Chayes and Chayes 1995, 17ff.). State commitment to the Rome Statute through ratification is crucial for the operation of the ICC both practically and operationally. Practically, the Rome Statute needed 60 ratifications for the ICC to become operational. Operationally, the ICC is not part of the UN organization, which increases its global legitimacy, as it is not directly controlled by the UNSC, but has three consequences. First, the ICC's budget and functioning rely on its States Parties' financial contributions. Second, the ICC depends on state cooperation when it comes to the enforcement of arrest warrants and sentences. Last but not least, the universalization of the ICC's jurisdiction depends on states' adherence to its mandate.

The first years following the adoption of the Rome Statute were the boom time of ratifications as altogether 87 states joined the ICC. Yet, in the year 2003 the ratification rate drastically declined and a record low was reached in 2007 as only Japan joined the ICC. By then, 104 states had joined the ICC. I suggest that the drastic decline in the ratification rate was the result of two developments. First, most countries that had intended joining the ICC had already done so by the year 2005, but, second, the economic coercion exercised by the Bush Administration influenced several states' possibility to ratify the Rome Statute. At the same time, when the USA used an enormous amount of time, diplomatic resources, and money to demote the ICC's jurisdiction, the EU started to invest millions of Euros and political persuasion to win countries for the ICC. Hence, during the years that followed the adoption of the Rome Statute, two powerful actors battled over the institution of the ICC in the international domain. These opposing policies of the USA and the EU between the years 2002 and 2008 created two competing fields of forces that states had to encounter, if they contemplated joining the ICC (Table 1.2).

Curiously, in March 2010, after the Obama Administration had revised the US stance on the ICC from opposition to friendly cooperation, the ratification rate started to increase again. Although the Obama Administration did not intend to ratify the Rome Statute, it encouraged further states to join the ICC (Belczyk 2010). I argue that this positive turn in the US policy—the "Obama effect"—provides a causal mechanism that explains the timing of late ratifications to the Rome Statute. The identification of the Obama effect offers grounds for a theoretical contribution. First, it provides the opportunity to argue that external

Table 1.2 Ratifiers, Signatories, and Non-Signatories to the Rome Statute as of December 31, 2017. **Ratifiers by year** (Italics: Did not sign the Rome Statute, Bold: Withdrawn from the Rome Statute)

Year	*Amount*	*Country*
2016	1	El Salvador
2015	1	State of Palestine
2013	1	Côte d'Ivoire
2012	1	*Guatemala*
2011	6	Cape Verde, *Grenada*, *Maldives*, Philippines, *Tunisia*, *Vanuatu*
2010	4	Bangladesh, Moldova, Saint Lucia, Seychelles
2009	2	Chile, Czech Republic
2008	3	*Cook Islands*, Madagascar, *Suriname*
2007	1	*Japan*
2006	4	Chad, Comoros, *Montenegro*, *Saint Kitts & Nevis*
2005	3	Dominican Republic, Kenya, Mexico,
2004	5	Burkina Faso, **Burundi**, Congo Brazz., Guyana, Liberia
2003	5	*Afghanistan*, Albania, Georgia, Guinea, Lithuania
2002	39	Australia, Barbados, Benin, Bolivia, Bosnia and Herzegovina, Brazil, Bulgaria, Cambodia, Colombia, Cyprus, Democratic Republic of Congo, Djibouti, *East Timor*, Ecuador, Estonia, Gambia, Greece, Honduras, Ireland, Jordan, Latvia, Macedonia, Malawi, Malta, Mauritius, Mongolia, Namibia, Niger, Panama, *Portugal*, Republic of Korea, Romania, *Saint Vincent & the Grenadines*, Samoa, Slovakia, Tanzania, Uganda, Uruguay, Zambia
2001	21	Andorra, Antigua and Barbuda, Argentina, Central African Republic, Costa Rica, Croatia, Denmark, *Dominica*, Hungary, Liechtenstein, Nauru, Netherlands, Nigeria, Paraguay, Peru, Poland, Serbia, Slovenia, Sweden, Switzerland, UK
2000	21	Austria, Belgium, Belize, Botswana, Canada, Finland, France, Gabon, Germany, Iceland, Lesotho, Luxembourg, Mali, Marshall Islands, New Zealand, Norway, Sierra Leone, South Africa, Spain, Tajikistan, Venezuela
1999	6	Fiji, Ghana, Italy, San Marino, Senegal, Trinidad and Tobago
	123	

Signatories

Algeria, Angola, Armenia, Bahamas, Bahrain, Cameroon, Egypt, Eritrea, Guinea-Bissau, Haiti, Iran, Jamaica, Kuwait, Kyrgyzstan, Monaco, Morocco, Mozambique, Oman, Russia, Sao Tome and Principe, Solomon Islands, Sudan,[a] Syria, Thailand, Ukraine, United Arab Emirates, USA,[b] Uzbekistan, Yemen, Zimbabwe (30, with ratifiers 138)

Outsiders

Azerbaijan, Belarus, Bhutan, Brunei, China, Cuba, Demorcatic People's Republic of Korea, Equatorial Guinea, Ethiopia, India, Indonesia, Iraq, Israel, Kazakhstan, Kiribati, Laos, Lebanon, Libya, Malaysia, Mauritania, Micronesia, Myanmar, Nepal, Nicaragua, Pakistan, Palau, Papua New Guinea, Qatar, Rwanda, Saudi Arabia, Singapore, Somalia, Sri Lanka, Swaziland, Togo, Tonga, Turkey, Turkmenistan, Tuvalu, Vietnam (40)

[a]Sudan withdrew its signature on August 26, 2008. UNTC 2018

[b]The G.W. Bush Administration withdrew the US signature on May 6, 2001. UNTC 2018

pressure is an important factor in state commitment to international treaties; an argument that flies in the face of theories emphasizing domestic preferences as the key explanatory variables for the ratification of the Rome Statute. Second, by juxtaposing the negative and positive US policies with the EU's support for the ICC, one can empirically assess whether material—US coercion—or normative—EU persuasion—incentives motivate states to commit to the Rome Statute. Third, the examination of the US pressure on third states allows further evaluation of the concept of normative binding as the EU's response to the US unilateralism. Lastly, such framing permits the evaluation of issue-linkages' effectiveness as a tool to realize normative foreign policy goals.

From this vantage point, the second research question of this book asks: Why do some states join the ICC considerably later than most of its States Parties? So far, the research on state commitment to the ICC has emphasized domestic preferences (Kelley 2007; Neumayer 2009; Simmons and Danner 2010; Chapman and Chaudoin 2013; Goodliffe et al. 2012). I claim that in the case of the stragglers—states that have ratified the Rome Statute more than ten years after its adoption—purely domestic factors do not explain ratification, because the vast majority of ICC States Parties had been able to overcome potential obstacles in the first six years after the adoption of the Rome Statute. Instead, external influence and the timing of ratification are fruitful aspects when trying to identify mechanisms that influence late and non-ratifications.

1.5 Research Design

> [...] social science research is not a purely empirical endeavor. What one finds is contingent upon what one looks for, and what one looks for is to some extent contingent upon what one expects to find. (Gerring 2004, 351)

This book has two consecutive aspirations. First, it aims at constructing a theoretical concept of normative binding to explain the emergence of the ICC and test it with case studies on Germany, the USA, and the EU. Second, by conducting case studies on the Philippines and Indonesia, it examines the claim that exogenous pressure exercised by the EU and the USA on third states affects late ratification decisions. As a by-product of the case studies, the conclusions present a rough categorization of different types of ratifiers deriving from a cross-case analysis. A case study approach is a useful tool to point out that although the decision to join the ICC is based on "complex configurations of events and structures" (Ragin 2004, 125), it can be traced back to foreign policy preferences that are influenced by external actors. This approach also allows the testing of the causal influence of normative binding against alternative explanations and the demonstration of the complexity of the ratification process.

Gerring defines case studies as "*an intensive study of a single unit for the purpose of understanding a larger class of (similar) units*" (Gerring 2004, 342). Accordingly, the distinctive feature of case studies is that by evidencing a covariation in a causal relationship, they aim at generalizing the attributes to a wider set of cases. By providing extensive empirical evidence, they "allow for both a holistic view of the story and a detailed view of events" (Bennett and Elman 2006, 260). In general, case studies are more suitable for identifying causal mechanisms than for calculating generalized causal effects and have two main weaknesses. First, unlike quantitative methods, case studies are not optimal tools for making robust generalizations. Adding more similar cases does not necessarily solve the problem of representativeness as case studies "remain much stronger at assessing *whether* and *how* a variable mattered to the outcome than at assessing *how much* it mattered" (George and Bennett 2005, 25; see also Bennett and Elman 2006, 260). Second, using cross-case studies—comparison of different units—is challenging, because the concepts and causal relationships are not always easily comparable in differing cases. Hence, theory confirmation is not the greatest strength of case studies, but this is not necessarily fatal for the purposes of this book, as its aim is to generate a new context-specific theoretical concept and to evaluate its plausibility and not to seek causal generalizations (Gerring 2004, 348ff.; Goldstein and Keohane 1993, 29).

Due to the weaknesses of the approach, case selection is central. As case studies unavoidably deal with a small-N sample, selection bias poses a problem. To avoid them, both the dependent variable (ratification of the Rome Statute) and the explanatory variable (normative binding) vary as I study states that joined the ICC early (Germany) and late (the Philippines) and have signed but not ratified (the USA) and neither signed nor ratified (Indonesia) the Rome Statute. Although the four cases are contrasting in terms of timing of ratification, they produce matching cases regarding the outcome (two ratifiers and two outliers).

The case selection rests not only on matching, but also on the motivation to have representative cases for cross-case analysis, which potentially generates different types of ratifiers (King et al. 1994, 128ff., 204ff.; George and Bennett 2005, 234ff.).

The method of process-tracing will be used to test the causal implications of normative binding and alternative explanations within the case studies. Process-tracing provides tools for causal inference of the ratification process and allows the identification of the mechanisms influencing the outcome—the ratification decision. As the name of the method connotes, process, "the unfolding of events or situations *over time*" (Collier 2011, 824), is its centerpiece and tracing is conducted through the characterization of key steps or events of the process. Detailed description of events at specific time points allows the analysis of change and sequence. Empirical evidence that describes events in detail is central and, accordingly, deep case knowledge is a prerequisite for a successful analysis of change and causation (Collier 2011, 823–24). Process-tracing is, according to George and Bennett, "an indispensable tool for theory testing and theory development not only because it generates numerous observations within a case, but because these observations must be linked in particular ways to constitute an explanation of the case" (George and Bennett 2005, 207).

However, process-tracing has two main weaknesses. First, successful causal inference requires the demonstration of an uninterrupted causal path that connects the assumed causes to observed effects. Second, because process-tracing requires the consideration of alternative explanations "there may be more than one hypothesized causal mechanism consistent with any given set of process-tracing evidence" (George and Bennett 2005, 222). The elimination of alternative explanations is particularly challenging when human actors are involved in the process. For instance, external influence on the ratification decision, that has traditionally been considered a domestic matter, is a sensitive issue and policymakers might want to conceal the reasons leading to the ratification. While isolating one single causal effect or making generalizations might prove impossible, the exclusion of potential explanatory variables can serve for theory building too (George and Bennett 2005, 207, 218, 222; Bennett 2010, 211).

This book applies four empirical tests of process-tracing that enable causal inference. Hoop tests measure the potentiality and relevance of a hypothesis. Failing the hoop test eliminates the hypothesis and passing the test is a necessary condition for the hypothesis to remain under consideration, but it is not sufficient for confirming a theory. Considering the hypothesis of normative binding, passing a hoop test would, for instance, require evidence from primary sources to confirm that the EU has exercised pressure on third states. Second, passing a smoking gun test strongly corroborates a hypothesis and weakens its rival ones, but it does not provide indisputable evidence. In the case studies on the stragglers, smoking guns would be primary source evidence that the USA or the EU influenced the (non-)ratification decision. Third, doubly decisive tests confirm one hypothesis and eliminate all other explanations. Since such tests are rarely successful in political science, a combination of positive loop and smoking gun tests provide similar leverage. Fourth, the least indecisive evidence is provided by straw-in-the-wind tests. They provide useful information, which however is neither able to confirm a hypothesis nor to reject rival ones. Nevertheless, several straws in the wind may add up to affirmative evidence and combined with a smoking gun they can strongly support one hypothesis (Van Evera 1997, 31–32; Bennett 2010, 210–11; Collier 2011, 826ff.).

The primary sources used in the case studies include official state documents: legislative documents, congressional and parliamentary resolutions, draft resolutions, debates and press releases of the legislative and executive branches, and documents of judicial organs. Moreover, documentation of international institutions, especially the EU, the ICC, and the UN, the Web sites of regional institutions, NGO archives, and WikiLeaks provided a range of primary data. Confidential interviews with diplomats, policymakers, bureaucrats, academics, and NGO workers conducted in Brussels, Helsinki, Hiroshima, Mexico City, New York City, Osaka, and Tokyo provided a great amount of information and clues, which strongly loom in the background. Secondary sources include Web sites of NGOs, local parliamentarians, political parties, international news agencies, and main local English language newspapers for the case studies on the Philippines and Indonesia. While the evidence of primary sources is reliable enough to constitute smoking guns and successful hoop tests, newspaper sources provide mainly "straws-in-the-wind" kind of evidence.

To summarize, the case study approach and the method of process-tracing facilitate the testing of the normative binding argument against a set of alternative explanatory variables. Moreover, systematic study of alternative explanatory variables provides a thorough understanding of processes and sheds light onto a variety of structures, potentially influencing the dependent variable, while simultaneously implying causality. Thus, the case studies try to maximize a multifaceted understanding of events, although their primary purpose is to identify which mechanisms influence the institutionalization of the ICC and states' decision to join it (Bennett and Elman 2006, 255, 264).

1.6 Plan of the Book

This book is composed of three parts. Part I, including this introduction, lays out the empirical and theoretical framework for the book's argument. This introduction, as the book in general, deals mainly with the institutionalization process of the ICC and leaves untouched many events around the ICC, such as the cases in front of the court, the process on the crime of aggression, the 2010 Kampala Review Conference, and critique against the ICC. Chapter 2 starts with an overview of three theoretical explanations (realist, institutionalist, and reflectivist) for the institutionalization of the ICC. The aspiration is not to examine the theories in a particularly critical way, but to outline mainstream theories for which normative binding offers an alternative. It then proceeds to the concept of normative binding, which in the conclusion is compared to the three alternative theories.

Part II asks the question: What explains the creation of the ICC? In this part, I test the normative binding argument with case studies on Germany (Chapter 3), the USA (Chapter 4), and the EU (Chapter 5). I employ process-tracing to create a historical narrative outlining the policy development of these actors toward international criminal law. The cases on Germany and the USA pinpoint key steps in the preference formation process since the First World War, which I take to explain why Germany ended up supporting the ICC despite its exceptionally murderous past and the USA opposing the institution although it initially seemed to be twentieth century's beacon of international justice. These cases also provide an overview of the history of international criminal law and the negotiations on the Rome Statute. Part II closes with Chapter 5 on the EU's policy to the ICC, which shows how the common European policy on the ICC developed as a reaction to the US opposition. By empirically demonstrating that the USA and the EU intentionally pressured smaller states to realize their respective policies vis-à-vis the ICC, Part II establishes the point of departure for Part III.

Part III asks: What explains late ratification of the Rome Statute? The main hypothesis is that exogenous pressure works as the causal mechanism in late-ratifiers decision (not) to join the ICC. Part III starts with Chapter 6 on alternative explanations for state commitment to the ICC. Short studies on the policies of Australia, Czech Republic, East Timor, Japan, Tajikistan, Thailand, and Uganda toward the ICC enrich the theoretical discussion and generate additional explanations for late ratification. Throughout the cases on the Philippines (Chapter 7) and Indonesia (Chapter 8), I test whether the EU has been able to exercise normative binding by inducing late ratifications with issue-linkages or whether economic sanctions posed by the USA and the turn in the US policy, the Obama effect, would explain late ratifications. In these cases, the process-tracing is organized around explanatory variables: Liberal variables emphasize domestic preferences, reflectivist variables social influence, and external influence variables exogenous factors. To avoid confirmation bias and the risk of concepts and causal relationships being easily incomparable across cases, the dependent variable varies (Indonesia is a non-ratifier) and the cases test identical key variables and alternative explanations. The conclusion of the book starts by an evaluation of the strategy of normative binding at the Rome conference. It then reviews the highlights and results of each case study, followed by a short cross-case analysis and a discussion of how to facilitate further participation in the ICC. The book concludes with a discussion on the implications of the ICC for world order.

This book contributes to the research of international relations and international law in the following ways. The concept of normative binding puts forward a novel explanation for the institutionalization of the ICC. While it has not been tested on other institutions and clearly cannot be generalized with one single study, it has potential to elaborate how further international norms can be established against the will of powerful states and how regimes become binding also on those who want to remain outside their influence. Moreover, the study of single states' commitment to the ICC brings into the limelight the fact that the development and expansion of international rules, norms, and institutions is a result of a process that is not simple, but multifaceted, that is not steered by the interests of one actor, but multiple ones, and that, therefore, cannot be easily reduced to one explanatory variable. Accordingly, the process leading to state commitment to the ICC proceeds simultaneously at multiple levels. This has the implication that theories aimed at understanding state commitment to international institutions should take into account not just the interdependence of domestic and international spheres, but also an actor's bilateral interactions.

References

UN documents (references starting with A/... and S/...) available at documents.un.org or unbisnet.un.org.

2003/444/CFSP. 2003. "Council Common Position on the International Criminal Court." Council of the European Union.

Abbott, Kenneth W., and Duncan Snidal. 2000. "Hard and Soft Law in International Governance." *International Organization* 54 (3): 421–56.

Ainley, Kirsten. 2011. "The International Criminal Court on Trial." *Cambridge Review of International Affairs* 24 (3): 309–33.

Akhavan, Payam. 2001. "Beyond Impunity: Can International Criminal Justice Prevent Future Atrocities?" *The American Journal of International Law* 95 (1): 7–31.

Arsanjani, Mahnoush H. 1999. "The Rome Statute of the International Criminal Court." *The American Journal of International Law* 93 (1): 22–43.

Aust, Anthony. 2010. *Handbook of International Law*, 2nd ed. Cambridge: Cambridge University Press.

Belczyk, Jaclyn. 2010. "US War Crimes Ambassador Says US Unlikely to Join ICC in 'Foreseeable Future.'" *Jurist*, January 28.

Benedetti, Fanny, and John L. Washburn. 1999. "Drafting the International Criminal Court Treaty: Two Years to Rome and an Afterword on the Rome Diplomatic Conference." *Global Governance* 5 (1): 1–37.

Bennett, Andrew. 2010. "Process Tracing and Causal Inference." In *Rethinking Social Inquiry: Diverse Tools, Shared Standards*, edited by Henry E. Brady and David Collier, 2nd ed., 207–19. Lanham: Rowman & Littlefield.

Bennett, Andrew, and Colin Elman. 2006. "Complex Causal Relations and Case Study Methods: The Example of Path Dependence." *Political Analysis* 14 (3): 250–67.

Borek, Jamison. 1995. "Statement: Agenda Item 142: Establishment of an International Criminal Court. United Nations General Assembly." USUN Press Release #182. U.S. Department of State.

Brown, Bartram S. 2000. "The Statute of the ICC: From The Hague to Rome and Back Again." In *The United States and the International Criminal Court: National Security and International Law*, edited by Sarah B. Sewall and Carl Kaysen, 61–84. Lanham: Rowman & Littlefield.

Bush, George W. 2002. "Remarks Prior to Discussions with President Alvaro Uribe of Colombia and an Exchange with Reporters." *Weekly Compilation of Presidential Documents* 38 (39): 1618.
CB/MM-Doc.6. 1998. "Draft Declaration on the United Nations Diplomatic Conference of Plenipotentiaries on the Establishment of an International Criminal Court by the Ministerial Meeting of the Coordinating Bureau of the Non-Aligned Movement." NAM.
Chapman, Terrence L., and Stephen Chaudoin. 2013. "Ratification Patterns of the International Criminal Court." *International Studies Quarterly* 57 (2): 400–9.
Chayes, Abram, and Antonia Handler Chayes. 1995. *The New Sovereignty: Compliance with International Regulatory Agreements*. Cambridge: Harvard University Press.
Collier, David. 2011. "Understanding Process Tracing." *PS: Political Science & Politics* 44 (4): 823–30.
Crawford, James. 2003. "The Drafting of the Rome Statute." In *From Nuremberg to The Hague: The Future of International Criminal Justice*, edited by Philippe Sands, 109–56. Cambridge: Cambridge University Press.
George, Alexander L., and Andrew Bennett. 2005. *Case Studies and Theory Development in the Social Sciences*. Cambridge, MA: MIT Press.
Gerring, John. 2004. "What Is a Case Study and What Is It Good For?" *American Political Science Review* 98 (2): 341–54.
Gilligan, Michael J. 2006. "Is Enforcement Necessary for Effectiveness? A Model of the International Criminal Regime." *International Organization* 60 (4): 935–67.
Goldstein, Judith, and Robert O. Keohane. 1993. "Ideas and Foreign Policy: An Analytical Framework." In *Ideas and Foreign Policy: Beliefs, Institutions, and Political Change*, edited by Judith Goldstein and Robert O. Keohane, 3–30. Ithaca: Cornell University Press.
Goodliffe, Jay, Darren Hawkins, Christine Horne, and Daniel L. Nielson. 2012. "Dependence Networks and the International Criminal Court." *International Studies Quarterly* 56 (1): 131–47.
Grossman, Marc. 2002. "American Foreign Policy and the International Criminal Court: Remarks to the Center for Strategic and International Studies." U.S. Department of State.
Hall, Christopher Keith. 1998. "The Sixth Session of the UN Preparatory Committee on the Establishment of an International Criminal Court." *The American Journal of International Law* 92 (3): 548–56.
Henkin, Louis. 1979. *How Nations Behave: Law and Foreign Policy*, 2nd ed. New York: Columbia University Press.
Hoile, David. 2010. *The International Criminal Court: Europe's Guantánamo Bay?* Africa Research Centre.

ICC. 2017. “Situations under Investigation.” https://www.icc-cpi.int/pages/situations.aspx.

ICC-01/04-01/06. 2012. “Situation in the Democratic Republic of Congo in the Case of the Prosecutor v. Thomas Lubanga Dylio. Public Decision on Sentence Pursuant to Article 76 of the Statute”.

ICC-02/05-01/09. 2010. “Situation in Darfur, Sudan in the Case of The Prosecutor v. Omar Hassan Ahmad Al Bashir (‘Omar Al Bashir’). Public Document. Second Warrant of Arrest for Omar Hassan Ahmad Al Bashir”.

Kaul, Hans-Peter. 1998. “Durchbruch in Rom. Der Vertag Über Den Internationalen Strafgerichtshof.” *Vereinte Nationen* 4: 125–30.

Kelley, Judith. 2007. “Who Keeps International Commitments and Why? The International Criminal Court and Bilateral Nonsurrender Agreements.” *American Political Science Review* 101 (3): 573–89.

King, Gary, Robert O. Keohane, and Sidney Verba. 1994. *Designing Social Inquiry: Scientific Inference in Qualitative Research.* Princeton: Princeton University Press.

Kinkel, Klaus. 1998. “Statement on July 17, 1998.” Völkerrechtliche Praxis Der Bundesrepublik Deutschland Im Jahre 1998. Max-Planck-Institut für ausländisches öffentliches Recht und Völkerrecht.

Kirsch, Philippe. 2008. “Introductory Remarks.” In *The International Criminal Court and National Jurisdictions*, edited by Mauro Politi and Federica Gioia. Aldershot: Ashgate.

Kirsch, Philippe, and John T. Holmes. 1999. “The Rome Conference on an International Criminal Court: The Negotiating Process.” *American Journal of International Law* 93 (1): 2–12.

Lee, Roy S. 1999. “Introduction: The Rome Conference and Its Contributions to International Law.” In *The International Criminal Court: The Making of the Rome Statute—Issues, Negotiations, Results*, edited by Roy S. Lee, 1–40. The Hague: Kluwer Law International.

Mayerfeld, Jamie. 2003. “Who Shall Be Judge?: The United States, the International Criminal Court, and the Global Enforcement of Human Rights.” *Human Rights Quarterly* 25 (1): 93–129.

Mills, Kurt. 2012. “‘Bashir Is Dividing Us’: Africa and the International Criminal Court.” *Human Rights Quarterly* 34 (2): 404–47.

Neumayer, Eric. 2009. “New Moral Hazard? Military Intervention, Peacekeeping and Ratification of the International Criminal Court.” *Journal of Peace Research* 46 (5): 659–70.

Ragin, Charles C. 2004. “Turning the Tables: How Case-Oriented Research Challenges Variable-Oriented Research.” In *Rethinking Social Inquiry: Diverse Tools, Shared Standards*, edited by Henry E. Brady and David Collier, 123–38. London: Rowman & Littlefield.

Richardson, Bill. 1997. "Statement Before the Sixth Committee of the 52nd General Assembly, Regarding Agenda Item 150: Establishment of an International Criminal Court." U.S. Department of State.
Roach, Steven C. 2009. "Justice of the Peace? Future Challenges and Prospects for a Cosmopolitan Court." In *Governance, Order, and the International Criminal Court: Between Realpolitik and a Cosmopolitan Court*, edited by Steven C. Roach, 225–34. Oxford: Oxford University Press.
———. 2011. "The Turbulent Politics of the International Criminal Court." *Peace Review: A Journal of Social Justice* 23 (4): 546–51.
Rodman, Kenneth A., and Petie Booth. 2013. "Manipulated Commitments: The International Criminal Court in Uganda." *Human Rights Quarterly* 35 (2): 271–303.
Rudolph, Christopher. 2001. "Constructing an Atrocities of War Regime: The Politics of War Crimes Tribunal." *International Organization* 55 (3): 655–91.
Schabas, William A. 2007. *An Introduction to the International Criminal Court*, 3rd ed. Cambridge: Cambridge University Press.
———. 2010. "Victor's Justice: Selecting 'Situations' at the International Criminal Court." *John Marshall Law Review* 43 (2): 535–52.
———. 2011. *An Introduction to the International Criminal Court*, 4th ed. Cambridge, UK: Cambridge University Press.
Scheffer, David 1999. "The United States and the International Criminal Court." *American Journal of International Law* 93 (1): 12–22.
———. 2012. *All the Missing Souls: A Personal History of the War Crimes Tribunals*. Princeton: Princeton University Press.
Simmons, Beth A., and Allison Danner. 2010. "Credible Commitments and the International Criminal Court." *International Organization* 64 (2): 225–56.
UN Office of Legal Affairs, Treaty Section. 2006. *Treaty Handbook*. United Nations.
United States Delegation. 1998. "Statement: United States Delegation to the Preparatory Committee on the Establishment of an International Criminal Court".
United States Senate. 1998. "Is a U.N. International Criminal Court in the U.S. National Interest? Hearing Before the Subcommittee on International Operations of the Committee on Foreign Relations." S. Hrg. 105–724. Washington, DC: Congress of the United States of America.
Van Evera, Stephen. 1997. *Guide to Methods for Students of Political Science*. Ithaca: Cornell University Press.
Van Schaak, Beth. 2007. "The Establishment of the Permanent International Criminal Court." In An International Symposium, Working Paper, No. 7–40. Santa Clara, CA: Santa Clara University School of Law.
Washburn, John. 1999. "The Negotiation of the Rome Statute for the International Criminal Court and International Lawmaking in the 21st Century." *Pace International Law Review* 11 (2): 361–77.

CHAPTER 2

Theorizing the Institutionalization of the International Criminal Court

2.1 Theoretical Explanations for the International Criminal Court

2.1.1 Defining the ICC

Forums of international cooperation are called international organizations, regimes, and institutions. The study of international organizations refers to the system and functions of formal institutions such as the UN and, hence, rather to agents than structures (Milner 1997, 18). Regime theory introduced a more normative and social approach to the study of institutions. States address issue-areas, such as security or international criminal law, by establishing regimes, which are understood as a set of "implicit or explicit principles, norms, rules, and decision-making procedures around which actors' expectations converge in a given area of international relations" (Krasner 1983, 3). The grade of a regimes' institutionalization depends on states interests for cooperation, their (un)certainty about the costs and benefits of the regime, and whether a regime can create issue-linkages, which further institutionalize cooperation (Keohane and Victor 2011, 8–9; Haggard and Simmons 1987, 493ff.). The ICC could be called as a descendant of the regime of international criminal law. Some of its principles, rules, and norms[1] have existed for

[1] Norms are understood as standards of behavior, principles as purposes that actors are expected to pursue, and rules as specific rights and obligations of actors. Keohane (1984, 57–58).

S. Huikuri, *The Institutionalization of the International Criminal Court*,
https://doi.org/10.1007/978-3-319-95585-8_2

decades, such as the Genocide Convention, and centuries, such as *ius cogens* crimes (Byers 1999, 12–13; Bassiouni 2001, 108ff.), but until the establishment of the ICC, the UN bodies were the only international instances that had some decision-making power when these were violated.

As Simmons and Martin point out, the concept of regimes has provided definitional confusion and therefore the ICC is here referred to as an international institution, a set of rules that govern international behavior: "Institutions are viewed as explicitly normative – they specify what states should do" (Simmons and Martin 2002, 194). Institutionalization refers to the process in which rules, norms, and decision-making processes governing specific issue-areas are developed, adapted, and transformed. As Goldstein et al. put it,

> greater institutionalization implies that institutional rules govern more of the behavior of important actors – more in the sense that behavior previously outside the scope of particular rules is now within that scope or that behavior that was previously regulated is now more deeply regulated. (Goldstein et al. 2000, 387)

By defining core crimes as proscribed acts with legally prescribed consequences, the Rome Statute outlaws unacceptable behavior and provides proceedings in response to the violation of the rules. The grade of the ICC's institutionalization today is high since important actors, such as China, Russia, and the USA, which are not States Parties to the Rome Statute, have accepted its rules and proceedings in the cases of Darfur and Libya.

The ICC is a highly legalized institution as the Rome Statute creates legally binding, formal rules that describe certain acceptable behavior and provides the ICC with powers to implement, interpret, and apply these rules to its States Parties (Abbott et al. 2000, 401). As such, the Rome Statute constitutes hard law, "legally binding obligations that are precise [...] and delegate authority for interpreting and implementing the law" (Abbott and Snidal 2000, 421), which creates significant costs for the ICC States Parties. The costs for participating in the ICC's operation include: loss of state sovereignty—the Rome Statute restricts states' behavior and it has supremacy over national jurisprudence in some cases; domestic implementation of the Rome Statute—often expensive constitutional change and/or amendment of other national laws before ratification; international enforcement of the Rome Statute—there is no assurance that citizens are protected from ICC prosecutions and the costs of international enforcement for member states are high; and negative public image—if the state violates the established rules (Keohane 1984, 258). These costs touch the fundamental areas of what Krasner calls the "trinity of the sovereign state system": exclusive territorial control, non-interference in the internal affairs of the state, and the right to conduct foreign policy according to states' own preferences (Krasner 1993, 142–43). The Rome Statute balances the costs by the principle of complementarity and by giving the UNSC certain powers *vis-à-vis* the ICC (Abbott 1999, 375).

2.1.2 Power and the Emergence of the ICC

The institutionalization of the ICC would be explainable from the realist point of view as result of rational calculations or the exercise of statecraft. In general, realist thinkers do not place their bets on international cooperation as institutions have no real potential to pacify an anarchic system where maintaining and increasing one's hard power is paramount for survival. States decision to cooperate within an ICC would be based on pure self-interests and limited by the worry of others gaining more of the court and the fear of becoming dependent on others or losing state sovereignty (Carr 1939, 80, 102ff.; Morgenthau 1973, 27, 479ff.; Waltz 1979, 105–7). An order that accommodates an ICC would be created either by hegemonic stability or through equilibrium established by the balance of power. The desire for stability and survival is the point of departure for the balance of power that aims not simply at increasing power by combining it with others, but also at balancing unchecked, threatening power (Morgenthau 1973, 167; Haas 1953; Wight 1966; Bull 1977). If weaker states would jump straight into the bandwagon of the strongest one, the result would be global hegemony. Accordingly, in order to survive, they tend to join the weaker side and counterbalance (Morgenthau 1973, 178ff.; Walt 1987, 18–19, 263ff.). Compared to the coercive domination of a hegemon, balance of power can secure the international system without annihilating the plurality of the actors. Hegemonic order, based on the preponderance of one state, is another realist way of explaining international cooperation. With its power, the hegemon creates, controls, and maintains international institutions according to its own interests (Carr 1939; Kindleberger 1986; Krasner 1976; Gilpin 1981).

In contrast to a coercive hegemon, who controls the distribution of benefits in the system, Ikenberry argues that the USA used its power to set the standards and rules of the post-WWII system, which provides benefits for other states too. While such benevolent hegemonies initially base on power asymmetry, the relations are more reciprocal, consensual, and institutionalized and, as such, guarantee for weaker states. Accordingly, incentives to balance the hegemon lower and the system gradually ceases to reflect power asymmetry as the leader operates within common rules and other states participate in the management of the system. The system becomes rule-based and liberal (2001, 28–29, Ikenberry 2002b, 9–10, 2011, 70–75). Although the institutions correspond to the interests of the leader, it must limit its power and keep its commitments. Otherwise, the order would not be legitimate and likelihood to balancing would increase. The incentive for constraining power through binding institutions is that in the long term it is cheaper to secure one's interests through cooperation than through coercion and inducements (Ikenberry 2001, 51, 29). Moreover, once established, it becomes hard to replace institutions: States and other groups need them for their own functioning, and even if new institutions would be more efficient, their establishment costs are higher than the maintenance costs of the existing ones. Thus, thanks to its initial strategic restraint through institutional investment, the US preferences influenced the operation of the post-WWII system long after the zenith of its power (Ikenberry 2001, 72, see also 29, 70–71, 199; Bennett and Elman 2006).

Abbot suggests that the establishment of the ICC could be explained by realist theories with the powerful state's attempt to control the behavior of weaker states and to optimize the costs of potential prosecutions with a permanent institution. Furthermore, once multilateral institutions are established, they provide for stability when power relations start to change (Abbott 1999, 373–74). However, powerful states preference to establish ad hoc courts to prosecute losers of wars explains well the emergence of the international criminal law regime from the realist perspective too. Ad hoc courts provide the possibility to select which cases fall under international jurisdiction and, by so doing, provide room for maneuver for powerful states as they do not need to fear that their own actions would fall under international jurisdiction. Through their selectivity, ad hoc courts best protect states from the interference of external actors into their domestic matters and, thus, safeguard the principles of territorial integrity and state sovereignty Krasner (1999, 20ff.), which are of central importance in the state-centric world of realism and play a significant role in some states' considerations of whether to join the ICC or not.

2.1.3 *Joint Gains as Motivation for the Establishment of the ICC*

Liberal theories would explain the institutionalization of the ICC with states' desire to realize joint gains by developing stable international system. Especially, democracies institute common rules to overcome insecurity and potential conflicts resulting from interdependence, to solve common problems such as impunity for core crimes, and to integrate and facilitate cooperation within institutions like the ICC (Ikenberry 2011, 63–65; Keohane 1984, 50ff.; Keohane and Nye 1977, 8). While states are egoistic and rational actors trying to realize self-interests, they also have coinciding interests that make cooperation reciprocal and advantageous. The decision to build, join, maintain, and evolve the regime of international criminal law is a result of states decision to pursue their own and common interests (Keohane 1983, 150; Martin 1992, 776–77; Keohane 1984).

Hence, the emergence of the ICC bases on states anticipation that it would reduce uncertainty and increase reciprocal benefits of cooperation in three following ways. First, the institutionalization of cooperation within the ICC reduces transaction costs of addressing gravest crimes by providing a permanent court for investigations, negotiations, and prosecutions. Second, the ICC reduces uncertainty by providing more information about the preferences and intentions of others, for instance, regarding on how to proceed when the international community faces grave human rights violations. Third, the ICC increases the credibility of states' commitment to investigate and prosecute core crimes, because the violation of commonly agreed rules would cause reputational costs (Keohane 1984, 88, 100ff.; Hasenclever et al. 1997, 34–36). Once the ICC has been established, it becomes costly for states to abandon it as it is cheaper to evolve existing institutions. In fact, institutions develop without active efforts since changes in power relations, interests, and participating states as well as patterns of interdependence shape their functions. This means that states cannot calculate the exact costs and benefits of alternative solutions, the decision to create regimes at first place is based on anticipations, and the violation of established rules will likely be punished, because states fear precedents. This is how the shadow of the future helps the ICC "to link the future with the present" (Axelrod and Keohane 1985, 234; Keohane 1984, 85, 107; Axelrod 1984, 187–89; Young 1982, 290ff.).

According to Moravcsik's liberal theory, state preferences are paramount in explaining the institutionalization of the ICC. Unlike the realist and most liberal approaches, which assume that state preferences are fixed at the international level, Moravcsik argues that domestic actors and social groups form state preferences, define foreign policy goals, and thus play a central role in whether a state engages in building the ICC. Preferences vary among states, because states do not pursue the same goals and the decision to cooperate is explained by shifts in the domestic, and not in international, realm (Moravcsik 1997, 516–20; Doyle 2005, 464). The decision to cooperate within the ICC comes about through three stages. First, states define their preferences based on their assumptions over possible outcomes of the negotiations on the court. They then engage in multilateral bargaining, because they realize that it is more efficient than unilateral action. The outcome of the negotiations depends on the bargaining power of each state, its alternatives to the agreement, and potential issue-linkages or side payments. Lastly, states decide whether to commit to the ICC or not. Commitment is more likely when mutual gains are high, distributional conflicts moderate, and the future uncertain. Uncertainty about the future expands to the domestic domain as governments may commit to an institution in order to lock-in their policies, meaning that the commitment enforces domestic oppositions and the potential future rulers to follow the desired policies (Moravcsik 1998, 20ff., 63–66, 75–76).

To summarize, liberal approaches explain the institutionalization of the ICC by the rationalist logic of the expected consequences of cooperation (March and Olsen 1998, 949–51). With the ICC, states may expect the following positive consequences, among others, if they decide to cooperate: codification of international criminal law delimits unacceptable behavior, institutionalization improves state cooperation in the field of human rights and reduces the transaction costs of international trials, and these aspects possibly deter future atrocities. Negative consequences of cooperation would include relative loss of state sovereignty regarding jurisdiction over the crimes defined in the Rome Statute and reputational costs, if the participating state defies the rules (Fehl 2004).

2.1.4 ICC as a Result of Socialization

According to Wendt's constructivism, the ICC would be the result of continuous interaction between states, which leads to common expectations of others' behavior in favor of accountability for core crimes, socialization in the sense that a court to address grave human rights violations is needed, and, thus, institutionalization of the ICC. Common identities and ideas create the basis for preference formation. The way actors perceive the situation surrounding an issue-area—for instance, supportive toward cooperation—would explain their interest in creating the ICC. Here, institutions are fairly stable structures of states' interests and identities and cognitive by nature. Those who participate to the ICC believe that it exists and its existence is based on this self-fulfilling belief (Wendt 1999, 113ff., 316, 327–31; Kratochwil and Ruggie 1986, 768; Wendt 1992, 399). However, institutions can be codified in rules and norms and

> [a]s collective knowledge, they are experienced as having an existence "over and above the individuals who happen to embody them at the moment." In this way, institutions come to confront individuals as more or less coercive social facts, but they are still a function of what actors collectively "know". (Wendt 1992, 399)

Thus, identities and institutions presuppose each other.

Accordingly, the institutionalization of the ICC is socialization, because it is a cognitive process of participating actors' identity and interest internalization: It affects the "self" of the actors and not only their behavior (Wendt 1999, 43–44, 229, 309). The difference in would also explain in reflectivist terms why some countries do not support the ICC although they share similar interests with those that join the ICC. For example, the EU and the USA share interests that support liberal values, such as democracy and respect for human rights, but they do not have a common identity that would make them agree on how to achieve these values. One can fairly argue that the European identity is based on multilateralism and the US identity on state sovereignty (Wendt 1999, 231). Accordingly, common interests explain the USA and the EU's support for international trials in general, but their differing identities explain why European countries support the establishment of an independent ICC and the US easily controllable ad hoc courts.

The communicative action approach emphasizes persuasion as a tool of socialization that potentially leads to the institutionalization of norms that constitute the ICC (Habermas 1981, 286–87). While for rational theories preferences at negotiations are fixed and change only outside of the game—mostly at the domestic level—the communicative action theory recognizes that the interests are endogenous to the negotiation process and become the subject of bargaining. Negotiating actors are expected to find justifications for appropriate behavior, to define rules within a regime through persuasion, and arrive at reasoned consensus. Such negotiation style benefits smaller participants, as power is measured not in material strength, but in the most persuasive argument. It also implies risks, because the outcome of the negotiations is open in relation to the interests and identities of the actors (Risse 2000, 6–7, 33; Struett 2008, 137; Deitelhoff 2009, 43–44).

The premise for action here is that actors share constitutive values and want to maintain them, but this common identity does not necessarily imply common preferences. The process of persuasion starts when actors decide to negotiate about a certain issue, such as establishing an ICC, and develop a common understanding of the situation. In the negotiations, they try to find reasons why for instance defining common rules to investigate and prosecute core crimes should be favored. The requirement of legitimacy pushes actors to use norm-based arguments strategically, because the most legitimate argument wins. The legitimation process makes institutions robust in two ways. First, since rules and norms are not imposed from above, but agreed upon by reaching a common understanding, actors are motivated to follow them. Second, compliance is controlled collectively and defection needs acceptable reasons, which makes it more unlikely (Habermas 1981, 99ff.; Risse 2000, 11, 20–23; Schimmelfennig 2001, 62–63). Since international negotiations are often conducted in the public sphere, the likelihood that states engage in persuasion is high. The openness also allows the participation of non-state actors to the discourse and makes identity-related issues relevant (Risse 2000, 23). To summarize, reflectivist theories would explain the emergence of the ICC with socially constructed and commonly shared identities and norms that promote institutionalization of international criminal law (March and Olsen 1998, 952; Wendt 2001, 1024ff.).

2.2 Normative Binding

2.2.1 Normative Binding as a Reaction to the USA's Power After the Cold War

The end of the Cold War left behind a power vacuum in international relations, often called the unipolar moment, which was filled by the preponderance of the USA (Krauthammer 1990; Wohlforth 1999; Ikenberry 2002a; Nye 2002). The relatively non-threatening character of the USA, the benefits flowing from its power, the stability of unipolarity, and the difficulty of balancing in unipolarity have been offered as explanations for why other states did not challenge American power by means of classical balancing (Paul 2005, 48–49; Fortmann, Paul, and Wirtz 2004, 361–62). This lack of balancing attempts and the exceptionalist foreign policy of the USA[2] inspired the development of new models of power and balancing. The concepts of soft[3] and smart power[4] were introduced to the debate on the US power, while civilian[5] and normative[6] power are frequently mentioned while defining the EU. Moreover,

[2] "American exceptionalism has at least three separate elements. First, the United States signs on to international human rights and humanitarian law conventions and treaties and then exempts itself from their provisions by explicit reservation, nonratification, or noncompliance. Second, the United States maintains double standards: judging itself and its friends by more permissive criteria than it does its enemies. Third, the United States denies jurisdiction to human rights law within its own domestic law, insisting on the self-contained authority of its own domestic rights tradition" (Ignatieff 2005, 3; see also Byers and Nolte 2003).

[3] The logic of soft power is "getting others to want the outcomes that you want," (Nye 2004, 5) and it is based on cultural attractiveness, political values and behavior, and legitimate foreign policies.

[4] Smart power addresses the question of how the USA should combine its hard (Weber 1922, 28) and soft power in order to enhance its global role. Using smart power means investing more on global public goods and institutions, with which one can win strong allies and increase influence (Nye 2004, 11; Armitage and Nye 2007; Wilson 2008, 616).

[5] A civilian power is "an actor which uses civilian means for persuasion, to pursue civilian ends, and whose foreign policy-making process is subject to democratic control or public scrutiny" (Smith 2005, 68–69; see also Duchêne 1973; Maull 1990).

[6] Normative power is understood as the "ability to shape conceptions of 'normal'" (Manners 2002, 239). Arguably, the EU has normative power, if it can influence the perception of others about appropriate behavior. Normative power works through the logic of social diffusion, and its exercise takes the form of persuasion, invoking norms, shaping discourse, or showing an example (Diez and Manners 2007, 174; Pace 2007).

Kelley, Pape, and Paul, among others, developed the concept of soft balancing, which is a reaction to American unilateralism with nonmilitary means. Other states aim to "delay, frustrate, and undermine aggressive unilateral U.S. military policies" (Pape 2005, 10; See also Paul 2005, 70–71; Walt 2009, 104) through international institutions, economic statecraft, and diplomatic arrangements. According to this logic, the EU's efforts to strengthen the multilateral order would be strategic moves to increase its influence with respect to the USA and the promotion of the ICC is a good opportunity to profile oneself as an agenda setter (Kelley 2005, 154–55).

Compared to balancing, bandwagoning, and bargaining, binding as a foreign policy strategy term is rather novel. Ikenberry defines institutional binding as a multilateral decision to commit to institutions in order to limit power and to prevent uncertainty and conflict: "The logic of balance is to check power with power; the logic of institutional binding and supranationalism is to restrain power through the establishment of an institutionalized political process supervised by formal-legal authority" (Ikenberry 2001, 43, see also 63ff., Ikenberry 2003b, 14ff., Ikenberry 2011, 183ff.; Fearon 1997, 82). Here, binding is an act that both the preponderant power and secondary states mutually agree on. This is also the weakness of binding, because "Institutions cannot force strong states to behave in certain ways, and when the dominant powers no longer want to be bound, the strategy of binding is not likely to work" (Walt 2005, 148; Ikenberry 2003a, 534; Deudney 2007, 57). However, Walt admits that the establishment of new norms and institutions, such as the ICC, is potentially an effective strategy to circumvent US exceptionalism, because new norms may take root and change the existing practices and normative understandings (Walt 2005, 151; Ikenberry et al. 2009, 21).

Normative binding as understood here is similar to what Ikenberry calls baiting. Weaker states engage in baiting by developing groupings:

> that are designed, at least in part, to lure the dominant state into interaction with – and ultimately conformity with – this regional or functional grouping. The strategy is to develop principles and institutions that establish international standards or best practices that over time will become universal in scope. The leading state may resist the initial establishment of the regional or functional grouping but over time it will find it increasingly difficult to avoid or circumvent that alternative cooperative arrangement. (Ikenberry 2003b, 19)

The difference between baiting and normative binding is that the latter has little to do with fishing-related actions. Normative binding is triggered by unilateral policies of the leading state and power disparity between the leader and other actors. When secondary powers cannot balance in hard power terms without taking high security or economic risks, normative binding allows them to check the behavior of the leader. By resorting to normative binding, states initiate new norms and institutions that, once institutionalized, can limit the scope of maneuver of also reluctant states. Successful institutionalization of norms potentially increases the legitimacy of the norm entrepreneur, the binder, which in the case of the ICC is the EU, as it succeeds in shaping the standards of international behavior and in offering an alternative multilateral order to the existing one.

As already stated above, norms are standards of behavior. They are created by men and their existence depends on their validity, as Kelsen put it: "The norms which normative jurisprudence regards as valid are norms that are ordinarily obeyed or applied" (Kelsen 1945, 170). Accordingly, normative is an adjective describing values or conducts that follow these valid standards of behavior. Validity is central for successful binding, which refers to a way of tying or obliging someone to do something: in the case of normative binding, to obey and apply valid norms. International treaties constituting new institutions usually require a minimum amount of ratifications to become valid and, thus, operational. Moreover, the greater number of states follows a certain norm or rules of an institution, the more difficult it becomes for outliers to ignore them. Accordingly, normative binding presumes that the binder forms a coalition of states in support of the institutionalization of the desired norms. When most states accept the validity of the new institution and adapt their behavior within the scope of it, it starts shaping policies in the international domain and eventually its norms become binding also on those who do not officially adapt to it. In addition to the UNSC referrals of cases to the ICC, an example of such bindingness is the Vienna Convention on the Law of Treaties, which for instance the USA, as will be elaborated in Chapter 4, tends to use to justify its actions regarding treaties—without being party to it. I hypothesize that normative binding is a process that is produced through three mechanisms that presuppose each another. First, the binding potential of international institutions, their rationality, legitimacy, and legality explains why binding works. Second, the legitimacy and credibility of the binder explain who can use binding as an effective foreign policy strategy. Third, successful coalition building explains how binding works.

2.2.2 Rationality, Legitimacy, and Legality of International Institutions

The prospect of international institutions to further cooperation and peaceful conditions explains why binding is a strategy worthy of consideration. The ICC institutionalizes and therefore eases state cooperation on international criminal law and challenges the preceding impunity for core crimes. While international institutions advance multilateralism, their scope can become universal, when actors consider them as rational, legitimate, and legalized. Rationality gives states reasons to bind themselves in an institution in the first place. As liberal theories point out, cooperation within institutions is rational, because binding international agreements set out rules and procedures for problem-solving, decision-making, and communication, thereby linking states together and providing certainty about others' future behavior. This allows long-term calculations as institutions enable interaction between states and create mechanisms to influence other states. Rules may also shape and constrain governmental policies and push states to follow a certain desired direction (Ikenberry 2001, 65ff.). Such rational account represents the practical aspect of binding institutions: Based on self-interested calculations, states stick to the ICC and binding works, because established routines and procedures have the potential to force also reluctant actors to follow them. The concepts of legitimacy and legality, in turn, imply that the rules of an institution ought to be followed for social, normative, and formal reasons.

Legitimacy is a prerequisite for globally binding institutions. The logic here is that when most actors consider an institution legitimate, its authority can also extend onto those who do not participate in it. Legitimacy, however, "is an extremely slippery concept", (Hurrell 2005, 17) and has no absolute value. For Weber, legitimate rule derives from the right of the rule(r) to rule and the willingness of the ruled to be ruled (Weber 1922, 214–15). Weberian legitimacy has deep systemic effects as it shapes the structure of the society through internalization and resulting expectations of behavior (Hurd 2007, 44f.; Buchanan and Keohane 2008, 30; Franck 1990, 17). The most standardized definition of legitimacy today incorporates two aspects. The normative aspect presumes that an institution acts according to common rules and the sociological aspect requires the acceptance of the institution by the society (Franck 1990, 24; see also Beetham 1991, 16–17; Hurrell 2005, 29). However, there are different accounts on what produces legitimacy. According to the rationalist approach, states should have the moral right to invoke rules and people should have normative reasons to follow them (Buchanan and Keohane 2008, 33ff.). For the English School, legitimacy derives from the institution's ability to persuade the actors of an appropriate order or action, in other words, from actors' notion of obligation (Hurrell 2005, 22ff.; Clark 2005, 20ff.). While the two views differ, they agree on that legitimacy does not emerge simply from state consent and compliance or the sheer notion of justice (Buchanan and Keohane 2008, 34). This extends the definition of legitimacy in that normatively an institution becomes legitimate when it has the right to rule and sociologically when it is believed to have the right to rule (Buchanan and Keohane 2008, 25; Hurrell 2005, 18, 20). Accordingly, the Rome Statute is considered of having legitimacy when states have internalized its rules and norms and comply with it even against their interests (Hurd 2007, 45; Hurrell 2005, 16).

Legality lends practical bindingness to specific rules, as they are codified in multilateral treaties, and by so doing provides institutions with powers in their sphere of action. In the absence of coercive power, the grade of legalization of institutions can be measured by the degree of their binding force, precision, and enforcement power. First, binding force means that states are obligated by legal commitments to treaties and the commitment is observed under the rules, procedures, and discourses of the treaty. The degree of obligation varies from hard to soft law, where either the obligation, precision, or enforcement dimension is weakened (Abbott and Snidal 2000, 422). Considering the grade of obligation, the Rome Statute as a multilateral treaty creates a legal obligation for its States Parties to investigate core crimes, or to allow the ICC to do so, and provides for a set of rules, procedures, and discourses to observe the commitment. Second, the grade of precision "implies not just that each rule in the set is unambiguous, but that the rules are related to one another in a noncontradictory way, creating a framework within which case-by-case interpretation can be coherently carried out" (Abbott et al. 2000, 413). While the Rome Statute provides for a coherent set of rules and procedures, its precision is contested not least by its opponents, as Parts II and III will elaborate. Third, the enforcement power comprises "the extent to which states and other actors delegate authority to third parties [...] to implement agreements" (Abbott et al. 2000, 415). The Judges of the ICC have the authority to interpret and apply the Rome Statute, and, hence, the degree of delegation is high although the enforcement remains in the hands of the ICC States Parties. To conclude, as Abbott et al. point out, hard or customary law can be created from soft law (Abbott et al. 2000, 412). This is a powerful virtue of international law and a persuasive argument in favor of normative binding, which success to institutionalize new global norms is observable in the long run, when actors start adapting their behavior to the desired rule.

2.2.3 The Binder: Legitimacy and Credibility as Sources of Influence

As Henkin pointed out almost 40 years ago, hard power does not automatically translate into law in multilateral negotiations (Henkin 1979, 34). This is the point of departure for explaining what kinds of actors—I call those attempting to employ normative binding as "binders"—can successfully respond to unilateral politics with normative binding. The aim here is neither to examine power per se nor to create yet another concept of power, but to formulate a strategy, with which the unilateralism of powerful actors can be restricted. Subsequently, power is understood as a relational concept (Baldwin 1985, 20) and the central question is what can be achieved with what kind of statecraft in a specific setting. Baldwin's definition of political power helps to understand the role of power in normative binding: "political power is multidimensional and political power resources are low in fungibility, more power in one policy-contingency framework may mean less in another" (Baldwin 1989, 145). This challenges the traditional division of states into great, middle, and small powers and instead helps to concentrate on the issue-area where influence is at work, here the domain of international law and human rights (Baldwin 1989, 135, 166).

In order to promote a normative order, the binder needs to be persuasive, that is, able to convince others of the alternative she offers. An extreme form a communicative action process would offer any actor, regardless of her attributes, the possibility to convince others of her alternative, if her argument is persuasive enough. However, legitimacy and credibility significantly ease the binder's ability to convince others of her alternative (Schimmelfennig 2001, 63–64; Hurrell 2005, 16). For a binder to have legitimacy in the international sphere, three conditions should be met. First, political legitimacy requires that the exercise of power follows established rules and is morally justified (Buchanan 2004, 233–34; Beetham 1991, 16; Clark 2005, 227). Second, legitimacy reveals itself through the beliefs and calculations of other states. If the beliefs are temporary or purchased rather than internalized, the power is not legitimate and vice versa (Hurrell 2005, 32). Lastly, legitimate power expresses itself through legitimation, "the need to 'bind in' at least the most significant members among the subordinate, [...] so as to establish or reinforce their obligation to a superior authority, and to demonstrate to a wider audience the legitimacy of the powerful" (Beetham 1991, 19). Accordingly, subordinate states' voluntary expression of consent is the third condition of legitimate power, and non-cooperation becomes a sign of delegitimation (Beetham 1991, 20). These two latter manifestations of legitimacy are sociological ones, and hence, legitimacy is revealed through other actors' actions: Whether they commit to the desired rules or not.

Legitimacy is the *sine qua non* of credibility. As the first condition of an actor's legitimacy proposes, credibility presupposes commitment to common rules, and as the second condition points out, "commitment works only if the intended recipient knows of it and believes it. [...] Credibility refers to the correspondent's belief that what is promised or threatened will indeed be carried out" (Schelling 2006, 3). Thus, commitments and the intention to keep one's promises do not automatically translate into reliability and eliminate others' uncertainty (Morrow 1999, 85). As Schelling elaborates, credibility originates from being committed to something, not from becoming committed. Accordingly, credibility is an attribute that cannot be acquired simply through costly commitments, although they do advance it (Schelling 2006, 18–20; Simmons and Danner 2010, 233; Moravcsik 2000, 244). As such, the grade of credibility is harder to measure than legitimacy. However, for a binder credibility is important when it starts persuading reluctant actors, or those thwarted by external influences, to commit to the desired norms. Especially in the latter case where a state faces potential (economic or political) losses as a result of its commitment, as was the case with the US campaign against the ICC, the binder and the alternative he offers must be perceived as credible.

2.2.4 *Strategies of Binding*

Without states' wide acceptance of, and adherence to, their norms, institutions have poor prospects to become globally binding. Accordingly, the success of normative binding depends on state cooperation and a coalition to back the desired institution is needed. The ratification of the Rome Statute and support for the ICC's operation serve here as signals of cooperation. Half of the UN member states ratified the Rome Statute in the first four years following the Rome conference, and in all probability, most of them made a rational choice and realized mutual gains by establishing the ICC (Keohane 1984, 78). Moreover, many deliberately engaged in normative binding, because the US stance toward the ICC was on the record. Accordingly, participation in the normative binding coalition has most likely two purposes: first, to indicate commitment to the ICC's norms and, second, to respond to developments that threaten the multilateral order. For the outlier states, the ICC either generates more costs than benefits or is not of central importance. To motivate these states to commit to the ICC, the attraction of legitimacy is presumably not enough and bargaining is needed. In the bargain over the support for the ICC, coercive tactics, such as economic sanctions, would send a wrong signal about the normativity and legitimacy of the undertaking and therefore the coalition building should be based on positive exogenous pressure, namely persuasion and side payments (Beetham 1991, 43–44).

Regarding persuasion, advocacy networks composed of *inter alia* NGOs, research centers, media, scholars, churches, trade unions, and parliamentarians (Keck and Sikkink 1998, 8ff.), can substantially assist the binder to advance its normative binding agenda in international negotiations and beyond. To realize their common goals, advocacy networks raise international awareness and pressure norm-violating states (Risse and Sikkink 1999, 5). If successful, the pressure leads to the socialization of states and the globalization of new norms. Models emphasizing the role of networks in norm internalization explain socialization with the logic of argumentation. For instance, Struett explains the ratification of the Rome Statute and Deitelhoff the emergence of the ICC with discursive practices, used by the NGOs and like-minded states (Deitelhoff 2009, 43ff.; Struett 2008, 132–33). Finnemore and Sikkink's norm life cycle model starts with norm entrepreneurs; advocate networks that aim at persuading enough states to embrace a certain norm. In the norm emergence phase, domestic entrepreneurship plays a significant role. Once a critical number of states has adopted the norm, it reaches a tipping point. Like-minded states become "norm leaders" that try to socialize other states to follow it. After the tipping point, a norm cascade occurs, as more states start to adopt the norm rapidly and sometimes even without pressure. Optimally, the norm finally becomes internalized and so self-evident that it will not be contested anymore (Finnemore and Sikkink 1998; Risse and Sikkink 1999, 11).

For states that do not respond to persuasion, positive economic sanctions, e.g., trade agreements and development aid (Baldwin 1985, 42, 102), and side payments, e.g., vote trading, reciprocity, concessions, and issue-linkages (Milner 1997, 109–11), might prove to be successful. For binders who challenge the economic coercion of the USA, the use of issue-linkages helps gaining support from states that initially are neither interested or willing to commit to the binding norms. Issue-linkages as "simultaneous discussion of two or more issues for joint settlement" (Poast 2012, 278) have the potential to produce mutually beneficial outcomes when states have differing interests, but want either to resolve conflicts or reach agreements (Koremenos et al. 2001, 785ff.; Sebenius 1983, 314–15; Moravcsik 1998, 65; Davis 2004, 153). Since the assumption here is that states to be convinced are not keen to cooperate with the ICC, the linkages made by binders are expected to be tactical inducements aimed at optimizing the bargaining leverage of the binder through offering an arrangement in return for the commitment to the norm (Haas 1980, 371ff.; McGinnis 1986, 142).

Since domestic actors are expected to carry the costs of the linkage deals, the likelihood of a successful linkage depends on whom the costs are imposed (Moravcsik 1998, 65–66). While some domestic actors will favor and others oppose cooperation with the ICC, the opponents are expected to be louder and the potentiality of the linkage influencing electoral behavior makes issue-linkages easier or more difficult to make (Milner 1997, 16–17, 46, 60–61). The influence of the legislature *vis-à-vis* international cooperation needs to be emphasized here in particular, since in most countries the ratification of international treaties requires legislative approval (Martin 2000, 39, 48). To conclude, issue-linkages are hypothetically the most effective tactic in shaping the preferences of states whose demand for cooperation in the field of international criminal law is not particularly high. This is so especially when states do not simultaneously face political or economic coercion from other actors, as was the case with the US campaign against the ICC, meaning that economic incentives become more appealing under the Obama effect, when the reluctance to join the ICC is not caused by the fear of economic sanctions.

2.3 Conclusions

Institutionalization does not require the exercise of coercive power, as proposed by realist theories. While states undoubtedly share interests when they create new institutions—including information sharing, economic gains, reputation, the establishment of legitimate norms, or multilateralism—they estimate the costs and benefits of institutions based on their specific domestic preferences. Due to policy interdependence, state behavior is also shaped by external actors as is the case with the ICC, where the EU promoted its institutionalization and the USA imposed direct costs on the commitment to the court. Normative binding challenges coercive policies by taking advantage of the binding nature of norms and institutions and aims at constraining unilateralist policies by promoting a multilateral order. Other actors opt for binding institutions, because of their legitimate and durable character, as Ikenberry suggests (Ikenberry 2001), and because they realize mutual gains, as Keohane elaborates (Keohane 1984). Once established and legalized, binding institutions not only substitute hegemonic power, as regime theory suggests, but they also work as tools of influence in international agenda setting.

Like the constructivist socialization process, normative binding does not work overnight, because for norms to become globally binding most states need to observe them. However, for normative binding, institutionalization does not presume the creation of common identities through processes of interaction and internalization. It is enough for states to share preferences, which support binding institutions. While states' adherence to a legitimate institution can be considered socialization, the promotion of international norms can simultaneously serve as a tool to realize self-interests. With the case of normative binding, the self-interest is to uphold a multilateral order based upon state cooperation and binding institutions, which limit the unilateral use of power and increase the influence of secondary states. Accordingly, normative binding by no means rejects the values of the ICC, but binder intentionally tries to realize his own preferences not only for the values sake,

Table 2.1 Emergence of international institutions: Theories and hypotheses

	Realist	*Rationalist*	*Reflectivist*	*Normative binding*
Motivation	In unipolarity and multipolarity: dominance of the powerful In bipolarity: maintenance of stable system	To realize joint gains and to avoid conflicts resulting from interdependence or defection	Shared interests, understandings, and values of states	To protect the multilateral system and institutions by binding the behavior of the unilateralist power with norms and institutions
Initiator	Hegemon or powerful states	Either a powerful state at the zenith of its power or shared interests	No one initiator. Continued interaction or persuasion between states initiates cooperation	Secondary powers, with the help of advocacy networks
Other participants	Do not have choices due to power disparity	Want to reduce insecurity and transaction costs and facilitate problem solving and cooperation through information	Socialize through interaction, which leads to common expectations of appropriate behavior	Cooperate because of the binding features of institutions: rationality, legality, and legitimacy
Negotiations	Powerful states coerce others to the system	Cost and benefit calculations.	Cooperation produced through social interaction or persuasion. Shared or common under-standings lead to institutionalization of political practices	Commitment is rationalized through the normative character of institutions Binding and exogenous pressure exercised on those, who do not respond to persuasion
Outcome	Balance of power or hegemonic stability. Due to the anarchic character and maintenance costs of the system, the order will not last	Stable system, based on interdependence. Creating new institutions and defection become costly. States choose cooperate and evolve existing institutions	Institutions are stable, because they result from social process and states are committed to them through common identities	Cooperation can emerge against the will of the most powerful, whose power will be bound by the normativity of the institutions. An order based on multilateralism and norms

but also because multilateralism has the potential to sideline undesired power policies.

These considerations generate the following hypotheses:

H1: States that prefer multilateral policies are likely to response to unilateralist policies by strengthening existing and evoking new binding institutions and norms;
H2: In international negotiations, binding behavior manifests itself by coalition building and legitimation;
H3: The likelihood of reluctant states to join the institution increases with the use of economic incentives.

The hypotheses are reflected against alternative explanations generated by realist, rational, and constructivist theories, which are summarized in Table 2.1. The following part consists of three case studies on the politics of Germany, the USA, and the EU toward the ICC. Each study takes a chronological form and tests the first two hypotheses with the method of process-tracing. The third part of the book starts with a chapter, which refines the third hypothesis and generates a set of alternative explanations, which are then tested in case studies on the Philippines and Indonesia.

References

Abbott, Kenneth W. 1999. "International Relations Theory, International Law, and the Regime Governing Atrocities in International Conflicts." *The American Journal of International Law* 93 (2): 361–79.

Abbott, Kenneth W., Robert O. Keohane, Andrew Moravcsik, Anne-Marie Slaughter, and Duncan Snidal. 2000. "The Concept of Legalization." *International Organization* 54 (3): 401–19.

Abbott, Kenneth W., and Duncan Snidal. 2000. "Hard and Soft Law in International Governance." *International Organization* 54 (3): 421–56.

Armitage, Richard Lee, and Joseph S. Nye. 2007. *CSIS Commission on Smart Power: A Smarter, More Secure America*. Washington, DC: CSIS Press.

Axelrod, Robert. 1984. *The Evolution of Cooperation*. Rev. ed. New York: Basic Books.

Axelrod, Robert, and Robert O. Keohane. 1985. "Achieving Cooperation under Anarchy: Strategies and Institutions." *World Politics* 38 (1): 226–54.

Baldwin, David A. 1985. *Economic Statecraft*. Princeton: Princeton University Press.

———. 1989. *Paradoxes of Power*. New York: Basil Blackwell.

Bassiouni, M. Cherif. 2001. "Universal Jurisdiction for International Crimes: Historical Perspectives and Contemporary Practice." *Virginia Journal of International Law* 42 (1): 81–162.

Beetham, David. 1991. *The Legitimation of Power*. New York: Palgrave Macmillan.

Bennett, Andrew, and Colin Elman. 2006. "Complex Causal Relations and Case Study Methods: The Example of Path Dependence." *Political Analysis* 14 (3): 250–67.

Buchanan, Allen. 2004. *Justice, Legitimacy, and Self-Determination: Moral Foundations for International Law*. Oxford: Oxford University Press.

Buchanan, Allen, and Robert O. Keohane. 2008. "The Legitimacy of Global Governance Institutions." In *Legitimacy in International Law*, edited by Rüdiger Wolfrum and Volker Röben, 25–62. Berlin: Springer.

Bull, Hedley. 1977. *The Anarchical Society: A Study of Order in World Politics*, Third Edition with Forewords by Andrew Hurrell and Stanley Hoffmann. New York: Columbia University Press.

Byers, Michael. 1999. *Custom, Power and the Power of Rules: International Relations and Customary International Law*. Cambridge: Cambridge University Press.

Byers, Michael, and Georg Nolte, eds. 2003. *United States Hegemony and the Foundations of International Law*. Cambridge: Cambridge University Press.

Carr, Edward H. 1939. *The Twenty Years' Crisis 1919–1939: An Introduction to the Study of International Relations*. New York: Palgrave Macmillan.

Clark, Ian. 2005. *Legitimacy in International Society*. Oxford: Oxford University Press.

Davis, Christina L. 2004. "International Institutions and Issue Linkage: Building Support for Agricultural Trade Liberalization." *The American Political Science Review* 98 (1): 153–69.

Deitelhoff, Nicole. 2009. "The Discursive Process of Legalization: Charting Islands of Persuasion in the ICC Case." *International Organization* 63 (1): 33–65.

Deudney, Daniel H. 2007. *Bounding Power: Republican Security Theory from the Polis to the Global Village*. Princeton: Princeton University Press.

Diez, Thomas, and Ian Manners. 2007. "Reflecting on Normative Power Europe." In *Power in World Politics*, edited by Felix Berenskoetter and Michael J. Williams, 173–88. London and New York: Routledge.

Doyle, Michael W. 2005. "Three Pillars of the Liberal Peace." *The American Political Science Review* 99 (3): 463–66.

Duchêne, François. 1973. "The European Community and the Uncertainties of Interdependence." In *A Nation Writ Large? Foreign-Policy Problems Before the European Community*, edited by Max Kohnstamm and Wolfgang Hager, 1–21. London: MacMillan.

Fearon, James D. 1997. "Signaling Foreign Policy Interests: Tying Hands versus Sinking Costs." *The Journal of Conflict Resolution* 41 (1): 68–90.
Fehl, Caroline. 2004. "Explaining the International Criminal Court: A 'Practice Test' for Rationalist and Constructivist Approaches." *European Journal of International Relations* 10 (3): 357–94.
Finnemore, Martha, and Kathryn Sikkink. 1998. "International Norm Dynamics and Political Change." *International Organization* 52 (4): 887–917.
Fortmann, Michel, T.V. Paul, and James J. Wirtz. 2004. "Conclusions: Balance of Power at the Turn of the New Century." In *Balance of Power: Theory and Practice in the 21st Century*, edited by T.V. Paul, James J. Wirtz, and Michel Fortmann, 360–74. Stanford: Stanford University Press.
Franck, Thomas M. 1990. *The Power of Legitimacy Among Nations.* Oxford: Oxford University Press.
Gilpin, Robert. 1981. *War and Change in World Politics.* Cambridge: Cambridge University Press.
Goldstein, Judith, Miles Kahler, Robert O. Keohane, and Anne-Marie Slaughter. 2000. "Introduction: Legalization and World Politics." *International Organization* 54 (3): 385–99.
Haas, Ernst B. 1953. "The Balance of Power: Prescription, Concept, or Propaganda." *World Politics* 5 (4): 442–77.
———. 1980. "Why Collaborate?: Issue-Linkage and International Regimes." *World Politics* 32 (3): 357–405.
Habermas, Jürgen. 1981. *The Theory of Communicative Action, Volume One: Reason and the Rationalization of Society.* Boston: Beacon Press.
Haggard, Stephen, and Beth A. Simmons. 1987. "Theories of International Regimes." *International Organization* 41 (3): 491–517.
Hasenclever, Andreas, Peter Mayer, and Volker Rittberger. 1997. *Theories of International Regimes.* Cambridge: Cambridge University Press.
Henkin, Louis. 1979. *How Nations Behave: Law and Foreign Policy*, 2nd ed. New York: Columbia University Press.
Hurd, Ian. 2007. *After Anachy: Legitimacy and Power in the United Nations Security Council.* Princeton: Princeton University Press.
Hurrell, Andrew. 2005. "Legitimacy and the Use of Force: Can the Circle Be Squared?" *Review of International Studies* 31 (S1): 15–32.
Ignatieff, Michael. 2005. "Introduction: American Exceptionalism and Human Rights." In *American Exceptionalism and Human Rights*, edited by Michael Ignatieff, 1–26. Princeton: Princeton University Press.
Ikenberry, G. John. 2001. *After Victory: Institutions, Strategic Restraint, and the Rebuilding of Order after Major Wars.* Princeton: Princeton University Press.
———, ed. 2002a. *America Unrivaled: The Future of the Balance of Power.* Ithaca: Cornell University Press.

———. 2002b. "Introduction." In *America Unrivaled: The Future of the Balance of Power*, edited by G. John Ikenberry. Ithaca: Cornell University Press.

———. 2003a. "Is American Multilateralism in Decline?" *Perspectives on Politics* 1 (3): 533–50.

———. 2003b. "Strategic Reactions to American Preeminence: Great Power Politics in the Age of Unipolarity." *Paper*. National Intelligence Council.

———. 2011. *Liberal Leviathan: The Origins, Crisis, and Transformation of the American World Order*. Princeton: Princeton University Press.

Ikenberry, G. John, Michael Mastanduno, and William C. Wohlforth. 2009. "Introduction: Unipolarity, State Behavior, and Systemic Consequences." *World Politics* 61 (1): 1–27.

Keck, Margaret E., and Kathryn Sikkink. 1998. *Activists Beyond Borders: Advocacy Networks in International Politics*. Ithaca: Cornell University Press.

Kelley, Judith. 2005. "Strategic Non-cooperation as Soft Balancing: Why Iraq Was Not Just about Iraq." *International Politics* 42 (2): 153–73.

Kelsen, Hans. 1945. *General Theory of Law and State*. Translated by Anders Wedberg. Cambridge: Harvard University Press.

Keohane, Robert O. 1983. "The Demand for International Regimes." In *International Regimes*, edited by Stephen D. Krasner, 141–71. Ithaca: Cornell University Press.

———. 1984. *After Hegemony: Cooperation and Discord in the World Political Economy*. Princeton: Princeton University Press.

Keohane, Robert O., and Joseph S. Nye. 1977. *Power and Interdependence: World Politics in Transition*. Boston: Little, Brown and Company.

Keohane, Robert O., and David G. Victor. 2011. "The Regime Complex for Climate Change." *Perspectives on Politics* 9 (1): 7–23.

Kindleberger, Charles P. 1986. *The World in Depression, 1929–1939*, Revised and Enlarged Edition. Berkeley: University of California Press.

Koremenos, Barbara, Charles Lipson, and Duncan Snidal. 2001. "The Rational Design of International Institutions." *International Organization* 55 (4): 761–99.

Krasner, Stephen D. 1976. "State Power and the Structure of International Trade." *World Politics* 28 (3): 317–47.

———. 1983. "Structural Causes and Regime Consequences: Regimes as Intervening Variables." In *International Regimes*, edited by Stephen D. Krasner, 1–21. Ithaca: Cornell University Press.

———. 1993. "Sovereignty, Regimes, and Human Rights." In *Regime Theory and International Relations*, edited by Volker Rittberger and Peter Mayer, 139–67. Oxford: Clarendon Press.

———. 1999. *Sovereignty: Organized Hypocrisy*. Princeton: Princeton University Press.

Kratochwil, Friedrich V., and John Gerard Ruggie. 1986. "International Organization: A State of the Art on an Art of the State." *International Organization* 40 (4): 753–75.
Krauthammer, Charles. 1990. "The Unipolar Moment." *Foreign Affairs* 70 (1): 23–33.
Manners, Ian. 2002. "Normative Power Europe: A Contradiction in Terms?" *Journal of Common Market Studies* 40 (2): 235–58.
March, James G., and Johan P. Olsen. 1998. "The Institutional Dynamics of International Political Orders." *International Organization* 52 (4): 943–69.
Martin, Lisa L. 1992. "Interests, Power, and Multilateralism." *International Organization* 46 (4): 756–92.
———. 2000. *Democratic Commitments: Legislatures and International Cooperation*. Princeton: Princeton University Press.
Maull, Hanns W. 1990. "Germany and Japan: The New Civilian Powers." *Foreign Affairs* 69 (5): 91–106.
McGinnis, Michael D. 1986. "Issue Linkage and the Evolution of International Cooperation." *Journal of Conflict Resolution* 30 (1): 141–70.
Milner, Helen V. 1997. *Interests, Institutions, and Information: Domestic Politics and International Relations*. Princeton: Princeton University Press.
Moravcsik, Andrew. 1997. "Taking Preferences Seriously: A Liberal Theory of International Politics." *International Organization* 51 (4): 513–53.
———. 1998. *The Choice for Europe: Social Purpose and State Power from Messina to Maastricht*. Ithaca: Cornell University Press.
———. 2000. "The Origins of Human Rights Regimes: Democratic Delegation in Postwar Europe." *International Organization* 54 (2): 217–52.
Morgenthau, Hans J. 1973. *Politics Among Nations: The Struggle for Power and Peace*, 5th ed. New York: Alfred A. Knopf.
Morrow, James D. 1999. "The Strategic Setting of Choices: Signaling, Commitment, and Negotiation in International Politics." In *Strategic Choice and International Relations*, edited by David A. Lake and Robert Powell, 77–114. Princeton: Princeton University Press.
Nye, Joseph S. 2002. *The Paradox of American Power: Why the World's Only Superpower Can't Go It Alone*. Oxford: Oxford University Press.
———. 2004. *Soft Power: The Means to Success in World Politics*. New York: Public Affairs.
Pace, Michelle. 2007. "The Construction of EU Normative Power." *Journal of Common Market Studies* 45 (5): 1041–64.
Pape, Robert A. 2005. "Soft Balancing Against the United States." *International Security* 30 (1): 7–45.
Paul, T.V. 2005. "Soft Balancing in the Age of U.S. Primacy." *International Security* 30 (1): 46–71.

Poast, Paul. 2012. "Does Issue Likage Work? Evidence from European Alliance Negotiations, 1860 to 1945." *International Organization* 66 (2): 277–310.
Risse, Thomas. 2000. "'Let's Argue!': Communicative Action in World Politics." *International Organization* 54 (1): 1–39.
Risse, Thomas, and Kathryn Sikkink. 1999. "The Socialization of International Human Rights Norms into Domestic Practices: Introduction." In *The Power of Human Rights: International Norms and Domestic Change*, edited by Thomas Risse, Stephen C. Ropp, and Kathryn Sikkink, 1–38. Cambridge: Cambridge University Press.
Schelling, Thomas C. 2006. *Strategies of Commitment and Other Essays.* Cambridge: Harvard University Press.
Schimmelfennig, Frank. 2001. "The Community Trap: Liberal Norms, Rhetorical Action, and the Eastern Enlargement of the European Union." *International Organization* 55 (1): 47–80.
Sebenius, James K. 1983. "Negotiation Arithmetic: Adding and Subtracting Issues and Parties." *International Organization* 37 (2): 281–316.
Simmons, Beth A., and Allison Danner. 2010. "Credible Commitments and the International Criminal Court." *International Organization* 64 (2): 225–56.
Simmons, Beth A., and Lisa L. Martin. 2002. "International Organizations and Institutions." In *Handbook of International Relations*, edited by Walter Carlsnaes, Thomas Risse, and Beth A. Simmons, 192–211. London: Sage.
Smith, Karen E. 2005. "Beyond the Civilian Power EU Debate." *Politique Européenne* 17 (1): 63–82.
Struett, Michael J. 2008. *The Politics of Constructing the International Criminal Court: NGOs, Discourse, and Agency.* New York: Palgrave Macmillan.
Walt, Stephen M. 1987. *The Origins of Alliances.* Ithaca: Cornell University Press.
———. 2005. *Taming American Power: The Golbal Response to U.S. Primacy.* New York: W. W. Norton & Company.
———. 2009. "Alliances in a Unipolar World." *World Politics* 61 (1): 86–120.
Waltz, Kenneth N. 1979. *Theory of International Politics.* Boston: McGraw-Hill.
Weber, Max. 1922. *Wirtschaft Und Gesellschaft: Grundriß Der Verstehenden Soziologie.* Tübingen: Mohr Siebeck.
Wendt, Alexander. 1992. "Anarchy Is What States Make of It: The Social Construction of Power Politics." *International Organization* 46 (2): 391–425.
———. 1999. *Social Theory of International Politics.* Cambridge: Cambridge University Press.
———. 2001. "Driving with the Rearview Mirror: On the Rational Science of Institutional Design." *International Organization* 55 (4): 1019–49.

Wight, Martin. 1966. "The Balance of Power." In *Diplomatic Investigations: Essays in the Theory of International Politics*, edited by Herbert Butterfield and Martin Wight, 89–131. Cambridge, MA: Harvard University Press.
Wilson, Ernest J. III. 2008. "Hard Power, Soft Power, Smart Power." *The ANNALS of the American Academy of Political and Social Science* 616: 110–24.
Wohlforth, William C. 1999. "The Stability of a Unipolar World." *International Security* 24 (1): 5–41.
Young, Oran R. 1982. "Regime Dynamics: The Rise and Fall of International Regimes." *International Organization* 36 (2): 277–97.

PART II

Normative Binding and the Institutionalization of the International Criminal Court

CHAPTER 3

Germany and International Criminal Law

3.1 The Evil Itself: Germany and International Criminal Law After the First World War

For better and for worse, Germans have influenced the evolution of international criminal law more than any other nation. From the beginning of First World War I, Germany's aggression and war crimes outraged the European public. The invasion of neutral Belgium in August 1914, the treatment of Belgian civilians, and the subsequent terror in France, the Zeppelin bombings of Britain, and the U-boat war in 1915 made the European Allies seek for postwar war trials already during the first months of the Great War (Willis 1982, 7–14). After the war's end, the victorious Allied powers took advantage of their leverage and dictated the terms of the Treaty of Versailles in 1919 in a realist fashion. Despite strong opposition of the German delegation and the reluctance of the USA, the Part VII of the Versailles Treaty included a special tribunal to try the ex-German Kaiser Wilhelm II. von Hohenzollern and obligated Germany to surrender all war crimes suspects for the Allies' military tribunals: "For the first time, a major international peace treaty had established the principle in international law that war crimes punishment was a proper conclusion of peace, that the termination of war did not bring a general amnesty as a matter of course" (Willis 1982, 85, see also 82–6).

Since Germany was party to the Geneva Red Cross Convention of 1864, several conventions regulating naval warfare, and the 1899

S. Huikuri, *The Institutionalization of the International Criminal Court*,
https://doi.org/10.1007/978-3-319-95585-8_3

and 1907 Hague Conventions, the Allies had some legal grounds to prosecute Germans for war crimes and aggression (Commission on the Responsibility of the Authors of the War and on Enforcement of Penalties 1920b, 108, 113–15, 118). But, as Mullins wrote in 1921, "A desire for revenge is always the enemy of justice" (Mullins 1921, 217). None of the conventions incorporated hard law nor did they establish any form of international jurisdiction and there was no previous reference to terms such as "violations of international morality" and "principles of humanity" in international law, with which Germans now were charged. Hence, besides the violations of the 1907 Hague Convention, the jurisdiction of the intended war crimes tribunal was ambiguous. Although the Allies justified the tribunals with cosmopolitan words such as morality and humanity, in the absence of codified crimes the law derived from their authority as the winners of the war (Commission on the Responsibility of the Authors of the War and on Enforcement of Penalties 1920a, 134, 146; Mullins 1921, 212–16; Kaleck 2007, 94; Kress 2006, 16).

Despite the efforts and the power position of the Allies, neither an international tribunal nor any other form of justice followed First World War. As the result of an anti-monarchist revolution in Germany, Kaiser Wilhelm II fled to the Netherlands in November 1918, and as the Dutch refused to extradite him to the Allied powers, he never stood trial. In the terms of the Treaty of Versailles, the Allies handed Germany a list of approximately 900 alleged war criminals in 1920 (El Zeidy 2008, 14–5). The list included prominent military and political figures from Princes to Marshals, but also less known soldiers, such as Göring, commander of an air force unit, who would sit on the accused bench in Nuremberg 25 years later. Germany's government strictly refused to extradite the accused, pleading that the surrender would lead to political turmoil in the young republic. As a compromise, the Allies let the German *Reichsgericht* (Supreme Court) in Leipzig conduct the trials and handed the German government a list of 45 persons charged with outrages against the laws of war (named by Britain, France, Belgium, Italy, Poland, Romania, and Yugoslavia). Between 1921 and 1922, 13 trials took place and ten short sentences were adjudicated. The British cases were tried first and resulted with two sole judgments that were of importance for the future evolution of international criminal law: The sinking of the hospital ships Dover Castle and Llandovery Castle, which established precedents on the rejection of superior orders (Willis 1982,

120–24, 130–39; AJIL 1922; Royal Courts of Justice 1922; Malanowski 1985, 75; Kress 2006, 18; Schabas 2007, 4).

The following French and Belgian cases were unsuccessful and resulted in outrage. Hence, the Allies gradually gave up on the project:

> German war crimes trials were obviously not a success. Political and diplomatic considerations encroached upon impartial justice. Neither the Allied nor the Germans dealt with the problem of war criminals in a commendable fashion. But whatever the measure of Allied vindictiveness, German reverence for military honor prevented a proper handling of the issue. (Willis 1982, 147, see also 139–47)

If German judges and prosecutors had problems with prosecuting their compatriots for war crimes, so did the public. The Leipzig trials were broadly rejected in the Weimar Republic, and rallies and mass protests were held all over the country. In fact, Göring, future Reichsmarschall and Hitler's deputy, met Hitler for the first time at one of the protest meetings in Munich's Königsplatz. In addition to other influences, the Leipzig trials offered an opportunity for the rising Nazi movement to advance nationalist sentiments and contributed to the emergence of the monstrous Third Reich (Willis 1982, 141; Bass 2002, 60, 104–05).

3.2 Nuremberg Trials

The unwillingness of Germans to prosecute the crimes of First World War combined with the inconceivable nature of the Nazi crimes motivated the Allied powers to do it right after Second World War II. As Bass has documented, it was not self-evident that the Nazi leaders would end up in front of a military tribunal (Bass 2002, 147–205). However, this time the USA, which emerged from Second World War as the hegemonic power (Ikenberry 2001, 167), was supportive toward war crimes trials, and thus, the International Military Tribunal (IMT) was established in August 1945. The Allies had started to collect evidence well before the end of the war, and having learned from the failures of Leipzig, they carefully prepared the trials after Germany's capitulation. Now, there were more legal grounds to proceed with a tribunal than after Second World War, because before the Nazis took over, the Weimar Republic had joined the League of Nations and the Kellogg-Briand Pact. Yet, the Nuremberg Charter historically contributed to the institutionalization of international criminal law by establishing the personal responsibility of the "major war criminals of the European Axis" for crimes against peace, war crimes, and crimes against humanity (including crimes committed against civilian populations) and also by setting grounds for the codification of the Genocide Convention.

The judgment of the IMT against Göring et al. sentenced twelve of the 22 defendants, representing different parts of the Nazi elite, to death by hanging, seven to imprisonment, acquitted three, and declared several Nazi organizations (including Gestapo, SS, and SD) to be illegal (International Military Tribunal 1947a, 172–74, 252, 333). Probably, the most cited quotation of the trials summarizes the main contribution of the IMT: "Crimes against international law are committed by men, not by abstract entities, and only by punishing individuals who commit such crimes can the provisions of international law be enforced" (International Military Tribunal 1947b, 223). The concept and realization of individual responsibility follow in the footsteps of Grotius' notion that sovereigns are men too (Grotius 1625: Book I, Ch. I, § XIV), and although one can criticize the IMT for many reasons, its contribution to the development of international criminal law is significant.

Following the Nuremberg Charter, the Allied powers issued Control Council Law No. 10 in December 1945, providing a uniform legal basis for subsequent trials in Germany and authorizing the establishment of military tribunals in each of the four zones of occupation (Taylor 1949, 7). Law No. 10

> was really a form of domestic legislation because it applied to the prosecution of Germans by the courts of the civil authorities, largely borrowed the definition of crimes against humanity found in the Charter of the Nuremberg Tribunal, but omitted the latter's insistence on a link between crimes against humanity and the existence of a state of war, thereby facilitating prosecution for pre-1939 atrocities committed against German civilians. (Schabas 2007, 7)

All four occupying powers organized subsequent trials to the IMT, of which the most famous ones were the 12 Nuremberg trials held by the Americans under Law No. 10. Due to their concentration on specific perpetrator groups (such as industrialists, lawyers, diplomats, bankers, and doctors), these trials revealed the contribution of the German elite, the "not professional Nazis" (Taylor 1949, 109), to the horrors of the Third Reich (Taylor 1949, 77, 90, 120; Lippmann 1992, 9–82). Between the years 1946 and 1949, the American, British, and French military courts convicted roughly 5000 perpetrators (Bassiouni 1999, 532–33; Rogers 1990, 797–98). Other countries, such as Belgium, Czechoslovakia, Denmark, Netherlands, Norway, and Yugoslavia, also tried German war criminals (Deák et al. 2000). When it comes to the trials conducted by the Soviet secret service, the NKVD, the exact number of convicted is unknown, but high, and the intelligence Taylor (the American Chief Counsel for War Crimes in the Law No. 10 trials) had about these trials in 1949 has not been significantly increased: "I am without reliable information on the war crimes program in the Soviet zone [...]" (Taylor 1949, 8).

The IMT and its successor trials exposed the magnitude of the Nazi crimes by providing an incredible amount of evidence: 800 kilometers of tapes and 750 million pages (or 4000 tons) of protocols and other documentation (*Der Spiegel* 1949, 9; Taylor 1949, 45). Despite the vengefulness of the Allied powers, the defendants stood a fair trial. They received their indictments 30 days before the trial started, they had the right to prepare their defense, they had access to counsels, and, thanks to the German accuracy, to a vast amount of evidence material (United Nations War Crimes Commission 1947, 190–99). The defense counsels in turn received generous allowances, including monthly 3500 Reichsmark per defendant, an office space, and a gratis carton of cigarettes each week. Also their travel expenses as well as those of witnesses were covered (Taylor 1949, 49). The IMT convened for 218 days to judge on the 22 defendants, and the Law No. 10 trials held altogether 1200 sessions for 12 cases. While the realist use of power and the rational desire of the winners of the war to selectively prosecute the ultimate loser best explains the emergence of the IMT, considering the initial situation and the outcome of the trials it is not an overstatement to label Nuremberg "legalism's greatest moment of glory" (Bass 2002, 203).

3.3 From Denial Toward Cooperation: First Decades After Nuremberg

Like the Leipzig trials, Nuremberg did not stand for an implicit acceptance of international criminal law for the Germans. The trials were criticized with three main arguments, deriving from the winners' selective use of law. First, the selectivity was obvious considering the personnel of the courts, since the judges and prosecutors only represented the victorious Allied powers and were carefully picked by them. Second, claims of retroactivity were raised, because the crimes were defined after the end of the war. Lastly, the Axis powers were not the only ones committing grave crimes during the war. The Soviet invasion of Finland in 1939 and the fire-bombings of Dresden provided *tu quoque*-grounds to argue that Nuremberg was victor's justice and that the victors too should face justice. The Allies vehemently negated the critique and rejected the accusations even thirty years later (Schmitt 1945; Kress 2006, 22–3; Jung 1992; Eser 2006, 54–56; A/C.6/33/SR.64 1978, 6; A/C.6/35/SR.12 1980, 9).

In addition to judicial critique, the German public was particularly dismissive toward the Law No. 10 trials and "the feeling of offended national dignity acquired from Leipzig resurfaced" (Kress 2006, 20; Reichel 2001, 45; Werle 2006, 657–58). The executions of those convicted under Law No. 10 by the USA faced widespread objections, and the Americans were accused for the allegedly inhumane conditions of the Landsberg prison where the Law No. 10 accused were detained and executed (*Der Spiegel* 1948b, 8; Appendix S, Taylor 1949). However, the Americans refused to hand over Landsberg:

> In the light of the increasing amount of "ultra-nationalist" sentiment expressed in the German press, attacks on the administration of Landsberg are likely to continue. [...] I further recommend that the administration of Landsberg be kept in American hands, and under no circumstances be turned over to the Germans. (Taylor 1949, 98)

It is intriguing how resentfully the Germans confronted the trials and international justice. On the one hand, Germans' reactions against the trials are surprising. In a due process, based on extensive and shocking evidence, far less than one percent of perpetrators and bystanders were convicted. It had taken approximately 500,000 Germans to accomplish the murder of more than six million Jews, and the Waffen-SS, Hitler's main instrument of terror, alone had according to SS-Oberführer Reinecke one million members during the war years (Kwiet 2007, 61; International Military Tribunal 1947a, 226–27; 1948, 472). Moreover, as the General Secretary of the League for Human Rights, Großmann, commented the Law No. 10 trial on employees of German ministries:

"Everything is really so totally different than we have heard or read. [...] I have never seen a court, in which the human rights of the defendants are so scrupulously respected than in the Wilhelmstraßen-trial"[1] (*Der Spiegel* 1948a, 18).

On the other hand, the reaction can be explained with the following two factors. First, one cannot expect that millions of Nazis would change their minds about the justifications of the war in a couple of months or years, because after all the Third Reich would not have been possible without the wide support of the population. The armed forces had altogether more than 18 million soldiers and as Göring put it to the IMT's prison psychologist in his cell: "Never mind what the people say *now!* [...] I know what they said *before!* I know how they cheered and praised us when things were going well. I know too much about people!" (Gilbert 1947, 12; see also Overmans 2004, 214). Second, the Allies' realist use of power, which did not allow room for the Germans' opinion on how to proceed with war criminals, likely served as a trigger to yet another nationalist reaction.

The trials of the Allied powers ceded with the establishment of the Federal Republic of Germany (BRD) and the German Democratic Republic (DDR) in 1949. The two republics became responsible for further Nazi prosecutions and took contrary positions toward international criminal law. In the BRD, the collective shame during the Nuremberg trials turned into a sentiment of collective victimhood, deriving from the Law No. 10 trials, material distress in the destroyed country, and denazification, the attempt to eliminate all Nazi influence from German public life (Herz 1948, 569). The humiliated West Germans wanted to "let the past rest" and the newly established *Bundestag* (the federal Parliament) agreed (von Merkatz, in Deutscher Bundestag, 221. Sitzung 1952, 9827–28; Reichel 2001, 68; Werle and Wandres 1995, 20; Frei 1997, 25). One day after the first convening of the *Bundestag*, laws terminating denazification and providing amnesty for lesser Nazi perpetrators were already being drafted. To the dismay of the Allies, the four-month-old *Bundestag* enacted amnesty for tens of thousands of Nazi crimes, including homicide (*Totschlag*). Further amnesty and limitation laws followed in the subsequent decades (Frei 1997, 51–52, 44ff., 2002, 2; Reichel 2001, 66).

[1] "Es ist in Wirklichkeit alles so völlig anders, als wir gehört oder gelesen haben" [...] "Ich habe niemals ein Gericht gesehen, in dem die Menschenrechte der Angeklagten so peinlich beachtet werden wie im Wilhelmstraßen-Prozeß." All translations by the author.

As the denazification ended during the fifties, more than 50,000 former Nazis returned to their civil servant posts. In general, the Adenauer government and the *Bundestag* rather undermined the legacy of the Nuremberg trials. Adenauer negotiated non-recognition of the IMT follow-up trials to the Settlement Convention with the Western Allies and refused to recognize the Nuremberg principles. In addition, his government successfully campaigned for the release of all convicted (including those sentenced to death) by the British, French, and American trials, the so-called war criminals as Dr. von Merkatz (Parliamentarian, who later became the Minister of Justice) scornfully called them (BGBl II 1954 1953, 14; von Merkatz, in Deutscher Bundestag, 221. Sitzung 1952, 9827–28; Adenauer, in Deutscher Bundestag, 217. Sitzung 1952, 9800; Kress 2006, 23; Werle 2006, 660). The dismissive attitude gradually started to turn in 1958, as the Central Office for the Investigation of NS-Crimes was established. Between the years 1958 and 2017, more than 118,000 cases have been examined by the Office, and 18,000 cases have been pending in courts and public prosecutors' offices (The Central Office of the Judicial Authorities for the Investigation of National Socialist Crimes 2018). Although the sixties marked a new, positive turn in the investigation and prosecution of Nazi crimes, the limitation laws had negative effect on further trials and several investigations of the Office remained without judicial consequences (Greve 2003, 197–99).

Unlike the BRD, the DDR unconditionally accepted the Nuremberg principles and incorporated them into Art. 91 of its Constitution and Chapter 2 of its Criminal Code. In the name of anti-fascism, investigations and proceedings against Nazi criminals were carried out most prominently in Waldheim. However, as is well known, the DDR was not exactly a rule-of-law state and, accordingly, its criminal courts violated human rights as much as did the rest of its state machinery. For this reason and especially because the DDR did not exist by 1998 when the ratification of the Rome Statute became topical, this chapter concentrates on the BRD (Werle 2006, 661; Reichel 2001, 68–9)

3.4 Confronting the Past: Positive Outcome of a Rule of Law Crisis

In the 1960s, the West German public started to face the brown past more extensively. *Das Dritte Reich*, the first documentary TV series about the Nazi years, was followed by up to 69% of the population.

Simultaneously, new trials, such as Eichmann in Jerusalem 1961 and the Auschwitz-trial in Frankfurt 1963–1965, were opened and the Nazi connections of German politicians as well as the amnesty debates of the *Bundestag* came to the public consciousness (Schildt 2001, 9; Fischer and Lorenz 2007, 162). At the same time, a leftist student movement picked up on the question of the Nazi past. The year 1968 marked a turning point in the political situation of the BRD, as student protests became increasingly violent. The 68er-student movement protested against the prevailing system in the name of anti-fascism, anti-capitalism, and anti-imperialism. The critique pointed to the reluctance of the society to tackle the Nazi past, the inequality of the economic system, the political system of the republic, the Vietnam War, and the subjugation of Third World countries (Kraushaar 2001, 15ff.; 2006b, 56). The most interesting legal aspect of the student protests was the opposition to the, allegedly fascist, undertaking of the Conservative Party to incorporate emergency laws into the German Constitution for the first time after the Weimar Republic. In May 1968, the Bundestag under the coalition government of Conservatives and Social Democrats adopted a constitutional amendment, which indeed was quite authoritarian as it widely limited the privacy of correspondence in case of national emergency (Borowsky 1998; Heinz 2007, 161ff.).

However, the emergency law was not the biggest threat to the German rule-of-law state. A terrorist organization called the *Rote Armee Fraktion* (RAF) emerged from the aftermath of the 68er-protests and kept Germany in fear for two decades with bomb attacks, taking hostages, and murders, as well as attempted murders, of economic and political personalities (Daase 2007). The worst, but not the first, escalation of the RAF crisis started on September 5, 1977, as the RAF blackmailed the Liberal-Social Democratic government under Chancellor Schmidt to free detained members of the organization or else they would murder the abducted President of the German Associations for Employers and Industries—and a former SS-Officer—Schleyer. Instead of evoking the emergency laws or negotiating with the RAF, Schmidt established a crisis squad, which acted as a shadow government for 45 days without legal basis, legislative control, or communication to the outside world (Kraushaar 2006a, 1013–14).

After the government refused to negotiate with the RAF, the Constitutional Court became involved with the matter and ruled on October 16 that the security of the collective overrules the life of one person and the government could not guarantee collective security, if it negotiates with terrorists (BVerfGE 46, 160—Schleyer 1977; Polzin 2006, 1026–29, 1036–41). The crisis ended three days later, as Schleyer was found dead. During the crisis, the government violated the Constitution and other laws. It invoked a news embargo, illegally wire-tapped telephones, forbid detained terrorists all contact to the outside world, and prevented the legislative to exercise control over the executive (Kraushaar 2006a, 1021–23; di Lorenzo 2007). Had the crisis lasted longer than 44 days, it might have created potential obstacles for further commitments to international law (Wesel 2006, 1053).

Another development during the 1970s that could have potentially turned Germany on a different track, considering its future role in advancing cooperation in international criminal law, was the Constitutional Court's rather reluctant attitude toward non-German courts. The *Solange I*-ruling of 1974 granted primacy for the German Constitution over the European Court of Justice (ECJ) as long as (*solange*) the ECJ could not guarantee effective protection of fundamental human rights. Although the ruling had realist, state sovereignty-oriented connotations as it aimed at protecting national laws, it was justified with the following legalist arguments. First, the decisions of the ECJ did not correspond with the German Constitution; second, the European Community (EC) suffered under a democratic deficit; and third, the ECJ lacked a codified catalogue for fundamental rights (BVerfGE 73, 339 1986). This negative ruling, however, turned out to have positive influence as it eventually strengthened human rights guarantees inside the EC. France ratified the European Convention on Human Rights (ECHR), and the European Parliament, Commission, and Council issued a joint declaration in 1977, underlining the importance of the protection of fundamental rights and confirming the applicability of the ECHR to the EC. Also, the first direct elections to the European Parliament were held in 1979, and most importantly for Germany, the ECJ developed due process guarantees on a case-by-case basis. Acknowledging these developments, the German Constitutional Court overruled *Solange I* with *Solange II* that recognized the jurisdiction of the ECJ also for conflicts concerning fundamental personal rights incorporated in the German Constitution (BVerfGE 73, 339 1986; Pernice 2006, 28; Lanier 1988, 1, 7, 26ff.). While the RAF crisis and the *Solange I*-ruling had the potential to precipitate Germany into being a rather authoritarian state, in particular *Solange* had positive effects for the development of human rights at the European level.

3.5 Commitment to International Law

In 1973, the BRD and the DDR joined the UN. West Germany had ratified the Genocide Convention and the Geneva Conventions already in 1954 and it joined the ICCPR and the ICESCR in 1973. At the UN, Germany took the promotion of human rights as one of its main agendas, and in 1976, the Schmidt government started to promote the establishment of an international court for human rights in the UN framework. The arguments and motivations in favor of facilitating international cooperation in the field of human rights were rational. At the international level, Germany considered the UN Human Rights Commission's protection of universal human rights ineffective and wanted to import the efficient model of the ECHR into the international domain. At the domestic political level, the RAF problem and the vast increase in aircraft hijackings during the 1970s contributed to Germany's willingness to negotiate a Convention against the Taking of Hostages: The international court for human rights was first brought up in connection with this convention proposal (A/C.6/31/SR.55 1976; A/31/PV.7 1976). Furthermore, incidents at the border of the BRD and the DDR had resulted in public concern and demands of the political opposition to address the border matter at the UN. The proposal for the world human rights court was Foreign Minister Genscher's and his Liberal Party's answer to the demands as Federal elections were approaching in the fall of 1976. Despite diplomatic *démarches* and the fact that the Hostage Convention was widely greeted among states, the proposal for a world human rights court did not catch fire. Canada was the only Western country explicitly supporting the initiative, which the Eastern Bloc decisively rejected in the name of state sovereignty (Rock 2010, 250–51, 258–62).

In 1978, the UNGA Sixth Committee started to reconsider an ICC in the framework of the Draft Code of Offences Against the Peace and Security of Mankind. Suddenly, the reelected Schmidt government was reserved about further codification of international criminal law. The main reason for the hesitance was the fact that the Soviet Bloc now considered the matter urgent and might have been able to shape the Draft Code and the potential court according to its interests. Yielding leverage to the rival bloc on such an important issue certainly was not in the interests of the Western states (A/C.6/35/SR.12 1980, 7–8; A/C.6/36/SR.69 1981, 8; A/C.6/37/SR.52 1982, 5; Kress 2006, 24–5). Ten years later, this view had not considerably changed. The first official West German reaction on a permanent ICC emphasized the need of a thorough definition of crimes and the importance of *nullum crimen, nulla poena sine lege* principle and Germany, now under Chancellor Kohl, voted with France, UK, Israel, and the USA against the ILC's further preparation of the Draft Code while 137 states voted in favor (A/43/PV.76 1988; A/C.6/43/SR.34 1988; A/C.6/42/SR.37 1987; A/C.6/45/SR.33 1990).

The fall of the Iron Curtain changed the power politics at the UN and the reunited Germany became more accommodating to the ICC. The Kohl government expressed its commitment to European integration and a multilateral world order, based on international law. According to Germany, the new multilateral order should include an ICC and Foreign Minister Genscher's call for the establishment of an ICC at the UNGA in 1991 marked a definitive turn in Germany's politics toward cooperation in international criminal law (A/46/PV.8 1991, 29–30). During this time, the cost-benefit calculations were shaped by a desire for multilateralism and binding norms and Genscher's call could be seen as providing the momentum for Germany to become a normative binder. However, the main motivation for an ICC originated from the Gulf war and the idea of creating a tribunal to judge Saddam (Steinke 2012, 87). While an international tribunal for Saddam was not realized, Germany did not give up the idea of establishing binding institutions and norms in the realm of international criminal law. In fact, the Kohl government was so excited about an ICC that Genscher's successor Kinkel even credited Germany with having proposed its establishment although this was only partially true. Granted, Germany had mentioned the ICC in the Sixth Committee in 1988, but the question had been referred to the UNGA due to Trinidad and Tobago's initiative (A/47/PV.8 1992, 61; A/48/PV.8 1993, 13). However, even before the ILC started working on the first draft of the Rome Statute, Germany emphasized that the establishment of an ICC was urgently needed and "a political necessity which did not lend itself to further delay" (A/C.6/48/SR.19 1993; A/C.6/47/SR.23 1992).

While the emerging new world order triggered Germany's interest in, and support for, an ICC, atrocities in the Former Yugoslavia and in

Rwanda also contributed to the growing demand for cooperation in the field of international criminal law (A/C.6/48/SR.19 1993). Although in the endgame the USA was the driving force behind the ad hoc tribunals ICTY and ICTR, Kinkel together with France was the first to support an international tribunal for Yugoslavia in 1992 (Gow 1992; United Nations 2001, 13, 46; Schabas 2006, 14, 19–22; Wilkitzki 2003, 924; Steinke 2012, 90). By coincidence, and because of the NATO forces' reluctance to arrest war criminals, Germany also provided the ICTY with its first case, Tadić (ICTY Case No. IT-94-1-I 1995; Schabas 2006, 187–88, 233–34). The fact that a country transferred a case from the domestic level to international proceedings was unusual indeed, but the Tadić case also made German legislation more accommodating toward cooperation in the field of international criminal law. In 1995, the *Bundestag* enacted a cooperation law with the ICTY (similar law was enacted for the ICTR in 1998) and Germany significantly revised its attitude toward retroactivity. It first ignored the potential retroactivity of the Tadić case, and one year later, the Constitutional Court decided to accept retroactivity, if a state has seriously violated fundamental human rights. Moreover, in 2001 the German government withdrew its reservation to the Art. 7, 2 (exception for *nulla poena sine lege*) of the ECHR (BGBl I 1995 1995, 485; BGBl I 1998 1998, 843; ICTY Case No. IT-94-1-I 1995; Kress 2006, 29–30).

Since the Tadić case, the ICTY has made more than 600 legal assistance requests to German authorities and Germany has contributed to the working of the ICTY by being its third largest financer. The conflict in the former Yugoslavia also resulted in the first Genocide Conviction by German courts (Wilkitzki 2003, 926–33; BVerfG 2 BvR 1290/99 2000). Considering Germany's reserved statements toward an ICC in the mid-1980s, the end of the Cold War definitely changed its attitude. The Kohl government's emphasis on international multilateralism, European integration, and cooperation in the field of international criminal law provides smoking guns in support of the argument that when the negotiations on the ICC were launched in 1995, Germany had abandoned its state sovereignty-oriented approach to international law and was on its way to becoming a supporter of institutionalization. Moreover, bearing in mind the multilateral emphasis of the Kohl government, it is no wonder that the US agenda on the ICC triggered normative binding attempts already during the negotiations on the Rome Statute.

3.6 Binding Attempts at the Negotiations on the Rome Statute

When the preparations of the Rome Statute had been launched, the Ministries of Foreign Affairs and Justice were already supportive of the idea of an ICC, but the Ministries of Interior and Defense (like their counterparts in most other states) were concerned about an ICC's implications on German soldiers. According to Steinke and Kress, the *primus motors* behind Germany's policy on the ICC were the liberal Foreign Minister Kinkel and the Head of Ministry of Foreign Affairs' International Law Department, Kaul, who later became Judge of the ICC. While Kaul shaped Germany's agenda especially after the 1997, when he became head of Germany's delegation on the ICC, already before that he had started to persuade skeptical ministries and the *Bundestag* into supporting the ICC. Kaul's strongest argument in support of the ICC was the principle of complementarity that gives priority to domestic prosecution. This argument provides grounds to maintain that even states (or at least central state agencies) that supported the ICC from the beginning onward made rational calculations about the potential costs of the ICC before and during the negotiations (Steinke 2012, 109ff.; Kress 2006, 36).

Although there was still some suspiciousness inside the federal government when the negotiations on the ICC were launched in 1995, to the outside world Germany seemed to be a frontline supporter of an ICC. Throughout the negotiations, the German delegation pleaded for a multilateral ICC that would be independent from the power politics of the P-5. Moreover, Germany was one of the leaders of the LMS that comprised, among others, Canada, Australia, South Africa, Senegal, and by the end of the conference, all 15 EUMS. Considering the idea of coalition building in support of normative binding, the German delegation and the LMS initially put efforts into getting powerful states, such as India, on board. However, as the attempt to persuade India was unsuccessful, the idea of the "one country one vote" rule inspired the LMS to turn to small and middle powers. Eventually, the coalition comprised sixty middle powers and developing states that persuaded in favor of a strong and independent court. Considering the outcome of the conference, this tactic of coalition building turned out to be effective (Steinke 2012, 116ff.). As is well known, the LMS agenda was more or less opposed by the P-5 of the UNSC (the UK and later also France joined the LMS), who, in rather realist terms, were concerned with their state sovereignty and wanted to secure UNSC control over the ICC (Kirsch and Holmes 1999, 4–5; Benedetti and Washburn 1999, 30–1).

Supported by the Kohl government (A/52/PV.5 1997; Schmidt-Jortzig 1998), Federal President Herzog (Herzog 1996), the *Bundestag* (BT-Drs. 13/10935 1998), and inline with other LMS, the German delegation to the Rome conference aimed at negotiating a strong, independent, and effective ICC. The agenda was based on four "building blocks," which would provide solid fundamentals for a functioning court: universal jurisdiction, complementarity, an independent Prosecutor, and strict obligation to cooperate with the ICC (Kaul 1997a; German Delegation 1996; A/C.6/52/SR.14 1997; Schmidt-Jortzig 1998). These cornerstones clearly reflected multilateral values and norms and offered grounds for the establishment of a highly legalized institution, which is of central importance for normative binding attempts. Unsurprisingly, the defenders of state sovereignty—P-5 states and in particular the US—opposed the German agenda, but the LMS coalition had grown strong and Germany went to the conference with high self-esteem. In fact, taking into account the state sovereignty-oriented US stance in the negotiations, the tone of the German Minister of Justice, Schmidt-Jortzig, in the opening ceremony of the conference was defiant and the following line a self-fulfilling prophecy regarding the outcome of the conference: "in an interdependent world and a global society, sovereignty will be served better by cooperation than by a futile attempt to stand alone" (Schmidt-Jortzig 1998). Hence, Germany wanted to cooperate with other states and build a coalition in order to gain legitimacy for an independent, multilateral ICC.

Universal jurisdiction, the first "building block" of an independent ICC, offered fertile grounds for legitimacy claims as the concept derives from multilateralism and equality of states before the law. Germany had long been concerned over the reach of the ICC, and the initial solution for gaining universal support was to include the ICC in the UN organization, which would also bind the USA to the court (A/C.6/47/SR.23 1992; A/C.6/48/SR.19 1993; A/C.6/49/SR.20 1996).[2] Yet the USA was powerful enough in its opposition to universal jurisdiction

[2] Interestingly, in 1992 Germany had favored a permanent ICC, but one which would convene only when necessary. See A/C.6/47/SR.23 1992.

and during the negotiations, it became clear that a multilateral treaty was a more realistic option. However, Germany did not give up its idea of a politically independent ICC with at least limited universal jurisdiction and, hence, before the Rome conference it promoted automatic jurisdiction for all ICC States Parties through diplomatic *démarches*, among other means (Kaul 1997a, 1998b, 368; A/AC.249/1998/DP.2 1998; A/C.6/51/SR.29 1996). Germany persuaded in favor of universal jurisdiction with the argument that considering the crime of genocide, crimes against humanity, and war crimes, it was already widely practiced and therefore there should be no problem to transfer it to the ICC (A/AC.249/1998/DP.2 1998; Kaul 1998b, 369).

Somewhat ironically, universal jurisdiction had been the cornerstone of the Nuremberg trials, but it now made the US delegation see red. This points out that the American delegation indeed preferred the realist use of ad hoc courts on a pick-and-choose basis to an independent ICC (Weschler 2000, 97). Germany's activism on the ICC's jurisdiction did not remain unnoticed in the US Congress either. The influential Chair of the US Senate Foreign Relations Committee, Helms, who loudly opposed an independent ICC, got it right:

> I understand that Germany was the intellectual author of this universal jurisdiction provision. [...] we have thousands of American soldiers stationed in Germany right now. Will the German Government now consider those American forces under the jurisdiction of the International Criminal Court? (United States Senate 1998, 7)

However, during the negotiations, the universal jurisdiction proposal did not succeed, and Germany, like other LMS, aligned with South Korea's proposal, suggesting that the ICC would exercise jurisdiction, if either the territorial or custodial state or the state of nationality of the victim or the offender were a State Party to the Rome Statute (A/CONF.183/C.1/L.6 1998). Faithful to its idea of universal jurisdiction, Germany opposed all opt-in/opt-out options for crimes under the jurisdiction of the ICC, but this undertaking failed as the P-5 eventually were able to include a 7 years opt-out possibility for war crimes (A/C.6/50/SR.26 1995; Westdickenberg 1998).

The independent Prosecutor was Germany's second "building block." If Germany had initially been suspicious of an independent Prosecutor (A/C.6/49/SR.20 1996), it changed this view during the negotiations for the sake of universal jurisdiction and the ICC's credibility (German Delegation 1996; Schmidt-Jortzig 1998). Again, the German and American delegations disagreed on the *proprio motu* power of the Prosecutor. And again, the preceding US policy on ad hoc war crimes trials turned against the Americans, as Germany was able to argue that the prosecutors of the ICTY and ICTR also had the power to initiate investigations *ex officio*, exposing the selectivity of the US policy on international trials (Kaul 1997a).

Complementarity was the third "building block" and the only one on which Germany and the USA agreed. Considering the negotiations on complementarity, Germany made a normative binding move by inviting delegations from Africa, Asia, the Caribbean, and Latin America to engage in the discussion (Kaul 1997a). The fact that Germany and nearly all other states were interested in securing primary jurisdiction to its own courts provides smoking gun evidence in favor of the rationalist assumption that state agendas are shaped not only by the logic of appropriateness or legitimacy-centered arguments in favor of multilateralism, but also by domestic cost-benefit calculations. Having a functioning domestic judicial system, Germany has nothing to fear from the ICC as long as the principle of complementarity is part of the Rome Statute.

State cooperation with the ICC was the last "building block" of Germany's agenda. According to Kaul, cooperation with the ICC should not be founded upon the traditional understanding of cooperation and extradition between sovereign states, but, at least regarding the ICC States Parties, upon an obligation to cooperate with the court. In 1997, Kaul made a legitimacy-oriented point of state cooperation being of central importance:

> What we now have to do is to make sure that this new Court will be a fair, just, impartial, independent and, above all, an efficient institution. [...] When I mention [efficiency], we all are aware, that the Court will have no police, no executive arm of its own and will be entirely dependent on international cooperation forthcoming from Member States. (Kaul 1997b)

In addition to the "building blocks," a short discussion of Germany's approach to the definition of crimes is in order, not least because it posed one of the bones of contention between the USA and Germany during the negotiations.

From the outset, Germany was in favor of including only genocide, crimes against humanity, war crimes, and the crime of aggression to the Rome Statute, meaning that the delegation did not support the codification of, for instance, terrorism or drug trafficking. While Germany emphasized the importance of precise and exhaustive definitions of crimes and individual responsibility, which would increase the legality of the ICC, it opposed the idea of the USA to separately annex an Elements of Crimes document to the Rome Statute (L/2770 1996; A/C.6/51/SR.29 1996; Kress 2006, 31–2). The US delegation, in turn, was irritated by Germany's successful efforts to include the crime of aggression to the Rome Statute. With the crime of aggression, the logic of the Nuremberg trials yet again turned against the Americans: The German delegation reasoned the inclusion of aggression from the Nuremberg legacy and also with the deterrence and prevention effects it would have on future perpetrators (A/C.6/50/SR.26 1995; A/AC.249/1997/WG.1/DP.3 1997; A/AC.249/1997/WG.1/DP.20 1997; A/AC.249/1998/DP.12 1998; A/C.6/52/SR.14 1997).

The nexus between the UNSC and the ICC played a central role throughout the negotiations. Considering the crime of aggression, the German and American views somehow coincided as both countries agreed that the ICC should be able to exercise its jurisdiction only if the UNSC, acting under Chapter VII of the UN Charter, determined that aggression has occurred. However, Germany was not willing to let the UNSC control the definition of the crime itself, since that would "ruin the concept of a self-sustained, autonomous definition of the crime of aggression" (A/AC.249/1997/WG.1/DP.20 1997; A/C.6/50/SR.26 1995; A/C.6/51/SR.29 1996). Furthermore, the overall views of Germany and the USA on the ICC's functioning did differ significantly. Germany's perception of an effective ICC was of a highly legalized multilateral institution that has universal jurisdiction over core crimes, exclusive powers to decide whether a state is unwilling or unable to prosecute, and an independent Prosecutor. This was an antithesis to the realist US perception, which was centered on the UNSC's control over the ICC, providing the US government with veto-power over the institution. According to Germany's multilateral approach, the UNSC should not be able to refer specific cases to, or deter investigations of, the ICC (Kaul 1997a; for different German proposals on complementarity, see Non-Paper/WG.3/NO.3 1997; Non-Paper/WG.3/NO.8 1997).

The result of the Rome conference was a last-minute compromise and neither the LMS nor the P-5 were able to impose all their proposals. South Korea's proposal on automatic jurisdiction, although supported by 85% of states, was replaced by a state consent-oriented approach, reflecting the position of the P-5. Germany felt sidelined by the P-5, who, according to Kaul, "negotiated away" the automatic jurisdiction:

> As so often in critical phases of the UN decision-making process, the well-established co-ordination mechanisms among the permanent members of the Security Council came into play. Of course, it was France, in particular, which had since the beginning of the conference been looking for a way to exempt war crimes and crimes against humanity from compulsory jurisdiction. The US, too, wanted the ICC to have a merely optional competence for [these] crimes. [...] On 15 July, the permanent Security Council members apparently met to agree, in the usual way, on a 'compromise' proposal that was in keeping with their interests (the German side was not informed and not involved). (Kaul 1998b, 371, 373)

The UK and France introduced the P-5 compromise proposal—an opt-out for war crimes and crimes against humanity for ten years, no jurisdiction on non-States Parties' military missions, and jurisdiction only if the territorial state is a State Party—in an EU coordination meeting to which Germany made a counter-proposal—three years opt-out for war crimes and jurisdiction also if custodial or victim's state is a State Party—and won immediate support from the majority of the EU and other LMS. This proposal, according to Kaul, played a key role in the compromise on the final package (Kaul 1998b, 371–73; Benedetti and Washburn 1999, 29).

Although the final outcome of the conference, especially considering the jurisdiction, was not optimal from the German point of view, the LMS were successful in their normative binding attempts. They created a coalition in support of their agenda and with the power of the majority they were able to resist most of the attempts to weaken the court and to secure a relatively strong and independent ICC. Before the final vote, Foreign Minister Kinkel declared that the Rome Statute accommodated essential elements of the German position, including complementarity, limitation of the Rome Statute to core crimes, *proprio motu* Prosecutor, the ICC's independence from political institutions, and cooperation mechanisms with the court. Hence, Germany, which throughout the negotiations had been able to build its legitimacy and sideline the USA with legalist arguments deriving from the Nuremberg experience, joined 119 other states in supporting the establishment of the ICC (Kinkel 1998; Kaul 1998a, 129–30).

3.7 Setting a Legalist Example: Ratification and Implementation of the Rome Statute

After the Rome conference, federal elections brought about a governmental change as the red-green coalition under Chancellor Schröder took office. Although Foreign Minister Kinkel had emphasized human rights, the conservative coalition had been selective on the issue especially considering bilateral relations with human rights abusing governments. In contrast, Fischer, the new Foreign Minister, declared human rights to be the guideline of the government's foreign policy and was committed to promote them through international law and multilateral structures, in particular the UN Human Rights Commission and the EU (Pfeil 2003, 179). Consistent to this agenda, the Schröder government signed the Rome Statute less than six months after its adoption on the fiftieth anniversary of the Universal Declaration of Human Rights.[3] Also the continuous support of the *Bundestag* played an important role in the swift ratification and implementation of the Rome Statute (Kreß 2010, 1114; Röttgen in BT Plenarprotokoll 14/90 2000, 8376).

However, before Germany could ratify the Rome Statute, two constitutional obstacles had to be overcome. First, Art. 16, 2 of Germany's Constitution prohibited the extradition of Germans to foreign courts. The *Bundestag*, with the approval of the *Bundesrat* (the Federal Council), amended the paragraph, which since December 2000 accommodates extradition of Germans to international courts and to EUMS (BGBl I 2000 2000, 1633ff.; Jarasch and Kreß 2000, 96ff.). Second, and more conventionally, according to Art. 59 of the Constitution, the *Bundestag* had to enact a ratification law (BGBl II 2000 2000, 1393ff.; Kreß and MacLean 2005, 131). According to the government, the motivation for an early ratification was twofold. First, Germany wanted to show that it is particularly committed to the enforcement and

[3] Germany made two declarations that considered cooperation with the ICC: Requests of cooperation should be directed to the Federal Ministry of Justice and include a German translation (UNTC 2018).

development of international law and to the work of the UN. Second, timely ratification was part of a common European plan, aimed at expediting the entry into force of the Rome Statute and thereby positively affecting states, which were reluctant or hostile toward the ICC (BT-Drs. 14/2682 2000, 6). Both of these motivations are smoking guns verifying normative binding attempts. The first point shows that Germany clearly wanted to profile itself as a supporter of multilateralism and international law, and the latter proves that Germany wanted to influence other states' policies regarding their ratification.

In addition to ratification and constitutional amendment, the government also wanted to demonstrate its support for the ICC by implementing the Rome Statute *stricto* sensu. This undertaking consisted in a Law on Cooperation with the ICC (LCICC) and a novel Code of Crimes against International Law. The LCICC entered into force in June 2002, and as its name reveals, it aims at complementing and adjusting German laws to the provisions of the Rome Statute (BGBl I 2002 2002, 2144ff.). While Germany already had a law dealing with interstate cooperation, the government decided to enact a separate law—as with the ICTY and ICTR—in order to avoid the swelling of interstate cooperation law. The main aim of the LCICC is to accommodate, as broadly and friendly as possible, the obligations arising from the Rome Statute, but also to maximize the efficiency of the ICC by facilitating judicial assistance (BT-Drs. 14/8527 2002, 29). Accordingly, the law is generous considering Germany's prospective cooperation with the ICC (Kress 2006, 33). The LCICC has seven sections, 73 articles, and includes, among other things, detailed regulations of arrest, surrender, and the enforcement of sentences. Some parts are quite groundbreaking as they facilitate witnesses' appearances before the ICC and allow international proceedings and investigations in Germany. In general, the LCICC displays Germany's commitment to the ICC and is peculiar as, instead of merely adhering to State Party obligations, it exceeds the duties described in Parts 9 and 10 of the Rome Statute (Wilkitzki 2005, 101; BGBl I 2002 2002, 2144ff.; Kreß and MacLean 2005, 135–54).[4]

Simultaneous to the cooperation law, a working group composed of legal scholars and representatives of ministries (justice, foreign affairs,

[4] In addition to the adoption of the LCICC, Germany has, among others, changed the Law on the Organization of Courts to provide the ICC with decision power on immunities under Art. 98 of the Rome Statute. See Art. 21, Gerichtsverfassungsgesetz [Judicature Act] 1950.

and defense) drafted a Code of Crimes against International Law. While many other states simply copied Arts. 6, 7, and 8 of the Rome Statute to their legal orders, Germany had several reasons for accommodating the crimes defined in the Rome Statute into a new body of law (Zimmermann 2003, 980). Due to the Nuremberg legacy, the Art. 103 of Germany's Constitution obeys the principle of *nullum crimen sine lege*, meaning that criminal acts can only be prosecuted if they are legally defined. Therefore, a simple reference to international norms would not have been sufficient to make ICC crimes punishable under German law. Although most of the core crimes could have been prosecuted as violations of national laws (such as murder, rape, and pillaging) or international law (such as apartheid and transferring civilian population), German laws only accommodated watertight prosecution of genocide since Germany had not taken measures to implement the Geneva Conventions (Jarasch and Kreß 2000, 92, 95; Wirth 2002, 2–3; Werle and Jessberger 2002, 198). Hence, Germany decided to adopt new laws in order to avoid inconsistencies between domestic laws and the Rome Statute, to guarantee that it can take advantage of the principle of complementarity by having jurisdiction over the crimes defined in the Rome Statute and, thus, to reduce the likelihood of Germans landing in front of the ICC. The *Bundestag* and *Bundesrat* unanimously adopted the Code of Crimes against International Law, which entered into force on the same day as the Rome Statute, July 1, 2002. As the Minister of Justice Däubler-Gmelin put it, this Code constitutes "legal virgin soil in the interface of international law and criminal law" (Däubler-Gmelin 2002, vii).[5]

The aim behind the Code of Crimes against International Law was not simply to synchronize German laws with the Rome Statute, but also to reflect other binding treaties (especially the Geneva Conventions) and to define core international crimes as specifically as possible. Therefore, the Code complements the shortfalls of the ICC's jurisdiction, strengthens its institution, develops the definitions of crimes under international law (Jarasch and Kreß 2000, 92; Werle and Jessberger 2002, 199), and by so doing maximizes the ICC's grade of legalization. It exceeds the ICC's definitions of crimes by following customary international law and expands the scope of war crimes into non-international conflicts. It

[5] "juristisches Neuland an der Schnittstelle zwischen Völkerrecht und Strafrecht."

also does not rule out the possibility of deferring cases to the ICC even though Germany could use territorial, personal, or universal jurisdiction to prosecute the alleged crimes. Most importantly, Art. 1 of the Code establishes a strictly universal jurisdiction for genocide, crimes against humanity, and war crimes (Werle and Jessberger 2002, 208ff.; Kress 2006, 34; Zimmermann 2003, 980ff.).

The intentions behind this far-reaching, deeply legalized implementation of the Rome Statute were not only motivated by legal ambitions. According to Werle, legal expert in the working group on the Code of Crimes against International Law, one of the Code's aims was to promote the ideas of international humanitarian law. Furthermore, the Code was supposed to provide precedence for other countries considering the implementation of the Rome Statute and for these purposes it was immediately translated into all official UN languages. As Däubler-Gmelin put it, the Code was an important signal for other countries (Werle and Jessberger 2002, 199; Däubler-Gmelin 2002, vii; BT Plenarprotokoll 14/233 2002, 23271). The swift ratification and the over-the-top implementation of the Rome Statute express Germany's particular desire to support the ICC and provide two smoking guns to evidence that Germany aimed at building a coalition in support of the ICC along the lines of the normative binding argument. First, with a highly legalized Code, Germany was able to increase its own legitimacy and credibility as a supporter of the ICC. Second, the novel legislation and its swift translation provided Germany with grounds to engage in third states' ratification and implementation processes by offering materials and the assistance of legal experts that would potentially contribute to further coalition building in support of the ICC.

3.8 Making the ICC a Binding Institution: Promotion of the Rome Statute

Domestic legal implementation of the Rome Statute was only one part of Germany's plan to support and promote the ICC. Soon after the end of the Rome conference, the EU expressed its hope that the Rome Statute would quickly reach sixty ratifications (10398/98 (E/98/78) 1998). Germany had emphasized the importance of the widest possible acceptance of the ICC throughout the negotiations and inline with the

EU policy the German Permanent Representative to the UN declared in October 1998 that Germany stands

> ready to cooperate closely with our EU partners, the like-minded and the NGOs to encourage all countries to sign and ratify the Statute soon. This includes [...] the United States [...]. [W]e will make sure that during our term of the EU Presidency the promotion of the ICC will be a matter of priority. (Kastrup 1998)

Hence, the coalition building in support of the ICC started right after the Rome conference and in the years to come, Germany became very active in promoting the ICC and using persuasion tactics. While Germany consistently brought up the ratification in the framework of the UN (A/54/PV.8 1999; A/55/PV.14 2000), direct persuasion took the form of diplomatic *démarches* in third countries. Furthermore, Germany funded conferences on the ratification and implementation of the Rome Statute, sent panelists to such conferences, and sponsored the participation of outside experts. In addition to other EU countries and the LMS, Germany also worked in close cooperation with pro-ICC NGOs, which received considerable funding from it. The undertaking to globally promote the ICC gained support from the *Bundestag*: "In the field of international cooperation, the Federal Government has always in view that all parties of the German Bundestag have continuously supported the ICC-project"[6] (BT-Drs. 14/9990 2002; see also European Commission 2002, 18; Röttgen in BT Plenarprotokoll 14/90 2000, 8377).

The normative binding agenda was strengthened as the goal of sixty ratifications was achieved in April 2002, enabling the ICC to become operational in July 2002. Germany expected that the USA and other reluctant states would start to adhere to the ICC once it became operational, as the Minister of Justice put it: "the work of the permanent International Criminal Court will help to ensure that global law will increasingly apply also for these large states"[7] (BT Plenarprotokoll

[6] "Auf dem Gebiet der internationalen Zusammenarbeit hat die Bundesregierung stets im Blick, dass alle Parteien des Deutschen Bundestages das IStGH-Vorhaben kontinuierlich unterstützt haben."

[7] "die Arbeit des ständigen Internationalen Strafgerichtshofs wird dazu beitragen, dass dieses globale Recht immer stärker auch für diese großen Staaten gelten wird."

14/233 2002, 23271). However, the USA did not welcome the emergence of the ICC. The *Bundestag* and the government were irritated by the US stance toward the ICC and did not share the concerns of the USA (BT-Drs. 14/9990 2002). Fischer and Däubler-Gmelin assured that they were eager to solve the conflict as soon as possible, but when the USA exercised its power at the UNSC to secure immunity to its service members through Resolution 1422, they did not hide their disappointment and clearly labeled the US actions an example of realist power politics (Fischer-Lescano 2002, 204–05; Röttgen in BT Plenarprotokoll 14/90 2000, 8377; BT-Drs. 14/9912 2002; *Der Spiegel* 2002):

> It is annoying and sad, though, that the current US government withdrew its signature of the Rome Statute and has last Sunday even made the necessary extension of the UN peacekeeping mission in Bosnia dependent on the UN Security Council's approval for an immunity of US soldiers. This veto has completely isolated the US in the Security Council. In the era of globalization, such an approach must face particular suspicion, since it aims quite openly at double rights, double standards and special privileges for the powerful.[8] (Fischer-Lescano 2002, 204)

While Germany cooperated with other EU member states to find a compromise with the USA, the government also got active bilaterally, when the US Congress was legislating the American Service-Members' Protection Act. The government repeatedly tried to convince the Bush Administration and Congressmen to refrain from enacting the law (BT-Drs. 14/9990 2002). It goes without saying that Germany refused to sign a BIA with the USA.

In addition to EU-level coordination and bilateral consultations with the Bush Administration, in September 2003 Germany responded to the US actions against the ICC by deepening the normative binding coalition through the establishment of a "Friends of the ICC" group in New York (A/C.6/59/SR.6 2004). The Friends of the ICC are

[8] "Ärgerlich und traurig ist allerdings, dass die derzeitige US-Regierung ihre Unterzeichnung des Römischen Statuts zurückgezogen und am vergangenen Sonntag sogar ihre Zustimmung zur notwendigen Verlängerung der UN-Friedensmission für Bosnien von einer Immunitätserklärung des UN-Sicherheitsrats für die US-Soldaten abhängig gemacht hat. Dieses Veto hat die USA im Sicherheitsrat völlig isoliert. Im Zeitalter der Globalisierung muss ein solches Vorgehen auf besonderes Misstrauen stoßen, zielt es doch ganz offen auf zweierlei Recht, zweierlei Maßstäbe und Sonderrechte für Mächtige ab."

states, committed to promote universal ratification of the Rome Statute, to safeguard its integrity and deepen state cooperation with the ICC. Shortly after the establishment of the New York branch, the Embassy of Germany in the Netherlands founded another "Friends of the ICC" branch in The Hague and the work of the group became more organized. The New York branch provides for a link between the UN and the ICC as it coordinates UNSC and UNGA matters, host country relations, financial issues, and matters concerning the crime of aggression. The Hague branch in turn is in charge of, among other things, the ICC's relation to the UN and the EU and affairs concerning the organs of the ICC. While the Group is informal and open to all states, it operates systematically by coordinating strategies through regular communications. Having more than 110 members, the Group is a powerful player in the promotion of the ICC and works as a tool to maintain an ICC friendly coalition (CICC 2004, 7; ICC 2006, 8).

In addition to international cooperation in support of the ICC, Germany continued its work on the Rome Statute's jurisdiction. During the Rome conference, Germany had opposed the US proposal of annexing a separate Elements of Crimes to the Rome Statute, because it considered the listing of crimes exhaustive enough. In return, the USA had opposed Germany's proposal of including the crime of aggression to the ICC's jurisdiction. While the USA imposed its will considering the Elements of Crimes and they were drafted by the Preparatory Commission succeeding the Rome conference, Germany was successful with the definition of aggression, which, with overwhelming support, ended up being part of the Rome Statute and was defined at the 2010 Kampala Review Conference (A/C.6/52/SR.14 1997; PCNICC/1999/DP.13 1999; PCNICC/2000/WGCA/DP.4 2000). As the Kampala Review Conference approached, the German government and the *Bundestag* got active on the issue. Germany's interest in the inclusion of aggression to the Rome Statute was justified by the Nuremberg legacy, Germany's special obligations arising from history, and with the will to avoid victor's justice and to maintain the integrity of the ICC. In June 2010, the ICC Assembly of States Parties adopted the definition of aggression and three years later Germany became the sixth state to accept the crime of aggression amendment to the Rome Statute (BT-Drs. 17/1767 2010; Deutscher Bundestag 2010; for an overview of Kampala negotiations, see Kreß and von Holtzendorff 2010).

3.9 Conclusions: From an Outlaw to a Binder

Looking back to 1919 and 1949, dedication to international criminal law was not really an attribute of Germany, and the enthusiasm with which the executive, legislative, and judicative branches greet the ICC today is astonishing. While, for instance, the Liberal Party trivialized the Nazis as so-called war criminals in the 1950s, the statement of former Minister of Justice, Schmidt-Jorzig, shows a 180 degree policy turn of the party: "The establishment of a permanent international criminal court is indeed progress par excellence in humanitarian international law. [...] I shy a bit of the attribute historical, but here it would actually be appropriate"[9] (BT Plenarprotokoll 14/90 2000, 8380–81). Considering Germany's domestic politics, it is impressive that there are not too many issues on which all German political parties would agree so clearly as on the ICC. But how did a neglectful aggressor turn into one of the strongest supporters of international criminal law?

In a long-term perspective, the success of the post-Second World War years, including the European integration, democratization, and economic development, has probably had greatest impact on Germany's changed attitude toward international criminal law. The significance of the EU is especially striking, as Chancellor Schröder put it at the UNGA in 2003:

> Thirty years ago, Germany was a country with limited sovereignty, divided by the Iron Curtain. Today, Germany is a sovereign nation, a civil Power in the heart of a united Europe. We live in a common area of freedom, the rule of law, prosperity and social responsibility. This goes to show that development towards justice and peace is indeed possible and we shall not cease to support endeavours to that end anywhere in the world, be it in the Middle East, in Africa or in any other crisis area. Bearing in mind our own history, we are indeed assuming responsibility for cooperative policy of peace. This we do by employing economic, political and humanitarian means. (A/58/PV.9 2003)

Two issues in this statement are striking while evaluating Germany's normative binding desires. First, Schröder defines Germany as a civil power,

[9] "Die Bildung eines ständigen Internationalen Strafgerichtshofs ist im humanitären Völkerrecht in der Tat ein Fortschritt par excellence. [...] Ich scheue mich ein wenig vor dem Prädikat 'historisch,' aber eigentlich wäre es hier angebracht."

pointing out that it does not wish to use coercive politics. Second, he mentions justice, peace, and cooperation as the core aims of Germany's policy. These concepts presuppose multilateralism and binding norms that, according to this statement, are best achieved by economic, political, and humanitarian means. As such, Schröder's statement makes a normative binding point.

Going back to the question of what explains Germany's turn into a supporter of multilateral order, Schröder's statement goes back to two further important factors: the end of the Cold War and the ideals of the 68er generation. The fall of the Iron Curtain and the change in the political alignments in UN diplomacy opened new avenues for the codification of international law. Even if the establishment of a world human rights court had been high on Germany's agenda in 1976, it opposed the further drafting of the Draft Code of Offences Against the Peace and Security of Mankind in 1980, because it was the Soviet Bloc's undertaking. Yet, the generation of the 1968ers and their ideals of a multilateral order definitely guaranteed Germany's role as the supporter of international justice. The cabinets of Kohl and Schröder did not have to confront the Nuremberg trauma in the same way as their predecessors and, thus, were less ambivalent toward international jurisdiction and more receptive to the idea of a permanent ICC. Moreover, had the conservative coalition won the elections in 1998, it certainly would have ratified the Rome Statute, but Kohl's geopolitical approach to international affairs might not have produced as assertive a response to the US opposition to the ICC than that of Schröder's government. The leading figures of the coalition government of Social Democrats and Greens—Schröder, Fischer, and Däubler-Gmelin—represented the 68er generation that had forced Germans to confront the Nazi past. Now their generation ruled the country during the years when the ratification, implementation, and protection of the Rome Statute were a central question. Correspondingly, the reasoning in support of the ICC became colored by peace ideals.

The Schröder government perceived the ICC as a step toward a peaceful world order, in which the force of law and not the law of force (or power) prevails, as Däubler-Gmelin stated in 2000: "The power of law should take the place of the right of the powerful"[10]

[10] "Die Stärke des Rechts soll an die Stelle des Rechts des Stärkeren treten."

(BT Plenarprotokoll 14/90 2000, 8378). Such expressions, which the government used to describe the importance of the ICC, come very close to the idea of normative binding. For instance, strengthening the rule of law at the expense of hard power is central to a multilateral world order, based on binding institutions. It shows Germany's trust in binding norms and the importance of credibility, legitimacy, and legality—the "building blocks" for successful use of normative binding (Däubler-Gmelin in BT Plenarprotokoll 14/90 2000, 8378).

In addition to binding norms, another essential element of this envisioned multilateral order is the system of cooperative global security, where the ICC offers an alternative, peaceful, solution for violent conflicts. From Germany's perspective, collective security should secure human rights and be based on the rule of law. This perspective is a counterpoint to the realist theory, as it aims at addressing causes of terrorism and insecurity through ending lawlessness, not by using military means. As Fisher put it at the UNGA in September 2002, collective security

> will have to measure up to the binding legal framework in which it is embedded. It is imperative for the globalization process to be flanked by a growing set of international rules, because international law and the rule of law constitute the indispensable foundations for peaceful and ordered coexistence. That is why the establishment of the International Criminal Court is so important to us. (A/57/PV.6 2002; see also BT-Drs. 14/2682 2000, 99; Herzog 1996; Fischer in BT Plenarprotokoll 14/90 2000, 8375, Schmidt-Jorzig in 2000, 8381; A/58/PV.9 2003)

This statement, again, testifies that Germany's post-Cold War strategy was indeed to build binding multilateral institutions in order to overcome traditional power politics and the use of force as stabilizing elements of the international order. In this normative binding undertaking, the ICC played and plays a central role.

While the ICC provides peaceful conditions and promotes the rule of law for the international system, its further virtue lies in the consolidation of international justice. Ultimately, as seen by the Schröder government, from the codification of international criminal law follows the abolition of impunity and the establishment of personal accountability for violations of humanitarian law. As Däubler-Gmelin put it: "The message of the permanent International Criminal Court is: the torturers and the desk criminals of this world cannot feel protected from a fair trial nowhere and at no time"[11] (BT Plenarprotokoll 14/233 2002, 23272; See also BT-Drs. 14/2682 2000, 99; Herzog 1996; BT-Drs. 13/10935 1998). This hope for, and confidence in, the deterrence effect pays tribute to the legacy of the Nuremberg trials. Accordingly, this case study concludes with the acknowledgment that Germany is a supporter of the ICC and promotes the universalization of the Rome Statute, because "*Fiat iustitia ne pereat mundus*" (Däubler-Gmelin in BT Plenarprotokoll 14/90 2000, 8378, see also Fischer in 2000, 8375; A/AC.249/1997/WG.1/DP.20 1997).

References

UN Documents (references starting with A/…, L/…, and PCNICC/) available at documents.un.org or unbisnet.un.org.

10398/98 (E/98/78). 1998. "Declaration by the Presidency on Behalf of the European Union on the International Criminal Court." Council of the European Union.

AJIL. 1922. "German War Trials: Report of Proceedings Before the Supreme Court in Leipzig." *The American Journal of International Law* 16 (4): 628–31.

Bass, Gary Jonathan. 2002. *Stay the Hand of Vengeance: The Politics of War Crimes Tribunals*. Princeton: Princeton University Press.

Bassiouni, M. Cherif. 1999. *Crimes Against Humanity in International Criminal Law*, 2nd rev. ed. The Hague: Kluwer Law International.

Benedetti, Fanny, and John L. Washburn. 1999. "Drafting the International Criminal Court Treaty: Two Years to Rome and an Afterword on the Rome Diplomatic Conference." *Global Governance* 5 (1): 1–37.

BGBl I 1995. 1995. "Gesetz über die Zusammenarbeit mit dem Internationalen Strafgerichtshof für das Ehemalige Jugoslawien (Jugoslawien-Strafgerichtshof-Gesetz)." Bundesgesetzblatt, Teil I, Nr. 18, Z 5702. Bonn: Deutscher Bundestag.

BGBl I 1998. 1998. "Bundesgesetzblatt, Teil I, Nr. 25." Bonn: Deutscher Bundestag.

BGBl I 2000. 2000. "Gesetz zum Änderung des Grundgesetzes (Artikel 16)." Bundesgesetzblatt, Teil I Nr. 52, G 5702. Bonn: Deutscher Bundestag.

[11] "Die Botschaft des Ständigen Internationalen Strafgerichtshofs ist: Die Folterknechte und Schreibtischtäter dieser Welt können sich nirgendwo und zu keiner Zeit mehr vor einer gerechten Strafverfolgung sicher fühlen."

BGBl I 2002. 2002. "Gesetz zur Ausführung des Römischen Statuts des Internationalen Strafgerichtshofes vom 17. Juli 1998." Bundesgesetzblatt, Teil I Nr. 41. Bonn: Deutscher Bundestag.

BGBl II 1954. 1953. "Bekanntmachung über das Inkrafttreten der Konvention zum Schutze der Menschenrechte und Grundfreiheiten." Bundesgesetzblatt, Teil II. Bonn: Deutscher Bundestag.

BGBl II 2000. 2000. "Gesetz zum Römischen Statut des Internationalen Strafgerichtshofs vom 17. Juli 1998 (IStGH-Statutgesetz)." Bundesgesetzblatt, Teil II Nr. 35, G 1998. Bonn: Deutscher Bundestag.

Borowsky, Peter. 1998. "Große Koalition und Außerparlamentarische Opposition." Informationen zur politischen Bildung Heft 258. Zeiten des Wandels. Bonn: Bundeszentrale für politische Bildung.

BT Plenarprotokoll 14/90. 2000. Berlin: Deutscher Bundestag.

BT Plenarprotokoll 14/233. 2002. "Herta Däubler-Gmelin." Berlin: Deutscher Bundestag.

BT-Drs. 13/10935. 1998. "Antrag der Abgeordneten Gerald Häfner, Dr. Uschi Eid, Gerd Poppe und Der Fraktion BÜNDNIS 90/DIE GRÜNEN, Schaffung eines Ständigen Internationalen Strafgerichtshofes." Deutscher Bundestag.

BT-Drs. 14/2682. 2000. "Gesetzentwurf der Bundesregierung. Entwurf eines Gesetzes zum Römischen Statut des Internationalen Strafgerichtshofs vom 17. Juli 1998." Deutscher Bundestag.

BT-Drs. 14/8527. 2002. "Gesetzentwurf der Bundesregierung. Entwurf eines Gesetzes zur Ausführung des Römischen Statuts des Internationalen Strafgerichtshofes vom 17. Juli 1998." Deutscher Bundestag.

BT-Drs. 14/9912. 2002. "Kleine Anfrage der Abgeordneten Dr. Evelyn Kenzler, Wolfgang Gehrcke, Roland Claus und der Fraktion der PDS, Der Internationale Strafgerichtshof und die USA." Deutscher Bundestag.

BT-Drs. 14/9990. 2002. "Antwort der Bundesregierung auf die Kleine Anfrage der Abgeordneten Dr. Evelyn Kenzler, Wolfgang Gehrcke, Roland Claus und der Fraktion der PDS – Drucksache 14/9912 – Der Internationale Strafgerichtshof und die USA." Deutscher Bundestag.

BT-Drs. 17/1767. 2010. "Antrag, Einigkeit über die Definition des Tatbestandes des Aggressionsverbrechens im IStGH-Statut Erzielen." Deutscher Bundestag.

BVerfG 2 BvR 1290/99. 2000. "In dem Verfahren über die Verfassungsbeschwerde." Entscheidungen des Bundesverfassungsgerichts. Karlsruhe: Bundesverfassungsgericht.

BVerfGE 46, 160—Schleyer. 1977. "Urteil." Entscheidungen des Bundesverfassungsgerichts. Karlsruhe: Bundesverfassungsgericht.

BVerfGE 73, 339, Entscheidungen des Bundesverfassungsgerichts. 1986. "Solange II." Karlsruhe: Bundesverfassungsgericht.

CICC. 2004. "'Friends of the ICC' Revived at the European Parliament." *The International Criminal Court Monitor* 26 (February): 7

Commission on the Responsibility of the Authors of the War and on Enforcement of Penalties. 1920a. "Annex II: Memorandum of Reservations Presented by the Representatives of the United States to the Report of the Commission on Responsibilities, April 4, 1919." *American Journal of International Law* 14 (1): 95–154.

———. 1920b. "Report Presented to the Preliminary Peace Conference, March 29, 1919." *American Journal of International Law* 14 (1): 95–154.

Daase, Christopher. 2007. "Die Zweite Generation Der RAF (1975–1981)." Dossier. Die Geschichte Der RAF. Bonn: Bundeszentrale für politische Bildung.

Däubler-Gmelin, Herta. 2002. "Geleitwort Der Bundesministerin Der Justiz." In *Materialien Zum Völkerstrafgesetzbuch. Dokumentation Des Gesetzgebungsverfahrens*, edited by Sascha Lüder and Thomas Vormbaum. Münster: Lit Verlag.

Deák, István, Jan Tomasz Gross, and Tony Judt. 2000. *The Politics of Retribution in Europe: World War II and Its Aftermath*. Princeton: Princeton University Press.

Der Spiegel. 1948a. "Ein Spiegel Seite für Robert M. W. Kempner. Nichts Menschliches ist mir Fremd." *Der Spiegel*, August 21.

———. 1948b. "Wenn in Landsberg. Keine Grundsätzlichen Handhaben." *Der Spiegel*, November 13.

———. 1949. "Gott Hat Kain Bestraft. Kleinliche Einwände Uninteressant." *Der Spiegel*, May 19.

———. 2002. "Internationaler Strafgerichtshof. Fischer Ruft zu Kompromiss Auf." *Der Spiegel*, July 7.

Deutscher Bundestag. 2010. "Aggressionsverbrechen als Straftatbestand beim Den Haager Strafgerichtshof Umstritten. Ausschuss für Menschenrechte und Humanitäre Hilfe (Anhörung)." Deutscher Bundestag.

Deutscher Bundestag, 217. Sitzung. 1952. "Verhandlungen des Deutschen Bundestages, I Wahlperiode, Stenographische Berichte Band 12." Bonn.

Deutscher Bundestag, 221. Sitzung. 1952. "Verhandlungen des Deutschen Bundestages, I Wahlperiode, Stenographische Berichte Band 12." Bonn.

El Zeidy, Mohamed. 2008. *The Principle of Complementarity in International Criminal Law: Origin, Development and Practice*. Leiden: Martinus Nijhoff.

Eser, Albin. 2006. "Das International Militärtribunal von Nürnberg aus Deutscher Perspektive." In *Die Nürnberger Prozesse: Völkerstrafrecht Seit 1945*, edited by Herbert R. Reginbogin and Christoph Safferling, 53–59. München: K.G. Saur.

European Commission. 2002. "Report of the Conference Held in Brussels 28 and 29 January 2002 and Follow-Up." Brussels.

Fischer, Torben, and Matthias N. Lorenz. 2007. *Lexikon der „Vergangenheitsbewältigung" in Deutschland: Debatten und Diskursgeschichte des Nazionalsozialisums Nach 1945*. Bielefeld: Transcript Verlag.

Fischer-Lescano, Andreas. 2002. *Völkerrechtliche Praxis Der Bundesrepublik Deutschland in Den Jahren 2000 Bis 2002, 1. Teil. Allgemeine Fragen Des Völkerrechts Und Individualrechte.* Max-Planck-Institut für ausländisches öffentliches Recht und Völkerrecht.

Frei, Norbert. 1997. *Vergangenheitspolitik: Die Anfänge Der Bundesrepublik Und Die Nazi-Vergangenheit*. 2. Auflage. München: C. H. Beck.

———. 2002. *Adenauer's Germany and the Nazi Past: The Politics of Amnesty and Integration*. New York: Columbia University Press.

German Delegation. 1996. "Non-Paper, Articles 21–25." United Nations Negotiations on the Establishment of an International Criminal Court (ICC).

Gilbert, G. M. 1947. *Nuremberg Diary*. New York: Farrar, Straus, and Company.

Gow, David. 1992. "Germany to Call for War Crimes Trials." *Guardian*, August 20.

Greve, Michael. 2003. "Täter oder Gehilfen? Zum Strafrechtlichen Umgang mit NS-Gewaltverbrechern in der Bundesrepublik Deutschland." In *Bestien und Befehlsempfänger: Frauen und Männer in NS-Prozessen Nach 1945*, edited by Ulrike Weckel and Edgar Wolfrum, 194–221. Göttingen: Vandenhoeck & Ruprecht.

Grotius, Hugo. 1625/2007. The Rights of War and Peace: Including the Law of Nature and of Nations. New York: Cosimo.

Heinz, Wolfgang S. 2007. "Germany: State Responses to Terrorist Challenges and Human Rights." In *National Insecurity and Human Rights: Democracies Debate Counterterrorism*, edited by Alison Brysk and Gershon Shafir, 157–76. Berkeley: University of California Press.

Herz, John H. 1948. "The Fiasco of Denazification in Germany." *Political Science Quarterly* 63 (4): 569–94.

Herzog, Roman. 1996. "Rede von Bundespräsident zur Friedenspolitik und Internationalen Gerichtsbarkeit".

ICC. 2006. "New Coordinator for the Friends of the ICC in the Hague." *International Criminal Court Newsletter* 8 (July): 8.

ICTY Case No. IT-94-1-I. 1995. "The Prosecutor of the Tribunal Against Dusan Tadic a/k/a 'Dule' Goran Borovnica, Decision on the Defence Motion for Interlocutory Appeal on Jurisdiction." The Hague: International Tribunal for the Prosecution of Persons Responsible for Serious Violations of International Humanitarian Law Committed in the Territory of Former Yugoslavia Since 1991.

Ikenberry, G. John. 2001. *After Victory: Institutions, Strategic Restraint, and the Rebuilding of Order After Major Wars*. Princeton: Princeton University Press.

International Military Tribunal. 1947a. "Judgment and Sentences." *American Journal of International Law* 41 (1): 172–333.

———. 1947b. "Trial of Major War Criminals Before the International Military Tribunal, Nuremberg, 14 November 1945–1 October 1946, Volume I, Official Documents." Nuremberg.

———. 1948. "Trial of Major War Criminals Before the International Military Tribunal, Nuremberg, 14 November 1945–1 October 1946, Volume XX, Proceedings 30 July 1946–10 August 1946." Nuremberg.

Jarasch, Frank, and Claus Kreß. 2000. "The Rome Statute and the German Legal Order." In *Rome Statute and Domestic Legal Orders Volume I: General Aspects and Constitutional Issues*, edited by Claus Kreß and Flavia Lattanzi, 91–112. Baden-Baden: Nomos Verlagsgesellschaft.

Jung, Susanne. 1992. *Die Rechtsprobleme der Nürnberger Prozesse*. Tübingen: Mohr Siebeck.

Kaleck, Wolfgang. 2007. "German International Criminal Law in Practice: From Leipzig to Karlsruhe." In *International Prosecution of Human Rights Crimes*, edited by Wolfgang Kaleck, Michael Ratner, Tobias Singelnstein, and Peter Weiss, 93–112. Berlin: Springer Verlag.

Kastrup, Dieter. 1998. "Permanent Representative of Germany to the United Nations, Speech on the Occasion of Today's Meeting with European Commissioner Emma Bonino in Support of the International Criminal Court Convened by the NGO 'No Peace without Justice.'" No. 27. Permanent Mission of Germany to the United Nations.

Kaul, Hans-Peter. 1997a. "Statement—Complementarity, Trigger Mechanism—Permanent Mission of Germany to the United Nations." New York: United Nations Negotiations on the Establishment of an International Criminal Court (ICC).

———. 1997b. "Statement: International Cooperation and Judicial Assistance." Preparatory Committee on the Establishment of an International Criminal Court. New York: United Nations General Assembly.

———. 1998a. "Durchbruch in Rom. Der Vertag Über Den Internationalen Strafgerichtshof." *Vereinte Nationen* 4: 125–30.

———. 1998b. "Special Note: The Struggle for the International Criminal Court's Jurisdiction." *European Journal of Crime, Criminal Law and Criminal Justice* 6 (4): 364–76.

Kinkel, Klaus. 1998. "Statement on July 17, 1998." Völkerrechtliche Praxis der Bundesrepublik Deutschland im Jahre 1998. Max-Planck-Institut für ausländisches öffentliches Recht und Völkerrecht.

Kirsch, Philippe, and John T. Holmes. 1999. "The Rome Conference on an International Criminal Court: The Negotiating Process." *American Journal of International Law* 93 (1): 2–12.

Kraushaar, Wolfgang. 2001. "Denkmodelle der 68er-Bewegung." *Aus Politik und Zeitgeschichte* B 22–23: 14–27.

———. 2006a. "Der Nicht Erklärte Ausnahmezustand: Staatliches Handeln Während des so Genannten Deutschen Herbstes." In *Die RAF und der Linke Terrorismus, Band II*, edited by Wolfgang Kraushaar, 1011–25. Hamburg: Hamburger Edition.

———. 2006b. "Einleitung: Zur Topologie des RAF-Terrorismus." In *Die RAF und der Linke Terrorismus, Band I*, edited by Wolfgang Kraushaar, 13–61. Hamburg: Hamburger Edition.

Kress, Claus. 2006. "Versailles – Nuremberg – The Hague: Germany and International Criminal Law." *International Lawyer* 40 (1): 15–39.

Kreß, Claus. 2010. "Der Internationale Strafgerichtshof vor der Überprüfungskonferenz. Zur Entscheidung über das Verbrechen der Aggression." Kurzstellungnahme für den Ausschuss für Menschenrechte und Humanitäre Hilfe. Cambridge.

Kreß, Claus, and Leonie von Holtzendorff. 2010. "The Kampala Compromise on the Crime of Aggression." *Journal of International Criminal Justice* 8 (5): 1179–217.

Kreß, Claus, and Jan MacLean. 2005. "Germany." In *Rome Statute and Domestic Legal Orders Volume II: Constitutional Issues, Cooperation, and Enforcement*, edited by Claus Kreß, Flavia Lattanzi, Bruce Broomhall, and Valeria Santori, 131–54. Baden-Baden: Nomos Verlagsgesellschaft.

Kwiet, Konrad. 2007. "Rassenpolitik und Völkermord." In *Enzyklopädie des Nationalsozialismus*, edited by Wolfgang Benz, Hermann Graml, and Hermann Weiss, 46–64. München: Deutscher Taschenbuch Verlag.

Lanier, E. R. 1988. "Solange, Farewell: The Federal German Constitutional Court and the Recognition of the Court of Justice of the European Communities as Lawful Judge." *Boston College International and Comparative Law Review* 11 (1): 1–29.

Lippmann, Matthew. 1992. "The Other Nuremberg: American Prosecutions of Nazi War Criminals in Occupied Germany." *Indiana International & Comparative Law Review* 3 (1): 1–100.

di Lorenzo, Giovanni. 2007. "Ich Bin in Schuld Verstrickt, Interview Mit Helmut Schmidt." *Die Zeit*, August 30.

Malanowski, Wolfgang. 1985. "'Revolution' oder 'Riesenhaftes Theater'?" *Der Spiegel*, November 18.

Mullins, Claud. 1921. *The Leipzig Trials an Account of the War Criminals' Trials and a Study of German Mentality*. London: H. F. & G. Witherby. http://www.gale.com/ModernLaw/.

Non-Paper/WG.3/NO.3. 1997. "Canadian-German Draft Proposal on Complementarity".

Non-Paper/WG.3/NO.8. 1997. "Modified German Draft Proposal of 1996".

Overmans, Rüdiger. 2004. *Deutsche Militärische Verluste im Zweiten Weltkrieg: Schriftenreihe des Militärgeschichtlichen Forschungsamtes*. München: Oldenbourg Wissenschaftsverlag.

Pernice, Ingolf. 2006. *Das Verhältnis Europäischer zur Nationalen Gerichten in Europäischen Verfassungsverbund*. Berlin: Gruyter Recht.

Pfeil, Florian. 2003. "Bleibt Alles Anders? Kontinuität und Wandel Rot-Grüner Menschenrechtspolitik." In *Deutschland im Abseits? Rot-Grüne Aussenpolitik 1998–2003*, edited by Hanns W. Maull, Sebastian Harnisch, and Constantin Grund, 177–92. Baden-Baden: Nomos Verlag.

Polzin, Carsten. 2006. "Kein Austausch! Die Verfassungsrechtliche Dimension der Schleyer-Entscheidung." In *Die RAF und der Linke Terrorismus, Band II*, edited by Wolfgang Kraushaar, 1026–47. Hamburg: Hamburger Edition.

Reichel, Peter. 2001. *Vergangenheitsbewältigung in Deutschland. Die Auseinandersetzung mit der NS-Diktatur in Politik und Justiz*. Zweite Auflage. München: C. H. Beck.

Rock, Philipp. 2010. *Macht, Märkte und Moral – Zur Rolle der Menschenrechte in der Außenpolitik der Bundesrepublik Deutschland in der Sechziger und Siebziger Jahren*. Frankfurt am Main: Peter Lang.

Rogers, A. P. V. 1990. "War Crimes Trials Under the Royal Warrant: British Practice 1945–1949." *International and Comparative Law Quarterly* 39 (4): 780–800.

Royal Courts of Justice, Law Officers' Department. 1922. "The British Cases." *American Journal of International Law* 16 (4): 633–40.

Schabas, William A. 2006. *The UN International Criminal Tribunals: The Former Yugoslavia, Rwanda, and Sierra Leone*. Cambridge: Cambridge University Press.

———. 2007. *An Introduction to the International Criminal Court*, 3rd ed. Cambridge: Cambridge University Press.

Schildt, Axel. 2001. "Vor der Revolte: Die Sechziger Jahre." *Aus Politik und Zeitgeschichte* B 22–23: 7–13.

Schmidt-Jortzig, Edzard. 1998. "Statement of the German Federal Minister of Justice, German Delegation to the United Nations Diplomatic Conference of Plenipotentiaries on the Establishment of an International Criminal Court." Rome.

Schmitt, Carl. 1945. *Das Internationalrechtliche Verbrechen des Angriffskrieges und der Grundsatz "Nullum Crimen, Nulla Poena Sine Lege,"* edited by Helmut Quaritsch. Berlin: Duncker & Humblot.

Steinke, Ronen. 2012. *The Politics of International Criminal Justice: German Perspectives from Nuremberg to The Hague*. Oxford: Hart Publishing.

Taylor, Telford. 1949. "Final Report to the Secretary of the Army on the Nuremberg War Crimes Trials Under Control Council Law No. 10." Washington, DC.

The Central Office of the Judicial Authorities for the Investigation of National Socialist Crimes. 2018. "Information Sheet".

United Nations, International Criminal Tribunal for the Former Yugoslavia. 2001. *The Path to The Hague: Selected Documents on the Origins of the ICTY*. The Hague: United Nations.

United Nations War Crimes Commission. 1947. "Law Reports of Trials of War Criminals, Volume XV: Digest of Laws and Cases." London: His Majesty's Stationery Office.

United States Senate. 1998. "Is A U.N. International Criminal Court in the U.S. National Interest? Hearing Before the Subcommittee on International Operations of the Committee on Foreign Relations." S. Hrg. 105-724. Washington, DC: Congress of the United States of America.

UNTC, United Nations Treaty Collection. 2018. "Status of Treaties: Multilateral Treaties Deposited with the Secretary-General".

Werle, Gerhard. 2006. "Von der Ablehnung zur Mitgestaltung: Deutschland und das Völkerstrafrecht." In *Völkerrecht als Wertordnung: Festschrift für Christian Tomuschat*, edited by Pierre-Marie Dupuy, Bardo Fassbender, Malcolm N. Shaw, and Karl-Peter Sommermann, 657–58. Kehl: N.P. Engel Verlag.

Werle, Gerhard, and Florian Jessberger. 2002. "International Criminal Justice Is Coming Home: The New German Code of Crimes Against International Law." *Criminal Law Forum* 13 (2): 191–223.

Werle, Gerhard, and Thomas Wandres. 1995. *Auschwitz vor Gericht: Völkermord und Bundesdeutsche Strafjustiz.* München: C. H. Beck.

Weschler, Lawrence. 2000. "Exceptional Cases in Rome: The United States and the Struggle for an ICC." In *The United States and the International Criminal Court: National Security and International Law*, edited by Sarah B. Sewall and Carl Kaysen, 85–111. Lanham: Rowman & Littlefield.

Wesel, Uwe. 2006. "Strafverfahren, Menschenwürde und Rechtsstaatsprinzip: Versuch Einer Bilanz der RAF-Prozesse." In *Die RAF und der Linke Terrorismus, Band II*, edited by Wolfgang Kraushaar, 1048–58. Hamburg: Hamburger Edition.

Westdickenberg, Gerd. 1998. "Statement, Head of German Delegation in the Committee of the Whole." German Delegation to the United Nations Diplomatic Conference of Plenipotentiaries on the Establishment of an International Criminal Court.

Wilkitzki, Peter. 2003. "The Contribution of the Federal Republic of Germany and the German Länder to the Work of the ICTY." In *Man's Inhumanity to Man: Essays on International Law in Honour of Antonio Cassese*, edited by Lal Chand Vorah, Fausto Pocar, Yvonne Featherstone, Olivier Fourmy, Christine Graham, John Hocking, and Nicholas Robson, 923–33. The Hague: Kluwer Law International.

———. 2005. "The German Law on Cooperation with the ICC." *Revue Internationale de Droit Pénal* 76 (1): 97–102.

Willis, James F. 1982. *Prologue to Nuremberg: The Politics and Diplomacy of Punishing War Criminals of the First World War*. Westport: Greenwood Press.

Wirth, Steffen. 2002. "International Criminal Law in Germany: Case Law and Legislation. Presentation to the Conference Combating International Crimes Domestically, Ottawa".

Zimmermann, Andreas. 2003. "Implementing the Statute of the International Criminal Court: The German Example." In *Man's Inhumanity to Man: Essays on International Law in Honour of Antonio Cassese*, edited by Lal Chand Vorah, Fausto Pocar, Yvonne Featherstone, Olivier Fourmy, Christine Graham, John Hocking, and Nicholas Robson, 977–94. The Hague: Kluwer Law International.

CHAPTER 4

The USA and the International Criminal Court

4.1 Beacon of International Justice

In the aftermath of the First World War, President Wilson was keen to pursue liberal policies and international law. However, unlike other Allied powers, the USA was not interested in international tribunals, probably because the 100,000 American casualties were considerably low in comparison with 900,000 British and 1.4 million French battle deaths (Knock 1998, 126). Nevertheless, war crimes trials had been in the US agenda after a German U-boat sank the RMS Lusitania in 1915, killing 1198 people (including 128 Americans) and shocking the American public. But Wilson had a bigger project in mind: the establishment of a new, liberal order based on a novel organization, the League of Nations (Bass 2002, 95, 92–104).

Considering an international tribunal, Wilson was suspicious about its legality that would only vaguely derive from existing law. Instead, he favored separate national commissions and tribunals to prosecute crimes committed against the respective states' nationals or property: "the nations should use the machinery at hand […] rather than to create an international tribunal with a criminal jurisdiction for which there is no precedent, precept, practice, or procedure" (Commission on the Responsibility of the Authors of the War and on Enforcement of Penalties 1920, 142; Willis 1982, 75). As Bass notes: "American objections were not based on a lack of faith in law, but on an excess of it" (Bass 2002, 59, see also 100–3). While Wilson pursued his vision of the

S. Huikuri, *The Institutionalization of the International Criminal Court*,
https://doi.org/10.1007/978-3-319-95585-8_4

League of Nations, Articles 227–229 of the Treaty of Versailles doomed Kaiser Wilhelm II to being tried in a special tribunal and provided for further military tribunals to prosecute persons who had violated the laws and customs of war. The succeeding Leipzig trials turned into show trials due to Germany's resistance and the Allies' lack of political will to pursue justice. Also, the League of Nations failed, because of the growing isolationist desires of the US Congress and because the USA was not powerful enough to induce European countries to commit to the new order (Ikenberry 2001, 159–60; Bassiouni 1997, 20).

The USA emerged from the Second World War as a hegemon, so powerful that with its preponderance it was able to shape the postwar milieu to respond its interests and this time international justice was on the agenda too. Thus, the IMT ended up being an American creation, but initially it was not an obvious solution for dealing with the Nazi criminals: Stalin wanted to kill 100,000 German soldiers, Churchill 50–100 top Nazis, and the US Secretary of the Treasury Morgenthau proposed 2500 summary executions plus an industrial destruction of the *Ruhrgebiet* and demilitarization of Germany (Bass 2002, 181; Senate Committee on Foreign Relations 1950, 502–5). However, the US Secretary of War Stimson successfully insisted on the establishment of a tribunal "because of America's own domestic respect for due process" (Bass 2002, 148). The proceedings against the top Nazi leaders and the following Law Nr. 10 trials against specific perpetrator groups reflected the US preferences. Before and throughout the proceedings, President Roosevelt and the US prosecutors, Supreme Court Justice Jackson and his successor Taylor, followed a rather rationalist track of self-interest and selectivity. Instead of emphasizing crimes against humanity, the USA was almost exclusively concerned about prosecuting the Nazis for waging war against it and for war crimes against American soldiers. As Justice Jackson stated in his opening statement before the IMT: "to start or wage an aggressive war has the moral qualities of the worst of crimes" (International Military Tribunal 1947, 155). Subsequently, the extermination and terror of Jews and other minorities were subordinated to aggression and war crimes (Bass 2002, 178).

Also in postwar Japan, international justice served the purposes of the hegemon. Unlike the IMT, the International Military Tribunal for the Far East (IMTFE) was not based on a treaty, because the USA did not want to have Soviet influence over the proceedings. Instead, jurisdiction derived from a special order of American General MacArthur, the

Supreme Commander for the Allied Powers, who had almost full control over the establishment of the IMTFE. The IMTFE has been perceived as being more politicized than the IMT—internally because it had judges from eleven Allied countries and externally because the defendants were chosen by political criteria and the judgments were inconsistent. "Some have claimed that the trial was [...] America's revenge for the treacherous attack on Pearl Harbor [...]" (Cassese 2003, 332; see also Bassiouni 1997, 32–34). Such claims are not completely unfounded. Neither the IMT nor the IMTFE dealt with crimes committed by the USA or other Allies—including the atomic bombings of Hiroshima and Nagasaki—and, hence, protected the sovereignty of powerful states while serving as tools to punish losers of the war.

4.2 The Idea of an ICC Within the Genocide Convention

The most significant development of international criminal law after the Nuremberg trials was the adoption of the Genocide Convention. One of the most central and complex issues during its drafting was the question of whether the jurisdiction of an ICC should be included in the treaty. The UN Secretariat prepared the first draft of the Genocide Convention in 1947, which included an international court (Article IX, X, and Annex I, A/RES/77 (V) 1947; A/362 1947). During the negotiations on the Convention, the US delegation was the most vocal supporter of the inclusion of an ICC in the convention: "It was precisely because it had been felt that national courts might not be sufficiently effective in the punishment of genocide that States had realized the need for an international convention [and court] on the subject" (A/C.6/SR.98 1948, 378). The Soviet Union opposed the idea as "an infringement of the principle of sovereignty" (A/C.6/33/SR.64 1978, 14; A/C.6/SR.74 1948, 103; A/C.6/SR.98 1948, 379). Although the US proposals to maintain an ICC as part of the convention were rejected in the Ad Hoc committee for Genocide (E/794 1948, 30) and later at the UNGA Sixth Committee (A/C.6/SR.98 1948, 381), the Truman Administration remained persistent. Less than two weeks before the adoption of the Convention, the USA proposed, again, the inclusion of an ICC to the treaty and suggested to refer the establishment of the ICC to the consideration of the ILC. In this proposal, the jurisdiction of a prospective ICC was optional, responding to many states' concerns over being bound by a tribunal, the competences of which were yet unknown. Now previously reluctant states were willing to include an ICC into the Convention (A/C.6/SR.129 1948, 669, see also 677ff.). As a result and to dissatisfaction of the Soviet bloc, Article VI of Genocide Convention mentions an ICC.

However, the Truman Administration's support for the incorporation of an ICC into the Genocide Convention should not be understood as a desire to establish a court with broad powers. The court should have jurisdiction only when the state in question has failed to punish the crime of genocide, an idea that is nowadays known as the principle of complementarity and that to an extent protects state sovereignty (A/C.6/235 1948). The Truman Administration did not promote a universal jurisdiction for the prosecution of genocide either. Instead,

> the scope of the international tribunal should be limited strictly to cases of denial of justice. [...] The principle of universal punishment [promoted by France] was one of the most dangerous and unacceptable of principles, and [U.S. representative Maktos] hoped, consequently, that the Committee would reject it. (A/C.6/SR.100 1948, 399)

The Genocide Convention was adopted on December 9, 1948, and although President Truman recommended its ratification, it took forty years for the US Senate to do so. Truman's successor Eisenhower and his Secretary of State, Dulles, shared the Senate's reluctance to the Convention (Power 2003, 79ff.). In general, by the beginning of the 1950s, the USA had lost interest in an ICC. As the USA stated at the Sixth Committee in 1978, the lack of time had made the consideration of an ICC impossible (A/RES/260 (III) A 1948; A/C.6/33/SR.64 1978).

4.3 From Hesitance to Assertive Multilateralism: New Hope for International Criminal Law in the 1990s

After more than two decades, interest in an ICC slowly reemerged at the end of the 1970s. At the request of South American and Caribbean countries, the Philippines, and Syria, the Sixth Committee started to reconsider the question of an ICC in the framework of the Draft Code of Offences Against Peace and Security of Mankind in 1978. The Carter Administration was not excited about the project (A/C.6/33/SR.64

1978; A/C.6/35/SR.12 1980), but the American Bar Association started to lobby the Department of State to open negotiations on the ICC (American Bar Association 2000, 2). A few years later, the Congress urged the Reagan Administration to engage with the matter (H.R. 4151 1986, 15). The Congress's emerging interest toward the ICC can be explained with reference not only to several airplane hijackings, kidnappings, and terrorist attacks against US armed forces in the 1980s, but also to increased drug trafficking from South America to the USA. As a response to drug smuggling and the rapid growth in Americans' use of cocaine, crack, and marijuana, Reagan declared a war on drugs in the beginning of the 1980s (Bagley 1988). The Congress enacted several new anti-drug laws, including the Anti-Drug Abuse Act of 1988, which expressed the Senate's wish to start negotiations with other governments on an ICC to prosecute drug smuggling and other international crimes.

In 1990, the Congress recommended G.H.W. Bush to explore the need for the establishment of an ICC (H.R. 5114 1990), but he did not think an ICC would be advantageous to the national interests of the USA: "Were the courts to become politicized, we might find it acting contrary to U.S. interests on a whole range of issues [...]" (Pickering et al. 2003, 128, see also 135). The USA considered the codification of international criminal law to be premature. It raised doubts over whether an ICC would ever receive enough support from the states, because it derogates state sovereignty, whether it would contribute to the existing system of international law, and whether states would ever be able to agree on its jurisdiction (A/C.6/44/SR.40 1989; A/C.6/45/SR.36 1990; A/C.6/46/SR.31 1991; A/C.6/47/SR.21 1992; Pickering et al. 2003, 127, 134). In fact, the G.H.W. Bush Administration was not willing to agree on anything about an ICC and wanted to make the initiative go away:

> To accomplish this, the United States proposed that the issue be assigned to the International Law Commission, [...] known for taking several decades to complete its projects. When the International Law Commission submitted a preliminary report on the ICC a year later, the United States responded by listing several problems requiring further study, but purposely avoided any mention of possible solutions. [...] The strategy worked – the International Law Commission might still be debating the matter to this day were it not for developments in the Balkan States [...]. (Scharf 1999, 98–99)

The strategy to sabotage unwanted enterprises by retarding the process is interesting. However, the Administration's hesitance was shared by all state agencies, vital for international criminal matters. The Department of State was suspicious toward all international courts because of the International Court of Justice's (ICJ) controversial Nicaragua ruling that resulted in the US withdrawal from the ICJ's jurisdiction (ICJ 1986). The Department of Defense was worried about the ICC's consequences for the contentious US military activities abroad—particularly in Panama and Libya—and the Justice Department was not willing to let an ICC jeopardize its own, disputed, efforts to enforce international law (Scharf 1999, 98).

One month after his inauguration, Clinton gave the first signs of his new foreign policy approach, assertive multilateralism, as his Administration started to strive for the establishment of an ad hoc war crimes tribunal for the Former Yugoslavia at the UNSC (S/PV.3175 1993). The ICTY and the ICTR emerged from conflicts to which the USA and European states were not willing to intervene: "U.S. and European policymakers felt a need to respond to the emotional issue of war crimes, but did not want to be drawn into the Bosnian war as combatants or policemen" (Mikung Lee et al. 1998). The ICTY and the ICTR were established by the UNSC acting under Chapter VII of the UN Charter, and the Clinton Administration willingly portrayed itself as an active supporter of the tribunals (S/RES/827 1993; S/RES/955 1994; Cummins and Stewart 2005, 580–81). The USA indeed supported the ICTY and the ICTR. Its financial contribution to the establishment of the courts was bigger than any other country, it repeatedly put pressure on states to surrender suspects to the courts, it offered rewards of USD 5 million for information leading to arrests or convictions, and it provided the courts with intelligence and professional staff. The USA also enacted laws, enabling the surrender of fugitives to the ICTY and ICTR (Office of the Ambassador-at-Large for War Crimes Issues 2000; Scheffer 1998a; Peskin 2008, 51–52; Murphy 2002c, 377).

With the ICTY and ICTR on their way, the Clinton Administration was hopeful that the UNSC could establish similar courts also elsewhere in the world. As the rational and realist theories suggest, a powerful country tends to perceive ad hoc courts as safe tools for advancing foreign policy interests. Since the USA can control the courts and their jurisdiction through the UNSC, the risks of American citizens being prosecuted in front of them are significantly lower (Scharf 1999, 99). Clinton's foreign policy considerations combined with the horrors of

Rwanda and Srebrenica contributed to a growing interest in international justice. With the support of the Congress, Clinton launched investigations on the Cambodian Genocide (Pickering et al. 2003, 121ff.), he kept Iraq on the agenda, and his Administration's support for the investigations of the massacre in Burundi and the National Truth Commission in Haiti was crucial. However, the establishment of the ICTY and ICTR leads, according to Clinton's Ambassador-at-Large for War Crimes Issues, Scheffer, to "tribunal fatigue" at the UNSC: "Council Members are unenthusiastic about the prospect of reinventing the wheel–and financing it–every time an outrage against humanity merits judicial intervention" (Scheffer 1996, 49, see also 47–48). A certain sentiment spoke just as much for the establishment of a permanent ICC, as it did for the 1992 US Presidential Election—it's the economy, stupid!

4.4 Clinton's Rationalist Agenda on the ICC

During the negotiations of the PrepCom between the years 1996 and 1998, the Clinton, Administration and the US Congress frequently expressed their support for an ICC and its rapid establishment before the new millennia. Due to tribunal fatigue, the main US motivation behind establishing a permanent ICC was to decrease the transaction costs of international justice through avoiding new, costly ad hoc courts (Clinton 1995; A/52/PV.5 1997, 10; Scheffer 1999a, 13; S. J. RES. 32 1993). Even though the general attitude was benevolent toward the ICC, the USA stuck to the same, rationalist loaded policy it had had toward the jurisdiction of international trials since 1945, easily described with one word: control. The UNSC, enabling the USA to veto any referral that would not be in its national interest, should be the tool to exercise the control: "the United States believes that only the Security Council should have authority to refer war crimes, crimes against humanity and genocide cases to the court" (A/CN.4/458 and Add. 1–8 1994, 10). The 1994 ILC's Draft Statute for an ICC, providing the point of departure for the PrepCom negotiations, reflected the statute of the ICTY and thus the US interests: Article 23 guaranteed broad, but not exclusive powers for the UNSC *vis-à-vis* the prospective court's jurisdiction (A/CN.4/SER.A/1994/Add. 1 (Part 2) 1997; Crawford 1995, 411). Although the US delegation submitted more than twenty pages of observations to the draft (A/AC.244/1/Add.2 1995), Scheffer, the chief negotiator of the US delegation, noted that it "constituted [...] a good starting point for far more detailed and comprehensive discussions" (Scheffer 1999a, 13).

Lead by Scheffer from 1997 onward, the US delegation was the largest one throughout the negotiations. At the Rome conference, the delegation was composed of "forty strong, and easily best prepared and most professionally disciplined" (Weschler 2000, 91) lawyers and officials from, *inter alia*, the Departments of State, Justice, and Defense. The goal of the team was to negotiate a "fair, effective, and efficient" ICC that would accommodate US national interests (Scheffer 1997). To fulfill these expectations, three main issues, concerning the future court's jurisdiction, were on the negotiation agenda.

First, the ICC should only address codified core crimes, namely crimes against humanity, war crimes, and genocide. While the USA was willing to accept automatic jurisdiction for genocide, it together with other P-5 states wanted to have an opt-out-possibility from war crimes and crimes against humanity. To safeguard its interests, the US delegation was particularly active in the definition of war crimes and crimes against humanity (United States Delegation 1996a; A/AC.249/1997/WG.1/DP.1 1997; Scheffer 1999a, 19; United States Delegation 1998). Furthermore, the USA favored the exclusion of drug crimes and terrorism from the ICC's jurisdiction, because such organized crimes require complex investigative and police activities and would complicate the design of the court. Most of all, the USA opposed the inclusion of aggression to the Rome Statute. The US stance was somewhat inconsistent with the core of the IMT's jurisdiction—international crimes are committed by men and not by abstract entities—as the argument for excluding aggression was that it usually is committed by states and would therefore not be in line with the personal jurisdiction of the ICC. Moreover, the American delegation was of the opinion that the definition of aggression was controversial and problematic due to humanitarian interventions and wars of liberation. Hence, incorporating aggression to the Rome Statute "presents all the risks of politicization in a serious form" (Borek 1995) and would compromise the fairness of the court. Since many other states strongly supported the inclusion of aggression, during the last session of the PrepCom the P-5 states worked hard to at least guarantee the exclusive power of the UNSC to define aggression (Scheffer 1999a, 14; A/CONF.183/2/Add.1 1998, 14).

Secondly, to avoid politically motivated and unnecessary referrals to the ICC, the Clinton Administration initially insisted that the UNSC should have exclusive rights to trigger the ICC's jurisdiction. Since, from the US perspective, the main purpose of establishing the ICC was to avoid further ad hoc tribunals, it was justified to guarantee the UNSC with similar powers *vis-à-vis* the ICC. This reasoning features two central aspects of the rationalist theory: first, states are egoistic actors that try to realize their self-interests through institutionalization and, second, they favor the establishment of international institutions in order to reduce transactions costs. The reasoning also has exceptionalist and hegemonic connotations of a powerful state's desire to control the design and functioning of the system. However, the USA also had joint interests in mind, because a further argument in support of UNSC control was state cooperation. Since most ICC situations were expected to concern the UNSC's mandate to maintain international peace and security, its authority would ensure higher cooperation with the court. To address other states' concerns of the judicial independence of the ICC, the USA suggested that after referral, the Prosecutor and the Judges would have exclusive capacity to decide which cases should proceed to investigations and trials. During the negotiations, the USA had to get comfortable with state referrals, but it continued opposing the idea of states being able to refer specific persons to an ICC's investigation: "An individual state should not be able to pick and choose who to investigate and to dictate this to the Prosecutor, by filing a selective complaint" (Richardson 1997; See also Borek 1995). From the US view—and this view prevailed—if states were allowed to make referrals, they should only be able to refer a situation to the Prosecutor, who then would have powers to decide how to proceed. The Prosecutor's right to initiate investigations *proprio motu* was clearly unacceptable for the USA (Richardson 1997).

Third, the USA like most other states wanted the Rome Statute to be complimentary to national jurisdictions, meaning that the ICC could intervene only when domestic instances were not investigating the case in good faith:

> This […] is extremely important to the United States Government. In our view, it takes account of our interest in protecting against unwarranted prosecutions of our nationals, as well as nationals of other responsible members of the international community, while ensuring the prosecution of those who should be brought before an international tribunal. (Scheffer 1998a; L/2771 1996)

Moreover, the USA supported a possibility to opt-into the ICC jurisdiction on a case-by-case basis, which allegedly would increase the ICC's universal acceptance. Further issues on the American agenda were the funding of the ICC, which should be provided by the States Parties and not the UN, the independence of the ICC from the UN organization, and the number of ratifications (sixty), which the Rome Statute should receive before it enters into force (Richardson 1997; United States Delegation 1996b).

4.5 The Defeat in Rome

When the Rome conference started on June 15, 1998, all main issues regarding the jurisdiction of the ICC were open and the US delegation had all the reason to believe that the outcome of the conference could be successful. This is not a "mission impossible," Scheffer said few months before the conference (Scheffer 1998a). However, domestic politics played a significant role in shaping the US agenda, and by mid-June, it was clear that the mission's success would depend on the delegation's ability to negotiate guarantees that no American citizen would ever be subject to the judgment of the ICC. Otherwise, according to the powerful Republican Head of the Senate Foreign Relations Committee, Helms, the Rome Statute would be "dead on arrival" in his Committee, whose consent is necessary for the ratification of international treaties (Helms 2001, 9). As before in the PrepCom, the initial setting was polarized, because the closest US allies, namely European states and Canada, pleaded together with other LMS for a strong and independent ICC with universal jurisdiction. The US delegation, in turn, presented itself as the voice of realism: "The International Criminal Court could be truly powerful and effective only if it were built on a firm foundation of international consensus and support and if it adopted a realistic and workable approach" (A/CONF.183/13 (Vol. II) 1998, 95).

Both the dynamics of the conference, controlled by the LMS, and the domestic political situation complicated the US delegation's work at the Rome conference. First, unlike most states that worked in coalitions, the Americans had to build support for their positions in time-consuming bilateral negotiations (Scheffer 1999a, 15; Scharf 1999, 102). Second, the US proposals often came late to the negotiation table and failed to gain support or were displaced by other, more carefully drafted proposals, because the delegation received last minute instructions from Washington. This problem was caused by the time difference, but also because the Clinton Administration was battling at home not only with the Republican Congress, but also with the Lewinsky sex-scandal. In addition, Clinton traveled to China in June 1998 and the Administration was divided on the ICC. While the Department of State initially supported the ICC, the Republican Secretary of Defense and Pentagon opposed the jurisdiction of the ICC (Scheffer 2012, 227–29; Halper and Clarke 2004, 122; Feinstein and Lindberg 2009, 38.). By the end of the conference, also Albright started to get irritated and asked Scheffer how "to blow up the entire conference?" (Scheffer 2012, 207), hence, trying to utilize the same retardation tactics to which the G.H.W. Bush Administration had reached for earlier.

Already during the PrepCom negotiations, the USA had adjusted to the reality that the UNSC would not have the exclusive right to refer cases to the ICC. However, the *proprio motu* Prosecutor remained a central issue. In essence, the USA, again, feared the Prosecutor would have to deal with an enormous amount of politically motivated referrals and was of the opinion that it was not her task to decide on political issues, such as which situations would fall under the jurisdiction of the court (United States Senate 1998, 148; L/ROM/11 1998). The LMS did not sympathize with the fears over the Prosecutor turning into an international Kenneth Starr, as some US officials had referred to it (United States Senate 1998, 36). Accordingly, the *proprio motu* Prosecutor was included to the final package.

The ultimate deal breaker for the USA ended up being state consent, although statements prior to the conference did not imply that the preconditions for the exercise of the ICC's jurisdiction would be so crucial. By the end of the conference, the USA seemed to be willing to make compromises on many issues, including the Prosecutor and the UNSC powers *vis-à-vis* the ICC, but Germany's proposal of universal jurisdiction was as unacceptable for the USA as it had been during the negotiations for the Genocide Convention (A/AC.249/1998/DP.2 1998; Weschler 2000, 99, 105). According to Scheffer: "If the principle of universal jurisdiction were adopted, many Governments would never sign the treaty and the United States would have to actively oppose the Court" (A/CONF.183/C.1/SR.29 1998). The proposal of South Korea—the ICC could exercise jurisdiction if the territorial state, the state of nationality of victim or accused, or the custodial state was a States Party— was also intolerable for the USA although it enjoyed wide support among other states (A/CONF.183/C.1/L.6 1998, 1; Kirsch and Holmes 1999, 9).

Overall, the offender's state of nationality was central to the USA, and in the last four days of the conference, it made two counterproposals: first suggesting that the ICC has jurisdiction only if the territorial state *and* the state of nationality of the suspect have accepted its jurisdiction and, second, suggesting the creation of a protocol allowing states to opt out of the ICC's jurisdiction for war crimes and crimes against humanity for ten years (Kaul 1998, 368; A/CONF.183/C.1/L.70 1998; A/CONF.183/C.1/L.90 1998).

While the final package was being prepared in Rome, the ICC started to receive intensified attention from Washington too, as Clinton, Albright, and the Secretary of Defense Cohen started to call their counterparts all around the world. Cohen was even said to have threatened to reconsider the stationing of American troops in the territory of its key allies, if the ICC would have universal jurisdiction (United States Senate 1998; Weschler 2000, 104). The final package was introduced in the last morning of the conference, and it incorporated a compromise between the proposals of South Korea and the USA. The court would have jurisdiction only in cases where *one or more of* the following states are States Parties to the ICC: the state where the crime has been committed or the state of the nationality of the accused. In addition, the package offered a possibility to opt out from war crimes for seven years (Kirsch and Holmes 1999, 9–10; Kaul 1998, 371–73).

In the evening of July 17, the Committee of the Whole assembled and its Chair proposed to adopt the final package without vote. However, the USA stuck to its two proposals and India also put two proposals for vote—an overwhelming majority rejected all four proposals (A/CONF.183/C.1/SR.42 1998). In response, the US delegation asked for a non-recorded vote, acting against the prevailing wish to adopt the treaty with consensus. The Rome Statute was adopted with 120 votes to 7 and with 21 abstentions (A/CONF.183/SR.9 1998). This was a defeat for the USA that voted against the ICC in the rather dubious company of China, Libya, Iraq, Israel, Yemen, and Qatar (Van Schaak 2007; Lee 1999, 26; Scheffer 2012, 222, 224). Scheffer had reasons to feel overrun:

> There was enormous applause and glee throughout the large room. [...] They knew they had buried us, and they were ecstatic over achieving a treaty after so many years of tough negotiations. I remained seated, however, as I could hardly stand and applaud my own defeat on the vote. (Scheffer 2012, 223)

According to Scheffer's statement on the vote, in the end it was only about four words, *one or more of*: "he did not accept the concept of universal jurisdiction as reflected in the Statute, or the application of the treaty to non-parties, their nationals or officials, or to acts committed on their territories" (A/CONF.183/SR.9 1998, Scheffer 2012, 223). The outcome of the conference showed that the USA was no longer powerful enough to impose its will and to dictate the terms of an emerging international institution—its hegemony had been eroded.

However, the primary goal of the LMS was not to contest with, and rule out, the USA. The Rome Statute shows that the support of the USA was in fact perceived to be crucial by other states, because the Americans achieved almost all their objectives, most of which were not in the interest and even opposed by the LMS. As Scharf stated at the US Senate shortly after the conference:

> Scheffer should be applauded; because, really, the United States bullied its way into getting the U.S. stamp on almost every single provision in the International Criminal Court statute. It is really a U.S. statute with just a couple of exceptions, a couple of things that we did not get. (United States Senate 1998, 38)

Scheffer negotiated, among other things, for the right for the UNSC to block the ICC's investigations for one year at a time (Weschler 2000, 93), the exclusion of war nexus for crimes against humanity, and the inclusion of internal conflicts and gender crimes into the treaty. Moreover, significant improvements in the complimentary system, a guarantee that the ICC will not be financed from the UN budget, and the requirement of sixty ratifications before the ICC can become operational were incorporated into the Rome Statute (United States Senate 1998, 12; United States Delegation 1996a; A/AC.249/1997/WG.1/DP.1 1997; Scheffer 1999a, 19; United States Delegation 1998).

Although the LMS made significant concessions, in the endgame the independence of the ICC was more important to them than having the USA on board. Furthermore, it was clear that concerning state consent the US delegation had to rigorously follow the "mandate" from Senator Helms and the Pentagon to guarantee that no American citizen would ever be prosecuted in front of the ICC:

> "David Scheffer could draft the entire document, every single word of it," David Matas, a lawyer with the Canadian delegation, commented toward week's end, "and the Senate would never ratify it. It took America forty years to ratify the Genocide Convention. The United States still hasn't ratified the Convention on the Rights of Child. [...] So, one has to wonder, why even bother trying to meet such demands?" (Weschler 2000, 100; Goldsmith 2003, 100–1)

This statement also explains why the final package was "mysteriously" prepared by a small group of states behind closed doors and without US participation—other states did not believe that the USA would join the ICC anyway. The closed-door policy irritated Scheffer: "I will not belabor the final hours of the conference except to say that it could have been done differently and the outcome might have been far more encouraging" (Scheffer 1999b). In the beginning of the conference, Scheffer had hoped that the ICC would become a community accommodating concerns of states and not a club of states. However, for the LMS the US view of a community, whose rules the club of the P-5 would control, threatened to compromise the independence of the court (Scheffer 1998b).

4.6 Making the Best Out of the Defeat

Less than one week after the defeat in Rome, the Subcommittee on International Operations of the Senate Committee on Foreign Relations convened to discuss whether the ICC is in the national interest of the USA. Republican Senators Helms, Grams, and Ashcroft characterized the ICC as a serious threat to US foreign policy and national security interests. According to Helms, the Rome Statute was irreparably flawed due to the independent Prosecutor. Moreover, he argued in a realist fashion that the ICC undermines the power of the UNSC and the veto power of the USA and, therefore, "The United States must fight this treaty. [...] So long as there is breath in me, the United States will never—and I repeat never, never—allow its national security decisions to be judged by any international criminal court" (United States Senate 1998, 6). So it was clear that it would not make much sense to seek the Senate's consent for ratification of the Rome Statute (Senator Helms passed away in July 2008).

Clinton was "not prepared to go forward with this treaty in its current form" (United States Senate 1998, 23) either. His Administration's objections did not change much after Rome and can be summarized in following five points. First, states cannot delegate universal jurisdiction to the ICC, because according to the Art. 34 of the Vienna Convention on the Law of Treaties, treaties are not binding for non-party states:

> While certain conduct is prohibited under customary international law and might be the object of universal jurisdiction by a national court, the establishment of, and a state's participation in, an international criminal court are not derived from custom but, rather, from the requirements of treaty law. (Scheffer 1999a, 18)

Scheffer's statement is intriguing and points out that at least the Vienna Convention has normative binding leverage in the eyes of the USA, because it is not party to it and yet consider its rules as binding.

Second, the main problem for the USA remained Art. 12, 2 (b) of the Rome Statute. It allows the ICC to prosecute citizens of non-States Parties if they commit core crimes in the territory of a States Party or a state that recognizes the jurisdiction of the ICC ad hoc and, according to Scheffer, could potentially lead to the prosecution of Americans (A/C.6/53/SR.9 1998). As a principal military power, that possesses capabilities and the responsibility to intervene in international conflicts and to lead humanitarian missions, the USA has a unique position in the world. On this basis, its citizens are exceptionally vulnerable in the face of the ICC and would be attractive objects for political prosecutions. Hence, it would be untenable to expose such a powerful state to the jurisdiction of an international court (Scheffer 1999a, 18).

Third, the possibility of opt-out for war crimes for seven years (Art. 124 of the Rome Statute) and the amendment process of new crimes (esp. the crime of aggression) could lead to the prosecution of Americans, because ICC States Parties can opt out for war crimes and non-States Parties cannot. For instance, if Saddam had committed war crimes, but not crimes against humanity or genocide, he could ad hoc accept the jurisdiction of the ICC and opt out for war crimes, meaning that he would avoid the ICC's jurisdiction. However, if American citizens had committed crimes against humanity in Iraq, they could be prosecuted while Saddam travels free around the world. Fourth and fifth, the *proprio motu* Prosecutor and the failing linkage between the UNSC and aggression were among the most serious concerns of Clinton Administration (United States Senate 1998, 13–14; Scheffer 1998c, 1999b).

With these objections, the Clinton Administration decided to realize its preferences through cooperation and actively participated in the Preparatory Commission (PrepCommission) that had been established to prepare supplemental documents for the Rome Statute, such as Elements of Crimes (EOC) and Rules of Procedure and Evidence (RPE). The USA had, against the will of nearly all other states, been able to include an EOC in the Rome Statute, and it had strongly supported the establishment of a PrepCommission. After the defeat, the Administration hoped the PrepCommission would modify the jurisdiction of the ICC and contributed substantially to the EOC, mainly with the motivation of exempting Americans from the ICC's jurisdiction (A/53/PV.83 1998, 11; See also A/AC.249/1998/DP.11 1998; A/CONF.183/10 1998 Annex I F; A/RES/53/105 1999).

In addition to the EOC, Scheffer started to discuss additional ways to secure US citizens' immunity from the ICC. At the Senate hearing in July, he mentioned the possibility to revise the current status of forces agreements with ICC States Parties, which under Art. 98 of the Rome Statute would guarantee immunity for American military personnel (United States Senate 1998, 20–21). Accordingly, the aim was to include a Rule to the RPE, which, by taking advantage of Art. 98, would allow the USA to conclude an agreement with the ICC, preventing the surrender of its citizens to the court. The "U.S. secretaries of state and defense wrote letters to their counterparts around the world, urging their support for the [...] proposal" (Hall 2000, 786; PCNICC/2000/WGRPE(9)/DP.4 2000). Although nearly 90% of states opposed the proposal, there was a willingness for compromise because the American Service-members' Protection Act (ASPA) was simultaneously introduced in the US Congress and, if adopted, it would prohibit all US cooperation with the ICC. Consequently, Rule 195, 2 of the RPE prohibits the ICC to proceed with requests for surrender without the consent of the sending state, if under Art. 98, 2 of the Rome Statute the request would conflict with obligations under international agreements. In June 2000, the USA joined the consensus for the adoption of the EOC and RPE (Hall 2000, 786). More or less satisfied with the outcome of the EOC and RPE, the Clinton Administration now concentrated on the relationship agreement between the UN and the ICC. It wanted to preclude the automatic surrender of non-States Party nationals to the ICC in the absence of a UNSC referral (A/C.6/55/SR.9 2000, 5). This was the last US proposal (PCNICC/2000/WGICC-UN/DP.17 2000), since after the inauguration of Bush, the USA did not actively involve in the work of the PrepCommission (United States Delegation 2001; Women's Caucus for Gender Justice 2001).

On December 31, 2000, the day when the Rome Statute closed for signatures, Clinton authorized Scheffer to sign it. Clinton, however, clearly indicated that he did not recommend the ratification for his successor and that the signature only served the purpose of securing for the USA the possibility to influence the development of the ICC in the PrepCommission (Murphy 2001, 399). The signature was based on Scheffer's rational considerations: It would render the attitude of the prospective Judges and other ICC personnel more positive toward the USA, which would protect US interests, discourage actions against the USA, and enhance prospects for negotiating Bilateral Immunity Agreements with other signatories. Furthermore, opposition to the ICC had never been in the Administration's interest and without the signature, Scheffer "could not press hard for concessions from others" (Scheffer 2002, 58–59) during the negotiations on a relationship agreement between the UN and the ICC. It also seems that the strategy was to make the best out of the situation through cooperation, not least because other countries were willing and able to leave the USA behind, if necessary. Senator Helms published a press statement immediately after the signature, which he described as outrageous and inexplicable:

> for two years, the Administration has tried in vain to secure additional protections for American citizens, but was rebuffed at every turn by our so-called allies. […] I have a message for the outgoing President: This decision will not stand. I will make reversing this decision, and protecting America's fighting men and women from the jurisdiction of this international kangaroo court […]. (Helms 2000)

4.7 Bush Administration's Campaign Against the ICC at the UN

After the Rome conference, Senator Biden predicted that the ICC was "not going to come to fruition anyway, and if it does, it is a long way off" (United States Senate 1998, 21). Yet, the Rome Statute received its 60th ratification in April 2002, meaning that the ICC would become operational on July 1, 2002. The Bush Administration started its campaign against the ICC in May 2002 by withdrawing the US signature to the Rome Statute. Withdrawal of a signature is an unconventional act, which, however, according to Bush's Undersecretary of State Grossman, was legally admissible according to the Vienna Convention on the Law of Treaties. One should note, again, that the USA is not a States Party to the Convention (Grossman 2002). The Bush Administration also started to criticize the ICTY and the ICTR for being inefficient. Both courts were struggling with financial problems, lack of personnel and capacity, and the ICTY with the unwillingness of NATO forces to arrest indicted war criminals (Murphy 2002b, 483; Bass 2002, 221–22, 247–48; Prosper 2002). Only few weeks after the Milošević trial had commenced in 2002, the USA urged both courts to end the trials by 2008. Although this encountered criticism from Europe, in 2003 the UNSC called both tribunals to complete their activities by 2010 (The Council of Europe 2002; S/RES/1503 2003).

The official objections of the Bush Administration to the "illegitimate" ICC did not significantly differ from its predecessor. The ICC, and in particular the Prosecutor, is an unaccountable and unchecked power, open to abuse and unable to afford the same rights as the Bill of Rights. The court undermines the role of the UNSC and threatens US sovereignty because it has jurisdiction over its citizens (Bolton 1999; Grossman 2002). The choice to define the ICC as an unchecked power is interesting, because according to the realist theory the motivation for balancing attempts arises from other actor's unchecked and threatening power. Hence, the US campaign against the ICC could be perceived as power-balancing against the ICC, which threatened US domestic interests and national security. Bolton, Bush's Undersecretary for Arms Control and later UN Ambassador, perceived the ICC issue as a EU–US divide: "The Europeans may be comfortable with such a system, but that is one reason why they are Europeans and we are not" (Bolton 1999). According to Bolton, the ICC erodes American standards of structural constitutionalism, therefore its liberty, and should be perceived as an attack against the USA. The "no reservations" clause was directed against the Senate and the reservations it had made to the Genocide Convention. Furthermore, the definition of war crimes implied the atomic bombings of Hiroshima and Nagasaki. Regarding the deterrence effect of the ICC, the view was that only democracy promotion would prevent atrocities. Bolton, like many other neoconservatives, followed traditional realist reasoning by considering military action as the only effective deterrent for core crimes (Bolton 1999; United States Senate 1998, 2; Grossman 2002).

As the operationalization of the ICC approached, so did also the renewal of the UN Peacekeeping Mission in Bosnia and Herzegovina (UNMIBH) mandate. On the day when the Rome Statute received its 60th ratification, five Congressmen (including Senator Helms) urged the Bush Administration to secure immunity for American peacekeepers in all UN missions (Murphy 2002a, 725). In May, the USA unsuccessfully tried to secure immunity to its UN peacekeepers through a UNSC resolution that would automatically renew every year. As the UNSC rejected the proposal again in June, the USA vetoed the extension of the UNMIBH mandate (S/PV.4563 2002; Cummins and Stewart 2003, 157). That the USA decided to use its veto power at the UNSC was an exceptional move. After the end of the Cold War, between January 1990 and June 2002, the USA had taken advantage of its veto power fourteen times: thirteen times because of the situation in the Middle East—in support of Israel—and now because of the ICC (United Nations 2013).

Other UNSC members were not willing to provide blanket immunity for peacekeepers. From their view, the Rome Statute offered sufficient checks against unwarranted prosecutions and, as India's representative stated, peacekeepers already enjoyed immunity under Status of Forces Agreements. The UN Secretary-General Annan found the concerns unfounded and wrote to the US Secretary of State Powell: "I can state confidently that in the history of the United Nations [...] no peacekeeper or any other mission personnel have been anywhere near the kind of crimes that fall under the jurisdiction of the ICC" (Murphy 2002a, 727; S/PV.4568 2002; S/PV.4568 (Resumption 1) 2002). After two short extensions of the UNMIBH mandate, the withdrawal of American peacekeepers from East Timor, and strong pressure from other members of the UNSC, the USA agreed to settle with a resolution that provides immunity for non-ICC States Parties' peacekeepers. The Res. 1422 was adopted on July 12 and on the same day the UNSC extended the mandate of the UNMIBH. The idea of the resolution was to defer the ICC's jurisdiction for one year, after which it had to be renewed annually by an affirmative vote of the UNSC. In case of a failed renewal, the ICC would have jurisdiction for crimes committed during the time of the deferral (S/RES/1420 2002; S/RES/1421 2002; S/RES/1422 2002; Murphy 2003, 711). In June 2003, the renewal of Res. 1422 was due. Other UNSC members contested the renewal, and Annan hoped that this would "not become an annual routine" (S/PV.4772 2003). While the resolution was renewed (France, Germany, and Syria abstained), in

2004 the UNSC refused to issue another renewal, not least because of the US torture scandals in Iraq, Afghanistan, and Guantánamo Bay (S/RES/1487 2003; Johansen 2006, 309).

In addition to Res. 1422, the Bush Administration kept opposing ICC-related resolutions at the UN. Due to its power position, it was able to delete all references to the ICC in UNSC resolutions and when, for instance, the UN recommended Burundi to refer the Gatumba massacre to the ICC and Burundi was willing to do so, the USA blocked this undertaking by refusing to support the renewal of the UN Operation in Burundi, if it would cooperate with the ICC (S/PV.5093 2004; S/RES/1577 2004; SC/8258 2004). Moreover, although the USA was not able to prevent the UN–ICC cooperation agreement at the UNGA, it succeeded in guaranteeing that the UN would not pay for any expenses arising from its cooperation with the ICC. However, other undertakings of the Bush Administration at the UNGA and its committees were overruled by an EU-led coalition (A/RES/58/79 2003; A/C.6/58/SR.9 2003; A/C.6/58/SR.10 2003; A/C.6/58/SR.13 2003; A/RES/58/318 2004; A/C.6/59/SR.6 2004; A/C.6/59/SR.27 2004). The advantage of the EU at the UNGA was that here all countries have one vote, no one holds veto powers, and resolutions are adopted by two-thirds majority. Hence, while the USA was able to use its veto power at the UNSC, it was not able to influence the multilateral diplomacy of the UNGA and was overruled by a normative binding coalition.

4.8 Protecting National Interests Through Coercion

4.8.1 American Service-Members' Protection Act and Article 98 of the Rome Statute

Actions at the UN-level were not enough for the USA. Already in 2000, the Senate had started to include a prohibition of extradition to the ICC to all new extradition treaties with other countries (Cummins and Stewart 2001, 173) and nearly fifty Congressmen introduced the ASPA to the Congress. The ASPA prohibits the cooperation of all US-agencies with the ICC and any military assistance to ICC States Parties, with the exception of major US-allies Argentina, Australia, Egypt, Israel, Japan, Jordan, South Korea, New Zealand, and Taiwan (Sec. 2007, H.R. 4775 2002). It also restricts US participation to UN peacekeeping missions, unless participating US military personnel are permanently exempted from the ICC's jurisdiction. Moreover, the ASPA authorizes the US President to free American military personnel held captive by the ICC (S. 2726 2000; H.R. 4654 2000). For this reason, the ASPA is also called "The Hague Invasion Act" as it authorizes the President "to use all means necessary and appropriate [except bribes and other inducements] to bring about the release of any [United States and allied person] who is being detained or imprisoned by, on behalf of, or at the request of the International Criminal Court" (Sec 2008, H.R. 4775 2002). While the Clinton Administration, including Pentagon, did not support the ASPA (United States House of Representatives 2000, 39–40), Helms and DeLay reintroduced the bill in May 2001 (S. 857 2001; H.R. 1794 2001) and in 2002 President Bush signed the ASPA into law as part of the Anti-Terror Bill (H.R. 4775 2002). The ASPA constitutes coercive use of economic (prohibition of military aid) and military (invasion to The Hague) threats and, as such, can be perceived as an attempt to weaken international cooperation, norms, and institutions.

With the ASPA on its way, the Bush Administration launched a campaign for Bilateral Immunity Agreements (BIAs) in July 2002, at the same time when it was pressing the UNSC to adopt Res. 1422. The BIAs are also called Article 98 agreements and non-surrender agreements, because Art. 98, 2 of the Rome Statute prohibits the ICC from requesting surrender, if this would require the surrendering state to breach an international agreement with another state. The strategy of the USA was to take advantage of this paragraph and to conclude bilateral agreements in order to protect American citizens against ICC prosecutions (Bolton 2003). As Bush stated in September 2002:

> we want an Article 98 with all countries, absolutely. I strongly reject the ICC. I'm not going to accept an ICC. I'm not going to put ourselves in a position where our soldiers and diplomats get hauled into a court over which we have got – the prosecutors whom we don't know, the judges – I mean, we're not going to allow ourselves to do that. (Bush 2002, 1618)

Several cases under universal jurisdiction were filed for national courts in France, Great Britain, Germany, and Belgium against Rumsfeld, G.H.W. Bush, Powell, and Cheney between the years 2002 and 2007 and fueled the Administration's paranoia against international criminal law (Langer 2011).

The legality of the BIAs is questionable for two reasons. First, it is argued that the original intent of Art. 98 was only to recognize the existing Status of Forces Agreements (SOFAs), commonly concluded between the receiving and the sending states (and also with international and non-governmental organizations) to regulate a broad range of issues concerning the sending state's military presence in the host country. Second, the reason why the SOFAs are addressed in the Rome Statute is that they can also exclude the sending state's military personnel from local jurisdiction and the drafters wanted to solve potential legal conflicts arising from existing SOFAs. While, according to Scheffer, the intent of the USA in the negotiations on Art. 98 was to guarantee a means to negotiate new non-surrender agreements, the Bush Administration's interpretation of Art. 98 went much further, because it wanted blanket immunity not just for US military personnel, but for all American citizens (Scheffer 2005, 338; Erickson 1994, 139–40; United States Senate 1998, 20–21; Meyer 2005, 100).

Bolton claimed that the original initiative to conclude BIAs came from European countries during the negotiations on the UNSC Res. 1422. Indeed, France and Ireland had discussed the use of Art. 98, but they did not have a global campaign for immunity agreements in mind (S/PV.4563 2002; S/PV.4568 2002). While a BIA between the USA and a non-States Party to the ICC is unproblematic, serious issues of treaty conflict arise when an ICC States Party signs a BIA. Art. 27, 2 of the Rome Statute prohibits all forms of immunity, and Art. 86 establishes a general obligation to cooperate with the ICC. Therefore, a States Party that refuses to comply with Art. 89, 1 (States Parties shall comply with requests for arrest and surrender), because it has signed a BIA, acts inconsistently with its obligations to the ICC (Tallman 2003, 1034). Moreover, Art. 18 of the Vienna Convention on the Law of Treaties obliges states to refrain from acts that defeat the object and purpose of a treaty they are parties to. And, after all, one of the oldest principles of international law is *pacta sunt servanda*, agreements must be kept.

4.8.2 Worldwide Run for Bilateral Immunity Agreements

Organized and supported by the Department of State and in particular Bolton, American embassies started to persuade their host countries into signing a BIA with economic coercion as their main tool of diplomacy. When diplomatic persuasion combined with cuts in military aid did not have the desired effects, President Bush signed the Consolidated Appropriations Act 2005 into law in December 2004. The Act contained the Nethercutt Amendment, which made development aid from the US Economic Support Fund conditional on signing a BIA and, hence, threatened countries all over the world with losing aid in the amount of tens, or even hundreds, of millions of US-dollars (H.R. 4818 2004, Sec. 574; Human Rights First 2004). The scope of the BIA campaign was unparalleled in the history of diplomacy. The strongest pressure was put on European NATO-candidate states and African, Latin American, Caribbean, and Central Asian countries and cuts in military and development aid were effective means of coercion in poorer countries such as Romania—ICC States Party since April 2002—which became the first state to sign a BIA in August 2002 (Reeker 2002).

CARICOM-states, highly dependent on US economic aid, refused to conclude BIAs despite strong economic and diplomatic pressure (Ribando 2007, 5). As a result, the USA suspended all aid to Caribbean ICC States Parties. The CARICOM was "deeply disturbed at the punitive action taken by the US Government" (CARICOM 2003). The Bush Administration canceled not only projects for hurricane relief, health care, and infrastructure, but also programs that were in the US national interest, such as support to fight drug trafficking, which has wider consequences for the USA too. After the suspension of US economic aid, Antigua & Barbuda, for instance, experienced a significant increase in cocaine smuggling and criminality and eventually it signed a BIA (CICC 2006b, c).

African countries faced similar treatment. Namibia was one of the ICC States Parties refusing to sign a BIA, and as a consequence, it lost some 225,000 USD of military assistance (Amupadhi 2003). Also in Kenya, politicians were defiant: "They can keep their dollars as long as they [do not] respect our dignity" (Kristof 2005). Accordingly, Kenya, and South Africa too, lost tens of millions of US-dollars. However, Kenya and Namibia were exceptions and 24 out of the 30 African ICC States Parties ended up concluding a BIA. The large amount of BIA's in the continent can be explained with the fact that most countries could not afford to lose the US aid.

Most Latin American countries, including Argentina, Brazil, Mexico, Paraguay, Peru, and Uruguay, opposed the BIAs, and also here the main regional organization, MERCOSUR, adopted a critical stance toward the US campaign (Ribando 2007, 5; MERCOSUR 2005). Peru lost more than 4 million USD of military aid that was supposed to be used against drug dealing. In Ecuador, host to one of the largest US military bases in Latin America, the whole political scene opposed the US attempts and the BIA campaign was characterized as blackmail. Ecuador has traditionally cooperated with the USA on money laundering, border control, and illegal immigration. Due to its unwillingness to submit to US demands, it lost up to 22 million USD. However, not all Latin American states could afford to resist the USA. In 2003, Colombia lost approximately 5 million USD in aid and when the USA threatened to cut further 130 million USD of development and military aid, including aid for the fight against drug traffickers and terrorists, Colombia signed a BIA (Los Angeles Times 2005; Ribando 2007, 5; CICC 2006a, b).

In the Middle East, North Africa, and Asia, the situation was not as dramatic, since most of the countries were not ICC States Parties. Of Middle Eastern countries, only Jordan was a States Party and signed a BIA in December 2004 after it was threatened with the loss of more than 250 million USD from USAID. In Central Asia, Asia, and Pacific, many non-ratifiers signed BIAs without antagonism and the signatures were followed by celebratory statements such as: "This is another step in the developing closer ties between the U.S. and the Lao PDR" (U.S. Embassy 2003). Allegedly, there were cases, where the USA not only "asked" states to sign a BIA, but also affected their decision to ratify the Rome Statute. In Georgia, for instance, the "Government sources have told [...] that ratification of the ICC Treaty is stalled in the President's office as 'a direct consequence of U.S. pressure'" (HRW 2003b). Major non-NATO allies Japan, South Korea, Australia, New Zealand, and Taiwan were exempted from the restrictions and of the other ICC States Parties in the region, and only the Cook Islands and Samoa did not sign a BIA (Balais-Serrano 2006; CICC 2006b, c) (Table 4.1).

The EU-countries actively opposed the BIAs. With 42 ratifications, European continent is best represented at the ICC, and only Belarus, Turkey, Russia, and Ukraine have not ratified the Rome Statute. As NATO-allies, most of the Western European countries were exempted from the ASPA-restrictions and only a few states even considered a BIA. However, NATO-candidate countries were targets of intensive BIA-diplomacy, but in addition to Romania only Albania, Bosnia-Herzegovina, Macedonia, and Montenegro signed a BIA (Hawkins 2008, 114). In the Balkans, the BIA campaign took bizarre forms. "US Ambassador in Croatia even published a public (!) letter in the Zagreb

Table 4.1 Bilateral Immunity Agreements with the USA[a]

ICC states parties in 2007	*Non-states parties in 2007*
Afghanistan, Albania, Antigua and Barbuda, Belize, Benin, *Bolivia*, Bosnia and Herzegovina, Botswana, Burkina Faso, Burundi, Cambodia, Central African Republic, Chad, Colombia, Comoros, Congo Brazz., Democratic Republic of Congo, Djibouti, Dominica, Dominican Republic, East Timor, Fiji, Gabon, Gambia, Georgia, Ghana, Guinea, Guyana, Honduras, *Jordan*, Lesotho, Liberia, Macedonia, Malawi, Marshall Islands, Mauritius, Mongolia, Montenegro, Nauru, Nigeria, Panama, *Romania*, Saint Kitts and Nevis, Senegal, Sierra Leone, Tajikistan, Uganda, Zambia (total 49)	Algeria, Angola, Armenia, Azerbaijan, *Bahrain*, Bangladesh, Bhutan, Brunei, Cameroon, Cape Verde, Cote d'Ivoire, Egypt, *El Salvador*, Equatorial Guinea, Eritrea, *Ethiopia*, Grenada, Guinea-Bissau, Haiti, India, Israel, Kazakhstan, Kiribati, *Kuwait*, *Kyrgyzstan*, Laos, Madagascar, Maldives, Mauritania, Micronesia, Morocco, Mozambique, Nepal, Nicaragua, Oman, Pakistan, Palau, Papua New Guinea, Philippines, Rwanda, Sao Tome and Principe, Seychelles, Singapore, Solomon Islands, Sri Lanka, *Suriname*, Thailand, Togo, Tonga, Tunisia, Turkmenistan, Tuvalu, United Arab Emirates, Uzbekistan, Yemen (total 55)

[a]The data is compiled from four different sources. The most reliable source is the Georgetown Law Library's Article 98 Agreements Research Guide that provides full texts of 95 BIAs. That listing, however, does not include all BIAs as, for instance, the BIA with Romania is not included in the listing. In addition to the Georgetown Law Library, NGO sources have reported more than one hundred BIAs. Those BIAs that are not listed in the Georgetown Law Library's Web site, but are reported by NGO sources, are highlighted in italics. See Georgetown Law Library (2009), AMICC (2007), CICC (2006c), and HRW (2003a)

press [...] warning that Croatia would lose 19 million $ of military aid if it did not sign an agreement" (Aguirrezabal Quijera 2003, 201; Boucher 2002; Boduszyński and Balalovska 2004, 25). In 2003, the USA threatened to withhold all assistance from Serbia and Montenegro unless they fully cooperated with the ICTY. Two weeks later, Serbia's military aid was suspended, because it refused to grant US citizens immunity for crimes against humanity, war crimes, and genocide—the same crimes for which the ICTY had jurisdiction over Serbian citizens. Moreover, although Baltic states, Bulgaria, and Slovakia supported the US Operation Iraqi Freedom and Bulgaria allowed the USA to use its air base, the USA suspended millions of USD of military funding after they refused to sign a BIA (Diehl 2003; Gardner 2003, 3).

Many African, European, and Latin American states reasoned their unwillingness to conclude a BIA with their obligations emerging from the ratification of the Rome Statute. Also, the desire to protect the integrity of the Rome Statute and state sovereignty, which both were undermined by the US actions, was given as reasons to ignore the US requests (Gardner 2003; CICC 2006b, c). It is indeed intriguing that while the USA was deeply concerned about its own state sovereignty potentially being violated by the ICC, it did not hesitate to directly intervene into other states' domestic matters, such as treaty ratification. This brings into the limelight the Bush Administration's realist perception of international cooperation and international law being tools of powerful states' domestic politics.

4.8.3 Gradual Change of Mind

The first signs of *détente* in the Bush Administration's stance toward the ICC became visible in 2005, when it tolerated the UNSC referral of the Darfur-situation to the ICC. However, the Administration considered the ICC as the last resort to address the violence in Sudan. During the negotiations on the resolution, the USA, along the lines of its selective policy *vis-à-vis* international tribunals, offered to sponsor an ad hoc tribunal in the facilities and under the jurisdiction of the ICTR. However, other UNSC members resisted the idea, the Human Rights Watch calculated that the costs of a hybrid court would drastically exceed the costs of an ICC referral, and there were also rumors that Bush would be too ashamed to use his veto power at the UNSC, because his Administration had led the way in denouncing the situation in Darfur as genocide (H. CON. RES. 467 2004; Powell 2006; Kostas 2006, 115–16, 118). Hence, the UNSC referred the Darfur case to the ICC, and the USA abstained in the vote and declared:

> it is important that the international community speaks with one voice in order to help promote effective accountability. The United States continues to fundamentally object to the view that the ICC should be able to exercise jurisdiction over the nationals, including government officials, of states not party to the Rome Statute. That strikes the essence of the nature of sovereignty. (S/PV.5158 2005)

The referral significantly strengthened the ICC's international standing, while another ad hoc or hybrid tribunal would have weakened its legitimacy as a cooperative solution for the international criminal law regime. Furthermore, even though the USA would never ratify the Rome Statute, from now on it was impossible to outlaw the ICC completely (Ralph 2007, 175–78). Although the USA made sure that the UN would not carry the costs of the ICC's actions in Darfur, it did not exclude the possibility of cooperation in terms of the handover of information to the ICC (McCormack 2008; S/PV.5158 2005; S/RES/1593 2005).

Around the same time as the Darfur referral, some officials in the Department of Defense started to express concerns regarding the unwanted consequences of the BIA policy and were joined in the first half of 2006 by members of the Congress and Bush Administration. In 2006, Senator McCain stated that the USA was paying "a very heavy price" (Ribando 2007, 10) in countries where aid had been cut. Only few days earlier, Secretary of State Rice had admitted that the BIA campaign was "sort of the same as shooting ourselves in the foot" (Rice 2006). Indeed, in Latin America, the fight against drug trafficking, transnational crime, and money laundering had suffered. In Africa, regional peacekeeping capacities were seriously weakened, and in Eastern Europe, as the Serbian Prime Minister Živković said, "it would be very difficult to explain to our people that on the one hand we will sign a bilateral agreement with the United States in which we agree to protect their citizens, while at the same time we are arresting and extraditing our citizens for [the ICTY]" (Gardner 2003, 3). The Bush Administration's Eastern European allies in the Iraq War even lost funds for night vision goggles, because they declined to sign a BIA (Heindel 2003, 374). Starting from the fall of 2006, a series of bills and waivers relinquished the sanctions provided by the ASPA and the Nethercutt Amendment and four days before leaving office, Bush issued final waivers. The BIA campaign came to its end in March 2009 as the Nethercutt Amendment expired, but the BIAs remain in force (Taft et al. 2009, 13–14).

While the campaign was more of a disadvantage for US foreign policy interests, for emerging powers, such as the EU and China, cuts in the US foreign and military aid opened opportunities for cooperation with developing countries. The US Southern Commander General Craddock acknowledged already in 2005 that in Latin America "Extra-hemispheric actors are filling the void left by restricted U.S. military engagement with partner nations. [...] An increasing presence of the People's Republic of China (PRC) in the region is an emerging dynamic that must not be ignored" (Taft et al. 2009, 12). The tendency to seek alternative partners of cooperation was observable in many countries. For instance, after being three years on the "black list" of the USA, Barbados signed a military aid agreement with China that produced USD 1.5 million of aid (CICC 2006b, c). For the EU-candidate countries, such as Bulgaria and Croatia, the choice was even easier. These countries did not just feel morally obligated to follow the EU stance on the BIAs, but they also balanced the loss of the US aid with much larger EU pre-accession funds (CICC 2006b). Moreover, the US exceptionalism allowed the EU to signal a multilateral alternative to coercive policies and to engage in normative binding.

4.9 Cooperative Turn: The Obama Effect

Although the Obama Administration made clear that it primarily supports justice through national and not international courts (Rapp 2010a), the policy toward the ICC changed significantly after Obama's inauguration. In January 2009, Secretary of State Clinton stated, in a rationalist fashion, that the USA ends its hostility toward the ICC and will look for opportunities to support the ICC in ways that promote US interests (United States Senate 2009, 65–66). The US Ambassador to the UN, S. Rice, referred to the ICC in her first speech at the UNSC, noting that the ICC "looks to become an important and credible instrument [...]" (Rice 2009). According to Koh, the Legal Advisor of the Department of State, the Administration applied a "pragmatic, case-by-case approach towards ICC issues" (Koh 2012). In 2009, the USA participated as an observer delegation in the ICC Assembly of States Parties (ASP) for the first time in eight years and confirmed its support for international justice (Rapp 2009). According to Koh, the participation was motivated by the Obama Administration's "smart power" policy, meaning that instead of simply disagreeing, the Administration tries to reach mutually beneficial outcomes regarding the ICC (Koh 2012).

The USA also participated with a very large interagency delegation to the 2010 Kampala Review Conference (RC/INF.1 2010). The Bush Administration's withdrawal of the US signature could have prevented the participation as Art. 112 of the Rome Statute allows only signatories' participation in ICC conferences, but the Obama Administration renounced the withdrawal (Koh 2010). The main agenda of the USA at the ASP and in Kampala was the definition of aggression that had been addressed by a special working group since 2004. In line with traditional US policy toward the crime of aggression, the Obama Administration considered the working group's definition vague, because it did not provide the UNSC with exclusive rights to determine aggression (Rapp 2009, 2010a). While the USA failed to achieve veto power over aggression, it succeeded in realizing many of its preferences. First, an opt-out possibility for the crime was included in the amendment, and second, nationals of non-States Parties will not be prosecuted for aggression. Furthermore, the ICC cannot exercise its jurisdiction over the crime before 2017 and before two-thirds of ICC States Parties have ratified the amendment to the Rome Statute (Rapp 2010a). However, since the USA was not able to guarantee the UNSC control over the crime of aggression, it interfered with other states' commitment to the amendment by repeatedly stating that it does not support the ratification of the amendment (Koh 2012; Rapp 2013).

Although the Obama Administration did not approve the crime of aggression amendment, significant improvements in the context of US cooperation with the ICC took place. In November 2010, the USA promised to support all current ICC proceedings and urged other states to provide cooperation and assistance to the ICC (Rapp 2010b). In 2011, it supported the UNSC referral of the Libya case to the ICC and played a significant role in the surrender of Ntaganda to the ICC. Furthermore, under the War Crimes Reward Program, the USA offered USD 5 million rewards for information leading to the arrest of ICC fugitives (Rapp 2013).

While the attitude toward the ICC significantly changed, the Obama Administration did not ratify the Rome Statute. As Rapp, Obama's Ambassador-At-Large for War Crimes, put it: "while the US has an important role in international criminal justice, it is unlikely to join the ICC anytime soon" (Belczyk 2010). Instead of ratifying the Rome Statute, the Obama Administration designed an own solution for dealing with accountability:

> "Smart Power Approach" to international criminal justice [...] sees accountability as part of a broader approach to diplomacy, development, rule of law, and atrocities prevention. To that end, a year ago the President announced the formation of an Atrocities Prevention Board, stating that "preventing mass atrocities and genocide is a core national security interest and a core moral responsibility of the United States of America." Through focused coordination, training, enhancing our civilian surge capacity, and many other efforts, the United States is working to put in place a whole-of-government approach to atrocities prevention. (Koh 2012)

To conclude, although the Obama Administration accommodated the ICC, it preferred to set its own mechanism—a mechanism it can control—for the punishment and prevention of core crimes instead of relying on an existing institution, the ICC.

4.10 Conclusions

This case study allows to conclude that since Second World War all American Presidents have more or less constantly followed three guidelines when it comes to international tribunals. They, first, seek to safeguard national sovereignty and oppose universal jurisdiction, second, pursue international justice through ad hoc tribunals, and, third, try to control the system through the UNSC. These guidelines aim at protecting and advancing national, and not primarily international, interests in common with the realist perception of international institutions to the extent that maintaining state sovereignty is of central importance. In an extreme case, such as the Bush Administration, international cooperation is perceived as a potential threat, because it may not maximize domestic interests, but instead may erode state power as the distribution of benefits is not controllable.

The core of the US policy preferences has not significantly changed in the last six decades, but there clearly are nuances among different Administrations and one could claim that Republicans tend to follow rather realist tracks, while Democrats choose a rationalist course. To describe the Republicans' policy toward international criminal law as somewhat realist is justified. First, all Republican Presidents who had to confront the issue of a permanent, independent ICC—Eisenhower, Reagan, G.H.W. Bush, and G.W. Bush—were dismissive of the cooperative solution. Second, while the majority of states considered binding norms and institutions the key to suppress impunity for grave human rights abuses, neoconservatives did not put their bets on cooperation or international law but questioned their power. As Bolton put it: "Why should anyone imagine that bewigged judges in The Hague will succeed where cold steel has failed?" (Bolton 1999; United States Senate 1998, 2). Third, the BIA campaign showed that neoconservatives do not shy away from economic pressure, military means—the invasion of The Hague—and ad hoc coalitions when they disagree with other states on the rules of cooperation. Clearly, such policies do not leave much space for multilateralism.

While the examples of the G.H.W. Bush and G.W. Bush Administrations showed that the Bush family does not prefer to negotiate on the issues of international tribunals, Clinton and Obama sent their envoys to the negotiation tables although their room for maneuver is not very spacious—not least because of the partisan Senate. Along the lines of rationalist theory, Clinton and Obama acknowledged that they could not afford to stay outside international institutions and, accordingly, they tried to realize self-interest through cooperation. However, when the USA enters negotiations, its preferences are already fixed in the domestic realm and thus exogenous to the negotiation situation. This leaves less room for compromises and cooperation, and, at least in the case of the ICC, there is not much support for the explanatory power of socialization and communicative action-theories considering the US policies. The "smart power" approach of the Obama Administration declared that the USA is interested in realizing mutual interests (increasing accountability) through cooperation. However, national interests seemed override mutual gains as the Obama Administration sought for ways to modify the ICC from the outside and to maximize the gains of the institution without investing its power and assets into it. Moreover, the Administration interfered somewhat in the development of the treaty by discouraging other states from ratifying the crime of aggression amendment.

Compared to the EU, international treaties serve mainly the domestic purposes of the USA (Cummins and Stewart 2005, 731). In contrast, European countries have an institutional picture in mind: an order that would be based on the international rule of law, multilateralism, and binding institutions. Looking back to the post-Second World War institutionalization from the point of view of Ikenberry's liberal theory, the USA could have secured the design of, and thus control over, the regime of international criminal law—at least it had the power and cause to do so. By integrating an amended version of the Nuremberg Charter to the UN system or by investing more authority into the negotiations on the Genocide Convention, the USA may have been able to save a lot of diplomatic effort in the decades that were to come. By the end of the Cold War, US hegemony had declined and it was no longer able to dictate the rules of cooperation. Although the USA remains a powerful actor, it is not supreme at least in the framework of international criminal law: A normative binding coalition of middle powers and small states was able to overrule its authority and establish one of the most important post-Second World War institutions against its will. This defeat reveals that in the domain of human rights there was no such thing as a "unipolar moment" or "American empire," but quite the contrary. While also in the future, the USA will have enough economic power to coerce many states into signing agreements like the BIA, such coercive tactics can easily turn against its interests and cause a legitimacy crisis. Hence, the emergence of the ICC cannot be explained as a result of hegemonic stability or coercive power, but with state cooperation, successful coalition building of the LMS, and perhaps with power balancing, which, however, is not based on traditional sources of power, but on state cooperation.

References

UN Documents (references starting with A/…, E/…, L/…, PCNICC/…, SC/…, and S/…) available at documents.un.org or unbisnet.un.org.

Aguirrezabal Quijera, Irune. 2003. "The Integrity of the Rome Statute: Political Aspects from an European and American Perspective." In *Der Internationale Strafgerichtshof: Fünf Jahre Nach Rom*, edited by Gunnar Theissen and Martin Nagler, 38–45. Berlin: Deutsches Institut für Menschenrechte.

American Bar Association, Criminal Justice Section. 2000. "Report to the House of Delegates".

AMICC. 2007. "Bilateral Immunity Agreements: Breakdown of Countries." American Non-Governmental Organizations Coalition for the International Criminal Court.

Amupadhi, Tangeni. 2003. "Namibia: Country Snubs US on ICC." *AllAfrica*, July 30.

Bagley, Bruce Michael. 1988. "The New Hundred Years War? US National Security and the War on Drugs in Latin America." *Journal of Interamerican Studies and World Affairs* 30 (1): 161–82.

Balais-Serrano, Evelyn. 2006. "Rome Statute of the International Criminal Court, Ratification and Implementation in Asia: Some Prospects and Concerns." In *Experts Meeting and Delegation on ICC Organized by FORUM-ASIA and INSEC*. Kathmandu.

Bass, Gary Jonathan. 2002. *Stay the Hand of Vengeance: The Politics of War Crimes Tribunals*. Princeton: Princeton University Press.

Bassiouni, M. Cherif. 1997. "From Versailles to Rwanda in Seventy-Five Years: The Need to Establish a Permanent International Criminal Court." *Harvard Human Rights Journal* 10: 11–62.

Belczyk, Jaclyn. 2010. "US War Crimes Ambassador Says US Unlikely to Join ICC in 'Foreseeable Future.'" *Jurist*, January 28.

Boduszyński, Mieczyslaw P., and Kristina Balalovska. 2004. "Between a Rock and a Hard Place: Croatia, Macedonia, and the Battle over Article 98." *Problems of Post-Communism* 51 (1): 18–30.

Bolton, John R. 2003. "American Justice and the International Criminal Court: Remarks at the American Enterprise Institute." Washington, DC.

———. 1999. "Speech Two: Reject and Oppose the International Criminal Court." In *Toward an International Criminal Court? Three Options Presented as Presidential Speeches*. New York: Council on Foreign Relations.

Borek, Jamison. 1995. "Statement: Agenda Item 142: Establishment of an International Criminal Court. United Nations General Assembly." USUN Press Release #182. U.S. Department of State.

Boucher, Richard. 2002. "Daily Press Briefing." U.S. Department of State.

Bush, George W. 2002. "Remarks Prior to Discussions with President Alvaro Uribe of Colombia and an Exchange with Reporters." *Weekly Compilation of Presidential Documents* 38 (39): 1618.

CARICOM. 2003. "Statement Issued by the Conference of Heads of Government of the Caribbean Community on Bilateral Agreements Under Article 98 of the Rome Statute Establishing the International Criminal Court, Press Release 95/2003." Caribbean Community.

Cassese, Antonio. 2003. *International Criminal Law*. Oxford: Oxford University Press.

CICC. 2006a. "Countries Opposed to Signing a US Bilateral Immunity Agreement (BIA): US Aid Lost in FY04&FY05 and Threatened in FY06." Coalition for the International Criminal Court.

———. 2006b. "Quotes from High Officials Opposing the US Campaign for Bilateral Immunity Agreements." Coalition for the International Criminal Court.

———. 2006c. "Summary of Information on Bilateral Immunity Agreements (BIAs) or So-Called 'Article 98' Agreements as of July 8, 2006." Coalition for the International Criminal Court.

———. 2006d. "Status of US Bilateral Immunity Agreements (BIAs)." Coalition for the International Criminal Court.

Clinton, Bill. 1995. "A Commitment to Human Dignity, Democracy, and Peace, Speech at the University of Connecticut Dodd Human Rights Center." American NGO Coalition for the International Criminal Court.

Commission on the Responsibility of the Authors of the War and on Enforcement of Penalties. 1920. "Annex II. Memorandum of Reservations Presented by the Representatives of the United States to the Report of the Commission on Responsibilities, April 4, 1919." *American Journal of International Law* 14 (1): 95–154.

Crawford, James. 1995. "The ILC Adopts a Statute for an International Criminal Court." *The American Journal of International Law* 89 (2): 404–16.

Cummins, Sally J., and David P. Stewart, eds. 2001. *Digest of United States Practice in International Law 2000.* Washington, DC: U.S. Department of State, Office of the Legal Adviser, International Law Institute.

———, eds. 2003. *Digest of United States Practice in International Law 2002.* Washington, DC: U.S. Department of State, Office of the Legal Adviser, International Law Institute.

———, eds. 2005. *Digest of United States Practice in International Law 1991–1999.* Washington, DC: U.S. Department of State, Office of the Legal Adviser, International Law Institute.

Diehl, Jackson. 2003. "Allies and Ideology." *The Washington Post*, November 24.

Erickson, Richard J. 1994. "Status of Forces Agreements: A Sharing of Sovereign Prerogative." *The Air Force Law Review* 37: 137–53.

Feinstein, Lee, and Tod Lindberg. 2009. *Means to an End: U.S. Interest in the International Criminal Court.* Washington, DC: Brookings Institution Press.

Gardner, Maggie. 2003. "Sanctioning Allies: Effects of the 'Article 98' Campaign." *World Federalist Association*, December.

Georgetown Law Library. 2009. "International Criminal Court—Article 98 Agreements Research Guide." December.

Goldsmith, Jack. 2003. "The Self-Defeating International Criminal Court." *University of Chicago Law Review* 70 (1): 89–104.

Grossman, Marc. 2002. "American Foreign Policy and the International Criminal Court: Remarks to the Center for Strategic and International Studies." U.S. Department of State.

H. CON. RES. 467. 2004. "Declaring Genocide in Sudan." Washington, DC: Senate of the United States, Congress of the United States of America.

Hall, Christopher Keith. 2000. "The First Five Sessions of the UN Preparatory Commission for the International Criminal Court." *The American Journal of International Law* 94 (4): 773–89.

Halper, Stefan, and Jonathan Clarke. 2004. *America Alone: The Neoconservatives and the Global Order.* Cambridge: Cambridge University Press.

Hawkins, Darren. 2008. "Power and Interests at the International Criminal Court." *SAIS Review* 28 (2): 107–19.

Heindel, Anne K. 2003. "The Counterproductive Bush Administration Policy Toward the International Criminal Court." *Seattle Journal for Social Justice* 2 (2): 345–92.

Helms, Jesse. 2000. "Helms Press Release of Clinton Signature. Helms on Clinton ICC Signature: 'This Decision Will Not Stand'".

———. 2001. *Empire for Liberty: A Sovereign America and Her Moral Mission.* Washington, DC: Regnery Publishing.

H.R. 1794, Title II. 2001. "American Servicemembers' Protection Act of 2001." Washington, DC: House of Representatives, Congress of the United States of America.

H.R. 4151. 1986. "Omnibus Diplomatic Security and Antiterrorism Act of 1986." Washington, DC: House of Representatives, Congress of the United States of America.

H.R. 4654, Title II. 2000. "American Servicemembers' Protection Act of 2000." Washington, DC: House of Representatives, Congress of the United States of America.

H.R. 4775, Title II. 2002. "American Service-Members' Protection Act." Washington, DC: House of Representatives, Congress of the United States of America.

H.R. 4818. 2004. "Consolidated Appropriations Act, 2005." Washington, DC: House of Representatives, Congress of the United States of America.

H.R. 5114. 1990. "Foreign Operations, Export Financing, and Related Programs Appropriations Act, 1991, SEC. 599E, International Criminal Court." Washington, DC: House of Representatives, Congress of the United States of America.

HRW. 2003a. "Bilateral Immunity Agreements." Human Rights Watch.

———. 2003b. "Letter to US Secretary of State Colin Powell on US Bully Tactics Against the International Criminal Court." Human Rights Watch.

Human Rights First. 2004. "U.S. Threatens to Cut Aid to Countries That Support the ICC." *CICC*, December 7.

ICJ. 1986. "Summary of the Summary of the Judgment of 27 June 1986, Case Concerning the Military and Paramilitary Activities in and Against Nicaragua (Nicaragua v. United States of America)." The Hague: International Court of Justice.

Ikenberry, G. John. 2001. *After Victory: Institutions, Strategic Restraint, and the Rebuilding of Order After Major Wars.* Princeton: Princeton University Press.

International Military Tribunal. 1947. "Trial of Major War Criminals Before the International Military Tribunal, Nuremberg, 14 November 1945–1 October 1946, Volume II, Official Documents." Nuremberg.

Johansen, Robert C. 2006. "The Impact of US Policy Toward the International Criminal Court on the Prevention of Genocide, War Crimes, and Crimes Against Humanity." *Human Rights Quarterly* 28 (2): 301–31.

Kaul, Hans-Peter. 1998. "Special Note: The Struggle for the International Criminal Court's Jurisdiction." *European Journal of Crime, Criminal Law and Criminal Justice* 6 (4): 364–76.

Kirsch, Philippe, and John T. Holmes. 1999. "The Rome Conference on an International Criminal Court: The Negotiating Process." *American Journal of International Law* 93 (1): 2–12.

Knock, Thomas J. 1998. "Wilsonian Concepts and International Realities at the End of the War." In *The Treaty of Versailles: A Reassessment After 75 Years*, edited by Manfred F. Boemecke, Gerald D. Feldman, and Elisabeth Glaser, 111–30. Cambridge: Cambridge University Press.

Koh, Harold Hongju. 2010. "Briefing on the International Criminal Court Conference in Kampala." U.S. Department of State.

———. 2012. "International Criminal Justice 5.0: Justice Address 2012 at the Vera Institute of Justice, The Paley Center, New York, NY." U.S. Department of State.

Kostas, Stephen A. 2006. "Making the Determination of Genocide in Darfur." In *Genocide in Darfur: Investigating the Atrocities in the Sudan*, edited by Samuel Totten and Eric Markusen, 111–26. New York: Routledge.

Kristof, Nicholas D. 2005. "Schoolyard Bully Diplomacy." *The New York Times*, October 16.

Langer, Máximo. 2011. "The Diplomacy of Universal Jurisdiction: The Political Branches and the Transnational Prosecution of International Crimes." *The American Journal of International Law* 105 (1): 1–49.

Lee, Roy S. 1999. "Introduction: The Rome Conference and Its Contributions to International Law." In *The International Criminal Court: The Making of the Rome Statute—Issues, Negotiations, Results*, edited by Roy S. Lee, 1–40. The Hague: Kluwer Law International.

Los Angeles Times, Editorial. 2005. "Courting Ill Will," November 26.

McCormack, Sean. 2008. "Daily Press Briefing." U.S. Department of State.

MERCOSUR. 2005. "Presidential Declaration on the 'Commitment of the MERCOSUR to the Rome Statute of the International Criminal Court', Adopted at the XXVIII Meeting of the Council." Asuncion: Southern Common Market.

Meyer, Eric M. 2005. "International Law: The Compatibility of the Rome Statute of the International Criminal Court with the US Bilateral Immunity Agreements Included in the American Servicemembers' Protection Act." *Oklahoma Law Review* 58: 97–133.

Mikung Lee, Margaret, Raphael Perl, and Steven Woehrel. 1998. "Bosnian War Crimes: The International Criminal Tribunal for the Former Yugoslavia and U.S. Policy." CRS Report for Congress. Washington, DC: Congressional Research Service.

Murphy, Sean D., ed. 2001. "U.S. Signing of the Statute of the International Criminal Court." *The American Journal of International Law* 95 (2): 397–400.

———, ed. 2002a. "Efforts to Obtain Immunity from ICC for U.S. Peacekeepers." *The American Journal of International Law* 96 (3): 725–29.

———, ed. 2002b. "State Department Views on the Future for War Crimes Tribunals." *The American Journal of International Law* 96 (2): 482–84.

———. 2002c. *United States Practice in International Law Volume 1, 1999–2001*. Cambridge: Cambridge University Press.

———, ed. 2003. "U.S. Efforts to Secure Immunity from ICC for U.S. Nationals." *The American Journal of International Law* 97 (3): 710–11.

Office of the Ambassador-at-Large for War Crimes Issues. 2000. "War Crimes Tribunals: Financial Figures at a Glance." Washington, DC: U.S. Department of State.

Peskin, Victor. 2008. *International Justice in Rwanda and the Balkans: Virtual Trials and the Struggle for State Cooperation*. Cambridge: Cambridge University Press.

Pickering, Margaret S., Sally J. Cummins, and David P. Stewart, eds. 2003. *Digest of United States Practice in International Law: 1989–1990*. Washington, DC: U.S. Department of State, Office of the Legal Adviser, International Law Institute.

Powell, Colin L. 2006. "U.S. Secretary of State Testimony Before the Senate Foreign Relations Committee, Washington D.C. 9 September 2004 (9:35 a.m. EDT). Reprinted." In *Genocide in Darfur: Investigating the Atrocities in the Sudan*, edited by Samuel Totten and Eric Markusen, 259–67. New York: Routledge.

Power, Samantha. 2003. *"A Problem from Hell" America and the Age of Genocide*. New York: Harper Perennial.

Prosper, Pierre-Richard. 2002. "Statement in Hearing Before the Committee on International Relations, Serial No. 107–71." House of Representatives, Congress of the United States of America.

Ralph, Jason G. 2007. *Defending the Society of States: Why America Opposes the International Criminal Court and Its Vision of World Society*. Oxford: Oxford University Press.

Rapp, Stephen J. 2009. "Address to Assembly of States Parties." U.S. Department of State.

———. 2010a. "U.S. Engagement with the International Criminal Court and the Outcome of the Recently Concluded Review Conference, Special Briefing with Harold Hongju Koh." U.S. Department of State.

———. 2010b. "Remarks at Opening of the Nuremberg Trials Memoriam." U.S. Department of State.

———. 2013. "Statement of the U.S. at the Twelfth Session of the Assembly of States Parties of the International Criminal Court." U.S. Department of State.

RC/INF.1. 2010. "Delegations to the Review Conference of the Rome Statute of the International Criminal Court, Kampala." International Criminal Court.

Reeker, Philip T. 2002. "Press Statement: U.S. and Romania Sign Article 98 Agreement." U.S. Department of State.

Ribando, Claire M. 2007. "Article 98 Agreements and Sanctions on US Foreign Aid to Latin America." Library of Congress. Washington, DC: Congressional Research Service.

Rice, Condoleezza. 2006. "Trip Briefing: En Route to San Juan, Puerto Rico." Coalition for the International Criminal Court.

Rice, Susan E. 2009. "Statement Ambassador Susan E. Rice US Permanent Representative Respect International Humanitarian Law Security Council." U.S. Mission to the United Nations.

Richardson, Bill. 1997. "Statement Before the Sixth Committee of the 52nd General Assembly, Regarding Agenda Item 150: Establishment of an International Criminal Court." U.S. Department of State.

S. 857. 2001. "American Servicemembers' Protection Act of 2001." Washington, DC: Senate of the United States.

S. 2726. 2000. "American Servicemembers' Protection Act 2000." Washington, DC: Senate of the United States.

S. J. RES. 32. 1993. "Calling for the United States to Support Efforts to Conclude an International Agreement to Establish an International Criminal Court." Washington, DC: Senate and House of Representatives of the United States.

Scharf, Michael P. 1999. "The Politics Behind the U.S. Opposition to the International Criminal Court." *The Brown Journal of World Affairs* 6 (1): 97–104.

Scheffer, David J. 1996. "International Judicial Intervention." *Foreign Policy* 102: 34–51.

———. 1997. "U.S. Policy and the Proposed Permanent International Criminal Court: Address Before the Carter Center." U.S. Department of State.

———. 1998a. "U.S. Policy on International Criminal Tribunals: Address at Washington College of Law, American University." U.S. Department of State.

———. 1998b. "Statement on the Status of Negotiations." U.S. Department of State.

———. 1998c. "Statement on Creating an International Criminal Court." U.S. Department of State.

———. 1999a. "The United States and the International Criminal Court." *American Journal of International Law* 93 (1): 12–22.

———. 1999b. "Deterrence of War Crimes in the 21st Century, Twelfth Annual U.S. Pacific Command, International Military Operations and Law Conference, Honolulu, Hawaii." U.S. Department of State.

———. 2002. "Staying the Course with the International Criminal Court." *Cornell International Law Journal* 47: 47–100.

———. 2005. "Article 98(2) of the Rome Statute: America's Original Intent." *Journal of International Criminal Justice* 3 (2): 333–53.

———. 2012. *All the Missing Souls: A Personal History of the War Crimes Tribunals*. Princeton: Princeton University Press.

Senate Committee on Foreign Relations, Staff of the Committee and the Department of State. 1950. "The Morgenthau Plan, 1943: Program To Prevent Germany From Starting a World War III." In *A Decade of American*

Foreign Policy: Basic Documents, 1941–49, 502–5. Washington, DC: Government Printing Office.

Taft, William H., IV, and Patricia M. Wald, et al. 2009. "U.S. Policy Toward the International Criminal Court: Furthering Positive Engagement, Report of an Independent Task Force." Washington, DC: American Society of International Law.

Tallman, David A. 2003. "Catch 98 (2): Article 98 Agreements and the Dilemma of Treaty Conflict." *Georgetown Law Journal* 92: 1033–56.

The Council of Europe. 2002. "Parliamentary Assembly: President's Statement on International Criminal Tribunals, 115a (2002)."

United Nations. 2013. "United Nations Research Guides, UN Documentation: Security Council." December 22. http://research.un.org/en/docs/sc.

United States Delegation. 1996a. "Crimes Against Humanity: Lack of a Requirement for a Nexus to Armed Conflict." International Criminal Court.

———. 1996b. "'Trigger Mechanism,' First Question—Acceptance of and Exercise of Jurisdiction, Articles 21 and 22."

———. 1998. "Statement: United States Delegation to the Preparatory Committee on the Establishment of an International Criminal Court."

———. 2001. "Crime of Aggression, Statement by the United States."

United States House of Representatives. 2000. "The International Criminal Court: Hearings Before the Committee on International Relations." House of Representatives, Congress of the United States of America.

United States Senate. 1998. "Is a U.N. International Criminal Court in the U.S. National Interest? Hearing Before the Subcommittee on International Operations of the Committee on Foreign Relations." S. Hrg. 105–724. Washington, DC: Congress of the United States of America.

———. 2009. "Questions for the Record: Senator John Kerry. Nomination of Hillary Rodham Clinton, Department of State, Secretary of State." U.S. Senate Foreign Relations Committee.

U.S. Embassy, Vientiane. 2003. "U.S., Laos Sign Article 98 Agreement." Vientiane: U.S. Department of State.

Van Schaak, Beth. 2007. "The Establishment of the Permanent International Criminal Court." In *An International Symposium, Working Paper, No. 7–40*. Santa Clara, CA: Santa Clara University School of Law.

Weschler, Lawrence. 2000. "Exceptional Cases in Rome: The United States and the Struggle for an ICC." In *The United States and the International Criminal Court: National Security and International Law*, edited by Sarah B. Sewall and Carl Kaysen, 85–111. Lanham: Rowman & Littlefield.

Willis, James F. 1982. *Prologue to Nuremberg: The Politics and Diplomacy of Punishing War Criminals of the First World War*. Westport: Greenwood Press.

Women's Caucus for Gender Justice. 2001. "Report of the 26 February–9 March 2001 Preparatory Commission for the International Criminal Court."

CHAPTER 5

The European Union's Support for the International Criminal Court

5.1 Creating a New, Just Dimension of International Relations: European Union at the Negotiations on the Rome Statute

When the preparations of the Rome Statute commenced, the member states of the European Union (EUMS) and the European Parliament voiced their support for the establishment of the ICC. In 1995, at the UNGA Sixth Committee, "The European Union was convinced that establishment of an international criminal court would help to create a more just international order, and urged as many [UN] Member States as possible to participate in that endeavour." (A/C.6/50/SR.25 1995; see also A/C.6/51/SR.26 1996; COM (95) 567 1995; European Parliament 1995). However, although the European Parliament called on the EUMS to adopt a common position on the ICC prior to the Rome conference, it did not materialize (European Parliament 1996, 1997; Strapatsas 2002, 406–8). This was because the UK and France, and especially France, did not support as wide a jurisdiction of the ICC as most other European countries did (A/AC.249/L.3 1996; Groenleer and Van Schaik 2007, 977).

Despite the absence of a formal common policy, the EUMS did agree on the rough characteristics of the Rome Statute that followed the German agenda. They wanted the ICC to be a permanent and independent institution and emphasized the principle of complementarity, clear definition of crimes, cooperation with the ICC, and the importance

S. Huikuri, *The Institutionalization of the International Criminal Court*,
https://doi.org/10.1007/978-3-319-95585-8_5

of the rights of the accused. Furthermore, the widest possible ratification of the Rome Statute was considered central from the beginning (A/C.6/50/SR.25 1995; A/C.6/51/SR.26 1996; A/C.6/52/SR.11 1997). The EUMS' desire for a strong ICC opposed the goal of the USA, which wanted to negotiate a fair and efficient court that would accommodate its national interests Scheffer (1997). As the previous chapters have elaborated, the negotiations in Rome were a complex enterprise, with 160 states (accompanied by numerous intergovernmental organizations, UN-agencies, and NGOs) negotiating in simultaneously convened working groups on highly legal and political issues (Lee 1999, 21). However, the dynamics and the organization of the negotiations favored the EU and its strategy of normative binding. In particular, four actor groups contributed to the EU agenda's success in Rome: the group of the LMS, small states, NGOs, and the organizers of the negotiations.

First, as the concept of normative binding suggests, throughout the negotiations the EUMS, steered by Germany, actively sought to build a coalition of LMS that shared their agenda of an independent ICC. The LMS was composed of middle powers and developing states from all regions except Asia and lead by the EUMS, Canada, Australia, Argentina, and South Africa. As Schabas put it: "The beauty of the like-minded caucus, indeed the key to its great success, was its ability to cut across the traditional regionalist lines" (Schabas 2007, 19). Another key to the LMS success was the fact that they were the only coalition with an organizational strategy. Unlike the USA, whose proposals often came to the negotiation table at last minute, the LMS were carefully prepared for meetings. "The Like-Minded Group planned and thought through the entire progress of the conference" (Benedetti and Washburn 1999, 30) pointing out that they had a strong strategy with clear preferences in mind. By the end of the Rome conference, the coalition had 62 members and the fact that small states stuck to the LMS agenda played a decisive role in the outcome of the negotiations, as each country, whether China or Belize, had one vote (Washburn 1999, 368; Scheffer 2012, 18–9; Schabas 2011, 19).

Second, the EU's successful coalition building was not based merely upon its persuasiveness or well-argued preferences, but also on economic assistance. In the beginning of the preparatory negotiations, the Dutch Chairman of the Preparatory Committee, Bos, had initiated the establishment of UN Trust Funds to sponsor the participation of developing countries to the Preparatory Committee and the Rome conference. By the request of the UNGA, the UN Secretary-General founded Trust Funds, which had also been used before, but never for conferences codifying public international law (A/C.6/51/SR.27 1996; A/AC.249/CRP.l/Rev.l 1996; A/RES/51/207 1997; A/RES/52/160 1997). The only contributors to the Funds were Belgium, Denmark, Finland, Netherlands, Sweden, the UK, the European Commission, Canada, and Norway, who now sponsored 52 developing states' participation to the Rome conference (A/CONF.183/2 1998; Lee 1999, 9).[1] The almost exclusive European participation to the Trust Fund indicates that the EU was more interested than other countries in bringing as many small countries as possible into the conference. Conveniently, small states increased the power of the LMS coalition, and if the plan behind the Fund was to bind the sovereignty-oriented interests of the P-5 and push through a strong ICC in a one state one vote situation, it was successful (Groenleer and Rijks 2009, 178; Struett 2008; Deitelhoff 2009).

Third, the European agenda considerably profited from an active NGO lobby. The EU had started to finance pro-ICC NGOs already in 1995 (COM (95) 567 1995) and at the Rome conference the investment paid off. Only the largest delegations were able to participate in all working groups, and smaller states had difficulties to keep up with the negotiations, not only due to the simultaneously convening working groups, but also because of their lack of substantial knowledge of the issues. This opened a window of opportunity for the NGOs, which, organized under the umbrella of the "Coalition for an ICC," formed the largest delegation by far with 450 individuals. Their strategy was to lobby pro-ICC arguments by preparing daily legal analyses of the negotiations and by providing small delegations with judicial assistance (Benedetti and Washburn 1999, 9, 17; Pace and Thieroff 1999, 392–394; Struett 2008, 7; Welch and Watkins 2011, 928). Accordingly, the EU's alliance with the NGOs was profitable not just in terms of general lobbying, but also in terms of substantial legal issues.

Fourth, although the seats in the committees of the Rome conference were distributed regionally, coordinators in key roles, including the President of the Assembly of the Whole, Kirsch from Canada, who

[1]The list of states that received assistance from the Turst Fund is not publicy available. For the listing of delegations to the Rome Conference, see A/CONF.183/13 (Vol. II) 1998.

organized and conducted the negotiations, were citizens of the LMS and shared the EU's vision of an independent ICC. Also, the UN Secretary-General Annan had mutual interests with the EU and wanted the conference to be successful. This facilitated the Europeans success at least indirectly (Kirsch and Holmes 1999; Lee 1999, 10, 16ff.; Benedetti and Washburn 1999, 32–3; Schabas 2007, 19). With the backing of small states, NGOs, and the organization of the Rome conference, the LMS provided a counterbalance to the US agenda and the Americans had reasons to feel overwhelmed by the coalition:

> the middle powers - and especially the middle powers in Europe - who controlled the ICC process were less concerned with punishing serious human rights abusers than they were with increasing their relative influence by inhibiting and controlling militarily powerful nations. (Goldsmith 2003, 100–1; see also Lee 1999, 26; Arsanjani 1999, 22–3)

However, the aim of the European states was not to rule out the USA, but to secure the establishment of a relatively strong and independent ICC. The undertaking was successful, although the jurisdiction of the Rome Statute ended up being weaker than most of the EUMS had preferred (Kinkel 1998; Kaul 1998, 129–30).

So far, the coalition building in Rome has mostly been explained by persuasion, the success of justifications, and most persuasive arguments, which override material strength in international negotiations (Struett 2008, 137; Fehl 2004, 384; Deitelhoff 2009; Groenleer and Rijks 2009). While NGO persuasion was at play in Rome, the middle powers, especially the EUMS, and the economic assistance provided for small states played more a decisive role in coalition building than has so far been acknowledged. Cooper's concept of "new diplomacy," which comes close to the normative binding argument, explains well the outcome of the Rome conference with ad hoc cooperation initiated by NGOs and conducted by small and mid-sized countries coming together to build a strategic alliance to achieve normative change (Cooper 2002, 7). The EU's investment in the Trust Fund and in the NGOs provides two smoking guns in support of the argument that, unlike the majority of states, the EU was willing to invest in the establishment of the ICC. Without the EU's financial contribution, many small states and NGOs most probably would not have been able to attend the conference and the outcome of the vote might well have been different. Hence, the economic dimension played a decisive role in the building of a normative binding coalition in Rome.

Regarding the outcome of the Rome conference, "The European Union was extremely satisfied with" it, as the representative of Austria, speaking on behalf of the EU, put it few months later at the UNGA Sixth Committee. According to the EU, the ICC

> would make the world a safer place. The purpose of the Court was not only to punish those who committed crimes but through its mere existence to deter individuals from committing crimes in the first place. The culture of impunity had to end. Indeed, the Court would add a new dimension to international relations by reinforcing individual accountability. (A/C.6/53/SR.9 1998)

However, the vote in Rome was only for the adoption of the Rome Statute, not a promise for its ratification. The USA had succeeded in negotiating a condition of sixty ratifications for the ICC to become operational. The NGOs argued that the requirement of sixty ratifications was pushed through by the American delegation to guarantee that the ICC would never see the light of day. Moreover, delegations in support of universal jurisdiction argued that countries in post-conflict situations, such as Afghanistan, Burundi, Cambodia, the DRC, Serbia, or Uganda, would not enter the Rome Statute (Schabas 2007, 61–4; A/CONF.183/SR.4 1998; A/CONF.183/SR.6 1998). Despite all doubts, after the Rome conference, the EU expressed its hope that this number of ratifications would soon be reached (10398/98 (E/98/78) 1998).

5.2 Law and Justice for the World: The Struggle on the ICC

It took the EU almost three years after the Rome conference to adopt a common policy toward the ICC, although all EUMS signed the Rome Statute, more than half of them had ratified it by the end of the year 2000, and

> The European Union had consistently and strongly supported the idea of creating the Court [...]. All the States would do their best to proceed to ratification without delay. For the Court to succeed in its task it needed the widest support of the international community and he

> hoped that all States, whether or not they voted for the adoption of the Statute, would recognize the benefits of a universal criminal court. (A/C.6/53/SR.9 1998)

When the EU Council of Ministers adopted the first Common Position on the ICC, the timing seemed not to be a coincidence, because on the same day, June 11, 2001, President Bush started his first official visit in Europe. After Bush had been sworn into office, it became clear that his Administration would not be supportive of multilateral endeavors, including the ICC. One of Bush's first undertakings in the international arena was the rejection of the Kyoto protocol, which outraged European capitals (Black and Borger 2001; CNN 2001; Oakley 2001). Now, accelerating the ratifications to the Rome Statute, and hence expediting the operationalization of the ICC, was of central importance for the EU (PRES01-306EN 2001; Antoniadis and Bekou 2007). Along the lines of the normative binding argument, the EU policy formation was a response to the US policy on the ICC and other international agreements. Certainly, Europeans were well aware about Bush's visit when they adopted the Common Position on the ICC and they could have greeted him in another, friendlier way, if they had wanted to.

With the Common Position, EUMS committed themselves to facilitate an early establishment of the ICC by furthering the widest possible implementation and ratification of the Rome Statute. The promotion of the ratification should be undertaken by raising the issue in negotiations and political dialogues with third states, groups of states, and relevant regional organizations. While the USA perceived the ICC to be a threat to its national security, for the EU it was

> an essential means of promoting respect for international humanitarian law and human rights, thus contributing to freedom, security, justice and the rule of law as well as contributing to the preservation of peace and the strengthening of international security. (2001/443/CFSP 2001; A/C.6/56/SR.27 2001)

As Schabas notes, the pace with which states started to ratify the Rome Statute was unexpected, because, contrary to expectations, also countries with recent violent conflicts joined the ratifiers (Schabas 2007, 63). As the goal of 60 ratifications materialized in April 2002, the EU greeted the development with excitement: "The European Union salutes this event, which is a step of great importance for the defense of fundamental rights of human beings and for the affirmation of law and justice in the world." (7836/02 (Presse 97) 2002). The Bush Administration was all but thrilled and withdrew the US signature to the Rome Statute. The EU responded to the withdrawal with regret and disappointment and defined the action as unilateralist. It also stated that it does not share the US concerns—a trend that continued with all US actions (8864/02 (Presse 141) 2002; Garský 2013b, 7ff.).

When the Bush Administration started its campaign against the ICC, the EU was not willing to accommodate the US demands. In June 2002, as the American Servicemembers' Protection Act (ASPA) was under preparation in the US Congress, the EU expressed its unease over the legislation:

> The Council is particularly concerned about the current provision authorising the President to use all means necessary and appropriate to bring about the release of any person who is being detained or imprisoned by, on behalf of, or at the request of the ICC, including on the territory of EU Member States. The Council urges the US Administration to give full weight to these European Union concerns in considering whether to support ASPA. (9717/02 (Presse 178) 2002; Thomas 2009, 380–81)

Commissioner Byrne stated: "We will not allow the ICC to be handicapped from birth by excluding the work of the United Nations from its jurisdiction. There must be equality under the law, regardless of nationality" (Byrne 2002). At the same time as the ASPA was being prepared in Washington DC, the Council revised the EU Common Position to the ICC, which was now more detailed than a year earlier. The 2002 Common Position, which will be discussed in more detail below, pays more attention to the universal ratification of the Rome Statute and concretely outlines how the EUMS shall coordinate and provide political, technical, and financial support for the ICC (2002/474/CFSP 2002). As such, the new Common Position can be regarded as offering a counterweight to the ASPA legislation.

When the USA tried to secure immunity for its peacekeepers by blocking the extension of the UNMIBH mandate at the UNSC, the EU, again, did not show any sympathy to the US fears. On July 1, 2002, the EU stated that it would only accept a solution that respects the Rome Statute and does not undermine the ICC (PRES02-201EN 2002). Two days later, the EU Commissioner for External Relations, Patten, stated:

> The EU is wholeheartedly and unreservedly a supporter of the establishment of the International Criminal Court (ICC). We are sorry that the US walked away from this international undertaking. The International Criminal Court is the most important advance for international law since the establishment of the United Nations. We will allow nobody to water down the commitments contained in the ICC treaty. (Patten 2002a)

Thus, there were no realistic grounds for a compromise that would not sacrifice the ICC project of the EU and would convince the Bush Administration to follow a more accommodating policy. Accordingly, after Kagan had called the EU to be more sensitive about US concerns in an op-ed, Patten asked: "Why should people make concessions to America if the United States is going to walk away in any case?" He went on by pointing to the exceptionalism of the Bush Administration:

> The United States will be accused of putting itself above the law. It is happy enough to sit in judgment on others – indeed it is already doing so as part of the International Criminal Tribunal for the Former Yugoslavia – and it is ironic that it takes particularly tough positions in that context. But the United States now seems to be saying it must never itself be put in the dock. (Patten 2002b)

These statements, underlining the unilateralist and exceptionalist policies of the Bush Administration and the international character of the ICC, make an argument in support of multilateral policies and binding norms. Regarding the UNMIBH mandate, the European states together with other members at the UNSC were eventually able to pressure the USA to settle with a resolution that had to be renewed every year, although, as Thomas points out, the EU states initially had difficulties in agreeing on how to respond to the US demands (S/RES/1422 2002; Byrne 2002; Thomas 2009).

5.2.1 *Europe and the Bilateral Immunity Agreements*

Shortly after the US campaign for the BIAs was launched, the Political and Security Committee of the EU Council discussed the most recent turn in US policy and decided to return to the matter after consulting legal experts. However, Romania signed the first BIA already on August

1, 2002. Other EU-candidate countries, many of which were caught between a rock and a hard place, because they also wished to become NATO members, started to turn to the Commission, asking whether it could consider the BIAs as compatible with the Rome Statute. Hence, the Commission needed to respond to the issue quickly and initially advised the EU states not to sign a BIA. However, it took the EU another month and a half to reach a common policy on the issue. Among the EU countries, Italy and the UK were willing to accommodate the US concerns and enjoyed the support of Spain, Portugal, and Denmark, of which the latter held the EU Presidency at the time. In contrast, Germany and most other member states opposed the BIAs (European Parliament 2002a; Thomas 2009, 384ff.; Amnesty International 2002).

The official position toward the BIAs started to materialize at a meeting of EU foreign ministers in Elsinore, in which it was decided, on August 30, that the EU would not let the Rome Statute be undermined and would start to prepare a common approach to the issue. However, this decision also stated that the EU should try to accommodate the US concerns. Unlike with the Res. 1422, also the Commission was willing to find a compromise with the USA considering the BIAs, as Commissioner Patten said:

> At the moment, of course, the most controversial issue is that of bilateral agreements under Art.98 of the Rome Statute. The Commission supports the decision taken by the foreign ministers at Elsinore to develop an EU response on Art.98 that accommodates US concerns without undermining the Rome Statute. As soon as the details of the EU position on Art.98 are completed, hopefully by the end of this month, we will work with the candidate and EEA States to maintain a united front on the ICC. (Patten 2002c; see also European Parliament 2002a)

On September 26, the European Parliament regretted the US policy on the ICC, expressed its disappointment over Romania's decision to sign a BIA, and called for a common position on the issue (European Parliament 2002b). On September 30, the European Council published Common Conclusions on the BIA, which were accompanied by guiding principles concerning the agreements. The guiding principles stated: "Entering into US agreements – as presently drafted – would be inconsistent with ICC States Parties' obligations with regard to the ICC

Statute and may be inconsistent with other international agreements to which ICC States Parties are Parties" (12134/02 (Presse 279) 2002). While the message was perceived as an important policy direction by many non-European states (Groenleer and Van Schaik 2007, 983), the BIAs remained a bone of contention for the EU and the USA in the years to come.

The Americans were irritated by the EU's policy to consider the BIAs as a common rather than bilateral matter. As Bolton put it: "From our perspective, the EU is imposing an unfair choice upon our friends and allies, particularly those countries seeking to join the EU" (Bolton 2003; see also Bloomfield 2004). Already two weeks before the Elsinore meeting, the US Secretary of State Powell had arguably sent letters to European governments urging them to sign BIAs and to ignore the EU's request to wait for a common policy on the issue (Becker 2002; Groenleer and Van Schaik 2007, 979). According to the US Department of State's Spokesman, the EU's call for candidate states to wait for a common policy ignored the sovereign rights of the EU-candidate countries:

> I said the [EU] commission spokesman's comments, which I did see quoted this morning, suggesting that EU-candidate countries hold off any decision until the EU makes some decision of their own – we believe that those comments, in our view, are inappropriate in seeking to direct candidate-country foreign-policy choices in advance of EU accession. (Reeker 2002)

As the Bush Administration noticed that bilateral agreements with EUMS would not likely succeed, according to Groenleer and Van Schaik, it suggested an EU-wide BIA. Furthermore, the USA conducted a diplomatic *démarche* at the Council, complaining that the EU was mixing into third countries' policies. However, despite the initial willingness to accommodate the US concerns, Europe ignored all US suggestions and complaints and neither EUMS nor EU-candidate countries ratified any BIAs (Romania only signed one). It is noteworthy that while the USA coerced states into signing BIAs, there is no evidence that relationships between the EU and those states that signed BIAs were negatively affected (Groenleer and Van Schaik 2007, 982–83; Kelley 2007, 575).

5.3 The European Union's Universal Campaign in Support of the ICC

Instead of accommodating the US concerns, the EU did quite the opposite and started to deepen its campaign for the universalization of the ICC. At the first Assembly of States Parties to the ICC in September 2002, the EU declared that it "will do its utmost to ensure that the threshold of 100 States Parties be crossed before the 1st of April 2003" (PRES02-238EN 2002). Since the beginning of the preparations for the ICC in 1995, the universality of the Rome Statute had been of importance for the EU, and after the Rome Statute was adopted, it encouraged states to ratify it (A/C.6/53/SR.9 1998; A/C.6/54/SR.11 1999; A/C.6/55/SR.9 2000; A/C.6/56/SR.25 2001). By July 2002, when the ICC became operational, all EUMS had joined the ICC.

Along the lines of the argument that normative binding is a response to unilateralist policies, the US opposition opened a window of opportunity for the EU to profile itself in the international arena. As Commissioner Patten put it during the negotiations on Res. 1422 concerning UN peacekeepers' immunity: "We disagreed with the United States over Kyoto, but we didn't sit down and wait. We ratified and encouraged others to do so as well. The same thing has happened with the International Criminal Court" (Patten 2002a). As the hypothesis of normative binding predicts, the EU's support for the ICC also deepened in accord with growing US unilateralism, and hence, the common EU position on the ICC as of June 2002 paid much more attention to the ratification of the Rome Statute.

According to the Common Position of 2002, the EU member states should disseminate the values, principles, and provisions of the Rome Statute and cooperate with other states and NGOs to reach these objectives. While the position does not mention the US opposition to the ICC, its conclusions take the US campaign into account by stating: "States considering to ratify the Statute or to cooperate with the Court shall be encouraged to inform the Union of difficulties encountered on that path" (2002/474/CFSP 2002). As with the Common Position of 2001, the core of the new position of 2002 was the ratification campaign: "The Union and its Member States shall contribute to the worldwide ratification and implementation of the Statute [...]" (2002/474/CFSP 2002). In order to do so, the member states should raise the issue of widest possible ratification and implementation of the Rome Statute in negotiations and political dialogues with third states, groups of states, and regional organizations and cooperate with LMS, international institutions, and civil society. The member states were also called to contribute technical and financial assistance to the ratification and implementation in third countries and to coordinate and develop their country and region-specific strategies and policies. It is also noteworthy that in May 2002, the Council established an ICC subarea for its Working Group on Public International Law (COJUR), which deals with international law issues and prepares the EU's actions concerning international law. The COJUR-ICC, which convenes approximately four times a year and is the only subarea of the COJUR, follows closely ICC-related issues, including the ratification situation in third states (Hoffmeister 2008, 51; General Secretariat of the Council 2010, 27–8).

Hence, between the years 2001 and 2002, the ICC became an important issue in EU foreign policy and EUMS started to coordinate and channel their support for the ICC through the Common Foreign and Security Policy, while the Council coordinated the actions. The two Common Positions were replaced by a third one in June 2003, which emphasized more the institution of, and state cooperation with, the ICC, nevertheless still keeping the ratification campaign at the core of the issue (2003/444/CFSP 2003). To increase the effectiveness of the ratification campaign, the EU adopted an Action Plan in 2004, which specified the methods of the campaign as follows:

> In some cases, the primary objective with regard to third countries is to maximise their political will for the ratification and implementation of the Statute in order to achieve the desired universality. The realisation of this objective requires the use of a variety of means such as political dialogue, demarches or other bilateral means, statements in the UN and other multilateral bodies and support for the dissemination of the ICC principles and rules. It may also be important to assist countries, which are willing but may encounter difficulties with ratification, accession or implementation of the Statute. This could involve, inter alia, concrete expert assistance, financial support or access to data compiled by others. (Council of the European Union 2004)

According to the Action Plan, the EU should develop country and region-specific action plans that take into account each country's possible political, legal, and regional difficulties for the ratification.

The Action Plan also established a focal point at the EU Council to coordinate the implementation of the common position with focal points in all EU member countries (Council of the European Union 2004). Correspondingly, concrete attempts to generalize the norms of the ICC through bilateral diplomacy took advantage of three binding strategies: persuasion, issue-linkages, and the strategic use of NGOs.

First, considering persuasion as a tool to convince reluctant states on the ICC, the ratification campaign has indeed been global. In the European continent, the ratification has been an important discussion point in all EU enlargement negotiations and accession phases. Accordingly, all 27 EUMS as well as all current candidate countries, except Turkey, are ICC States Parties (10229/03 (Presse 163) 2003; General Secretariat of the Council 2010). In its external relations, the EU brings up the ICC actively, including in negotiations and dialogues with third countries such as Russia, China, and India. In addition to diplomatic dialogues, the EU exercises diplomatic pressure on non-ratifiers and those who have signed a BIA. It has carried out hundreds of diplomatic *démarches* in more than 110 countries to encourage the ratification and adherence to the Rome Statute. The *démarches* are written concerns issued by EUMS and delivered on behalf of the EU to a host government by a group of European Ambassadors, usually the troika. The content of the *démarches* is disclosed, but there are rumors that they begin by referring to the US policy on the ICC (Council of the European Union 2007; General Secretariat of the Council 2010, 2). The EU has also created a list of legal experts that third countries may employ for the technical implementation of the Rome Statute (General Secretariat of the Council 2010, 15–6).

Second, in addition to diplomatic persuasion and technical assistance, the EU uses explicit issue-linkages to induce countries to join the ICC. While multi- and bilateral donors increasingly link their development aid to a good human rights account, the EU also encourages states, with which it has development cooperation, to implement and ratify the Rome Statute. This encouragement takes the form of ICC clauses, which the EU negotiates into its cooperation agreements with developing countries and that obligates the contracting party to ratify the Rome Statute (Piron and O'Neil 2005). As the biggest donor and one of the largest economies of the world, the EU's development and economic cooperation is important to all countries and, hence, the power of its issue-linkages is remarkable.

Probably the most influential issue-linkage is found in Art. 11 of the Cotonou Agreement of 2000 (and its revised version of 2005), which is a binding legal instrument and sets the agenda of the EU's development, economic, and trade cooperation with nearly 80 African, Caribbean, and Pacific (ACP) states. Although cooperation with the EU is important to the ACP, the negotiation of the ICC clause, committing the contracting parties to ratify and implement the Rome Statute, was not easy:

> there was prolonged debate on the EC's proposals in respect of the International Criminal Court [...] to become an essential element of the Agreement. Consensus was reached some might say, as a result of the EC's status as dominant partner in the negotiations. (European Commission 2006, 9)

Similar ICC clauses have also become standard in European Policy Action Plans and Cooperation Agreements with third countries. These agreements set the agenda for EU cooperation with a particular country for three to five years, and here also the negotiation of the ICC clauses has not always been straightforward, as High Representative Ashton noted in 2013: "The negotiations on the PCA Thailand started in 2004 and had stalled since 2009 over a number of issues, in particular the ICC clause" (Ashton 2013). The fact that the negotiations stall for five years due to the ICC shows that the ratification of the Rome Statute is a significant issue for the EU and has consequences for trade relations too.

Third, the role of pro-ICC NGOs has been central to the EU's promotion of the Rome Statute. As already elaborated above, the EU started to sponsor NGOs, when the negotiations on the Rome Statute were launched in 1995. Between the years 2000 and 2008, the European Commission used €36 million to support the ICC and international criminal justice, and since 2003, the EU has been the main financial supporter of all major NGOs and numerous smaller ones, working on the ratification of the Rome Statute (General Secretariat of the Council 2008, 16; European Commission 2008; EuropeAid 2006). In addition, major NGOs receive significant bilateral financial support from altogether 15 EUMS.[2] By investing into pro-ICC NGOs, the EU

[2] Belgium, Czech Republic, France, Finland, Germany, Italy, the Netherlands, Spain, Sweden, and the UK support 'No Peace Without Justice' and Belgium, Denmark, Finland, Germany, Greece, Italy, Ireland, Luxembourg, the Netherlands, Portugal, Sweden, and the UK support the Coalition for the International Criminal Court.

gains an (indirect) access through civil society to third states' political and social life, which as a supranational organization it does not have. In other words, neither EU institutions nor EUMS could possibly start to lobby domestic parties, policy makers, or the society of third countries, nor could they be as persuasive about the ICC as the NGOs are. Thus, the funding and support for the NGOs can be assessed as a strategic move to advance the EU's interests in third countries through indirect means. The centrality of NGOs for the ratification campaign is also demonstrated by the fact that the COJUR-ICC is the only working party of the Council that regularly invites NGOs to its sessions (Wouters and Basu 2009, 18).

When talking about the effectiveness of its ratification campaign, the EU likes to mention Japan's accession to the Rome Statute. For years, the EU worked in cooperation with pro-ICC NGOs on Japan's accession within the framework of "EU-Japan ICC dialogue." This dialogue, or persuasion, included several conferences in Japan with legal experts from EUMS, representatives of the European Commission, and the EU Council Secretariat (Wellenstein 2004; General Secretariat of the Council 2008, 10). However, persuasion itself was not enough as by the end of the campaign, Japan's accession depended on its financial contribution to the ICC. Here, the EU arguably "played an important role in the 5th Assembly of States Parties of the ICC in finding agreement on the scale of assessments for Japan's contribution to the ICC's budget, which was influential on Japan's decision to ratify" (European Union 2007, 39; General Secretariat of the Council 2008). Yet, finding a compromise on Japan's membership fee was more complex than the EU indicates (Garský 2013a). Until Japan's accession to the ICC in 2007, the EU countries were by far the biggest financer group to the ICC's budget with a 75.6% share of the total contributions (General Secretariat of the Council 2008, 18). Due to its high gross national income, Japan was now slated to become the main contributor to the ICC. Art. 117 of the Rome Statute, defining the assessment of the contribution, left some room for interpretation, and Japan calculated that its contribution would be 28% of the ICC's total budget. Hence, it wanted to apply the UN ceiling of 22% to its ICC contribution, but the EU hesitated to accept the proposal. Eventually, after complex negotiations and with the support of Australia, Canada, and New Zealand, Japan was able to get its way and in November 2006 the ICC-ASP approved the 22% ceiling and Japan's ratification began to materialize

(Komatsu 2009; Masaki 2008, 415ff.; ICC-ASP/5/Res.4 2006; GA/AB/3998 2011). The fact that the EU downplays the financial side of the deal is interesting indeed.

5.4 Making the ICC Normatively Binding

In international diplomacy, the EU did not sympathize with the USA either, but worked on gaining normativity for the ICC's institution by mainstreaming it into the "international business as usual." The first attempt to do so was the promotion of the adoption of a cooperation agreement between the UN and the ICC at the UNGA (A/C.6/58/SR.9 2003; A/C.6/59/SR.6 2004). While the Bush Administration clearly opposed the agreement, the EU was successful in its undertaking and the UN–ICC agreement was adopted in October 2004. In December 2004, the EU underlined its commitment to the agreement at the UNGA by stating that it "has relentlessly defended the integrity of the Rome Statute and will continue to do so." In the same statement, pointing to the divide with the USA, the EU also discussed at length the BIAs and its guidelines considering the BIAs:

> The European Union will continue to draw attention to those guiding principles. [...] The European Union [...] stands ready to help those States that might need assistance in ensuring that crimes falling within the jurisdiction of the Court do not enjoy impunity. (A/59/PV.65 2004, 10–11)

Although the UN–ICC agreement established a framework for cooperation between the two institutions, it was not optimal from the EU's perspective, because the USA succeeded in securing that the UN would not pay for any expenses arising from the UN cooperation with the ICC (ICC-ASP/3/Res. 1 2004; A/RES/58/318 2004, 318; A/C.6/59/SR.27 2004; Rosand 2004).

After the UN–ICC agreement, the EU also prepared its own cooperation and assistance agreement with the ICC, which was signed in April 2006. The preamble to the Agreement Between the International Criminal Court and the European Union on Cooperation and Assistance emphasizes "the fundamental importance and the priority that must be given to the consolidation of the rule of law and respect for human rights and humanitarian law, as well as the preservation of peace and the strengthening of international security […].” The Agreement is remarkable as the first legally binding agreement between the EU and another international institution and also as the first agreement between the ICC and a regional organization. As such, it regulates only cooperation between the EU and ICC and not between the ICC and EUMS. According to Arts. 13 and 14 of the Agreement, the EU offers gratis expertise of its personnel to assist the work of the ICC and commits to provide facilities and services as well as field-level support for the ICC.

Going back to the UN framework, the Bush Administration succeeded in deleting all referrals to the ICC in UNSC resolutions for a long time. However, most of these undertakings were overruled at the UNGA and its Sixth Committee. The EU, *inter alia*, prevented the US attempts to damage the UN–ICC relationship and a resolution calling all states to ratify the Rome Statute (A/RES/58/79 2003; A/C.6/58/SR.9 2003; A/C.6/58/SR.10 2003; A/C.6/58/SR.13 2003). Moreover, as the UNGA considered a draft resolution of the EU on the safety and security of humanitarian personnel, including two references to the ICC, the Bush Administration proposed an amendment deleting both references. Embarrassingly for the USA, the amendment was overruled by 89 votes to one vote (the USA) and with 27 abstentions (A/59/PV.74 2004). In general, when it came to multilateral diplomacy in the absence of the UNSC power politics, the EU was systematically able to get through with its agenda.

The most significant turn in mainstreaming the ICC came when the UN started to consider the Darfur crisis. While the EU, and in particular France, pleaded for a UNSC referral of the situation to the ICC (6072/2/05 REV 2 (Presse 19) 2005), for the Bush Administration the ICC was the last resort. As the preceding chapter pointed out, to the satisfaction of the EU the UNSC referred the Darfur case to the ICC in March 2005 and this development vastly strengthened the ICC's status *vis-à-vis* potential ad hoc courts (S/RES/1593 2005; SC/8351 2005; Cryer 2006; Power 2005). Since the referral, the EU has repeatedly expressed its support for the ICC's activities in Darfur and condemned, as well as considered measures against, those who do not cooperate with the court. It has also provided assistance to ICC investigations in Darfur and in the DRC by, for instance, facilitating local contacts and providing the ICC Prosecutor with reports on requested locations (General Secretariat of the Council 2010, 22058; CL07-058EN 2007; CL08-060EN 2008; EU10-152EN 2010; EU10-186EN 2010).

The UN–ICC cooperation agreement and the Darfur referral were crucial elements for elevating the ICC to the same level as established international institutions, and these developments might well not have been realized without the EU's efforts. Having now obtained an international standing for the ICC and the US government's approval—although a hesitant one—for its operation, the EU started to switch its focus more onto the cooperation with the ICC. After the European External Action Service (EEAS) was launched in December 2010, the Council replaced the Common Position of 2003 by a Decision on the ICC in March 2011. While the Common Position of 2003 concentrated mostly on the ratification of the Rome Statute, the new position reflects the current situation. Many countries that have joined the ICC have not implemented the Rome Statute in their national legislations and the cooperation with the ICC considering; for instance, the implementation of arrest warrants leaves room for hope. Therefore, the new Decision on the ICC pays increased attention to the implementation of the Rome Statute, including the principle of complementarity and state cooperation with the ICC (2011/168/CFSP 2011; Council of the European Union 2010, 24; 17218/09 (Presse 371) 2009; 16841/09 2009).

The new Decision on the ICC was followed by a Revised Action Plan in July 2011, which assigned the EU High Representative to share the coordination on the ICC with the Council. According to the Action Plan, the EEAS should mainstream the ICC across its different departments and the EU will provide political and diplomatic support to the ICC in the international arena. In terms of promoting the universality of the Rome Statute, the COJUR-ICC was assigned the task of picking target countries for the ratification campaign and, as a novelty, the effects of the ratification campaigns as well as the cooperation with the ICC should be monitored by the EU and EUMS. It is also remarkable that the Action Plan encourages EUMS to ensure that the media and the public understand the institution and mission of the ICC (12080/11 2011). Along this path, the EU "will continue to support the International Criminal Court both politically and diplomatically, as well as logistically and financially. In particular, the EU will keep on promoting the independence of the Court and helping to ensure its effective and efficient functioning" (EUUN11-148EN 2011).

5.5 Conclusions: The EU's Normative Binding Agenda

This chapter provided smoking guns in support of the argument that the EU used the strategy of normative binding with respect to the establishment of the ICC. Normative binding suggests that states supporting multilateralism respond to unilateral policies of powerful states by establishing binding institutions. Considering the ICC, the EU indeed took the lead in the domain of international criminal law and, together with 120 states, pushed through its agenda of an independent and effective court despite the US opposition. As Commissioner Byrne noted in 2002:

> The fact that the world's greatest military power is not with us is a blow - there is no denying this - but this is not the first time in recent history that Europe has taken the lead and set the international agenda. Many wrote off the Kyoto Protocol after the withdrawal of the United States, but the EU pressed on and ratified Kyoto, setting an example which was followed by the global community to deliver a genuine prospect for tackling the problem of climate change. We intend to do the same to make the ICC a working institution for global justice. (Byrne 2002)

What is striking in this statement is the fact that the USA is described as a military power, providing room for the claim that the EU might be powerful in another respect. The fact that the ICC ended up having a fairly independent institutional design regarding the UNSC supports this claim, because the EU succeeded in its undertaking to establish a binding institution against the will of arguably the most powerful states in the system as, in addition to the USA, China and Russia have not acceded to the ICC. This negates the realist assumption of international institutions being the product of hegemonic dominance or the traditional use of power.

Once the EU had succeeded in establishing the ICC, it started to build a coalition in support of the institution through its universalization campaign. The evidence presented in this chapter shows how the EU aimed at acting as a norm entrepreneur after the Rome conference too and, assisted by NGOs, persuaded other states into joining the ICC. Like the Bush Administration, the EU also approached third states bilaterally and used economic inducements to achieve its goal of a universal ICC. However, the linkages used by the EU were different to those of the USA. The Bush Administration linked development and military aid to the BIAs and threatened states with direct economic sanctions, unless they signed up to its proposed agreement. Such linkages are implicit, because the BIAs do not mention economic aspects. Yet, it is known that side payments played a significant role in their negotiation and states had reasons to believe that the ratification would have economic consequences. Unlike the side payments of the USA, the EU's economic inducements were not directly consequential, because it negotiated ICC clauses to trade agreements with third states. These linkages, however, were explicit, as ICC clauses were part of broader cooperation agreements concerning, among other things, trade relations (Poast 2012, 280). The effectiveness and consequences of persuasion and issue-linkages to third states' ratification decisions will be elaborated in more detail in Part III.

Further evidence for normative binding attempts is found in the EU's argumentation in support of the ICC. While promoting the ICC, the EU repeatedly pointed to the rationality, legitimacy, and legality of the institution. The rationality of the institution was reasoned by reference to the ICC's deterrence of most heinous crimes, which arguably is in the interest of all states. Furthermore, the codification of international criminal law and the prevention of core crimes contribute to the maintenance of international peace and security and the preservation of human rights. Lastly, since the ICC prioritizes domestic prosecution of crimes, the choice to support the institution does not interfere with national interests:

> The International Criminal Court will be an effective tool of the international community to buttress the rule of law and combat impunity for the gravest crimes. The Rome Statute provides all necessary safeguards against the use of the Court for politically motivated purposes. It should be recalled that the jurisdiction of the Court is complementary to national criminal jurisdictions and is limited to the most serious crimes of concern to the international community as a whole. (2002/474/CFSP 2002; see also 2001/443/CFSP 2001; A/C.6/53/SR.9 1998)

The normative side of the ICC's legitimacy and its legality, in other words the justification for the ICC to rule the realm of international criminal law, was reasoned by reference to the codification of international criminal law and the court's political independence, judicial integrity, its contribution to international rule of law and, subsequently, to a just world order (A/C.6/50/SR.25 1995; A/C.6/53/SR.9 1998; 2001/443/CFSP 2001; A/C.6/56/SR.27 2001; Patten 2002b). Considering a just world order, many EU's statements on the ICC mention international order, international legal order, or rule of law-based order (A/C.6/53/SR.9 1998; PRES02-201EN 2002; European Commission 2008; SP09-409EN 2009; EUUN11-148EN 2011), suggesting that it wants to offer an alternative to an order, based on military and economic dominance.

The references to international order also often mention the European Security Strategy of 2003 (ESS). According to the ESS, the EU wants to have a more orderly international system, an order based on effective multilateralism, not on the use of military force, as preferred by the Bush Administration:

> In a world of global threats, global markets and global media, our security and prosperity increasingly depend on an effective multilateral system. The development of a stronger international society, well functioning international institutions and a rule-based international order is our objective. [...] We are committed to upholding and developing International Law. (Council of the European Union 2003, 9)

This statement shows that the EU, unlike Bolton—"Why should anyone imagine that bewigged judges in The Hague will succeed where cold steel has failed?" (Bolton 1999)—places its bets on the capacity of rules, norms, and bewigged judges to maintain the international order. Accordingly, from the EU's point of view, the international order is best strengthened through the rule of law, protection of human rights, development of existing international institutions, and consolidation of new ones, including the ICC. This commitment to multilateralism mirrors the basic European values on which the EU is founded, according to Art. 2 of the Consolidated Version of the Treaty on European Union of 2012, namely the respect for human dignity, freedom, democracy, equality, the rule of law and respect for human rights. Compared to the Bush Administration's coercive policies, the EU's commitment to the Rome Statute combined with its liberal values and multilateral approach most likely provided Europe more legitimacy and credibility in the eyes of third states and contributed to the success of its normative binding attempts.

While the value-laden rhetoric facilitates the claim that the EU used values as tools to increase its international legitimacy and credibility, it also potentially supports a reflectivist understanding of the emergence of the ICC. Clearly, the ICC corresponds to the European identity, the ESS's idea of international society, and is therefore worthwhile supporting. In general, the EU is founded on the ideal of unity, and it is logical that its international identity and strategy emphasize international institutions and multilateralism. When it comes to the ICC, peaceful European countries with functioning judicial institutions have nothing to lose and a lot to gain from their support. The biggest gain might well be domestic and international reputation as a promoter and supporter of humanitarian values, such as international criminal law. However, reflectivist theories do not suffice for understanding the EU's direct bilateral attempts to universalize the ICC. The means of the ratification campaign—influencing the behavior and decisions of third countries through, among other things, binding agreements—do not correspond with what reflectivists would understand as a social formation of beliefs and identities. To put it simple, for a social understanding of state commitment to an international treaty, mere support for international organizations would suffice to live up to multilateral identity and expectations. The EU's ratification campaign did not have confidence in socialization, and it took advantage of binding agreements and direct persuasion.

Another rival, rational, explanation to normative binding would be the intentional formation of a common European foreign policy. Over time, the EU has been referred to as a (geo)political dwarf, which is not exactly flattering for an actor that wishes to become influential at the global level (Santer 1998; Mahbubani 2008). In order to claim its position among other world powers, the EU needs to act in unison and establish common preferences and, indeed, this has not always been easy. One could maintain that the ICC offered the EU an excellent opportunity to portray itself as a global actor with one voice and so the EU seized the moment. However, the EU did not hold a common position toward the ICC during the Rome conference and the more coordinated policy started at the time when the USA unsigned the Rome Statute and initiated its campaign against the ICC. This implies that the US policies, not the mere desire to formulate a common policy, pulled the EU countries closer together and served as a trigger for Europe's normative binding attempts (Groenleer and Van Schaik 2007, 970). It is also worthwhile mentioning at this stage that during the years of the Bush Administration, the EU's main points of interest in the framework of human rights were in addition to the ICC torture and death penalty—all three are very sensitive issues for the USA.

To conclude, the empirical findings of the three case studies on Germany, the USA, and the EU are summarized in Table 5.1. The idea is to provide a simplified evaluation of the theoretical hypotheses for the

Table 5.1 Summary of the theoretical findings of part II

	Realist	*Rationalist*	*Reflectivist*	*Normative binding*
Motivation	**No**: The ICC was not a policy priority of the Clinton Administration (or of other powerful countries except the EU)	**Yes**: Multilateralism was emphasized by the EU states, pointing out that cooperation was their preferred way to handle interdependence and to realize joint gains	**Yes**: The ICC can be claimed to institutionalize shared interests, understandings, and values of states	**Yes**: European countries were eager to establish legally binding norms and rules and reacted to US unilateralism through promoting the ICC
Initiator	**No**: The ICC was initiated by middle powers, small states, and the UN organization	**No and Yes**: Hegemony does not explain the emergence of the ICC, but shared interests do	**No**: The creation of the ICC was initiated by a group of states, of which not all interact intensively (cf. EU, Senegal, and Trinidad and Tobago), and the UN organization	**Yes**: The European countries actively increased the power of the LMS coalition with the assistance of small states and NGOs
Other participants	**No**: No single power was able to dominate the process	**Yes**: Through the codification and institutionalization of international criminal law, the ICC facilitates problem solving and decreases costs of cooperation	**Maybe**: The ICC was the result of a negotiation process. The amount by which socialization influenced the process is hard to estimate	**Maybe**: Germany and the EU emphasize rule-of-law, multilateralism, and human rights as the basic values of the ICC. These values correspond with rationality, legality, and legitimacy

(continued)

Table 5.1 (continued)

	Realist	*Rationalist*	*Reflectivist*	*Normative binding*
Negotiations	**Attempted coercion**: While the USA used coercive tactics after the Rome conference, they were not effective considering the ultimate outcome	**Yes**: Throughout the negotiations, the LMS made a series of concessions to the US demands, but were not willing to trade off the jurisdiction of the ICC for US participation	**Maybe**: If negotiations constitute social interaction, then the ICC can be seen as the product of socialization. However, there is no solid evidence of common understandings leading to institutionalization	**Maybe**: The EU legitimized the ICC with its positive influence on world peace and deterrence of grave crimes. It also tried to induce reluctant states to join the ICC
Outcome	**No**: The outcome was cooperation, not a balance of power or hegemonic stability	**Too early to say**: Since the establishment of the ICC, states have started to modify the institution, which indicates that they prefer to stick to existing institutions instead of creating new ones	**Too early to say**: So far, the ICC is a stable institution and despite its flaws, in, e.g., its prosecutorial tactics, the majority of its States Parties are committed to it. Whether it will be able to deter future atrocities through socialization remains to be seen	**Yes**: Cooperation emerged against the will of the USA. Eventually, the USA became bound to the ICC and cooperates with it. This indicates that the order is multilateral and normative

emergence of international institutions presented in the theory section (see Table 2.1). Accordingly, the layout of Table 5.1 corresponds with Table 2.1 and reviews the tenability of its hypotheses. The overall finding is that while both reflectivist and rationalist explanations provide plausible accounts for why the EU supports the ICC, neither one can explain why the EU was so eager to facilitate third states' ratifications. The evidence presented in this section shows that the EU did not universalize the Rome Statute simply because it wanted to nurture collective identities or deepen common policies. It also aimed at initiating a counter reaction to the US policy and offering an alternative rule of law order that binds the unilateral policies of powerful countries: "The EU stands in the strong tradition of being a staunch supporter of the Court. We share the aims of the Court to combat impunity and promote a rule of law-based international order" (EUUN11-148EN 2011).

5.6 Conclusions on Part II

The three case studies of this section illustrated that in the international criminal law regime, the USA and the EU are leaders that endeavor to get other states to follow their opposing policies. This undertaking is arguably justified as both actors have credibility in the field. The US leadership in international criminal law derives not only from its hard power, but also from past agreements and practices, such as the Nuremberg trials and the ad hoc courts for Yugoslavia and Rwanda (Rapp 2010). Currently, the USA, if it wants to, can prevent the establishment of ad hoc tribunals or put on hold the work of the ICC with its veto power at the UNSC. The EU in turn is building up its authority in the field. It profiles itself as the supporter of human rights, rule of law, and multilateralism and has excelled by establishing a whole new organization, the ICC. Clearly, the power of both is based not only on legitimacy claims, but also on economic influence. What the EU and the USA think and want others to do has an impact on third states, because for the majority of states the two are the most important partners in terms of development aid and economic cooperation. During the Bush Administration's campaign against the ICC, the economic aspect of being a State Party to the ICC became painfully evident for dozens of states, as they were threatened with losing economic and military aid unless they followed the US agenda. As for the EU, it declared the BIAs as inconsistent with regard to States Parties' obligations to the ICC and linked economic cooperation to the ratification of the Rome Statute. This section showed that the concept of normative binding explains the outcome of the multilateral negotiations on the ICC. The following chapters test whether the EU is able to entrench the norms of the Rome Statute by inducing states to join the ICC or whether the economic sanctions posed by the USA are more powerful tools to evoke bilateral commitments. Accordingly, while this section concentrated on testing whether legitimacy and credibility can serve as sources of influence *vis-à-vis* hard power when it comes to the establishment of international institutions, the next section discusses the use of persuasion and issue-linkages in the strategy of normative binding.

References

UN Documents (references starting with A/..., GA/..., SC/..., and S/...) available at documents.un.org or unbisnet.un.org.

2001/443/CFSP. 2001. "Council Common Position of 11 June 2001 on the International Criminal Court." Council of the European Union.

2002/474/CFSP, Council of the European Union. 2002. "Council Common Position of June 2002 Amending Common Position 2001/443/CFSP on the International Criminal Court." Council of the European Union.

2003/444/CFSP. 2003. "Council Common Position on the International Criminal Court." Council of the European Union.

2011/168/CFSP. 2011. "Council Decision." Council of the European Union.

6072/2/05 REV 2 (Presse 19). 2005. "Declaration by the Presidency on Behalf of the European Union on the Report by the International Commission of Inquiry on Darfur." Council of the European Union.

7836/02 (Presse 97). 2002. "Statement by the Presidency on Behalf of the European Union." Council of the European Union.

8864/02 (Presse 141). 2002. "Statement of the European Union on the Position of the United States Towards the International Criminal Court." Council of the European Union.

9717/02 (Presse 178). 2002. "Council Conclusions on the International Criminal Court (ICC) and the Draft US American Servicemembers' Protection Act (ASPA)." Council of the European Union.

10229/03 (Presse 163). 2003. "EU-Western Balkans Summit, Declaration." Council of the European Union.

10398/98 (E/98/78). 1998. "Declaration by the Presidency on Behalf of the European Union on the International Criminal Court." Council of the European Union.

12080/11. 2011. "Action Plan to Follow-Up on the Decision on the International Criminal Court." Council of the European Union.

12134/02 (Presse 279). 2002. "Council Conclusions on the International Criminal Court." Council of the European Union.

16841/09. 2009. "EU Guidelines on Promoting Compliance with International Humanitarian Law." Council of the European Union.

17218/09 (Presse 371). 2009. "Promoting Compliance with International Humanitarian Law." Council of the European Union.

Amnesty International. 2002. "International Criminal Court: Foreign Ministers of France, Italy, Spain and the UK Should Say No to Impunity Agreements." IOR 30/008/2002.

Antoniadis, Antonis, and Olympia Bekou. 2007. "The European Union and the International Criminal Court: An Awkward Symbiosis in Interesting Times." *International Criminal Law Review* 7 (4): 621–55.

Arsanjani, Mahnoush H. 1999. "The Rome Statute of the International Criminal Court." *The American Journal of International Law* 93 (1): 22–43.

Ashton, Catherine. 2013. "Letter A(2013)441726-516158." High Representative, Vice-President of the European Commission.

Becker, Elizabeth. 2002. "U.S. Issues Warning to Europeans in Dispute Over New Court." *The New York Times*, August 26.

Benedetti, Fanny, and John L. Washburn. 1999. "Drafting the International Criminal Court Treaty: Two Years to Rome and an Afterword on the Rome Diplomatic Conference." *Global Governance* 5 (1): 1–37.

Black, Ian, and Julian Borger. 2001. "EU Dismay as Bush Reneges on Kyoto: Blair Seeks 'Constructive' Talks as World Denounces Decision to Put US Trade Before Global Climate." *The Guardian*, March 30.

Bloomfield, Lincoln P., Jr. 2004. "Post-election Strategic Priorities for the United States, Remarks at the Chatham House Conference on Matching Capabilities to Commitments—Can Europe Deliver?" London.

Bolton, John R. 1999. "Speech Two: Reject and Oppose the International Criminal Court." In *Toward an International Criminal Court? Three Options Presented as Presidential Speeches*. New York: Council on Foreign Relations.

Bolton, John R. 2003. "American Justice and the International Criminal Court: Remarks at the American Enterprise Institute." Washington, DC.

Byrne, David. 2002. "Commission Statement on the Consequences for Transatlantic Relations of the American Service Members' Protection Act (ASPA), Delivered by Commissioner David Byrne at the European Parliament, Plenary Session (Strasbourg)." European Union at the United Nations.

CL07-058EN. 2007. "EU Presidency's Declaration on International Criminal Court's Investigation into Darfur." Council of the European Union.

CL08-060EN. 2008. "EU Council Conclusions on Sudan." Council of the European Union.

CNN. 2001. "Skeptical Leaders Await Bush on European Trip," June 11.

COM (95) 567. 1995. "The External Dimension of the EU's Human Rights Policy: From Rome to Maastricht and Beyond." Commission of the European Communities.

Cooper, Andrew F. 2002. "Like-Minded Nations, NGOs, and the Changing Pattern of Diplomacy within the UN System: An Introductory Perspective." In *Enhancing Global Governance: Towards a New Diplomacy?* edited by Andrew F. Cooper, John English, and Ramesh Thakur, 1–18. Tokyo: United Nations University Press.

Council of the European Union. 2003. "A Secure Europe in a Better World: European Security Strategy".

———. 2004. "Action Plan to Follow-Up on the Common Position on the International Criminal Court".

———. 2007. "EU's Reply to the Information Request of Paragraph h) of the Plan of Action for Achieving Universality and Full Implementation of the Rome Statute." Presidéncia Conselho da União Europeia.

———. 2010. "The Stockholm Programme—An Open and Secure Europe Serving and Protecting Citizens, 5731/10".

Cryer, Robert. 2006. "Sudan, Resolution 1593, and International Criminal Justice." *Leiden Journal of International Law* 19 (1): 195–222.

Deitelhoff, Nicole. 2009. "The Discursive Process of Legalization: Charting Islands of Persuasion in the ICC Case." *International Organization* 63 (1): 33–65.

EU10-152EN. 2010. "Statement by the Spokesperson of HR Ashton on President Al-Bashir." European Union at the United Nations.

EU10-186EN. 2010. "Statement by the Spokesperson of HR Ashton on Sudanese President Al-Bashir's Visit to Kenya." European Union at the United Nations.

EuropeAid. 2006. "EIDHR: European Initiative for Democracy and Human Rights 2000–2006." European Commission.

European Commission. 2006. "Partnership Agreement ACP-EC, Signed in Cotonou on 23 June 2000, Revised in Luxembourg on 25 June 2005." Directorate-General for Development and Relations with African, Caribbean and Pacific States.

———. 2008. "Programming Guide for Strategy Papers, Programming Fiche, the ICC and the Fight Against Impunity".

European Parliament. 1995. "Resolution on Human Rights in the World in 1993–1994 and the Union's Human Rights Policy, A4-0078/95, OJ C 126, 0015".

———. 1996. "Resolution on the Establishment of the Permanent International Criminal Court, B4-0992, OJ C 320, 0194".
———. 1997. "Resolution on Human Rights Throughout the World in 1995–1996 and the Union's Human Rights Policy, A4-0400/96, OJ C 020, 0161".
———. 2002a. "Debates: International Criminal Court".
———. 2002b. "Resolution on the International Criminal Court (ICC), P5_TA(2002)0449".
European Union. 2007. "EU Annual Report on Human Rights 2007." Luxembourg: European Communities.
EUUN11-148EN. 2011. "EU Statement—Assembly of States Parties to the Rome Statute of the International Criminal Court." European Union at the United Nations.
Fehl, Caroline. 2004. "Explaining the International Criminal Court: A 'Practice Test' for Rationalist and Constructivist Approaches." *European Journal of International Relations* 10 (3): 357–94.
Garský, Salla. 2013a. "Japan's Ratification of the Rome Statute of the International Criminal Court," 9. Voices from the Sylff Community. Tokyo: The Tokyo Foundation.
———. 2013b. "Strong, Independent, and Effective: The European Union's Promotion of the International Criminal Court." In *Global Power Europe—Vol. 2: Policies, Actions and Influence of the EU's External Relations*, edited by Astrid B. Boening, Jan-Frederik Kremer, and Aukje van Loon, 1–18. Berlin: Springer.
General Secretariat of the Council. 2008. *The European Union and the International Criminal Court*, Expert Series. Brussels: European Union.
———. 2010. *The European Union and the International Criminal Court*, Expert Series. Brussels: European Union.
Goldsmith, Jack. 2003. "The Self-Defeating International Criminal Court." *University of Chicago Law Review* 70 (1): 89–104.
Groenleer, Martin, and Louise Van Schaik. 2007. "United We Stand? The European Union's International Actorness in the Cases of the International Criminal Court and the Kyoto Protocol." *Journal of Common Market Studies* 45 (5): 969–98.
Groenleer, Martin, and David Rijks. 2009. "The European Union and the International Criminal Court: The Politics of International Criminal Justice." In *The European Union and International Organizations*, edited by Knud Erik Jørgensen, 167–87. London: Routledge.
Hoffmeister, Frank. 2008. "The Contribution of EU Practice to International Law." In *Developments in EU External Relations Law*, edited by Marise Cremona, 37–127. Oxford: Oxford University Press.

ICC-ASP/3/Res.1. 2004. "Negotiated Relationship Agreement Between the International Criminal Court and the United Nations." International Criminal Court.

ICC-ASP/5/Res.4. 2006. "Programme Budget for 2007, the Working Capital Fund for 2007, Scale of Assessments for the Apportionment of Expenses of the International Criminal Court and Financing Appropriations for the Year 2007".

Kaul, Hans-Peter. 1998. "Durchbruch in Rom. Der Vertag Über Den Internationalen Strafgerichtshof." *Vereinte Nationen* 4: 125–30.

Kelley, Judith. 2007. "Who Keeps International Commitments and Why? The International Criminal Court and Bilateral Nonsurrender Agreements." *American Political Science Review* 101 (3): 573–89.

Kinkel, Klaus. 1998. "Statement on July 17, 1998." Völkerrechtliche Praxis Der Bundesrepublik Deutschland Im Jahre 1998. Max-Planck-Institut für ausländisches öffentliches Recht und Völkerrecht.

Kirsch, Philippe, and John T. Holmes. 1999. "The Rome Conference on an International Criminal Court: The Negotiating Process." *American Journal of International Law* 93 (1): 2–12.

Komatsu, Ichiro. 2009. "Keynote Address by Ambassador of Japan to the Swiss Confederation." ICC Seminar at ITC Maurya Seraton Hotel. New Delhi: Ministry of Foreign Affairs of Japan.

Lee, Roy S. 1999. "Introduction: The Rome Conference and Its Contributions to International Law." In *The International Criminal Court: The Making of the Rome Statute—Issues, Negotiations, Results*, edited by Roy S. Lee, 1–40. The Hague: Kluwer Law International.

Mahbubani, Kishore. 2008. "Europe Is a Geopolitical Dwarf." *Financial Times*, May 21.

Masaki, Yasushi. 2008. "Japan's Entry to the International Criminal Court and the Legal Challenges It Faced." *Japanese Yearbook of International Law* 51: 409–26.

Oakley, Robin. 2001. "Bush Fails to Convert EU Leaders." *CNN*, July 10.

Pace, William, and Mark Thieroff. 1999. "Participation of Non-governmental Organizations." In *The International Criminal Court: The Making of the Rome Statute—Issues, Negotiations, Results*, edited by Roy S. Lee, 391–398. The Hague: Kluwer Law International.

Patten, Chris. 2002a. "Commissioner Patten's Statement on ICC and UN Mission Mandate in Bosnia-Herzegovina." European Union at the United Nations.

———. 2002b. "Why Does America Fear This Court?" *The Washington Post*, July 9.

———. 2002c. "Commissioner Patten's Statement on the ICC at the EP." European Union at the United Nations.

Piron, Laure-Hélène, and Tammie O'Neil. 2005. *Integrating Human Rights into Development: A Synthesis of Donor Approaches and Experiences*. London: Overseas Development Institute.

Poast, Paul. 2012. "Does Issue Likage Work? Evidence from European Alliance Negotiations, 1860 to 1945." *International Organization* 66 (2): 277–310.

Power, Samantha. 2005. "Court of First Resort." *The New York Times*, February 10.

PRES01-306EN. 2001. "EU Presidency Statement at the UNGA Sixth Committee—The International Criminal Court." European Union at the United Nations.

PRES02-201EN. 2002. "EU Presidency Statement at the 10th Meeting of the Preparatory Commission (New York)—The International Criminal Court." European Union at the United Nations.

PRES02-238EN. 2002. "EU Presidency Statement at the Assembly of States Parties of the Rome Statute of the International Criminal Court (New York)." European Union at the United Nations.

Rapp, Stephen J. 2010. "U.S. Engagement with the International Criminal Court and the Outcome of the Recently Concluded Review Conference, Special Briefing with Harold Hongju Koh." U.S. Department of State.

Reeker, Philip T. 2002. "State Department Regular Briefing." Federal News Service.

Rosand, Eric. 2004. "Explanation of Position on the Adoption of Resolution Concerning the Report of the International Criminal Court, in the Sixth Committee." USUN Press Release 257(04). U.S. Mission to the United Nations.

Santer, Jacques. 1998. "The EU in the 21st Century: Political Dwarf or World Actor. Speech at the Bologna Center of the Johns Hopkins University." Commission of the European Communities.

Schabas, William A. 2007. *An Introduction to the International Criminal Court*, 3rd ed. Cambridge: Cambridge University Press.

———. 2011. *An Introduction to the International Criminal Court*, 4th ed. Cambridge: Cambridge University Press.

Scheffer, David J. 2012. *All the Missing Souls: A Personal History of the War Crimes Tribunals*. Princeton: Princeton University Press.

———. 1997. "U.S. Policy and the Proposed Permanent International Criminal Court: Address Before the Carter Center." U.S. Department of State.

SP09-409EN. 2009. "'The Relationship Between the EU Institutions and the ICC'—Speech by Ambassador Valenzuela, Head of the EC Delegation to the UN".

Strapatsas, Nicolaos. 2002. "The European Union and Its Contribution to the Development of the International Criminal Court." *Revue de Droit Universite de Sherbrooke* 33: 399–424.

Struett, Michael J. 2008. *The Politics of Constructing the International Criminal Court: NGOs, Discourse, and Agency.* New York: Palgrave Macmillan.

Thomas, Daniel C. 2009. "Rejecting the US Challenge to the International Criminal Court: Normative Entrapment and Compromise in EU Policy-Making." *International Politics* 46 (4): 376–94.

Washburn, John. 1999. "The Negotiation of the Rome Statute for the International Criminal Court and International Lawmaking in the 21st Century." *Pace International Law Review* 11 (2): 361–77.

Welch, Claude E., Jr., and Ashely F. Watkins. 2011. "Extending Enforcement: The Coalition for the International Criminal Court." *Human Rights Quarterly* 33 (4): 927–1031.

Wellenstein, Edmond H. 2004. "EU–Japan ICC Dialogue: Introductory Statement/Press Briefing." Council of the European Union.

Wouters, Jan, and Sudeshna Basu. 2009. "The Creation of a Global Criminal Justice System: The European Union and the International Criminal Court." Working Paper No. 26. Leuven: Leuven Centre for Global Governance Studies.

PART III

Can Money Buy International Justice?

CHAPTER 6

Explaining Late Ratification of the Rome Statute

6.1 Ratification Decision

Treaties and their ratification are an essential part of international cooperation as they provide legal grounds for international institutions and thus for interstate cooperation. According to Art. 6 of Vienna Convention on the Law of Treaties, every state possesses the capacity to conclude treaties. Treaties have always an international character as they are concluded between states or with, within, or between international and regional organizations. However, their ratification has traditionally been considered a domestic matter. Indeed, every country deliberates the ratification of the Rome Statute from different legal perspectives and its implications for national legislation. The pre-ratification phase includes a domestic interpretation of the treaty, since the Rome Statute needs not only to be ratified but should also be implemented into national laws. Therefore, in most countries ministries responsible for the ratification will prepare memoranda for their respective parliament's and/or government's consideration before deliberations on the ratification. However, legal decisions ultimately depend on political will and, hence, political considerations are a central part of joining the ICC (Triffterer 2000, 2, 4–5).

A straightforward explanation for the ratification of the Rome Statute is that the treaty corresponds to the preferences, values, and practices of a state and the political decision makers decide to commit and comply with it by seeking national ratification (Simmons 2009, 65).

S. Huikuri, *The Institutionalization of the International Criminal Court*,
https://doi.org/10.1007/978-3-319-95585-8_6

This is probably true with many states that joined the ICC in the first wave between the years 1999 and 2002. In fact, the Like-Minded States arguably competed with the pace of their ratification in order to be included in the group of the first sixty ratifiers—the number that was needed for the ICC to become operational (Triffterer 2000, 6).

However, the underlying assumption here is that even for the most eager states, the ratification is not just normative and legal, but also a rational choice. The delegation of power to the ICC advances states' own and joint interests and the future gains of the ICC weigh more for most early ratifiers than the potential short-term costs of ratification. Hence, in the eyes of the early ratifiers, the ICC reduces the political costs of proceedings and raises the costs of defection in the domain of international criminal law (Martin 1992, 756–57). The benefits of the ICC as described in the Introduction and Chapter 2 form the basis for common interests and collective action. Furthermore, the normative side of the ICC provides grounds for legitimacy claims and reputation sensitivities, when the ratification is under consideration. Lastly, joining the ICC is a signal:

> Membership enables states to learn about each others' preferences if the membership mechanism can distinguish cooperators from noncooperators. Ideally, a state that values the goals of an organization will want to join, whereas one that wants a free ride will find it too costly to join a regime they intend to violate. In formal terms, membership is a costly signal. (Koremenos et al. 2001, 784)

Arguably, early ratifiers that joined the ICC between the years 1998 and 2002 deliberately signaled their support for the institution and dismissed US opposition to the ICC.

After the early ratifiers' accession, the heterogeneity of future ratifiers and their preferences expands (Koremenos et al. 2001, 785). Most likely, late ratification indicates that a country does not prioritize the development of international criminal law as much as the early ratifiers. Lethargy or averseness toward international criminal law offers the occasion for the EU and the USA to seek backing for their respective policies and to use exogenous pressure for shaping the preferences of late ratifiers. Accordingly, for latecomers that did not buy into the ICC in the first years after the Rome conference, the ratification decision becomes a functional choice. As Part II elaborated, for non-ratifiers, the world of international criminal law during the Bush Administration years was bipolar, as the EU and the USA battled for leadership. Both leaders approached third states bilaterally and used economic inducements to achieve their goals. The USA linked the BIAs to development and military aid and threatened states with direct economic sanctions, unless they would sign one. The linkage was implicit, because the BIAs do not mention economic aspects. However, the case studies to follow evidence that side payments played a significant role in the BIA negotiations and states had reasons to believe that the ratification would result in economic consequences.

Unlike the side payments of the USA, the EU's economic inducements were not directly consequential, because it negotiated ICC clauses to trade and partnership agreements with third states. The EU linkages, however, were explicit, as ICC clauses were a formal part of broader cooperation agreements concerning, among others, trade relations (Poast 2012, 280). The Obama Administration substantially revised the US policy toward the ICC, as Koh summed up: "After 12 years, I think we have reset the default on the U.S. relationship with the court from hostility to positive engagement. In this case, principled engagement worked to protect our interest, to improve the outcome, and to bring us renewed international goodwill" (Koh 2010). I hypothesize that this turn toward friendly cooperation, the "Obama effect," encouraged—or enabled—further states to join the ICC.

In the following chapters, most evidence for normative binding attempts and negative outside influence is found between the years 1998 and 2008. I expect that the type of ratifiers definitely changes from the core group of early ratifiers and lethargic latecomers to stragglers around the year 2009 onwards, since this is the period when the explanatory variable of US pressure switches to Obama effect. Stragglers' ratification was not motivated by normative binding aspirations, as those would be a reaction to the negative US policy. Moreover, it is unlikely that any country would consider the legal and political consequences of ratification for ten years. Therefore, stragglers are hypothesized to ratify human rights treaties when it is advantageous for them. This, however, does not mean that the effect of normative binding ceases, but quite the contrary: It is likely that the issue-linkages of the EU started to gain more weight in the policy considerations of stragglers after economic consequences of the ratification generated by the US sanctions dissolved. Hence, subsequent hypotheses follow:

H1: The stragglers' indifference to international justice opens a window of opportunity for external actors to realize their agendas through issue-linkages.
H2: Economic sanctions posed by the USA decrease the likelihood of ratification.
H3: Positive exogenous pressure influences ratification after the US policy toward the ICC relaxes.

The following provides a set of alternative explanations for testing the explanatory power of exogenous influence in the case studies on the Philippines and Indonesia.

6.2 Liberal Explanations

Extensive regression analyses explain the ratification of the Rome Statute and the commitment to human rights by domestic preferences, common identities, persuasion, and states' anticipations of other states' reactions (Kelley 2007; Neumayer 2009; Simmons and Danner 2010; Chapman and Chaudoin 2013; Goodliffe et al. 2012). Moravcsik's liberal theory argues that individuals and private groups are important in shaping state behavior in international politics. Hence, the ratification serves different purposes for different domestic actors (Moravcsik 1997). Liberal explanations for the commitment to human rights treaties argue that states follow domestic agendas and calculate the costs and benefits of the ratification. Hence, "treaty ratification is rationally expressive: It reflects a government's preferences and practices, subject to the potential net costs that ratification is expected to involve" (Simmons 2009, 64). Chayes and Chayes are skeptical whether a commitment originating from such calculations can be sincere: "If a state's decision whether or not to conform to a treaty is the result of a calculation of costs and benefits, as the realists assert, the implication is that noncompliance is premeditated" (Chayes and Chayes 1995, 9). Yet, without directly implying non-compliance, various rational theories explain the ratification by state agendas that are directly or indirectly related to the treaty and that influence the decision either positively or negatively.

6.2.1 Positive Influence

6.2.1.1 Credible Commitment

By using event history analysis, Simmons and Danner conclude that non-democratic countries, which have recently experienced civil wars and have a poor potential to prosecute ICC crimes, likely ratify the Rome Statute in order to demonstrate a "credible commitment." By exposing themselves to a potential ICC investigation, such governments want to signal their domestic public and opposition groups that they are committed to stopping violence and resolving conflicts (Simmons and Danner 2010, 227). Here, the least likely ratifiers are democracies that have recently experienced civil war and have functioning judicial systems. Not very surprisingly, peaceful democracies with low likelihood of being targeted by an ICC investigation are likely to join the ICC (Simmons and Danner 2010; see also Hathaway 2007, 613). Meernik and Aloisi argue that states with open political system and weaker executives issue more declarations to the treaties they ratify than those with strong executives. They also suggest that these states most likely keep their commitments, since many states that make declarations to treaties also prepare domestic implementation of the Rome Statute (Meernik and Aloisi 2009, 264–66, 272).

Tunisia is a good example of a country that likely made a credible commitment by joining the ICC. Under the Ben Ali government, Tunisia preferred state sovereignty to the ICC and did not sign the Rome Statute (A/CONF.183/13 (Vol. II) 1998, 148). Ali's policy followed the one of the League of Arab States and the African Union, which Tunisia joined, for instance, in regretting the ICC's issuance of an arrest warrant against al-Bashir and in calling for the respect of Sudan's sovereignty and territorial integrity (Foreign Affairs Ministry Tunisia 2009; Arab League Council 2009; African Union 2009). After Ali was unseated in January 2011 through the Tunisian Revolution that started the Arab Spring, the interim government announced right after its first cabinet meeting in February 2011 that Tunisia plans to accede to the Rome Statute (CICC 2011; ICG 2011a). Four months after the announcement, Tunisia became the first North-African country to join the ICC. As the ICC-ASP President Wenaweser stated on Tunisia's accession: "Ratifying the Rome Statute has become a symbol of a country's commitment to the fight against impunity and its commitment to the rule of law around the world" (UN News Centre 2011).

As such, it is reasonable to argue that Tunisia's accession was a credible commitment signal for the domestic and international public.

6.2.1.2 ICC as a Tool to Fight Global Crime

Chapman and Chaudoin find that democratic countries with stable legal institutions are most likely ratifiers. They conclude that the ICC's global effect is questionable, because governments that will most likely be targets of an ICC investigation are unlikely join the institution (Chapman and Chaudoin 2013). Also Neumayer finds that democratic states, but especially those which frequently engage in military interventions and contribute to peacekeeping, tend to be eager ratifiers. Such states perceive the ICC as another tool for fighting global crimes (Neumayer 2009). Brysk calls them "Global Good Samaritans," who pursue a global system and promote cosmopolitan values (Brysk 2009, 4; see also Hafner-Burton 2013). Such active peacekeepers and human rights promoters likely represent the early ratifiers camp and are prone to engage in binding. The ratification of the Rome Statute has no political costs for them, since they do not expect their nationals to be prosecuted and perceive the ICC as an institution that protects their interests and reaffirms their global values in the same way as peacekeeping operations do. As Simmons and Danner point out, most of these countries are presumably OECD member states, which participated in the LMS group and whose nationals hold ICC positions (Simmons and Danner 2010, 241–44).

6.2.1.3 Ratification as an Instrument of the Executive

Ratification of the Rome Statute can arguably serve the instrumental purposes of the executive. Hathaway argues that in an established democracy, the executive is often constrained by a strong political system but holds control over negotiating and ratifying international treaties. While the initiation of national legislative process is reserved for the legislative branch, the executive can use international treaties as a tool to achieve his own policy goals and set domestic or foreign policy agendas (Hathaway 2007, 595ff.). Similarly, Scheppele's study of the worldwide trend to adopt new anti-terrorism laws can be used as a starting point for analyzing how governments, witnessing domestic conflicts, use the ratification against their domestic opponents (Scheppele 2010, 451ff.).

The Ugandan ratification of the Rome Statute in 2002 could be argued to be instrumental. The Ugandan government, steered by President Museveni, has fought numerous rebel groups for decades and is involved in grave human rights abuses. The only significant survivor in Museveni's bloody war against rebel movements was the Lord's Resistance Army (LRA), which operates in the borderlands of Uganda, Sudan, the DRC, and the CAR (Furley 2008; ICG 2010). One year after ratification, Museveni referred the situation with the LRA to the ICC's consideration and the ICC subsequently opened a case against LRA leaders in 2004 (ICC-20040129-44 2004; ICC-OTP-20040729-65 2004). Arguably, the case was in the interest of Museveni and he used the ICC as a tool against violent opposition forces. The case also provided first grounds for claims that the ICC prosecutions would be politicized. ICC Prosecutor Moreno-Ocampo announced the opening of the investigations in a press conference together with Museveni, which offered reasons to argue that the ICC was acting on Museveni's behalf. Politicization rumors were strengthened as the ICC investigators were using government officials and vehicles in their investigations in Uganda (HRW 2005; Allen 2006, 99–127; Apuuli 2006, 185; Moreno-Ocampo 2005).

6.2.1.4 Locking-in Domestic Policies

Governments of newly established democracies, as Moravcsik argues, enter human rights regimes to "lock-in" domestic policies through international commitments. This tactic is used to overcome future political uncertainty and opposition forces (Moravcsik 2000; see also Ratner 2003, 2057). The lock-in logic is expected to have a deterring effect in a situation, where a regime change is likely. Governments try to protect the democratic system, hold future governments accountable for war crimes, and reduce impunity.

East Timor could qualify as a state that joined the ICC with the lock-in logic in mind. After gaining independence from Indonesia in May 2002, the new government of East Timor considered accession to the ICC of highest priority and deposited the instrument of acceptance only four months later. According to the statement of the Minister of Foreign Affairs Horta, the government perceived the ICC as an instrument, promoting the rule of law and justice: "There is a need to prevent violence and allow the rule of law to take its due course in trying to bring to justice those responsible for such horrendous crimes" (Ramos-Horta 2002; see also Borges 2011). No doubt the Rome Statute aims at promoting the rule of law and justice, but it is also likely that East Timor's accession had to do with the fact that Indonesia was still supporting pro-integration militias in the country and the threat of violence was concrete. As such, joining the ICC served as a potential deterrent (ICG 2002). The lock-in logic also finds support from the fact that the idealistic side of the ratification became somewhat muddled for two reasons. First, East Timor was one of the first countries to sign a BIA, arguably because the USA threatened to cut American personnel from the UN Mission for East Timor (Keller 2002).[1] Second, joining the ICC did not abolish the culture of impunity in the country (Amnesty International 2010, 5), which gives reason to claim that the ratification aimed at locking-in domestic politics, while the BIA served East Timor's international interests.

6.2.1.5 Insincere Commitment

Finnemore and Sikkink suggest that rogue states and Alcañiz argues that new democracies ratify human rights treaties to improve their domestic legitimacy, reputation, and credibility (Finnemore and Sikkink 1998, 903; Alcañiz 2012, 309). Along the same lines, Vreeland finds that dictatorships join the Convention against Torture (CAT) as a response to domestic interest groups' pressure. The commitment is a way to maintain power through cheap concessions, because dictators, or repressive governments, as Hafner-Burton and Tsutsui and Cole find, do not intend to comply with the treaty anyway (Vreeland 2008, 77–78; Hafner-Burton and Tsutsui 2005, 1398; 2007, 421; Cole 2005, 492). This is what Simmons calls an insincere ratification, aimed at polishing a state's public image and gaining short-term policy gains, such as membership to an organization or aid (Simmons 2009, 78–80). To extend a cynical argument, Goldsmith and Posner assume that the discrepancy in the ratification patterns can be explained by the fact that the costs and benefits of human rights treaties are so small for single states as well as in the international theater that their ratification does not matter anyway (Goldsmith and Posner 2005, 132). In fact, Hollyer and Rosendorff suggest that human rights violators may ratify human rights treaties

[1] The BIA was justified with national interests: "East Timor can not forget the role that the international community played in assisting it to achieve its long-desired status. In particular, it owes a debt of gratitude to the United States, which to a leading part in assisting East Timor on the road to independence […]. East Timor needed the support of all members of the international community in the past; it will continue to need their support in the future. History has proved that this tiny half-island, with a population of only 800,000 people is uniquely vulnerable. This new country is trying to protect its interests and its people in the new world in which it has found itself since May 20, 2002" (Camara 2002).

precisely because they want to signal to their opposition forces that such treaties will by no means restrict their actions, if the opposition attempts to remove them from power (Hollyer and Rosendorff 2011, 277).

It would be tempting to claim that an insincere commitment was made by Tajikistan, which joined the ICC in November 2000. Together with Georgia, it is one of only two Caucasian ICC States Parties and would qualify from many perspectives as an insincere committer. It is an authoritarian state, until today the poorest of Central Asian countries, and it gets, for instance, the largest share of the EU's assistance in the region, which would provide grounds for arguing that the ratification was aimed at pleasing international donors (Delegation of the European Union to the Republic of Tajikistan 2013). Tajikistan has serious problems with drug smuggling, corruption, and civil rights, in which the Rahmon government is allegedly closely intertwined (ICG 2001, 2011b). The government supported an independent ICC during the negotiations in Rome and has since then assured its support for the organization (A/CONF.183/13 (Vol. II) 1998, 92; Permanent Mission of the Republic of Tajikistan to the United Nations 2007). What speaks for insincerity is the fact that while Tajikistan was quick to ratify the Rome Statute, it scored even better in signing a BIA with the USA: It was the fourth country to do so (Boucher 2002). Moreover, like Azerbaijan and Kyrgyzstan, non-States Parties that supported an independent ICC during the Rome conference, Tajikistan's outspoken support for the ICC may also be cheap talk (A/CONF.183/13 (Vol. II) 1998, 77, 93). However, while the rule of law and human rights account of the government is suspicious, only the BIA has so far tested Tajikistan's commitment to the ICC.

6.2.2 Hindering Aspects

6.2.2.1 History of Violence and Human Rights Situation

The theories dealt with so far explain why states decide to join the ICC. The focus here, however, is also to explore reasons for late and non-ratification, which has hitherto been explained mostly via the by-products of inquiries. Rational explanations for non-ratification start with the argument that the commitment and compliance costs of human rights treaties vary among states. Hathaway's quantitative analysis points out that the higher the domestic enforcement and compliance costs of a treaty *vis-à-vis* the human rights practices of a country, the less likely is the ratification (Hathaway 2003, 1856; 2007, 602; Goodliffe and Hawkins 2006, 368). In the case studies on the Philippines and Indonesia, I will examine their human rights accounts and relationships to the ICC since the negotiations on the Rome Statute. I also test the hypothesis that past, recent, and ongoing domestic or regional conflicts, human rights violations as well as terrorism, truth commissions, and amnesties potentially influence domestic preferences toward the ICC negatively.

6.2.2.2 Political Players: Executive, Legislative, and Ministries

Late ratifications may be explained by governments' desires to use the ratification strategically, to advance their policy goals (Simmons 2009, 88), but political players may also delay or halt it for the same reasons (Hathaway 2007, 595ff.). An example of an executive that slowed down the ratification is the former President of the Czech Republic, Klaus. For six years, the Czech Republic was the only EU (candidate) country that had not joined the ICC, although it signed the Rome Statute in April 1999. After a long process steered by the Ministry of Foreign Affairs, both houses of the parliament approved the ratification by October 2008 and concluded that constitutional amendments were unnecessary. However, Klaus, famous for his skepticism toward international cooperation, halted the ratification for almost one year due to "serious juridical doubts." These included the extradition of Czechs to the ICC and the right of the President to pardon criminals (Klaus 2009; Pražský Hrad 2009; Parlament České republiky, Poslanecká sněmovna 2008; Parlament České republiky, Senát 2008; Hasenkopf 2009). However, somewhat unexpectedly Klaus ratified the treaty without further actions on July 8, 2009 (Ministry of Foreign Affairs of the Czech Republic 2009).[2]

[2] Funnily enough, the ratification occurred two days after my ex-Mother in Law, Ing. Studenovská, had personally approached Klaus on the issue. Mrs. Studenovská knows Klaus in person and I attended with her a service in honor of the Czech reformer Hus in Betlémská Chapel in Prague on July 6, 2009. Since Klaus was expected to come to the service too, I asked Mrs. Studenovská to inquire the President about the ratification. I was not close enough to hear their discussion, but she told me right afterwards that she had asked Klaus why he has not ratified the Rome Statute and he was annoyed by the question. While this is an anecdote and there is no further evidence on the issue, it might well be that Klaus reached his tipping point, because of this unexpected question. No doubt Czech Republic would have joined the ICC sooner or later, but the timing might have been different. For

In addition to reluctant executives, veto players in the legislative branch may also slow the process of ratification. Similar to the Czech Republic in Europe, Chile was for years the only South American country that had not joined the ICC. As Struett points out, the left-centrist government was supportive toward the ICC, but the legislature, biased toward conservative forces associated with the Pinochet government, blocked the ratification in the Senate (Struett 2008, 136). Chile ratified the Rome Statute a few weeks before the Czech Republic. Furthermore, ministries, and in particular the Ministry of Defense together with the armed forces, may pose potential hindrances for ratification. Simmons and Danner find that in contrast to "peacekeeper countries," states with strong militaries are more unlikely to join the ICC. When the military is used for national purposes, it easily becomes a potential target of the ICC (Simmons and Danner 2010, 241–44). Consequently, in countries with strong militaries, such as the USA, the Philippines, and Indonesia, the Department of Defense and the armed forces have been loud and powerful opponents of the ratification.

6.2.2.3 Legal System, Constitutional Restrictions, and Domestic Laws

In addition to political pro and contra calculations, the legal system, domestic laws, and judicial players hypothetically affect the ratification. Simmons concludes that common law countries are less likely to ratify human rights treaties. On the one hand, treaty interpretation tradition in common law systems poses a challenge to adjust potentially reluctant domestic lawyers and judges to the treaty. On the other hand, compared to civil law systems that strictly follow and interpret prescribed rules, the judges of common law systems have wide independence to interpret the treaty after ratification. This may decrease a government's enthusiasm toward the treaty, because the treaty effects are unpredictable and can lead to unwanted checks on government policies (Simmons 2009, 72–77; Goodliffe and Hawkins 2006, 369).

Moreover, there is some evidence that constitutional restrictions and amendments to national laws have delayed or hindered the ratification in certain countries. Thailand has not joined the ICC allegedly

a picture of Ing. Miroslava Studenovská talking with President Klaus after the service at the Betlémská Chapel, see Církev československá husitská (2009); report of Klaus' appearance at the service, see Týden (2009).

because according to the Art. 8 of the Constitution of the Kingdom of Thailand the King cannot do anything wrong and His Highness would require an exemption from the ICC jurisdiction, which is not possible according to Art. 27 of the Rome Statute (CICC 2008, 2013). At the same time, Cambodia and Norway, both monarchies with similar constitutional restrictions, have been able to convince their Kings to ratify (Asian Forum for Human Rights and Development 2002). Accordingly, if constitutional restrictions, personality cults, and other legal obstacles turn out to be insurmountable, I expect that the willingness to overcome them is low.

Yet, amendments to national laws are usually necessary when states join the ICC. While Japan was initially not very enthusiastic about the ICC, the government explained its late ratification of the Rome Statute in 2007 with slow legal review and implementation process (Goold 2002; Higashizawa 2007). The Japanese legal system is a mix of civil and common law with civil law characteristics dominating the system (Taylor et al. 2008; CIA 2013) and the ratification required the deliberation of three main legal issues. First, Japan had to consider whether and how to accommodate the ICC crimes with the national Criminal Code, which is very specific and, as such, time-consuming to amend. It decided to refrain from amendments, because Japanese laws already cover almost all crimes under the ICC's jurisdiction, with a few rather irrelevant exceptions (Arai et al. 2008, 365ff.). Second, a legal challenge was posed by Art. 9 of The Constitution of Japan, which states:

> [...] the Japanese people forever renounce war as a sovereign right of the nation and the threat or use of force as means of settling international disputes.
>
> In order to accomplish the aim of the preceding paragraph, land, sea, and air forces, as well as other war potential, will never be maintained. The right of belligerency of the state will not be recognized.

Because of this paragraph, legislating war-related laws was complicated, as it would imply the hypothetical possibility of Japan engaging in military activities. This obstacle was overcome in 2004 when the Diet adopted a package of emergency legislation that enabled Japan to ratify the 1977 Additional Protocols of the Geneva Conventions (Meierhenrich and Ko 2009, 237ff.). The last legal problem was cooperation with the ICC, which was resolved by adopting an ICC Cooperation Law (Takayama 2008, 388). As Chapter 5 already pointed out, financial matters also slowed down Japan's accession (Garský 2013) and therefore the economic side of the ratification considerations will be taken into account in the case studies too.

6.3 Reflectivist Explanations

Wendt would explain the ratification of the Rome Statute being driven by common identity. When actors share common knowledge and normative understanding of the principles and accepted behavior that supports human rights treaties, they act according to the logic of appropriateness and ratify them (Wendt 1992, 399, 417; March and Olsen 1998, 951–52). States may also ratify treaties just "because they want others to think well of them, and they want to think well of themselves" (Finnemore and Sikkink 1998, 903). Conditions where states comply with norms in order to belong to the "legitimate" group and non-ratifiers feel shame or guilt derive from a common worldview. However, domestic processes also influence identity politics. Brysk's Global Good Samaritans create their foreign policy identity as international humanitarians and global democracies from the inside: The foreign policy elite and civil society act as domestic norm entrepreneurs and once the identity of a Samaritan is established, the state becomes a promoter of global norms and values (Brysk 2009, 4, 35ff.). According to this logic, stragglers also could become Samaritans over time. Newly elected governments, in particular those that have fought hard to win repressive governments and to establish a rule of law tradition, can win domestic legitimacy and construct a new international identity through the promotion of human rights (Brysk 2009, 33ff.).

6.3.1 ICC as a Result of Diffusion

Both rationalist and reflectivist camps have theorized about policy diffusion. The core of the concept is interdependence, meaning that the policy decisions of a government depend on, and are affected by, other countries' prior decisions. The literature on diffusion identifies several mechanisms through which diffusion may occur, including learning, interdependence, emulation, and common identities and norms. Reflectivist approaches would explain the ICC as a result of diffusion among others with socialization, the self-evidence of its norms, and emulation; rationalists with the use of exogenous pressure (e.g., coercion, shaming, and acculturation), positive externalities, and states' fear of negative ones; and both strands with learning and the influence of powerful countries, epistemic communities, and advocacy networks (Simmons et al. 2006, 787, 800; Braun and Gilardi 2006, 311, see also 299ff.; Elkins and Simmons 2005, 35). Diffusion is often perceived as vertical (top-down) influence, but Sikkink extends the theory to include horizontal influence. She shows how domestic human rights prosecutions in Southern Europe and Latin America started twenty years before the establishment of the ICTY and allowed activists to pressure states to apply individual criminal accountability and design new legal doctrines. Such horizontal diffusion works better within than between regions, while vertical diffusion occurs through innovative states and results in international institutions (Sikkink 2011, 250ff.). The high ratification rates of the Rome Statute in Europe and Latin America provide grounds to argue that regional diffusion was at work in these continents, while Asia remains underrepresented in the ICC.

6.3.2 Persuasion

Risse and Sikkink extend the norm cascade theory presented in Chapter 2 to cover the socialization of human rights violators. According to their spiral model, "Norms influence political change through a socialization process that combines instrumental interests, material pressures, argumentation, persuasion, institutionalization, and habitualization" (Risse and Sikkink 1999, 37). The model explains how states or regions that did not adopt a norm during the norm cascade eventually may end up abiding it. The spiral starts with the rise of international attention to a certain government's human rights violation that leads to organized pressure from advocacy networks. The government begins to make tactical, insincere concessions, but as other actors keep on shaming and persuading, it gets trapped in the discourse and at some point it accepts the norm (Risse and Sikkink 1999, 17–18, 22ff.; Sikkink 2011, 250). Its validity claims are no longer controversial, concessions are more than instrumental, and it starts to ratify and implement human rights treaties. Finally, the state behaves in a rule consistent manner (Risse and Sikkink 1999, 16–17). But before that, a two-level game may occur at the domestic level as powerful domestic players, usually the military, keep on resisting the norms, which the (potentially newly elected) government already supports (Putnam 1988, 434; Risse and Sikkink 1999, 33). Correspondingly, persuasion of domestic and international NGOs, international and regional organizations, and other states will be considered potential explanatory variables in the case studies to follow.

6.4 External Influence and Late Ratifications of the Rome Statute

Considering the hypothesis about exogenous pressure and inducements influencing the ratification of the Rome Statute, Simmons and Danner's results suggest that they did not play a significant role in the ratification decisions made between the years 1998 and 2007. Military alliance with the EU had a positive impact on the ratification decision, but so did foreign aid assistance from the USA too, which arguably diminishes the significance of the EU's role. Moreover, one must note that the EU has no military alliances with non-EU member states, meaning that the countries Simmons and Danner refer to as the EU's military allies are the EUMS, which outspokenly supported the ICC. Interestingly, Simmons and Danner found some evidence that the conclusion of a BIA with the USA positively impacts the ratification. This may point to a state's willingness to show its support for the ICC despite the BIA and, accordingly, its latent disregard for the US policy (Simmons and Danner 2010, 245–46). Kelley has statistically analyzed the BIA campaign with the aim of finding out whether states care about human rights commitments or whether they abandon them when there are strong incentives, namely BIAs, to do so. She concludes that BIAs are rejected by democratic states, which belong to the LMS, respect human rights, and value the rule of law. Poor, US dependent states were more likely to sign a BIA, although in some cases the BIA campaign possibly deepened the trust in international law as respect for rule of law did not predict ratification, but played a significant role in not signing a BIA (Kelley 2007, 586–87).

6.4.1 Dependence Networks

Goodliffe et al. argue that an actor's dependency on, and in particular trade relationship with, either a supporter or opponent of the ICC predicts ratification (Goodliffe et al. 2012). Dependence networks are composed of close economic, military, and political allies that indirectly pressure countries to join the ICC, because governments tend to anticipate their partners' reactions and want to appear cooperative:

> To the extent that a government is dependent on other countries, it will want to appear both responsible and responsive to its partners. It will want both positive reactions and maintenance of relations. Thus, the government will try to anticipate how its partners might view its behavior. [...] [I]f the government depends on countries that have committed to a strong ICC, leaders will likely conclude that their partners will react positively to those who also commit to punish human rights violators. (Goodliffe and Hawkins 2009, 982–83; Goodliffe et al. 2012)

Hence, Goodliffe et al. emphasize diffuse reciprocity and anticipations of possible rewards and punishments. Their theory comprises a range of influential actors and ignores the fact that no other actor, except the USA and the EU, directly tried to influence third states policies on the ICC. The Organization of American States, for instance, only encourages its own members to ratify and Australia, which Goodliffe et al. use as an example of a country torn between the USA and the EU, has supported the ICC since the negotiations on the Rome Statute. The likelihood that Australia would not to ratify the Rome Statute was low from the very beginning (Goodliffe et al. 2012; Australian Government 2008; OAS 2003, 2010).

6.5 Conclusions

Part II provided empirical evidence that issue-linkages used by the EU and the USA shaped the preferences of third states *vis-à-vis* the ICC. The following case studies test the hypothesis that exogenous pressure to influence ratification decisions of third states has been successful at different points of time and that in the case of stragglers exogenous influence explains the timing of ratification. Moreover, I expect to find evidence for the EU's normative binding attempts starting to bear fruit with ICC skeptical states when the USA relaxes its policy toward the ICC.

This chapter generated alternative explanations for the exogenous influence hypothesis. The following case studies test the explanatory power of all the hypotheses put forward in Table 6.1. They aim at teasing out the

Table 6.1 The timing of ratification: theories and hypotheses

	External influence	*Liberal explanations*	*Reflectivist explanations*
Reinforcing Cooperation	*Normative binding* Unilateralist US-policies invoked binding attempts. Especially, states that were not dependent of the USA or opposed US policies likely engaged in normative binding by committing to the ICC Issue-linkages generated by the EU became more effective after the USA relaxed its opposition to the ICC	*Governmental motivations* The executive can use the ratification as a political tool to make a credible or an insincere commitment, lock-in future domestic politics, or to realize own policy goals A government may use the ICC against domestic opponents Internationally active democratic states use the ICC as another tool to fight global crime	*Persuasion* Advocacy of domestic society, NGOs, other countries, and international institutions furthers cooperation *Diffusion* Decisions of regional or international partners to cooperate produce vertical norm diffusion, while domestic and regional practice of international criminal law produces horizontal norm diffusion in favor of cooperation
Obstructing Cooperation	*US policy 1998–2009* Economic sanctions or threats likely hindered cooperation of US-dependent states and of countries that either did not prioritize the ICC and/or were reluctant to follow the EU policy	*Political and legal costs* Past, recent, or ongoing military conflicts, terrorism, poor human rights account, and strong military likely hinder cooperation Constitutional obstacles are more likely to be hindering factors than other legal issues	
Delaying cooperation	*Obama effect* Obama Administration's cooperation with the ICC encouraged international law friendly, but US-dependent states to ratify the Rome Statute	*Political and legal process* The political agenda of either the executive or legislative may delay cooperation Legal review of the Rome Statute and ICC-related domestic laws are potentially delaying factors *Financial contribution* A country's financial contribution to the ICC may delay ratification	
Alternate effects	*Dependence networks* Ratification decision depends on a state's closest military, economic, and political allies' policy toward the ICC		*Common identities* Common identity that defines a state's approach vis-à-vis international criminal law either promotes or hinders cooperation

process of ratification to the broadest possible extent and identifying its stakeholders and motives. A case study approach is meaningful, because for answering the question about the stragglers and non-ratifiers motives for (not) joining the ICC, the timing and process of the ratification are more important than the binary signal of whether states join the ICC or not. The case studies on the Philippines and Indonesia are built around three sets of explanatory variables that were presented in this chapter: The liberal set explains the ratification with domestic preferences and actors; the external influence variables test whether exogenous pressure and issue-linkages influence ratification; and the reflectivist variables test whether common identities, diffusion, and persuasion have influenced the ratification. For Indonesia, there is no intuitive explanation for its non-ratification—especially because it has repeatedly committed to ratification—and therefore I explore the grounds of non-ratification also from a historical perspective. In general, while the USA leads the sovereignty-oriented coalition of latecomers and the EU the early ratifiers, the non-ratifiers unlikely follow either one. Subsequently, in the international criminal law regime, today's non-ratifiers have no leader, who would be willing or able to establish mechanisms of control or sanctioning for the ratification.

As noted in the introduction while describing the method of process tracing, the same evidence can explain competing theories (George and Bennett 2005, 222). For instance, diffusion, dependence networks, and common identities are risky as explanatory variables, because they potentially share a regional aspect: It is not seldom that norms diffuse regionally, that states' closest allies or dependence networks are closely located, or that common identities follow cultural patterns. Furthermore, changes in the domestic political situation—such as a newly elected government or parliament favoring either the EU, the USA, or international cooperation—may produce similar effects as predicted by the external influence hypothesis, in particular if they overlap with the Obama effect. Considering external influence, the risk of coinciding evidence is the greatest with persuasion and dependence networks, because external influence is partly exercised through persuasion and the USA or EUMS may constitute a state's dependence network. Hence, if persuasion or dependence networks prove to influence the ratification, it potentially adds to the success of external influence. Vice versa, if the cases demonstrate that external pressure influenced the ratification, I expect to find evidence for persuasion. However, even if the variables on persuasion and dependence networks fail, it does not necessarily eliminate external pressure. Persuasion is only one tool of external pressure—economic inducements and sanctions are also central—and it may be that neither the EU nor the USA is close allies of the country. To demonstrate the centrality of external influence, a causal chain, where the connection between delayed ratification and external pressure is evident, needs to be constructed. The EU's external pressure would be successfully evidenced, if the case proves that the BIA campaign influenced state policies and the government acknowledged the EU's pressure before ratification. However, if the Obama effect finds strong verification, I will conclude that the US policy influenced the ratification more than the EU.

References

A/CONF.183/13 (Vol. II). 1998. "United Nations Diplomatic Conference of Plenipotentiaries on the Establishment of an International Criminal Court Rome, 15 June–17 July 1998, Official Records: Volume II".

African Union, PSC/PR/Comm(CLXXV). 2009. "Communique of the 175th Meeting of the Peace and Security Council".

Alcañiz, Isabella. 2012. "Democratization and Multilateral Security." *World Politics* 64 (2): 306–40.

Allen, Tim. 2006. *Trial Justice: The International Criminal Court and the Lord's Resistance Army*. London: Zed Books.

Amnesty International. 2010. "International Criminal Court. Timor-Leste: Justice in the Shadow." ASA 57/001/2010. London.

Apuuli, Kasaija Phillip. 2006. "The ICC Arrest Warrants for the Lord's Resistance Army Leaders and Peace Prospects for Northern Uganda." *Journal of International Criminal Justice* 4 (1): 179–87.

Arab League Council. 2009. "Resolution on the Decision of Pre-trial Chamber 1 to the International Criminal Court Against the President of the Republic of Sudan, Hassan Ahmad Al-Bashir, Unofficial Translation." Coalition for the International Criminal Court.

Arai, Kyo, Akira Mayama, and Osamu Yoshida. 2008. "Accession of Japan to the International Criminal Court: Japan's Accession to the ICC Statute and the ICC Cooperation Law." *Japanese Yearbook of International Law* 51: 359–83.

Asian Forum for Human Rights and Development. 2002. "The Second Regional Experts Meeting on the International Criminal Court." Bangkok.

Australian Government. 2008. "Australia-European Union Partnership Framework." Department of Foreign Affairs and Trade.

Borges, Sofia. 2011. "Statement at the General Debate of the Tenth Session of the Assembly of States Parties to the Rome Statute." República Democrática de Timor-Leste.

Boucher, Richard. 2002. "U.S., Tajikistan Agree to Implement Article 98 of Rome Statute: Excerpt from August 27 State Department Briefing." Daily Press Briefing. U.S. Department of State.

Braun, Dietmar, and Fabrizio Gilardi. 2006. "Taking 'Galton's Problem' Seriously: Towards a Theory of Policy Diffusion." *Journal of Theoretical Politics* 18 (3): 298–322.

Brysk, Alison. 2009. *Global Good Samaritans: Human Rights as Foreign Policy.* Oxford: Oxford University Press.

Camara, Joao. 2002. "Intervention of East Timor During the Assembly of States Parties of the Rome Statute of the International Criminal Court." ICC-ASP/1/3. Democratic Republic of Timor-Leste, Ministry of Foreign Affairs and Cooperation.

Chapman, Terrence L., and Stephen Chaudoin. 2013. "Ratification Patterns of the International Criminal Court." *International Studies Quarterly* 57 (2): 400–09.

Chayes, Abram, and Antonia Handler Chayes. 1995. *The New Sovereignty: Compliance with International Regulatory Agreements.* Cambridge: Harvard University Press.

CIA. 2013. "The World Factbook: Legal System." https://www.cia.gov/library/publications/the-world-factbook/fields/2100.html.

CICC. 2008. "Conference on the ICC Organized by Amnesty International Thailand and the National Commission on Human Rights." Coalition for the International Criminal Court.

———. 2011. "Tunisia Expresses Intent to Ratify the Rome Statute: First Steps of Interim Government Include Commitment to Human Rights." Coalition for the International Criminal Court.

———. 2013. "Letter to H.E. Ms. Yingluck Shinawatra, Prime Minister, The Kingdom of Thailand." Coalition for the International Criminal Court.

Církev československá husitská. 2009. "Betlémská Kaple 2009." http://www.ccsh.cz/galerie.php?id=236.

Cole, Wade M. 2005. "Sovereignty Relinquished? Explaining Commitment to the International Human Rights Covenants, 1966–1999." *American Sociological Review* 70 (3): 472–95.

Delegation of the European Union to the Republic of Tajikistan. 2013. "Projects: Overview".

Elkins, Zachary, and Beth A. Simmons. 2005. "On Waves, Clusters, and Diffusion: A Conceptual Framework." *ANNALS of the American Academy of Political and Social Science* 598 (1): 33–51.

Finnemore, Martha, and Kathryn Sikkink. 1998. "International Norm Dynamics and Political Change." *International Organization* 52 (4): 887–917.

Foreign Affairs Ministry Tunisia. 2009. "Tunisia: Country Expresses Deep Regret Following ICC Arrest Warrant Against Sudanese President".

Furley, Oliver. 2008. "Uganda: The Struggle for Peace." In *Ending Africa's Wars: Progressing to Peace*, edited by Oliver Furley and Roy May. London: Ashgate.

Garský, Salla. 2013. "Japan's Ratification of the Rome Statute of the International Criminal Court." Voices from the Sylff Community, 9. Tokyo: The Tokyo Foundation.

George, Alexander L., and Andrew Bennett. 2005. *Case Studies and Theory Development in the Social Sciences*. Cambridge: MIT Press.

Goldsmith, Jack L., and Eric A. Posner. 2005. *The Limits of International Law*. Oxford: Oxford University Press.

Goodliffe, Jay, and Darren Hawkins. 2006. "Explaining Commitment: States and the Convention Against Torture." *The Journal of Politics* 68 (2): 358–71.

———. 2009. "A Funny Thing Happened on the Way to Rome: Explaining International Criminal Court Negotiations." *The Journal of Politics* 71 (3): 977–97.

Goodliffe, Jay, Darren Hawkins, Christine Horne, and Daniel L. Nielson. 2012. "Dependence Networks and the International Criminal Court." *International Studies Quarterly* 56 (1): 131–47.

Goold, Benjamin. 2002. "Ratifying the Rome Statute: Japan and the International Criminal Court." *Focus, HURights Osaka*, 29.

Hafner-Burton, Emilie M. 2013. *Making Human Rights a Reality*. Princeton: Princeton University Press.

Hafner-Burton, Emilie M., and Kiyoteru Tsutsui. 2005. "Human Rights in a Globalizing World: The Paradox of Empty Promises." *American Journal of Sociology* 110 (5): 1373–1411.

———. 2007. "Justice Lost! The Failure of International Human Rights Law To Matter Where Needed Most." *Journal of Peace Research* 44 (4): 407–25.

Hasenkopf, Pavel. 2009. "K Ratifikaci Římského Statutu Mezinárodního Trestního Soudu Českou Republikou (To the Ratification of the Rome Statute)." *Fragmenty, Kulturně-Hospodářská Revue* XIV (4).

Hathaway, Oona A. 2003. "The Cost of Commitment." *Stanford Law Review* 55 (5): 1821–62

———. 2007. "Why Do Countries Commit to Human Rights Treaties?" *Journal of Conflict Resolution* 51 (4): 588–621.

Higashizawa, Yasushi. 2007. "Experiences in Japan for the Coming Accession to the Rome Statute." A Paper Prepared for the Symposium on the International Criminal Court. Beijing: International Centre for Criminal Law Reform and Criminal Justice Policy.

Hollyer, James R., and B. Peter Rosendorff. 2011. "Why Do Authoritarian Regimes Sign the Convention Against Torture? Signaling, Domestic Politics and Non-compliance." *Quarterly Journal of Political Science* 6 (3–4): 275–327.

HRW. 2005. "Uprooted and Forgotten: Impunity and Human Rights Abuses in Northern Uganda." *Human Rights Watch* 17 (12(A)).

ICC-20040129-44. 2004. "Press Release: President of Uganda Refers Situation Concerning the Lord's Resistance Army (LRA) to the ICC." International Criminal Court.

ICC-OTP-20040729-65. 2004. "Press Release: ICC—Prosecutor of the International Criminal Court Opens an Investigation into Nothern Uganda." International Criminal Court.

ICG. 2001. "Tajikistan: An Uncertain Peace." ICG Asia Report N° 30. Osh: International Crisis Group.

———. 2002. "Indonesia: Implications of the Timor Trials." Briefing Paper. Jakarta: International Crisis Group.

———. 2010. "LRA: A Regional Strategy Beyond Killing Kony." Africa Report N° 157. Nairobi: International Crisis Group.

———. 2011a. "Popular Protests in North Africa and the Middle East (IV): Tunisia's Way." Middle East/North Africa Report N° 106. Tunis: International Crisis Group.

———. 2011b. "Tajikistan: The Changing Insurgent Threats." Asia Report N° 205. Bishkek: International Crisis Group.

Keller, Anett. 2002. "US-East Timor Agreement on ICC Article 98 Detrimental to the Protection of Human Rights." *Indonesien-Information* 3.

Kelley, Judith. 2007. "Who Keeps International Commitments and Why? The International Criminal Court and Bilateral Nonsurrender Agreements." *American Political Science Review* 101 (3): 573–89.

Klaus, Václav. 2009. "Římský Statut: Míč Není Na Straně Prezidenta Republiky (Rome Statute: The Ball Is Not in the Hands of the President)." *Tisková Sdělení (Press Releases)*. February 4.

Koh, Harold Hongju. 2010. "U.S. Engagement with the International Criminal Court and the Outcome of the Recently Concluded Review Conference, Special Briefing with Stephen J. Rapp." Washington, DC: U.S. Department of State.

Koremenos, Barbara, Charles Lipson, and Duncan Snidal. 2001. "The Rational Design of International Institutions." *International Organization* 55 (4): 761–99.

March, James G., and Johan P. Olsen. 1998. "The Institutional Dynamics of International Political Orders." *International Organization* 52 (4): 943–69.

Martin, Lisa L. 1992. "Interests, Power, and Multilateralism." *International Organization* 46 (4): 756–792.

Meernik, James, and Rosa Aloisi. 2009. "I Do Declare: Politics, Declarations and the International Criminal Court." *International Criminal Law Review* 9: 235–73.

Meierhenrich, Jens, and Keiko Ko. 2009. "How Do States Join the International Criminal Court? The Implementation of the Rome Statute in Japan." *Journal of International Criminal Justice* 7 (2): 233–56.

Ministry of Foreign Affairs of the Czech Republic. 2009. "Statement of the Ministry of Foreign Affairs on the International Criminal Court." July 9.

Moravcsik, Andrew. 1997. "Taking Preferences Seriously: A Liberal Theory of International Politics." *International Organization* 51 (4): 513–53.

———. 2000. "The Origins of Human Rights Regimes: Democratic Delegation in Postwar Europe." *International Organization* 54 (2): 217–52.

Moreno-Ocampo, Luis. 2005. "Statement by Chief Prosecutor".

Neumayer, Eric. 2009. "New Moral Hazard? Military Intervention, Peacekeeping and Ratification of the International Criminal Court." *Journal of Peace Research* 46 (5): 659–670.

OAS, Organization of American States. 2003. "AG/RES. 1929 (XXXIII-O/03) Promotion of the International Criminal Court".

———. 2010. "AG/RES. 2577 (XL-O/10) Promotion of the International Criminal Court".

Parlament České republiky, Poslanecká sněmovna. 2008. "Usnesení PS č. 920 k Vládnímu Návrhu, Kterým Se Předkládá Parlamentu České Republiky k Vyslovení Souhlasu s Ratifikací Římský Statut Mezinárodního Trestního Soudu/Sněmovní Tisk 423/ (Czech Parliament Agrees to the Ratification of the Rome Statute)".

Parlament České republiky, Senát. 2008. "437. Usnesení Senátu, k Vyslovení Souhlasu s Ratifikací Římský Statut Mezinárodního Trestního Soudu/Senátní Tisk č. 188/(Czech Senate Agrees to the Ratification of the Rome Statute)".

Permanent Mission of the Republic of Tajikistan to the United Nations. 2007. "Letter." UNTAJ-291-2007. New York: Government of the Republic of Tajikistan.

Poast, Paul. 2012. "Does Issue Linkage Work? Evidence from European Alliance Negotiations, 1860 to 1945." *International Organization* 66 (2): 277–310.

Pražský Hrad. 2009. "Stanovisko Odboru Legislativy a Práva KPR k Ratifikaci Římského Statutu Mezinárodního Trestního Soudu." July 8.

Putnam, Robert D. 1988. "Diplomacy and Domestic Politics: The Logic of Two-Level Games." *International Organization* 42 (3): 427–60.

Ramos-Horta, Jose. 2002. "Statement on the International Criminal Court." República Democrática de Timor-Leste. http://www.iccnow.org/documents/East%20TimorRamos27Jun02.pdf.

Ratner, Steven R. 2003. "Precommitment Theory and International Law: Strating a Conversation." *Texas Law Review* 81: 2055–81.

Risse, Thomas, and Kathryn Sikkink. 1999. "The Socialization of International Human Rights Norms into Domestic Practices: Introduction." In *The Power of Human Rights: International Norms and Domestic Change*, edited by

Thomas Risse, Stephen C. Ropp, and Kathryn Sikkink, 1–38. Cambridge: Cambridge University Press.
Scheppele, Kim Lane. 2010. "The International Standardization of National Security Law." *Journal of National Security Law & Policy* 4 (2): 437–54.
Sikkink, Kathryn. 2011. *The Justice Cascade: How Human Rights Prosecutions Are Changing World Politics*. New York: W. W. Norton.
Simmons, Beth A. 2009. *Mobilizing for Human Rights: International Law in Domestic Politics*. New York: Cambridge University Press.
Simmons, Beth A., and Allison Danner. 2010. "Credible Commitments and the International Criminal Court." *International Organization* 64 (2): 225–56.
Simmons, Beth A., Frank Dobbin, and Geoffrey Garrett. 2006. "Introduction: The International Diffusion of Liberalism." *International Organization* 60 (4): 781–810.
Struett, Michael J. 2008. *The Politics of Constructing the International Criminal Court: NGOs, Discourse, and Agency*. New York: Palgrave Macmillan.
Takayama, Kanako. 2008. "Participation in the ICC and the National Criminal Law of Japan." *Japanese Yearbook of International Law* 51: 348–408.
Taylor, Veronica, Robert R. Britt, Kyoko Ishida, and John Chaffee. 2008. "Introduction: Nature of the Japanese Legal System." *Business Law in Japan* 1: 3–8.
Triffterer, Otto. 2000. "Legal and Political Implications of Domestic Ratification and Implementation Processes." In *Rome Statute and Domestic Legal Orders Volume I: General Aspects and Constitutional Issues*, edited by Claus Kreß and Flavia Lattanzi, 1–28. Baden-Baden: Nomos Verlagsgesellschaft.
Týden. 2009. "Hus Také Čelil Kritice z Francie, Připomněl Klaus." *Týden*, July 6.
UN News Centre. 2011. "Tunisia Becomes First North African Nation to Join International Criminal Court." United Nations.
Vreeland, James Raymond. 2008. "Political Institutions and Human Rights: Why Dictatorships Enter into the United Nations Convention Against Torture." *International Organization* 62 (1): 65–101.
Wendt, Alexander. 1992. "Anarchy Is What States Make of It: The Social Construction of Power Politics." *International Organization* 46 (2): 391–425.

CHAPTER 7

The Philippines' Late Ratification of the Rome Statute

7.1 The Philippines and International Criminal Law

The Republic of the Philippines is often called the most democratic country among the ASEAN states. The 1987 Philippine Constitution heavily emphasizes human rights not least because of the autocratic martial law era under the Marcos regime that ended in 1986 (Veloso Lao 1999, 229ff.; A/HRC/WG.6/1/PHL/1 2008, 2–4). At first sight, the Philippines seems to be a model student among ASEAN states when it comes to human rights. It was one of the first states in the world to ratify all seven core international human rights treaties and it has incorporated most human rights instruments into its domestic laws. Yet, in terms of the implementation of human rights treaties, the Philippines does not stand out in comparison with the rest of Asia, which is also the most underrepresented region in the ICC (A/HRC/WG.6/1/PHL/1 2008, 2; A/HRC/8/28 2008, 28).

Throughout the negotiations on the Rome Statute, the Philippines aspired to the codification of international criminal law and the establishment of a strong ICC. The sentiment of the Philippine President Ramos toward the ICC was supportive and before the Rome conference he established an interagency Task Force to study the proposed court and formulate the Philippine government's position on the ICC (Administrative Order No. 387 1998; Veloso Lao 1999, 234). In his opening speech at the Rome conference, the head of the ten men Filipino delegation confirmed his country's commitment to the ICC

S. Huikuri, *The Institutionalization of the International Criminal Court*,
https://doi.org/10.1007/978-3-319-95585-8_7

and its willingness to adjust its national laws to the Statute of the ICC (Baja 1998; A/CONF.183/13 (Vol. II) 1998, 82). Thus, the Philippines actively participated in the conference and worked mainly in the coalition of the Non-Aligned Movement (NAM). The NAM agenda preferred an independent ICC, emphasized the importance of creating a jurisdiction for the crime of aggression, and opposed universal jurisdiction (CB/MM-Doc.6 1998; A/CONF.183/C.1/SR.35 1998, 10). The Philippines was one of 23 NAM countries, which eventually joined the LMS and voted for the adoption of the Rome Statute, while some other Asian NAM states (Indonesia, Malaysia, Singapore, and Vietnam) arguably abstained in the vote (A/CONF.183/SR.9 1998; Schabas 2011, 19; Amnesty International 2003, 17; Van Schaak 2007).

During the Rome conference, the Philippines got a new President, Estrada, who was more doubtful over the ICC. At the UNGA Sixth Committee in 2000, the Philippines suggested that strong states might politically abuse the ICC to dominate weaker countries and drew attention to the UNSC's powers vis-à-vis the ICC. The Philippines further stated that it would only join the ICC if it were convinced that the court would be effective and fair (A/C.6/55/SR.12 2000). According to Foreign Affairs Secretary Ebdalin's statement, the Philippines was also concerned about EU countries: "President Estrada numbers among heads of states leery of the ICC [...]. Concern, [Ebdalin] said, stems from fear 'European countries could use that to harass developing countries for human rights reasons'" (BBC 2000). However, in the middle of his impeachment trial, President Estrada signed the Rome Statute on December 28, 2000. One month later, after the Philippine military withdrew its support for him, Estrada resigned from the Office and his Vice President, Arroyo, took the oath as President of the Philippines (Bernas 2003, 269–70).

It is interesting that while many ICC States Parties have not implemented the Rome Statute years after their ratification, the Philippines did so two years before its ratification. Over the decades, the Philippines had ratified a set of treaties concerning international humanitarian law, including the Genocide Convention and the Geneva Conventions, and in December 2009 President Arroyo signed Philippine Act on Crimes against International Humanitarian Law, Genocide and other Crimes against Humanity into law. This Act applies the Geneva Conventions, all their additional Protocols, and other relevant treaties acceded by the Philippines. By so doing, it provides, among other things, definitions of genocide, war crimes, and crimes against humanity, individual responsibility (including for superiors), and protection for victims and witnesses. Overall, the Act implements the Rome Statute and, hence, constitutional restrictions or legal obstacles do not explain why it took the Philippines another two years to join the ICC.

7.2 Liberal Explanations for Late Ratification

7.2.1 *The Executive Versus The Legislative*

Instead of legal hindrances, "problems of internal politics and differences in policy priorities [...] delayed ratification for some time" (Morales 2011) as the Philippine Ambassador to The Netherlands put it at the welcoming ceremony of the Philippines to the ICC in November 2011. Indeed, President Arroyo was able to hinder the ratification through the domestic process that is required for the ratification of treaties. According to Philippine laws, the President negotiates international treaties and has powers to sign them. After the signature, the Department of Foreign Affairs (DFA) prepares the ratification papers and submits them to the President's signature. After the President's ratification, the Philippines' Constitution requires a two-third concurrence of the Senate before the DFA can render the treaty effective and submit the instrument of ratification to the UN. Hence, both the President and the Senate have powers to block the ratification. As the following sections show, President Arroyo ignored the calls of the DFA, the Congress, and civil society and kept the treaty on her desk throughout her nine-year term for two main reasons. First, the numerous human rights violations committed during her term, especially extrajudicial killings, had the potential to qualify as crimes against humanity in front of the ICC. Second, Arroyo maintained close relationships with the Bush Administration and followed its "advice" not to ratify the Rome Statute.

Arroyo's reluctance to ratify the Rome Statute was repeatedly challenged by the legislative branch, and also in front of the Philippine Supreme Court. In March 2003, Senator Pimentel and Congresswoman Rosales (together with NGOs, a group of law students, and two children) filed a petition for mandamus to the Supreme Court, compelling the Office of the Executive Secretary and the DFA to transmit a signed text of the Rome Statute to the Senate's ratification. According to the plaintiffs, the signing of the Rome Statute in 2000 mandates the President to transmit the treaty to the Senate. In 2005, the Supreme Court ruled negative:

> under our Constitution, the power to ratify is vested in the President, subject to the concurrence of the Senate. The role of the Senate, however, is limited only to giving or withholding its consent, or concurrence, to the ratification. Hence, it is within the authority of the President to refuse to submit a treaty to the Senate or, having secured its consent for its ratification, refuse to ratify it. Although the refusal of a state to ratify a treaty which has been signed in its behalf is a serious step that should not be taken lightly, such decision is within the competence of the President alone [...]. (G. R. No. 158088 2005; PCICC 2009a; CICC 2004, 5)

According to this ruling, the ratification of international treaties is indeed a political question in the Philippines.

Throughout the Arroyo Presidency, both Chambers of the Philippine Congress made clear that they supported the ratification of the Rome Statute. From 1998 onwards, members of the House of Representatives drafted resolutions insisting Arroyo ratify the Rome Statute.[1] The most vocal supporters of the ICC in the House were representatives of small parties and in particular Rosales (Chair of the Committee on Human Rights, representing Akbayan-party) and Ocampo (Bayan Muna party). Both were long-term human rights defenders, who had fought against the Marcos dictatorship and their parties were critical of the conservative, and arguably corrupt, political mainstream and in particular the Arroyo Administration (Akbayan 2010; Bayan Muna 2013). Several Senators also worked on the ratification. In 2001, for instance, Senator Legarda (center-liberal Lakas party) introduced resolution number 11, urging the immediate ratification of the Rome Statute and also Senator Defensor-Santiago (Chair of the Foreign Relations Committee) was among the supporters of the ICC (PCICC 2011). By 2005, according to Senator Biazon (Chairman of the Committee on National Defense and Security), the whole Senate was more than willing to concur to the ratification: "'There is a consensus in the Senate. We are all for the ratification of the ICC, Rome statute. But we are waiting for it to be transmitted to the Senate. As soon as it is transmitted, the ratification process will pursue,' he told reporters" (Roncesvalles 2005; Senate of the Philippines 2011a).

[1] HR00094 (1998), HR01503 (2000), HR00341 (2001), HR00800 (2002), HR01391 (2003), HR00050 (2004), HR00417 (2004), HR00425 (2008). Some of the resolutions were later consolidated into HR00526 (2006) and HR00165 (2008).

While the Congress had been active on the ICC ever since the Rome conference, its engagement intensified in 2006. In April, the House approved the first bill, urging the Philippine government to support the ratification as an important step in the furtherance of the promotion and respect for human rights (HR00526 2006). In August, the Congress hosted the first Asian Parliamentarians' seminar on the Rome Statute, which was organized with NGOs. The conference gathered 80 representatives from Asian and European countries, the European Commission, and several NGOs (Rosales 2006). At the same time as the conference, the Senate unanimously adopted a resolution that for the first time called the President to submit the Rome Statute to the Senate (P. S. Res. No. 171 2006; adopted as P. S. Res. No. 94 2006). In this resolution, the Senators appealed to the Philippine Constitution and the International Covenant on Civil and Political Rights, which require the Philippines to protect and promote human rights. The resolution also mentioned a letter of the DFA to Arroyo, which recommended the ratification (P. S. Res. No. 171 2006). While reporting on the resolution in 2006, the Philippine Daily Inquirer newspaper linked Arroyo's reluctance to ratify the treaty to US pressure. The article also let understand that the reason why the resolution was enacted in 2006, and not earlier, was because the US war on terror had become increasingly questionable in the country, hence, providing straw-in-the-wind evidence for the Congress's growing interest in the ICC being a response to the US policies (Uy 2006a).

The pressure on the executive did not ease and the Senators became more outspoken about the US influence on Arroyo, hence, providing evidence in support of the hypothesis that the US policy influenced the Philippines decision to join the ICC. In 2007, a proposed resolution calling on the President to transmit the Rome Statute to the Senate mentioned the US pressure as the key factor for the Executive's inaction in the matter (P. S. Res. No. 90 2007). One year later, Senator Defensor-Santiago introduced two ratification-related resolutions, one paying particular attention to the changed US policy toward the ICC. The resolution discusses the willingness of President-elect Obama to cooperate with the ICC, the Bush Administration's policy change, and predicts that the USA might ratify the Rome Statute too. It concludes by noting:

> be it hereby resolved by the Philippine Senate that since the change of leadership in the United States may bring about a possible shift in US

> policy on […] the International Criminal Court, the President is respectfully requested to transmit the Rome Statute to the Senate for ratification proceedings. (P. S. Res. No. 748 2008; see also P. S. Res. No. 710 2008)

The Senate majority leader Pangilinan also urged the ratification in the media, but suspected that Arroyo followed the US decision not to join the ICC (Danao and Depasupil 2008).

7.2.2 *The Ministries: Proponents and Opponents*

The DFA and the Department of Justice were enthusiastic about the ICC in the first years after the Rome conference. In October 2001, together with the Ministry of Interior, the Office of the Executive, the Supreme Court, and the University of the Philippines, they organized a conference on the ICC that was sponsored by several European countries. Diplomats, ICC experts, and legal scholars, a delegation of the European Parliament, and members of the Philippine government and Congress attended the conference. As such, the event was exactly what a political dialogue of the EU's global ratification campaign was supposed to be. Also the Philippine Secretary of Justice hoped that the conference would "kick off of the campaign for the ratification of the ICC treaty by nations in the ASEAN region" (Panaligan 2001; Damaso 2001). While reporting on the conference, BusinessWorld newspaper wrote that the Undersecretary of Foreign Affairs, Ebdalin, had stated that the Rome Statute has already been endorsed by the Senate for ratification (*BusinessWorld* 2001).

Clearly, Arroyo did not ratify the Rome Statute, although her Vice President Guingona, who also acted as the Secretary of Foreign Affairs during the years 2001 and 2002, recommended the ratification. Guingona's successor at the DFA, Ople, arguably also "favored the ICC so that the Philippines will not be left behind in the international legal system" (Alcoseba 2003; Department of Foreign Affairs 2011b). However, in reality he kept up with Arroyo's policy and signed a BIA with the USA in 2003. In fact, by the end of Arroyo's first term, Vice President Guingona was the only devoted supporter of the ICC in the administration. In June 2003, as rumors about Arroyo's motivation for signing the BIA circulated in the public, he called for its full disclosure and "also told media the BIA was 'unfair' and contrary to the equal protection clause of the constitution" (Gamolo 2011; Concepcion

2004). Because of political controversies, including the ICC, Guingona was gradually eased out of the cabinet and did not run for the Vice Presidency in the 2004 elections (Agence France Presse 2003a; Xinhua 2002).

In contrast to the DFA under Guingona, the Philippine military and the Department of Defense were arguably the firmest opponents of the ICC. Due to the legacy of Marcos, who ruled the country with the military's support, the armed forces are influential in Philippine political affairs and are not the easiest domestic obstacles to overcome (Celoza 1997, 1–2). The politicized role of the military is evident, not least because after the People Power Revolution in 1986 all Presidents of the Philippines have faced *coup d'etats* by the military. The only exception is Ramos, who had been, among other things, the chief of staff of the armed forces and the Secretary of Defense before becoming the President (Plantilla 1997). To what extent the military's stance was a deal breaker for Arroyo is not entirely clear because throughout those years, military officials and the Department of Defense expressed quite differing opinions about the ICC.

In April 2001, according to Congresswoman Rosales, the Secretary of National Defense Reyes informed Senator Legarda that his department supported immediate ratification of the Rome Statute (Rosales 2006). However, years later military officials gave conflicting pictures of the Armed Forces' policy to the ICC. In 2008, General Bocobo told the Daily Inquirer newspaper that the Armed Forces supported the ICC, but the next day the *BusinessWorld* newspaper reported that according to the Chief of Staff, Yano, the ratification would only open up doors for politically motivated cases against the military (Torres 2008a; Pedrasa 2008). A few months earlier, the Vice Commander Cabayao had stated:

> The signing of an international treaty whatever its contents, conditions and consequences are political decisions left to the sound discretion between the executive department and the Senate [...] The AFP, as an apolitical government agency, would adhere and abide by the treaty if it gets ratified as part of the law of the land. (Bordadora and Uy 2008)

By February 2011, the military seemed to be more or less supportive of the ICC. "The good news is that the only remaining government agency hereabouts that had consistently opposed ratification, the Department of National Defense, has finally changed its stand" (Doyo 2011a). Curiously enough, in February 2011 the process of ratification started to materialize. This is not to say that the changed attitude of the military triggered the ratification process, but rather vice versa, as the process-tracing on the materialization of the ratification below will point out.

In addition to the military, the Cabinet Oversight Committee on Internal Security (COCIS) did not support the ratification. The COCIS is chaired by the Executive Secretary and composed by the Secretaries for Defense, Foreign Affairs, Justice, and Interior, the National Security Adviser, Chief General of the Armey, and the Chief Director General of the National Police. In September 2002, when Ople was the Secretary of Foreign Affairs, Arroyo's Spokesman stated: "none of the senior cabinet officials […] was in favor of ratification. The Philippines has no deadline to make a decision, Bunye said, although 'certain European Union members have asked us to sign it'" (Agence France Presse 2002b; Luib 2002). One year later, the Committee had not changed its view:

> Presidential Spokesman Ignacio Bunye, a member of COCIS, said yesterday President Arroyo's security advisers are in consensus that the country would not benefit from signing the treaty, but instead impair its law enforcement operations. 'So the initial reaction of those who attended the meeting is to recommend not to ratify this (ICC treaty)'. (BBC 2003a)

This statement provides smoking gun evidence that in 2003 the Arroyo Administration was not about to the join the ICC anytime soon.

Considering the US pressure, in 2008 the Secretary of Justice, Gonzales, said that financial concerns and not the US government or Arroyo's reluctance have delayed the ratification: "Gonzalez said the executive branch is not shelving the Rome Statute. However, he added, 'we have a lot of things to consider first,' foremost of these the expenses the government will have to shoulder if the country becomes an ICC member" (Torres 2008b). According to Gonzales, the millions spent for the ICC could be used to address the needs of the Philippine people. This argument, however, is not very convincing, if one considers that in 2011 Senator Santiago estimated the annual contribution of the Philippines to the ICC to be 8.3 million Philippine Pesos, which is less than 200,000 USD (Senate of the Philippines 2011b, 137). This amount of money in 2009, for instance, would have been 0.08% of the DFA budget and a small expenditure in the 2009 national budget of 1.4 trillion Philippine Pesos (Department of Foreign Affairs 2012; Bureau of the Treasury 2012). Accordingly, like most other governmental institutions, the Department of Justice also seemed not to favor the ratification of the Rome Statute during Arroyo's Presidency.

7.2.3 *The Executive, Again: Conflict and Violence as Reasons for Non-ratification*

For decades, Philippine Presidents have fought numerous communist insurgent and terrorist groups, mostly in the Southern parts of the Republic. During Arroyo's term, the military created a new counter insurgency strategy, focused on destroying leftist organizations. This program led to torture and executions of political activists, human rights defenders, judges, and lawyers. Depending on the source, the numbers of extrajudicial executions under Arroyo's watch vary between 100 and 800 cases. Although the Philippine military officers claimed that communist insurgents committed the killings as part of their internal purges, the UN Special Rapporteur on Extrajudicial Killings concluded that the military is responsible for most of the executions and "is in a state of denial concerning the numerous extrajudicial killings which its soldiers are implicated" (A/HRC/8/3/Add.2 2008, 13). Also journalists and farmers often fell victim to extrajudicial killings, when the corrupt elite and landowners were trying to protect their holdings. Apart from the military, the Philippine police has taken its share of the extrajudicial killings especially in the Southern parts of the country (A/HRC/8/3/Add.2 2008; UN News Centre 2007; Parreño 2011).

Because of international and local pressure, Arroyo established a commission to investigate the cases in 2006 and suddenly the number of extrajudicial killings and forced disappearances started to decline. However, the military has been involved in extrajudicial killings and forced disappearances, which continue until today. One particular reason for the continuing human rights violations is the atmosphere of impunity that has prevailed since the Marcos era. The judicial system has been more concerned of prosecuting the leftist activists than their assassins and neither the police nor the Office of the Ombudsman have been investigating the military. Despite the commission established by Arroyo and the fact that numerous government agencies are supposed to monitor and implement human rights, only few cases have been successfully investigated and prosecuted and not one senior military officer has been held accountable for the involvement in, or responsibility for, the human rights violations (A/HRC/8/3/Add.2 2008; HRW 2011; A/HRC/WG.6/1/PHL/1 2008; PCICC 2009b; Plantilla 1997).

Due to the internal armed conflict in Mindanao, the military and the COCIS were doubtful about the ICC. From their point of view, the ratification of the Rome Statute would hinder the government's campaign against rebel movements, as the COSIS put it in 2002: "The military and police establishments are concerned their forces could be hauled before the tribunal for actions related to a domestic campaign against Muslim separatist and communist insurgencies [...]" (Agence France Presse 2002b). In 2003, the COSIS defended its policy with reference to potential suits raised by the ICC:

> Bunye said law enforcers have to contend with 'harassment suits' like alleged human rights violations being filed in court by people who are arrested for rebellion. 'Imagine how much more if we ratify the ICC and their cases are elevated to international courts?' [...] Bunye said the COCIS was of the view that Senate ratification of the ICC treaty would tie the hands of law enforcers. (BBC 2003a)

In 2004, the Secretary of Foreign Affairs, Romulo, provided more evidence for internal conflict being one reason for the non-ratification by saying that in addition to the BIA with the USA, peace negotiations with the communist insurgents were the reason why the Philippines had not joined the ICC (Calderon 2004).

The rebels, in turn, considered the BIA a "major stumbling block" for the resumption of the peace talks. In 2003, they wanted the Philippines to ratify the Rome Statute, because the US–Philippines military cooperation had considerably increased after the 9/11 and included joint military operations against the rebels. For the rebels, a BIA was

> 'another despicable act of kowtowing by Mrs Arroyo to every wish and whim of (the US government).' Rosal said it was apparent that Malacanang and the White House wanted to 'deoperationalize the application of the ICC treaty in the Philippines.' The pact was meant to 'further heighten and widen the scope of US military intervention in the country,' he added. (BBC 2003b)

If potential suits of the ICC concerned the military, they might have concerned Arroyo herself too. The hundreds of extrajudicial killings, forced disappearances, and torture cases under her watch attracted international attention and hypothetically she may had been held accountable for them under the principle of command responsibility, prescribed in Art. 28, 1 of the Rome Statute. As Senator Pimentel put it after the Senate had passed resolution 94 in 2006: "Arroyo may not be interested in having the ICC convention ratified for fear she may find herself hailed before the international court to answer for the continued [...] human rights violations committed under her administration" (Uy 2006b). This point of view has been supported by Pangalangan, former Dean of the University of the Philippines' College of Law, and Panganiban, former Chief Justice of the Philippine Supreme Court (Pangalangan 2007; Panganiban 2008, 2009).

However, the human rights violations committed during the Arroyo Administration would probably not have qualified for ICC proceedings and even if so, the Philippines could have made use of the principle of complementarity. Accordingly, the problem was not so much with the ICC, but the potentiality of its jurisdiction and its consequences for the public discussion. As Pangalangan wrote in 2008, Arroyo was concerned about the press:

> When I gave one briefing [...] for the ratification of the Rome Statute, I noticed that the chief hesitation of our government was not just legal. I could give them all the assurances that the tribunal was perfectly okay. [...] I think they were concerned about the press, and how charges before the ICC might be discussed as if they were already formal indictments. (Pangalangan 2008a, 8–9)

Hence, by refusing to ratify the Rome Statute, Arroyo did not just try to protect herself and the military from ICC charges, but also from negative publicity.

7.3 External Pressure on the Philippines

7.3.1 The United States' Influence

In economic terms, the EU and the USA are equally strong partners to the Philippines: considering imports the USA is the main non-Asian trade partner and, in turn, exports to the EU are slightly greater than to the USA (National Statistics Office 2011, 44–45; U.S. Department of Commerce 2012; Eurostat 2010). However, there is no doubt that the USA is the Philippines' most important military ally. In matters of culture and politics, the Philippines tends to relate with the USA rather than with Europe, because of its colonial history (Salvador et al. 2009, 22, 32). In 1898, Spain surrendered the country to the USA, which exercised colonial rule until 1945 and, due to the Philippines strategic position, the US military remained heavily present also after 1945. Since 1951, a mutual defense treaty against external attacks has defined the bilateral military relationship and for years the air and naval bases in the Philippines were the largest US military bases outside the continental America (Colmenares 2002).

Over time, however, the US military presence became problematic for Philippine politicians. In 1992, due to increasing protests, the Senate decided not to renew the Military Bases Agreement of 1947 and forced US troops to leave the country. But the US military absence lasted only ten years. After the 9/11 attacks, President Arroyo was the first Asian President, and one of the few heads of states, to fully, openly, and loyally support the USA in its war on terror, including the Iraq invasion. The special military relationship was quickly revived as Arroyo made all Philippine military installations available for the US use—help that was highly valued by the Bush Administration (S. RES. 152 2003; H. CON. RES. 273 2001; S. CON. RES. 91 2001; Sandoval 2004, 464). As one can guess, the deal was not one-sided, but provided benefits for Arroyo too. The Bush Administration started to combat terrorist threats in Southeast Asia, in particular "Muslim terrorists" and "Communist insurgents" in Southern Philippines (S. RES. 152 2003).

In 2002, the US military presence in the Philippines exploded as the American and Filipino militaries started a joint-operation against the terrorist group Abu Sayyaf. The operation employed nearly 3000 US soldiers and later in 2002 the USA sent 1800 soldiers for training purposes to Luzon, the base of a leftist insurgency group called the New People's Army. The operations in the Philippines were the biggest US military deployment outside Afghanistan (Colmenares 2002). Simultaneously with the increasing military cooperation, US military aid and investments to the Philippines exploded: in 2001, the US military aid amounted USD 38 million, in 2002 USD 94.5 million, and in the first ten months of 2003 USD 114.6 million. Between 2002 and 2003, US military assistance and investments (including the joint-operations) was USD 808 million (Sandoval 2004, 463–64).

Since the US–Philippine relationship is close and involves vast economic stakes, the US campaign against the ICC touched close on the Philippines. Supporting the ICC against the will of the most important military ally was neither rational, in Arroyo's interest, nor consistent with the foreign policy tradition of the Philippines. As Magsino, governor of the Integrated Bar of the Philippines, put it in 2008:

> We are an ally and staunch supporter of the United States of America, and though it is not a declared foreign policy of the Philippines, we have always aligned our decisions in the international arena with the whims and desires of the US. [The] US and Israel's decision in 2002 to 'unsign' from the Rome Statute with no sign that they will again sign in the foreseeable future, strongly indicates that the Philippines will not affix its own signature to the treaty anytime soon. (Torres 2008a)

The Philippine newspapers (Calderon 2004; Bordadora and Uy 2008), human rights activists and lawyers (Pangalangan 2008b; Roque 2011b; Gamolo 2011), legislators (P. S. Res. No. 748 2008; Senate of the Philippines 2011a; Roncesvalles 2005; Uy 2006a; Osorio and Calderon 2004), and Obama's Ambassador for War Crimes, Rapp (Rapp 2011a), indicate that the US opposition to the ICC did indeed pose a major stumbling block to the Philippine ratification of the Rome Statute.

Pointing out how sensitive an issue external pressure is for states, Arroyo's Spokesman vehemently denied in 2002 that US pressure and potential cuts in military aid would influence the Philippines' decision regarding the ICC (Luib 2002). Also, the US Ambassador to the Philippines, Ricciardone, said that the USA did not try to hinder the Philippines' ratification of the Rome Statute. Yet, his media statement regarding the ratification in 2003 was somewhat intimidating: "This is the Filipino decision. If your government decides to ratify the ICC, that is certainly your right. The consequences though needed to be studied carefully" (Roncesvalles 2003).

While it is impossible to say with certainty that the USA ultimately hindered the Philippines' ratification, the amount of evidence is convincing. Moreover, it is quite certain that when the Bush Administration approached Arroyo with the quest to sign a BIA, money was involved in the matter. Several sources indicate that the USA offered USD 30 million additional military aid for the non-ratification of the Rome Statute or, depending on the source and the point of view, for signing into a BIA. The following quotation is from August 2002, after President Bush had signed the ASPA into law:

> 'US ambassador [...] Ricciardone wrote the Department of Foreign Affairs three weeks ago, assuring us that they will not put the Philippines in the blacklist as long as we sign an agreement with them,' one source said. 'We would have difficulty getting military assistance. For us to be entitled, we should enter into an agreement,' the source added. Defense Secretary Angelo Reyes confirmed Wednesday that Washington has held up a pledged 30 million-dollar supplementary military aid to the Philippines on top of 25 million dollars already approved by the US government. 'We will explore other ways' to get the 30 million dollars, he added without elaborating. (Agence France Presse 2002a; see also Alcoseba 2003; HRW 2003; CICC 2006; Filipino Youth for Peace 2003; Toon 2004, 229; Uy 2006a; Colmenares 2002; Kleiss 2003)

In 2004, Secretary of Foreign Affairs Romulo admitted that the BIA, among other factors, did hinder the Philippines ratification (Calderon 2004).

On May 2003, Secretary of Foreign Affairs Ople and US Secretary of State Powell concluded a Bilateral Immunity Agreement (Georgetown Law Library 2009). The timing of the BIA is intriguing, since only five days later Arroyo started a state visit to the USA and Bush promoted the Philippines into a major non-NATO ally. Even more interestingly, according to a draft House resolution, the Presidential palace estimated that Arroyo's visit generated USD 4.09 billion economic and military aid commitments (HR01188 2003; see also Agence France Presse 2003a), of which at least USD 356 were military-related assistance (Agence France Presse 2003b). In 2003, the USA was planning to increase its military presence in the Pacific and the aid may have had more to do with that purpose. However, since the Bush Administration and the US Congress were very outspoken on the consequences of not signing a BIA, it would not be surprising that at least some part of the USD 4 billion was related to the Philippines' cooperation regarding the BIA.

The BIA and its timing outraged many legislators. Congressmen were particularly worried about the US plans to stage a military comeback in the country and about the BIA's consequences for this potentially growing US presence. Thus, 20 legislators sponsored a resolution, urging Arroyo to make a public disclosure of the commitments she made during her visit to Washington, DC. They also wanted a clarification of "whether the bilateral agreement on immunity signed on May 13, is still a part of, or directly related to the Arroyo government's earlier unequivocal support to US President Bush's 'global war on terror'" (HR01188 2003; Corpuz 2003). The BIA was disclosed and, like all other BIAs, it does not mention anything about economic incentives or commitments. It simply confirms that neither the USA nor the Philippines will surrender, extradite, or transfer each other's citizens to international tribunals, unless the UNSC establishes them (Ople 2003; Ricciardone 2003). The Bayan Muna party tried to nullify the agreement by a Supreme Court decision in 2010, but in 2011 the Supreme Court ruled that the President has the powers to enter executive agreements and that the BIA does not violate the Philippines' obligations as a signatory to the Rome Statute (G. R. No. 159618 2011).

In addition to military aid, UN politics might also have been on the agenda, when the Philippines and the USA negotiated the BIA. As the USA started its campaign against the ICC, the Philippines had already decided to run for a non-permanent seat of the UNSC for the years 2004 and 2005. In October 2002, the USA promised to support the undertaking and a few weeks later the Asian caucus also lined up behind the Philippines (Ng and Valisno 2002; Malaysia General News 2002). During the Philippines membership at the UNSC, the Council worked on two important resolutions considering the ICC: the second renewal of Res. 1422 exempting US soldiers participating in UN missions from the ICC jurisdiction and the Darfur referral to the ICC. The renewal of Res. 1422 failed although the Philippines and three other countries were willing to support it. In the Darfur referral, the Philippines voted in favor while the USA abstained (Reilly 2004; S/RES/1593 2005; SC/8351 2005).

7.3.2 Gentle Push from Europe

The ties between Europe and the Philippines are not as close as the US–Philippine relationship. However, EU institutions and European countries are the Philippines' most important donors of development aid (Eurostat 2010; National Statistics Office 2011, 44–45; OECD 2012). As is well known, the EU links development aid to a good human rights account and throughout the years it has emphasized the importance of human rights in the Philippines. The death penalty was the main issue until Arroyo abolished it in 2006 (Roncesvalles et al. 2004; European Union 2006) and the EU has also funded various other human rights programs and conducted diplomatic *démarches* concerning human rights in general and women's rights, rights of displaced people, extrajudicial killings, torture, and children in armed conflicts in particular (European Union 1999; Lee-Brago 2010). In 2008, the EU and the Philippines started technical cooperation in criminal justice matters, which aims at strengthening the implementation and monitoring of human rights in the country (SFA-AGR-217-08 2008).

The EU's support for the Philippines' ratification of the Rome Statute started early. In 2001, when the Philippine government agencies organized an experts' meeting on the ICC, European countries were among its financial supporters and Members of the European Parliament among the participants. MEP Bonino urged the Philippines to ratify the Rome Statute and the participants of the conference were hopeful that 9/11 would change the US view on the ICC (*BusinessWorld* 2001). The contrary was the case. When the USA launched the BIA campaign, the EU's promotion of the ICC became more outspoken. In a draft House Resolution of October 2002, the legislators note that the EU had criticized the USA and urged the Philippines to join the Rome Statute. Also Arroyo's Spokesman confirmed in 2002 that some EU countries had requested that Philippines join the ICC (HR00800 2002; Luib 2002). In its campaign for the ICC in the Philippines, the EU used diplomatic persuasion, issue-linkages, and the help of NGOs.

First, considering diplomatic persuasion, both the Delegation of the European Commission to the Philippines and European Ambassadors, in particular the Italian one, were vocal about the Philippines' ratification (Panganiban 2008). In 2006, the Ambassador of the European Commission, de Kok, hoped that the Philippines would eventually join the ICC (Tan 2006) and one year later, Kok's successor MacDonald was more outspoken: "the EU wants the ICC implemented in the country. 'It's not an issue that we should be impatient about, but we want to see the Philippines sign it'" (Del Callar 2007). In 2008, the Italian Embassy together with the Philippine Supreme Court organized another international conference on the ICC, in which European Ambassadors voiced their support for the ICC (Philippines News Agency 2008b). In addition to public statements, the EU Ambassadors persuaded the Philippines with diplomatic *démarches.* The first official reference to a ratification *démarche* in the Philippines is from 2006 and, according to the EU's Human Rights Reports, further *démarches* were held in 2007, 2009, and 2010. Since 2008, some *démarches* were made jointly with Australia due to the 2008 Australia-European Union Partnership

Framework, for which objective number one, in addition to cooperation in the UN forums, was the promotion of the ICC in Southeast Asia (Australian Government 2008). This agreement shows how important the issue was both for the EU and Australia. As noted in the chapter on the EU, the contents of the *démarches* are not public, but they encourage states to join the ICC and discourage from signing a BIA with the USA (European Union 2006, 2007, 2008; EEAS 2010, 2011).

Second, to push the Philippines into joining the ICC, the EU linked the ratification to a formal partnership agreement. In 2004, the EU Council authorized the Commission to negotiate a bilateral Partnership and Cooperation Agreement (PCA) with the Philippines, which would become the first bilateral agreement between the EU and the Philippines. The negotiations on the PCA were officially launched in 2009, but already in 2007 the EU Human Rights Report mentioned that an ICC clause was under negotiation (European Union 2007). The ICC clause was not an easy one to negotiate and in the fourth round of the negotiations it reportedly became a stumbling block:

> The European Union (EU) and the Philippines remain deadlocked on the issue of human rights, particularly Manila's ratification of the 1998 Rome Treaty of the International Criminal Court (ICC) [...]. Negotiations [...] started in February last year, but Manila has yet to give commitments on whether it will ratify the 1998 Rome Statute of the ICC, as Malacanang, under President Arroyo, refused to transmit the instrument of ratification to the Philippine Senate. (TendersInfo 2010; see also Torres 2008; Lee-Brago 2009; Torres 2010)

As a compromise, the ICC clause does not mention the ratification, unlike for instance the EU–Indonesia PCA, but states that the "Parties agree to conduct a beneficial dialogue on the universal adherence to the Rome Statute in accordance with their respective laws" (COM (2010) 460 Final 2010). Although the PCA comprises topics from trade, investment, and intellectual property rights to justice, security, development, and energy, the ICC takes a central role in the agreement, as the EU's own introduction to the PCA points out: "The PCA contains legally binding commitments which are central to the EU's foreign policy, including provisions on human rights, nonproliferation, counter-terrorism, the International Criminal Court, migration and taxation" (COM (2010) 460 Final 2010). It is worthwhile mentioning that Manila's reluctance to commit to joining the ICC was also one of the reasons, why the EU–ASEAN negotiations on a regional Free Trade Agreement ended unsuccessfully (Garcia 2012, 68).

Third, in addition to persuasion and issue-linkages, the EU supported Philippine pro-ICC legislators, local civil society (The Philippine Coalition for the International Criminal Court, PCICC), and international NGOs (PGA and CICC) in their campaigns on the ratification (SOFRECO 2007, 13; European Union 2007). For instance, the EU Commission financed the PCICC's preparation and publication of a primer about the ICC for the Philippine Security Sector (Mostajo et al. 2008). For Arroyo, and especially for the DFA, the situation with the EU's promotion and the US demotion of the ICC was not easy (Department of Foreign Affairs 2011e). In September 2002, the Undersecretary of Foreign Affairs, Ebdalin, said

> the United States may have offered them US$30 million in military aid, but the European Union (EU) has also agreed to financial aid of 50 million euros over a five-year period. In fact, the Philippines Cabinet Oversight Committee is sandwiched between supporting the United States' anti-ICC stance and EU's pro-ICC stance because of the "need to balance the consequence" of both their relationship with the US and how they would be perceived by the international community. (de Leon 2004)

This quote is the only written evidence pointing to direct economic incentives coming from the EU for the exchange of the Philippines' support for the ICC and can only be considered a straw-in-the-wind for the argument that the EU used economic coercion to reach its goal. However, there is evidence enough that the EU did use persuasion and issue-linkages, the more diplomatic means, to encourage the Philippine ratification (Ledoux 2011; Gatdula 2011a).

7.4 Socialization and Non-ratification

7.4.1 Power of Civil Society and Persuasion

As the ICC President Song stated in his welcoming speech for the Philippines accession to the ICC, pro-ICC NGOs and in particular the PCICC tirelessly promoted the ICC in the country (Song 2011c). According to the Philippines' national Universal Periodic Review (UPR) report to the UNGA Human Rights Council in 2008, human rights NGOs in the country are numerous, heterogeneous, and often more or less loosely affiliated with political parties (A/HRC/WG.6/1/PHL/1 2008; see also SOFRECO 2007, 31; Mohamad 2002, 242). While the Philippines assures that the NGOs are valuable members of the political process, the NGOs in their joint submission to the UPR accused the state of limiting the participation of civil society from government (A/HRC/8/28 2008, 7; A/HRC/WG.6/1/PHL/3 2008, 6). The accusation is justified in the case of the pro-ICC NGOs at least to the extent that Arroyo did not change her course on the ICC despite strong calls from the civil society.

The Philippines' NGO coalition on the ICC, the PCICC, was established in 2000 and it is a member of the CICC. According to its own information, the PCICC was influential in the Philippine signing of the Rome Statute in December 2000 (PCICC 2012). Like CICC members all over the world, the PCICC together with other NGOs has been active in urging the government to ratify the Rome Statute, organizing events, publishing statements, and preparing and circulating educative information about the ICC. What is particularly interesting about the PCICC are the people behind it—the ICC advocates of the country. Until 2010, the PCICC was co-chaired by Congresswoman Rosales and Pangalangan, law professor of the University of the Philippines, who also participated in the Rome conference as part of the Philippines delegation. Since 2011, the coalition has been co-chaired by Pangalangan and Dr. Parong, the head of Amnesty International Philippines. Other previous and current board members of the PCICC include law professors, lawyers, and human rights activists (PCICC 2013). Hence, in addition to NGO workers and liberal politicians, legal scholars have also publicly advocated Philippine membership of the ICC over the years (Pangalangan 2007, 2008a, b, 2011a; Kim 2011). Moreover, the University of the Philippines (UP) and its law school have been active on the issue. For instance, Professor Roque (Director of the UP's Institute of International Legal Studies) and his students together with the PCICC, Senator Pimentel, and Congresswoman Rosales filed the above-mentioned case to the Supreme Court, urging Arroyo to submit the Rome Statute to the Senate (De la Paz 2003).

All presiding Chief Justices of the Supreme Court between 1998 and 2010 have also taken a positive stance toward the ICC. In 2001, Chief Justice Hilario emphasized the importance of the ICC and later his successor Panganiban recommended the Philippines to join the ICC (*BusinessWorld* 2001; Panganiban 2008, 2009). Also, according to Chief

Justice Puno, the Philippines would benefit from ratification of the Rome Statute. However, as the Supreme Court ruled in the Pimentel et al. case, the opinion of judiciary is not that influential: "the judiciary, Puno pointed out, has nothing to do in the treaty-making process and its [Rome Statute] ratification entirely depends on the Senate upon submission by the executive department" (Depasupil 2008; see also Philippines News Agency 2008a). In addition to supportive statements, the Supreme Court together with the Italian Embassy organized a conference on the tenth anniversary of the adoption of the Rome Statute in 2008, aimed at raising awareness of the ICC in regional and national context (Olivares-Cunanan 2008).

The last influential advocacy group is the Philippine media. Besides alternative newspapers, one of the biggest Philippine newspapers, The Daily Inquirer, has over the years criticized Arroyo's policy toward the ICC and published op-eds of Pangalangan and Panganiban in support of the ICC (Torres 2008a; Bordadora and Uy 2008; De Lima 2009; Corpuz 2003), while rather critical views have been voiced by the *BusinessWorld* (Gatdula 2011a, b). Although the newspapers wrote regularly about the ICC and the NGOs published information on the issue, decision-makers seemed not to be very familiar with ICC. As the ICC President Song put it in 2011:

> In my experience, the sheer lack of knowledge is one of the biggest obstacles to accession in many countries. Misconceptions are still persistent, and merely clarifying the principle of complementarity and the non-retroactive effect of ratification may often significantly clear the path for proper consideration of joining the ICC. (Song 2011d)

The Philippine Senate's deliberation on the ratification in August 2011 showed that some politicians were indeed uninformed about the ICC. For instance, the President of the Senate asked whether the ICC is part of the United Nations and there were misunderstandings about the retroactivity and complementarity of the Rome Statute (Senate of the Philippines 2011b, 137ff.).

7.4.2 Norm Diffusion and Common Identities in the Region of Laggards

At the time of the Philippines ratification in 2011, only 6 out of 24 Asian states were States Parties to the Rome Statute (shortly after the Philippines, the Maldives, and Vanuatu joined the court). The Philippines was also the first founding member and second ASEAN state (after Cambodia) to join the ICC and it is the only ASEAN country that has ratified the Genocide Convention (UNTC 2017). Under these circumstances, the lack of regional diffusion of human rights norms and potential dependence networks would better explain non-ratification than the decision to join the ICC. Although the current realities do not cherish human rights, the tendency to strengthen human rights protection—or at least the desire to polish the human rights image—is gradually growing. A good example is the establishment of a Working Group for an ASEAN Human Rights Mechanism in 2009 (ASEANhrmech 2017). Considering the ICC, the ASEAN as an organization has not independently taken a positive stance toward it. The only noteworthy statement resulted from the 2003 EU–ASEAN Ministerial Meeting, as the foreign ministers of European and ASEAN countries together with EU and ASEAN representatives acknowledged that the ICC is a "positive development in the fight against impunity for crimes against humanity, war crimes and genocide" (5400/03 (Presse 11) 2003). The fact that the only ASEAN statement on the ICC was made together with the EU provides a smoking gun in support of the argument that the EU plays an instrumental role in the promotion of the ICC.

While the diffusion of human rights norms in Southeast Asia does not explain the Philippines' ratification, there are two regional aspects that may have positively shaped the decision to join the ICC. First, the ASEAN region offers an excellent opportunity to stand out, if the Philippines wants to portray itself as a pioneer of human rights and international criminal law. Second, considering Asia more broadly, regional developments may have in fact influenced the Philippines' decision to join the ICC. In 2010, Bangladesh ratified the Rome Statute and shortly after the Philippines ratification, Maldives and Vanuatu joined the ICC too. In March 2011, the Malaysian government also announced its intention to ratify the Rome Statute, but so far the instrument of ratification has not been submitted to the UN (Song 2011b; PGA 2011). Having four ratifications and one prospective in less than two years is significant considering that Japan in 2007 was the last Asian country to accede the Rome Statute.

Considering the idea of a socially constructed identity that would support humanitarian values and the ratification of the ICC, the Philippines eagerness to accede to human rights treaties and its tendency to profile itself as an active member of the human rights community would speak in favor of this hypothesis. In 2008, the Philippines stated that it

> continues to work closely with other countries and regional and international organizations such as the European Union on human rights issues. The Philippines welcomed the expansion and deepening of human rights initiatives as a key pillar of international cooperation. (A/HRC/8/28 2008)

Moreover, according to its national UPR report of 2008, the Philippines works on strengthening domestic institutional mechanisms that are designed to monitor and protect human rights, including the national Commission on Human Rights, Office of the Ombudsma n, and the Presidential Human Rights Committee. Despite these developments, the reality is different. As already noted above, extrajudicial killings and human rights violations shadow the domestic politics and the implementation of human rights treaties seriously lags behind. From this vantage point, the Philippines' actions in the field of human rights would rather militate toward non-ratification (A/HRC/8/28 2008; A/HRC/WG.6/1/PHL/1 2008, 2–4).

7.5 The Timing of the Ratification

In June 2010, Senator Aquino III became the President of the Philippines. He is the son of anti-Marcos movement leaders (Thompson 1995) and following in the footsteps of his parents, he promised in his inaugural speech to fight the prevailing corruption and impunity in the country:

> To those who talk about reconciliation, if they mean that they would like us to simply forget about the wrongs that they have committed in the past, we have this to say: there can be no reconciliation without justice. When we allow crimes to go unpunished, we give consent to their occurring over and over again. (Aquino 2010)

Aquino kept his word and created a truth commission to investigate the corruption cases of the past administrations and, subsequently, Arroyo was arrested in November 2011 for electoral fraud (Executive Order No. 1 2010; Mogato 2011). While Arroyo was released on bail in July 2012, she was arrested, again, in October 2012 for plundering the states' lottery funds (BBC 2012). Also the human rights situation in the country was enhanced, although according to the Human Rights Watch the first one and half years of Aquino's Presidency did not fulfill all the promises of the presidential campaign (HRW 2012a, 376).

Shortly after the inauguration of Aquino, things started to move toward the Philippines accession to the ICC. In September 2010, the Presidential Human Rights Commission and the Departments of Justice, Foreign Affairs, and National Defense recommended the President ratify the Rome Statute. On February 28, 2011, he did so and transmitted the Rome Statute to the Senate for its concurrence on May 6, 2011 (Senate of the Philippines 2011d, e; Doyo 2011b). On August 4, 2011, Senators Defensor-Santiago (Chair of the Subcommittee on the ICC) and Legarda (Chair of the Committee on Foreign Relations) sponsored the concurrence resolution without amendments. In her sponsorship speech for the ratification, Defensor-Santiago listed four advantages of the ratification:

> 1. The Philippines would be able to influence the development of the Rome Statute and the International Criminal Court. 2. The Philippines would qualify to nominate a Filipino as one of the 18 judges of the ICC. 3. It will put the Philippines in a better position to protect Filipino overseas, when they might suffer crimes against humanity in pursuing work abroad. 4. It will keep the Philippines abreast with contemporary developments in international relations. (Senate of the Philippines 2011b, 134; see also Committee on Foreign Relations 2011)

Senator Legarda followed similar lines in her co-sponsorship speech. Two Senators, Arroyo (no relationship to President Arroyo) and Enrile (President of the Senate), opposed the motion.

The rationales of Senators Enrile and Arroyo against the ICC were similar to the reasons that explain Arroyo's reluctance to ratify the Rome Statute, namely the US opposition and the potential consequences of the ICC for the Philippine armed forces. When it comes to the USA, Senator Joker Arroyo stated that

> from the 12th Congress to the present Congress, the Senate has always thought that it was not fit to ratify the Treaty since the United States, the world's most powerful country, has not ratified it. [...] What concerned

> him [...] is that the U.S. Senate, under both Democratic and Republican presidents, has refused to ratify the Rome Statute. He clarified that he was not suggesting that the Philippines should not follow everything the U.S. does, but he advised that the country should acknowledge its size, that it is too small to play the role of a big power that can influence things. (Senate of the Philippines 2011b, 136)

Arroyo and Enrile were both concerned about Philippine military commanders deployed in multinational peacekeeping operations who might be held responsible for crimes of "various nationalities who may not respect him, may be exposed to charges for crimes committed by his troops under his command" (Senate of the Philippines 2011b, 136). During the interpellation in the Senate, Enrile furthermore questioned Senator Defensor-Santiago on a variety of issues such as the financial contribution to the ICC, the implementation of the arrest warrants, and why other ASEAN and Asian countries had not joined the ICC. China's reluctance to join the ICC in particular was discussed at length. Eventually, the Draft Resolution 546 was adopted for third reading and only Senators Arroyo and Enrile voted against the adoption (Senate of the Philippines 2011b, 137ff.; Pangalangan 2011b; HRW 2012b).

In the third reading on August 23, the Senate adopted Resolution number 57, concurring in the ratification of the Rome Statute (P. S. Res. No. 546 2011). At that time only Senator Enrile opposed the concurrence, because he did not want to hinder the army in its efforts to protect the country against communists (Senate of the Philippines 2011c, 191). In fact, Enrile tried to hinder the adoption at the last minute (Roque 2011a), but the resolution was adopted with 17 votes in favor and one against, while six Senators, among them Arroyo, were not present at the vote. One week later, the Permanent Representative of the Philippines to the UN deposited the Philippines instrument of ratification for the Rome Statute to the UN Office of Legal Affairs (Department of Foreign Affairs 2011d).

7.5.1 *Why Now and Not Earlier or Later?*

On August 30, 2011, the Philippines became the 117th State Party to the ICC. The ratification was a result of several domestic and international developments, but Aquino's rise to power clearly triggered the chain of events. As the Secretary of Foreign Affairs del Rosario stated in July 2011: "Only now and under President Aquino, our country is in the process of finally ratifying the Rome Statute" (Department of Foreign Affairs 2011a). As already pointed out above, with Aquino's policy of impunity came also the long desired support of the Department of Defense to the ICC (Doyo 2011a). The Senate resolution concurring with the ratification explicitly mentions the endorsement of all key domestic agencies—the Departments of Defense and Justice, the Commission on Human Rights, the Armed Forces of the Philippines, the Philippine National Police, and the National Security Council—and by so doing it points out that their support for the ICC played an important role in the ratification (P. S. Res. No. 546 2011). While a domestic momentum triggered the ratification, the exact timing was not random at all, but influenced by three factors at different stages of the ratification.

First, the ICC President Song visited the Philippines from March 7 to 8, 2011, as part of his awareness-raising trip, aimed at facilitating the ratification of the Rome Statute. "In view of his visit," the DFA "recommended the timely transmittal of the Rome Statute to the Senate [...]" (Legaspi 2011). Accordingly, one day before Song arrived, Aquino transmitted the Rome Statute to the Senate (ICC-CPI-20110302-PR632 2011; Song 2011e). In addition to the DFA, other instances persuaded the President. During February 2011, the Philippines was a target country of the CICC's universal ratification campaign (CICC 2012) and since there are rumors that the EU holds diplomatic *démarches* around the same time as NGO campaigns, one can guess that during February–March 2011 Aquino was also approached by EU Ambassadors.

Second, it was also not a coincidence that the Senate concurred to the Rome Statute on August 23. The press release informing of the concurrence ended with the following sentence: "With the Senate concurrence [...], the Philippines becomes qualified to nominate a Filipino as one of the 18 judges of the ICC" (Senate of the Philippines 2011d). The Philippines was indeed eager to have an international judge, because the last Filipino holding such high position had been Bengzon who served as an ICJ Judge more than forty years previous. Now, the deadline for the nomination of ICC Judges was September 2, 2011, and on August 30, the same day as the Philippines submitted its instrument of the ratification to the UN, it also officially announced Senator Defensor-Santiago's candidacy for an ICC Judge (Department of Foreign Affairs 2011c; Carvajal 2011; ICC-ASP/10/S/04 2011). Defensor-Santiago had unsuccessfully run for an ICJ seat in 2008 and now her prospects with the ICC were much better. Compared to the ICJ, where the Judges need the absolute majority of the UNGA and the UNSC (Department of Foreign Affairs 2008; Art. 10, Statute of the International Court of Justice 1945) in the case of the ICC the Assembly of States Parties elects the Judges. A bonus for Defensor-Santiago was the fact that the minimum voting requirements clearly advantage Asian women. When an independent Panel declared the only other Asian candidate as not qualified and the only other female candidate was competing in another category of expertise, her prospects of becoming a Judge were in fact fantastic (ICC Independent Panel 2011; ICC-ASP/3/Res. 6 2004). Accordingly, Defensor-Santiago was elected in the first round of the ballot (ICC 2011).

A third element that supported the ratification was the Obama effect and the fact that the USA had revised its policy toward the ICC already during the second Bush Administration (Bellinger 2008). The ICC President's note in March 2011 (a few days after Aquino had signed the Rome Statute) pointed at the Obama effect, as he assured that the USA did not oppose other states' ratifications of the Rome Statute:

> A few years ago, many countries were reluctant to join the ICC due to the hostile attitude of the Bush administration. But, those days are far behind us and the US has adopted a new policy of positive engagement with the ICC. Senior officials of the Obama administration have confirmed to me time and again that the US in no way opposes any country's ratification of the Rome Statute. (Song 2011a)

Four days after President Aquino had transmitted the Rome Statute to the Senate in May 2011, the Obama's Ambassador for War Crimes, Rapp, visited the Philippines and confirmed that the USA would not stand in the way of other countries, if they want to join the ICC:

> Recently [...] I saw the ICC President, Judge Song of South Korea. [...] He and I often talk about his worldwide travels to encourage ICC ratification and its implementation into national law. This time he spoke of his trips in March of this year to Malaysia and the Philippines in support of ICC ratification. He said to me, 'When I travel, I find people who have this impression that the ratification of the ICC will be viewed as an unfriendly act by the Government of the United States. Apparently, this is not the case. Why don't you just say it?' So I will. The United States respects the right of every country to join the ICC. (Rapp 2011b)

Rapp would hardly have brought up this issue, had there not been someone in the Philippines with the 'impression' that ratifying the Rome Statute would harm relations with the USA.

7.6 Conclusions

This case study provides strong evidence for the argument that the ratification decision of the Philippines was based on rational calculations and not on common identities, as the constructivist theory would suggest. The fact that the influence of the US policy toward the ICC is continuously brought up by parliamentarians, the media, NGOs, and later by the ICC President and the USA itself supports the argument that external pressure influenced the Philippines' calculations on whether to join the ICC or not. At the same time, the case study shows that Arroyo was also worried about the ICC's influence on the Philippines' state sovereignty and in particular on the military's room of maneuver. However, reading of the documents collected for this case allows to conclude that the US policies played a more decisive role, not least because the USA is much more often mentioned as a hindering factor than the military.

The Obama effect encouraged the Philippines' ratification, but since it coincided with the regime change from Arroyo to Aquino, its positive influence is not as evident as the Bush Administration's negative influence. Yet, an argument in support of the Obama effect is the fact that the timing of and the purely rational reasons for the ratification imply that Aquino's policies did not differ much from Arroyo. Aquino seemed to be very interested in having an international judge, perhaps more so than confirming common identities in support of the ICC. However, the Secretary of Foreign Affairs' comment on Defensor-Santiago's appointment could be understood in terms of a desire to raise the country's reputation as a defender of human rights: "The Philippines has found its rightful place in the International Criminal Court. As a strong democracy dedicated to the fight against impunity, the Philippines [...] considers this victory historic, as historic as the day we ratified the Rome Statute" (Department of Foreign Affairs 2011f) (Table 7.1).

The process-tracing also showed that the legislative branch, and at times the DFA, was supporting the ratification. Due to the ratification process of the Philippines, the judiciary was not able to force Arroyo to submit the Rome Statute to the Senate, because the Executive branch enjoys the exclusive right to decide whether an international treaty be

Table 7.1 Theoretical findings of the case study on the Philippines (PH)

	External influence	*Liberal explanations*	*Reflectivist explanations*
Reinforcing cooperation	***Normative binding*: Weak** Arroyo was US-dependent and not particularly motivated to support the ICC or to engage in normative binding PH was concerned about the EU stance. The ICC clause in the EU–PH PCA turned into a stumbling block during the negotiations on the agreement. Yet, the EU was able to include the clause to the PCA Binding attempts bore fruit after the USA relaxed its opposition to the ICC	***Governmental motivations*: Mixed** No hard evidence for lock-in or credible commitment desires, although the circumstances (Aquino's rise to power) support the hypothesis The timing of ratification provides smoking gun for the main domestic motivation being an international judge and improving the PH international profile	***Persuasion*: Weak** Local and global NGOs, the ICC, and the EU actively persuaded the PH. However, the evidence for persuasion being productive is vague ***Diffusion*: No** Considering the poor ratification rate in Asia, regional diffusion is not a tenable explanation for ratification, but it can explain non-ratification
Obstructing cooperation	***US policy 1998–2009*: Strong** There is strong evidence that the economic and political inducements of the USA hindered the ratification. In addition to straws in the wind, the evidence provides smoking guns in support of the hypothesis (PH was promoted into a major non-NATO ally military and received military aid right after signing a BIA)	***Political and legal costs*: Weak** The military opposed the ICC and Arroyo had vague reasons to be worried about ICC Legal issues did not pose hindrances: Arroyo adopted quasi-implementing legislation in 2009	

(continued)

Table 7.1 (continued)

	External influence	*Liberal explanations*	*Reflectivist explanations*
Delaying cooperation	***Obama effect*: Strong** US and ICC officials mention the Obama Administration's friendly policy towards the ICC in connection with the PH ratification	***Political and legal process*: Weak** Arroyo's considerations regarding the military and the US policy delayed ratification Legislative was supportive, and legal review did not slow down the process Financial contribution was discussed, but did not play a major role	
Alternate effects	***Dependence networks*: No** In economic terms, the EU and the USA are equally important partners; the USA is major military (and perhaps political) ally while the EU is significant provider of development aid. Asian allies not excited about the ICC		***Common identities*: No** Most statements of the PH do not point out socialization

submitted to the Senate or not. One of Arroyo's main motivations for blocking the ratification was her fear of potential ICC charges. How much she was influenced by the military in her decision is unclear, but it is evident that the military did not support the ICC. The case study also supports the hypothesis that internal armed conflicts, human rights abuses, and the atmosphere of impunity for human rights violations feed unwillingness to join the ICC. Moreover, Aquino's desire to ratify the Rome Statute shortly after becoming President could potentially imply lock-in desires or the wish to make a credible commitment. However, apart from the timing of the ratification, I was not able to find evidence for these arguments.

Lastly, the case study provides evidence for the normative binding-argument—the EU evidently and actively tried to influence the Philippines by promoting the ICC bilaterally and through NGOs. There is no support for the claim that the EU would have prevailed over the USA with its binding attempts as it did in the Rome conference, but when the situation with the US policy changed through the Obama effect, the EU got its way and the Philippines joined the ICC. Hence, the attempt to exercise normative binding was there and in the long term the result was that desired by the EU, although during the time of conflicting interests with the USA, persuasion and positive economic incentives were not as powerful as significant economic inducements deployed by the Bush Administration.

References

UN documents (references starting with A/…, SC/…, and S/…) available at documents.un.org or unbisnet.un.org.

5400/03 (Presse 11). 2003. "Joint Co-Chairmen's Statement, 14th EU–ASEAN Ministerial Meeting." Council of the European Union.

Administrative Order No. 387. 1998. "Providing for the Creation of a Task Force on the Proposed Establishment of the International Criminal Court." Fidel V. Ramos, President of the Republic of The Philippines.

Agence France Presse. 2002a. "Pressed for Military Aid, Philippines Thinking of ICC Immunity Deal with US," August 21.

———. 2002b. "Philippines Reluctant to Ratify ICC Treaty," September 5. LexisNexis Academic.

———. 2003a. "Philippines VP Calls for Full Disclosure of Immunity Pact with US," June 17.

———. 2003b. "Immunity Pact with US 'Unfair' and Discriminatory: Philippine VP," June 24.

Akbayan. 2010. "AKBAYAN in 2010: Reclaiming Hope Through Governance That Works," February 11.

Alcoseba, Hannah Ira V. 2003. "ICC Pact Now in Palace Hands." *BusinessWorld*, January 27.

Amnesty International. 2003. "International Criminal Court: The Unlawful Attempt by the Security Council to Give US Citizens Permanent Impunity from International Justice," May.

Aquino III, Benigno S. 2010. "Inaugural Address of President Benigno S. Aquino III (English Translation)." Official Gazette of the Republic of the Philippines.

ASEANhrmech. 2017. "About Us." The Working Group for an ASEAN Human Rights Mechanism.

Australian Government. 2008. "Australia–European Union Partnership Framework." Department of Foreign Affairs and Trade.

Baja, Lauro L., Jr. 1998. "Philippine Statement, Towards an Effective International Criminal Court."

Bayan Muna. 2013. "About Bayan Muna."

BBC. 2000. "Summary of World Broadcasts, Philippines Against Establishing International Criminal Court (Source: The Manila Times Web Site)," September 9.

———. 2003a. "Summary of World Broadcasts, Phillipines Unlikely to Ratify International Court Treaty Says Spokesman (Source: The Philippine Star Web Site)," June 10.

———. 2003b. "Summary of World Broadcasts, Philippine Speaker Says Talks with Communists to Resume in Oslo End of August (Source: The Philippine Star Web Site)," July 21.

———. 2012. "Philippines Arrests Gloria Arroyo on Plunder Charges," October 4.

Bellinger, John B. 2008. "Speech on International Criminal Justice, Fletcher School of Law and Diplomacy." Council on Foreign Relations.

Bernas, Joaquin G. 2003. *A Living Constitution: The Abbreviated Estrada Presidency*. Manila: Ateneo de Manila University Press.

Bordadora, Norman, and Veronica Uy. 2008. "PNP Backs Philippine Ratification of Int'l Criminal Court." *Philippine Daily Inquirer*, April 14.

Bureau of the Treasury. 2012. "Statistical Data: National Government Cash Operations, Yearly Cor-Summary." Republic of the Philippines.

BusinessWorld. 2001. "ICC Establishment Pushed by Experts." *BusinessWorld*, October 17.

Calderon, Ma Eloisa I. 2004. "RP Ties with US Preventing It from Okaying Crime Court." *BusinessWorld*, October 19.

Carvajal, Nancy C. 2011. "Santiago Is Philippines' Nominee for Judge of International Crime Court." *Philippine Daily Inquirer*, August 27.

CB/MM-Doc.6. 1998. "Draft Declaration on the United Nations Diplomatic Conference of Plenipotentiaries on the Establishment of an International Criminal Court by the Ministerial Meeting of the Coordinating Bureau of the Non-Aligned Movement." NAM.

Celoza, Albert F. 1997. *Ferdinand Marcos and the Philippines: The Political Economy of Authoritarianism*. Westport: Praeger.

CICC. 2004. "ICC Update, 40th Edition." Coalition for the International Criminal Court.

———. 2006. "Summary of Information on Bilateral Immunity Agreements (BIAs) or So-Called 'Article 98' Agreements as of July 8, 2006." Coalition for the International Criminal Court.

———. 2012. "Universal Ratification Campaign, Target Countries." Coalition for the International Criminal Court.

Colmenares, Neri Javier. 2002. "U.S. Military Operations in the Philippines: A Threat to Peace and Democracy." In Carbon Equity.

COM (2010) 460 Final, 2010/0241 (NLE). 2010. "Proposal for a Council Decision on the Signing of the Framework Agreement on Partnership and Cooperation Between the European Union and Its Member States, of the One Part, and the Republic of the Philippines, of the Other Part." Commission of the European Communities.

Committee on Foreign Relations. 2011. "Senate Committee Report No. 52." Senate of the Philippines.

Concepcion, Niza. 2004. "First Asian Victimes' Seminar on the International Criminal Court, Feb 26–27, 2004, Quezon City, Philippines." Asian Federation Against Involuntary Disappearances.

Corpuz, Gerry Albert. 2003. "GMA-Bush Secret Pact Seen to Restore U.S. Bases in Philippines: Groups Urge Macapagal-Arroyo's Impeachment." *Bulatlat* 17 (3), available at http://www.bulatlat.com/news/3-17/3-17-bases.html.

Damaso, Maria Felisa. 2001. "First Expert's Conference on the ICC Today in Manila." *The Manila Times*, October 17.

Danao, Efren L., and William B. Depasupil. 2008. "Miriam Prods Palace on International Court." *Manila Times*, October 16.

De la Paz III, Dean O. 2003. "From Nuremberg to Nothing." *BusinessWorld*, July 3.

Del Callar, Michaela P. 2007. "EU Presses RP Gov't to Ratify Rome Statute." *The Daily Tribune*, April.

De Lima, Leila. 2009. "Human Rights Violations Rise: Culture of Impunity Prevailing." *Philippine Daily Inquirer*, July 23.

Department of Foreign Affairs. 2008. "Without Miriam, ICJ Has No Woman Judge, Press Release." Republic of the Philippines.

———. 2011a. "Foreign Affairs Secretary Urges Senate Concurrence to Rome Statute Establishing International Criminal Court, Press Release." Republic of the Philippines.

———. 2011b. "DFA Welcomes Senate Concurrence on the Rome Statute, Press Release." Republic of the Philippines.

———. 2011c. "PHL Launches Senator Miriam Defensor-Santiago's ICC Bid, Press Release." Republic of the Philippines.

———. 2011d. "Sen. Legarda Witnesses, Lauds PHL's Deposit of ICC Rome Statute Instrument of Ratification, Press Release." Republic of the Philippines.

———. 2011e. "Ambassador Bataclan Meets EU Official." Republic of the Philippines.

———. 2011f. "Dr. Miriam Defensor Santiago Tops Election for International Criminal Court Judges, Press Release." Republic of the Philippines.

———. 2012. "DFA Budget in Graph, DFA Budget vs. National Budget, FY 2009, 2010 and 2011." Republic of the Philippines.

Depasupil, William B. 2008. "ICC to Benefit Justice System." *Manila Times*, September 26.

Doyo, Ceres P. 2011a. "PH as State Party in International Criminal Court." *Philippine Daily Inquirer*, February 17.

———. 2011b. "From Nuremberg to The Hague." *Philippine Daily Inquirer*, March 9.

EEAS. 2010. "Human Rights and Democracy in the World: Report on EU Action July 2008 to December 2009." Brussels: European External Action Service.

———. 2011. "EU Annual Report on Human Rights and Democracy in the World in 2010." Brussels: European External Action Service.

European Union. 1999. "European Union Annual Reports on Human Rights 1999–2006." Brussels: Council of the European Union.

———. 2006. "EU Annual Report on Human Rights 2006." Luxembourg: Council of the European Union.

———. 2007. "EU Annual Report on Human Rights 2007." Luxembourg: European Communities.

———. 2008. "EU Report on Human Rights 2008." Luxembourg: European Communities.

Eurostat. 2010. "External and Intra-EU Trade—Statistical Yearbook, Data 1958–2009." European Commission.

Executive Order No. 1. 2010. "Creating the Philippine Truth Commission of 2010." Official Gazette of the Republic of the Philippines.

Filipino Youth for Peace. 2003. "ICC Immunity Deal with US, GMA's Exchange Gift to Bush?" Bayan Muna Partylist.

Gamolo, Nora O. 2011. "Filipino Human Rights Activists Urge Ratification of Rome Statute." *AllVoices*, March 8.

Garcia, Maria. 2012. "Competitive Fears: The EU, US and Free Trade Agreements in East Asia." *EU External Affairs Review* 2 (1): 59–71.

Gatdula, Jemy. 2011a. "No to the ICC." *BusinessWorld*, April 1.

———. 2011b. "The Still-Unconvincing ICC." *Business World*, December 9.

Georgetown Law Library. 2009. "International Criminal Court—Article 98 Agreements Research Guide," December.

G. R. No. 158088. 2005. "Pimentel vs. Office of Exec Sec., En Banc, Decision." Supreme Court of the Philippines, July 6.

G. R. No. 159618. 2011. "Bayan Muna vs. Alberto Romulo and Blas F. Ople, Decision." Supreme Court of the Philippines, February 1.

H. CON. RES. 273. 2001. "Concurrent Resolution Reaffirming the Special Relationship Between the United States and the Republic of the Philippines." Washington, DC: House of Representatives, Congress of the United States of America.

HR00050. 2004. "Resolution of the House of Representatives, Congress of the Philippines." Consolidated into HR00526, July 26.

HR00094. 1998. "Resolution of the House of Representatives, Congress of the Philippines." Pending, July 27.

HR00341. 2001. "Resolution of the House of Representatives, Congress of the Philippines." Pending, December 18.

HR00417. 2004. "Resolution of the House of Representatives, Congress of the Philippines." Consolidated into HR00526, November 26.

HR00425. 2008. "Resolution of the House of Representatives, Congress of the Philippines." Adopted as Resolution No. HR00165, January 30.

HR00526. 2006. "Resolution of the House of Representatives, Congress of the Philippines," April 5.

HR00800. 2002. "Resolution of the House of Representatives, Congress of the Philippines." Pending, October 4.

HR01188. 2003. "Resolution of the House of Representatives, Congress of the Philippines." Pending, June 4.

HR01391. 2003. "Resolution of the House of Representatives, Congress of the Philippines." Pending, November 19.

HR01503. 2000. "Resolution of the House of Representatives, Congress of the Philippines." Pending, April 6.

HRW. 2003. "Bilateral Immunity Agreements." Human Rights Watch.

———. 2011. "'No Justice Just Adds to the Pain': Killings, Disappearances, and Impunity in the Philippines." New York: Human Rights Watch.

———. 2012a. "World Report 2012: Events of 2011." New York: Human Rights Watch.

———. 2012b. "Philippines: Arrest Ex-General Accused of 'Disappearances': Palparan's Prosecution Key to Ending Impunity." New York: Human Rights Watch.

ICC. 2011. "Final Results: Election of the Judges of the International Criminal Court. Tenth Session of the Assembly of States Parties." International Criminal Court, December 19.

ICC-ASP/3/Res. 6. 2004. "Procedure for the Nomination and Election of Judges of the International Criminal Court." International Criminal Court.

ICC-ASP/10/S/04. 2011. "Nomination and Election of Judges." International Criminal Court.

ICC-CPI-20110302-PR632. 2011. "ICC President to Visit Southeast Asia, Press Release." International Criminal Court.

ICC Independent Panel. 2011. "Report on International Criminal Court Judicial Nominations 2011." Independent Panel on ICC Judicial Elections.

Kim, Quilingin. 2011. "ICC President Argues for Philippine Ratification of Rome Statute." University of the Philippines Newsletter.

Kleiss, Karen. 2003. "Countries Must Choose: ICC or U.S. Dollars." *The Toronto Star*, June 29, Sunday Ontario Edition, sec. F.

Ledoux, Guy. 2011. "Feedback: The ICC as Court of Last Resort." *BusinessWorld*, June 2.

Lee-Brago, Pia. 2009. "Government Balks at European Union Rights Standard." *The Philippine Star*, February 12.

———. 2010. "EU's Priority: Promotion, Protection of Human Rights in Phl." *The Philippine Star*, December 11.

Legaspi, Amita O. 2011. "Aquino Signs Rome Statute of the Int'l Criminal Court." *GMA News*, March 6.

Leon, Max de. 2004. "RP Weighs ICC Stance; Admits U.S. Pressure. Newspaper Article Quoted In." In *International Criminal Court: Reservations of Non-state Parties in Southeast Asia*, by Valeriane Toon, 229. 26 (2): Contemporary Southeast Asia.

Luib, Romulo T. 2002. "Ratification of ICC Bucked." *BusinessWorld*, September 6.

Malaysia General News. 2002. "Philippines Assured of Non-permanent Seat in UNSC, Says Minister." *Pertubuhan Berita Nasional Malaysia*, November 1.

Mogato, Manuel. 2011. "Philippine Ex-President Arroyo Arrested in Hospital." *Reuters*, November 18.

Mohamad, Maznah. 2002. "Towards a Human Rights Regime in Southeast Asia: Charting the Course of State Commitment." *Contemporary Southeast Asia* 24 (2): 230–51.

Morales, Lourdes G. 2011. "Remarks at the Welcoming Ceremony International Criminal Court." Embassy of the Republic of the Philippines, The Hague.

Mostajo, Josel, Byron Bocar, Evelyn Balais-Serrano, and Aurora Parong, eds. 2008. *For Hope and Human Dignity: A Primer on the International Criminal Court for the Security Sector.* Quezon City: Philippine Coalition for the International Criminal Court.

National Statistics Office. 2011. "Philippines in Figures 2011." Republic of the Philippines.

Ng, Jennifer A., and Jeffrey O. Valisno. 2002. "US Inclined to Support RP Bid for UN Security Council Seat." *BusinessWorld*, October 10.

OECD. 2012. "Query Wizard for International Development Statistics, ODA from DAC-EU Members, USA, EU Institutions, and All Donors (incl. International Organizations) in Current USD Millions to Philippines 2002–2009." Organization for Economic Co-operation and Development.

Olivares-Cunanan, Belinda. 2008. "Pressures on Manila to Ratify ICC Treaty." *Philippine Daily Inquirer*, September 30.

Ople, Blass F. 2003. "Note No. 0470 to the Ambassador of the United States of America in Manila." Georgetown Law Library.

Osorio, Elisa P., and Ma Eloisa I. Calderon. 2004. "Arroyo Urged to Expedite Ratification of ICC Treaty." *Business World*, October 12.

Panaligan, Rey G. 2001. "Int'l Criminal Court Proposed by Davide." *Manila Bulletin*, October 17.

Pangalangan, Raul. 2007. "Either Knew or… Should Have Known." *Philippine Daily Inquirer*, June 29.

———. 2008a. "The International Criminal Court and Institutional Protection for Human Dignity." In *For Hope and Human Dignity: A Primer on the International Criminal Court for the Security Sector*, edited by Josel Mostajo, Byron Bocar, Evelyn Balais-Serrano, and Aurora Parong. Quezon City: Philippine Coalition for the International Criminal Court.

———. 2008b. "Ratify the Rome Statute." *Philippine Daily Inquirer*, October 3.

———. 2011a. "Embracing a Pact America Has Junked." *Philippine Daily Inquirer*, February 11.

———. 2011b. "Philippines Signs Rome Statute." *Philippine Daily Inquirer*, August 25.

Panganiban, Artemio V. 2008. "Justice Without Borders." *Philippine Daily Inquirer*, November 1.

———. 2009. "With Due Respect: Like Cory or Like Ferdie." *Philippine Daily Inquirer*, August 9.

Parreño, Al A. 2011. "Report on the Philippine Extrajudicial Killings (2001–Aug 2010)." Manila: Supreme Court of the Philippines, The Asia Foundation, and USAID.

PCICC. 2009a. "Coalition Urges Immediate Philippine Ratification of Treaty on the International Criminal Court." Philippine Coalition for the International Criminal Court.

———. 2009b. "Coalition Demands Justice for Maguindanao Massacre." Philippine Coalition for the International Criminal Court.

———. 2011. "Open Letter to the Philippine Senate." Philippine Coalition for the International Criminal Court.

———. 2012. "About PCICC." Philippine Coalition for the International Criminal Court.

———. 2013. "Archive for the 'Press Releases and Statements.'" Philippine Coalition for the International Criminal Court.

Pedrasa, Ira P. 2008. "Military Not Keen on International Criminal Court." *BusinessWorld*, September 27. Amnesty International Sweden.

PGA. 2011. "Press Release: The Philippines Becomes 117th State Party to the Rome Statute of the International Criminal Court." Parlamentarians for Global Action.

Philippines News Agency. 2008a. "SC Calls for Notification of ICCs Governing Law," September 26. LexisNexis Academic.

———. 2008b. "EU Concerned with Victims of International Crimes," September 27. LexisNexis Academic.

Plantilla, Jefferson. 1997. "Elusive Promise: Transitional Justice in the Philippines." Human Rights Dialogue 1.8. Carnegie Council for Ethics in International Affairs.

P. S. Res. No. 90. 2007. "Resolution of the Senate, Congress of the Philippines." Pending, August 22.

P. S. Res. No. 94. 2006. "Resolution of the Senate, Congress of the Philippines," August 15.

P. S. Res. No. 171. 2006. "Resolution of the Senate, Congress of the Philippines," August 15.

P. S. Res. No. 546. 2011. "Resolution of the Senate, Congress of the Philippines," August 23.

P. S. Res. No. 710. 2008. "Resolution of the Senate, Congress of the Philippines." Pending, October 15.

P. S. Res. No. 748. 2008. "Resolution of the Senate, Congress of the Philippines." Pending, November 11.

Rapp, Stephen J. 2011a. "Questions and Answers." Manila: Embassy of the United States.

———. 2011b. "Where Can the Victims of Atrocities Find Justice? Remarks at Forum Hosted by the Women of Ateneo." Manila: Embassy of the United States.

Reilly, William M. 2004. "U.S. Bid for Int'l Court Immunity KO'd." United Press International, June 23.

Ricciardone, Francis J., Jr. 2003. "Note No. BFO-028-03 to the Secretary of Foreign Affairs of the Philippines." Georgetown Law Library.

Roncesvalles, Carina I. 2003. "Ricciardone Says US Not Pressing Philippines on Int'l Crime Court." *BusinessWorld*, July 10.

———. 2005. "Senators Urge Malacanang to Submit Criminal Court Treaty." *BusinessWorld*, April 5.

Roncesvalles, Carina I., Karen L. Lema, and AFP. 2004. "EU Urges RP Gov't to Abolish Capital Punishment." *BusinessWorld*, January 16.

Roque, Harry, Jr. 2011a. "At Long Last." *Manila Standard Today*, August 25.

———. 2011b. "ICC: The Road Ahead." *Harry Roque's Blog: Thoughts of an Activist Lawyer*, September 23.

Rosales, Etta. 2006. "An Overview: Work for the Philippine Ratification of the Rome Statute: 1998–2006," September 6.

Salvador, Alma Maria O., Leslie V. Advincula-Lopez, and Manuel Enverga. 2009. "Orienatlism Reversed: Images and Perceptions of the EU in the Philippines." In *The EU Through the Eyes of Asia: Volume II. New Cases, New Findings*, edited by Natalia Chaban, Martin Holland, and Peter Ryan, 19–51. Singapore: World Scientific Publishing.

Sandoval, Raymond Vincent G. 2004. "The US–Philippines Impunity Agreement: Violating International Law and Municipal Law with Impunity." *Philippine Law Journal* 78 (3): 461–534.

Schabas, William A. 2011. *An Introduction to the International Criminal Court*, 4th ed. Cambridge, UK: Cambridge University Press.

S. CON. RES. 91. 2001. "Concurrent Resolution Expressing Deep Gratitude to the Government and the People of the Philippines for Their Sympathy and Support Since September 11, 2001, and for Other Purposes."

Senate of the Philippines. 2011a. "Asian Lawmakers Hail Pnoy on International Criminal Court, Press Release." Congress of the Philippines.

———. 2011b. "Journal, Session No. 9." Congress of the Philippines.

———. 2011c. "Journal, Session No. 12." Congress of the Philippines.

———. 2011d. "Senate Approves Ratification of Rome Statute on Final Reading, Press Release." Congress of the Philippines.

———. 2011e. "Miriam Lauds PH Membership to the International Criminal Court, Press Release." Congress of the Philippines.

SFA-AGR-217-08. 2008. "RP-EU Technical Cooperation on the Protection and Promotion of Human Rights, Press Release." Department of Foreign Affairs, Republic of the Philippines.

SOFRECO. 2007. "Comparative Evaluation of the Human Rights Projects and Interventions of the European Union in the Philippines and Cambodia: Final Report." European Union.

Song, Sang-Hyun. 2011a. "Keynote Address, Second Asia-Pacific Consultation on the Universality of the Rome Statute of the International Criminal Court.

Parliamentarians for Global Action & Parliament of Malaysia." International Criminal Court.

———. 2011b. "Remarks to the 20th Diplomatic Briefing." International Criminal Court.

———. 2011c. "Remarks at the Welcoming Ceremony for Philippines, the 117th State Party to the Rome Statute." International Criminal Court.

———. 2011d. "Keynote Remarks ASP Side Event 'Plan of Action: Universality of the Rome Statute and Implementing Legislation: Developments and Resources.'" International Criminal Court.

———. 2011e. "The Role of the International Criminal Court, Speech to Committee on Foreign Relations, Senate of the Republic of the Philippines." International Criminal Court.

S. RES. 152. 2003. "Welcoming the President of the Philippines to the United States." Washington, DC: Senate of the United States.

Statute of the International Court of Justice. 1945. "Annexed to the Charter of the United Nations." United Nations.

Tan, Reagan D. 2006. "Manila Urged to Ratify Treaty Backing World Court." *BusinessWorld*, August 16.

TendersInfo. 2010. "Philippines: EU, RP Talks Stall on Human Rights," February 9.

Thompson, Mark R. 1995. *The Anti-Marcos Struggle: Personalistic Rule and Democratic Transition in the Philippines.* New Haven: Yale University Press.

Toon, Valeriane. 2004. "International Criminal Court: Reservations of Non-state Parties in Southeast Asia." *Contemporary Southeast Asia* 26 (2): 218–32.

Torres, Estrella. 2008. "EU-Asean Meeting to Tackle Trade Barriers." *Business Mirror*, October 10. Bilaterals.org.

———. 2010. "RP, EU Conclude PCA After 2 Years." *Business Mirror*, June 7. Bilaterals.org.

Torres, Tetch. 2008a. "Sovereignty Should Protect People, Not Cover Up War Crimes: AFP Wants Rome Statute Ratified—Inspector General." *Philippine Daily Inquirer*, September 26.

———. 2008b. "Fund Concerns Delaying Rome Statute Nod: Not Fear of Losing US Aid." *Philippine Daily Inquirer*, October 8.

UN News Centre. 2007. "Philippines: Military Executing Leftist Activists, UN Independent Expert Finds." United Nations.

UNTC, United Nations Treaty Collection. 2017. "Status of Treaties: Multilateral Treaties Deposited with the Secretary-General." https://treaties.un.org.

U.S. Department of Commerce. 2012. "Trade in Goods with Philippines." United States Census Bureau.

Uy, Veronica. 2006a. "Senate Asks Arroyo to Submit Rome Statute for Ratification." *Philippine Daily Inquirer*, August 15.

———. 2006b. "'Arroyo Afraid She'll Be Tried as War Criminal'—Pimentel: President Slammed for Sitting on Rome Statute." *Philippine Daily Inquirer*, August 23.

Van Schaak, Beth. 2007. "The Establishment of the Permanent International Criminal Court." An International Symposium, Working Paper, No. 7–40. Santa Clara, CA: Santa Clara University School of Law.

Veloso Lao, Christine. 1999. "Safeguarding Sovereignty, Righting Human Wrongs: A Jurisprudential Justification for the Philippines' Ratification of the Rome Statute of the International Criminal Court." *Philippine Law Journal* 74 (2): 211–302.

Xinhua. 2002. "Philippine Vice President Resigns as Foreign Secretary." *Xinhua General News Service*, June 27.

CHAPTER 8

Why Indonesia Has Not Joined the ICC?

8.1 Indonesia at the Negotiations on the Rome Statute

Indonesia competes with the Philippines for the title of the most democratic Southeast Asian state (EEAS 2012b), and its standing as the most influential ASEAN state is indisputable. It is the fourth most populous country with the largest Muslim population in the world and a member of the G20. Thus, Indonesia has democratized after the thirty years rule of the repressive New Order regime of Suharto, which ended in 1998, but state violence remains. Intimidation of human rights activists, arbitrary detentions, forced disappearances, and extrajudicial killings are not unusual incidents (ICTJ and KontraS 2011; EEAS 2010b; CAT/C/IDN/CO/2 2008; A/HRC/WG.6/1/IDN/2 2008).

Indonesia participated in the preparations of the Rome conference under Suharto's rule, and the main aim of its negotiation agenda was to protect the principle of state sovereignty. According to Indonesia, the ICC's jurisdiction would be restricted to international conflicts, since international law arguably only governs interstate relations (Muladi 1998; GA/L/3080 1998; A/C.6/54/SR.14 1999). The moral authority of the court would be guaranteed by establishing an independent institution based on a consensually adopted treaty (A/C.6/50/SR.29 1995; A/C.6/52/SR.12 1998) and its political independence secured by allowing only States Parties that have direct concern over a case, to initiate investigations. Moreover, the prosecution of individuals would

S. Huikuri, *The Institutionalization of the International Criminal Court*,
https://doi.org/10.1007/978-3-319-95585-8_8

follow only after the approval of all parties concerned (A/C.6/51/SR.27. 1996; GA/L/3010 1996). Lastly, the ICC should complement domestic jurisdiction, and, for instance, arresting accused would be the prerogative of national authorities (L/2781 1996). Indonesia did not support universal jurisdiction, because it conflicted with the principle of complementarity (L/2775 1996). An ICC controlled by its States Parties would secure "effective prosecution of individuals responsible for serious crimes" (GA/L/2880 1995).

With the Rome conference approaching, Indonesia, Mexico, and India took the command in the NAM and drafted Declaration of Cartagena, which emphasized state sovereignty (CB/MM-Doc.6 1998). In contrast to most European countries, the NAM wanted a more limited jurisdiction for the ICC and unlike the USA, it wanted to include aggression to the Rome Statute and was concerned that the UNSC would control the functioning of the ICC (Terra Viva 1998; A/CONF.183/C.1/SR.30 1998). When the Rome conference started, President Habibie had been in power for few weeks and faced a plentitude of domestic problems, of which the biggest was the democratization of a large country in deep financial crisis (Liddle 1999, 35ff.). Yet, Indonesia sent a delegation of 14 men to Rome. Ideals, such as ending impunity, deterring future crimes, and promoting peace, justice, and rule of law, guided Indonesia's agenda side-by-side with the realist colored protection of state sovereignty. According to Indonesia, the Rome Statute should "protect citizens from inappropriate, frivolous, and politically motivated allegations" (Muladi 1998) and secure the rights of incorrectly accused states as much as it protects the rights of victims. Indonesia was concerned about politically motivated investigations, the *proprio motu* Prosecutor, and that the ICC would overrule national laws (A/CONF.183/C.1/SR.35 1998; A/CONF.183/C.1/SR.9 1998).

Few days before the end of the conference, Indonesia noted that over-politicization had complicated the negotiations and that consensual adoption of the Rome Statute was not realistic, if the ICC were to have automatic jurisdiction over crimes against humanity and war crimes (Muladi 1998). Some sources indicate that it was among those states, which abstained or voted against the adoption of the Rome Statute in the final, unrecorded vote (The Washington Times 1998; Newsweek 1998), but at the 2010 Kampala Review Conference, the head of the Indonesian delegation said that his country had supported the adoption (Wirana 2010). Since Indonesia did not make a statement on its vote in Rome, the issue remains unclear. Shortly after Rome, Indonesia emphasized that the effectiveness of the ICC depends on the universal coverage of the ICC. However, it also stated, in a rationalist fashion, that it did not want the ICC to become "a mechanism for interfering in State's internal affairs but [it] should fulfil its central objective of facilitating international cooperation and deterring the perpetration of heinous acts" (A/C.6/54/SR.14 1999; GA/L/3080 1998).

8.2 Liberal Explanations for Non-ratification

8.2.1 Potential Legal Obstacles

According to Art. 11, 2 of the Constitution of Indonesia, the President, with the approval of the House of Representatives, has the power to accede to international treaties. According to Law No. 24/2000 on Treaties, the accession procedure can be initiated by the state or a governmental institution, which then prepares a draft bill, other necessary documents, and coordinates their deliberations. Once the Parliament has enacted a law permitting the ratification, the Minister of Foreign Affairs submits the treaty to the President for ratification. Hence, the Parliament, the Minister of Foreign Affairs, and the President can potentially prevent the ratification of treaties. Before discussing the policies of domestic stakeholders on the ICC, I examine legal obstacles as a potential explanation for Indonesia's non-ratification, although according to Art. 7, 2 of Law No. 39/1999 Concerning Human Rights all international human rights treaties are legally binding in the country after their ratification.

In addition to the Constitution, Indonesian human rights legislation comprises Law No. 39/1999, which defines civil, political, social, economic, cultural, and legal rights and according to which "human rights are basic rights bestowed by God on human beings." Some crimes related to the Rome Statute are addressed in Law No. 26/2000 concerning human rights courts, which was adopted as a response to international pressure to address crimes committed in East Timor. It follows the Rome Statute as far as genocide and crimes against humanity are concerned, and although it brings many important enhancements to Indonesian legislation, it also has serious flaws: The definition of crimes is narrow, sporadic human rights violations remain outside the courts' jurisdiction, the definition of genocide does not include ancillary crimes, and the legislation allows retroactivity and capital punishment, which conflict not only with the Rome Statute, but also with the Constitution of Indonesia and Law No. 39/1999 (AHRC 2006; A/HRC/WG.6/1/IDN/3 2008; Linton 2006, 15–16; Amnesty International 2001; Huikuri 2017, 78).

Regarding constitutional restrictions, the right of the President to grant amnesties and drop charges could potentially be interpreted by the ICC as unwillingness to prosecute according to Art. 17 of the Rome Statue. Moreover, immunity of Indonesian parliamentarians is prohibited by Art. 27 of the Rome Statute, but neither of these issues necessarily hinder the ratification. According to the official notes to Law No. 26/2000, the prohibition of retroactivity of Art. 28I of the Constitution is overruled by Art. 28 J of the Constitution, which obligates *every person* to respect human rights and to accept legal restrictions that guarantee others' rights and freedoms. Since genocide, crimes against humanity, and war crimes violate human rights, which *every person* needs to respect, amnesties and immunities would not pose an obstacle for the ICC's jurisdiction (ICG 2001a, 16–17). Moreover, these crimes can be prosecuted as *jus cogens* crimes and under customary international law, and therefore, their prosecution at the domestic level does not necessitate Constitutional amendments. Other domestic laws do not pose insurmountable obstacles for the ratification of the Rome Statute either, and, legally, the greatest challenge is the implementation of the Rome Statute. In its 2012 national UPR report to the UNGA, the government noted that the implementation could follow after ratification (A/HRC/WG.6/13/IDN/1 2012, 22). This would require fundamental changes to domestic legislation, including the drafting of a new procedural law, as current legislation lacks standards for fair trial, including *habeas corpus* and the right to legal counsel (A/HRC/WG.6/1/IDN/3 2008, 5).

8.2.2 Empty Promises of the Executive

In the first years after the New Order regime, Indonesia saw three Presidents, Habibie, Wahid, and Megawati, and a series of major changes, mostly thanks to Habibie, who disempowered the military, decentralized the government, and introduced economic reforms (Thompson 1999; Vickers 2005, 210). Habibie was replaced by Wahid in 1999 after the first competitive presidential elections in Indonesia. After the elections, Indonesia stated at the UNGA Sixth

Committee that it would continue its "careful consideration of the [Rome] Statute, which it hoped to disseminate to the entire Indonesian population" (A/C.6/54/SR.14 1999). Educating 200 million Indonesians, spread over 6.000 islands, about the ICC is challenging and could almost be interpreted as hesitance to join the court (CICC 2005). Wahid drifted into conflict with his party and the Congress and was replaced, with the help of the military, by his Vice President Megawati in July 2001 (Vickers 2005, 211; ICG 2001b, 2011b). Megawati, President Sukarno's daughter, had been an important figure of the resistance against Suharto (ICG 2003, 6) although she had close ties to the Indonesian military (TNI) and her conservative agenda aimed suppressing autonomous movements in the provinces (Kingsbury 2003, 11, 140, 187, 240; Miller 2009, 61).

The first national conference on the ICC in Indonesia was held in 2001 and the conference report called Megawati to ratify the Rome Statute (ASIA-Pacific Human Rights Information Center 2002). However, the Administration "decided not to rush into ratifying a convention on the International Criminal Court [...] for fear of prejudicing the country's sovereignty" (The Jakarta Post 2001). According to the Ministry of Law and Human Rights (MLHR), the government needed to revise national legal procedures to accommodate the Rome Statute before the ICC becomes operational, otherwise "we would be obliged to comply with its rules, even though we had not yet ratified the Statute" (The Jakarta Post 2001). Seemingly, the motivation for creating an accommodating legislation was not the implementation, but the possibility to take advantage of the principle of complementarity and to prevent possible ICC actions. However, in the end of her term, Megawati adopted a National Action Plan on Human Rights (RANHAM) for the years 2004–2009, according to which Indonesia would ratify 12 human rights instruments in the following five years, including the Rome Statute in 2008 (Ministry of Justice and Human Rights 2011). Until the end of President Yudhoyono's second term in 2014, Indonesia had ratified only five out of the twelve treaties (UNTC 2018).

In February 2007, everything seemed to go according to the RANHAM, and Indonesian government officials and parliamentarians assured that Indonesia would ratify the Rome Statute before the deadline (CICC 2007a; A/HRC/WG.6/1/IDN/4 2008, 11). According to a discussion of the US Embassy with Harkrisnowo, who prepared the ratification at the MLHR, the ratification bill was under preparation and on the Parliament's agenda for 2008. The embassy also points out that Indonesian government officials were aware of the non-retroactivity of the ICC, and this played a major role in the willingness to accede to the ICC (U.S. Embassy 2008; Hamid and Pangaribuan 2012; Maulia 2008). The deadline of 2008 passed, and Indonesian Parliamentarians agreed that "there was no outstanding political or legal obstacle to Indonesia's Accession to the Rome Statute" (PGA 2009a). Likewise, as the ICC President Song visited Indonesia in 2009, he told that government officials "indicated their strong commitment to ratifying the Rome Statute, yet there are some technical problems to be further considered [...]. They all said it is not a matter of whether Indonesia will ratify it or not, but a matter of when Indonesia will ratify and how soon" (Song 2009).

Since 2008, Indonesia has confirmed its willingness to join the ICC at many official occasions, including the 2010 Kampala Review Conference, its 2012 UPR of UNGA Human Rights Council, and a Thematic Debate of the UNGA on International Criminal Justice in 2013 (Wirana 2010; A/HRC/WG.6/13/IDN/1 2012, 5; GA/11357 2013). Yet, Yudhoyono did not facilitate the accession to the Rome Statute. As an Indonesian NGO notes, "the lack of coordination and support among government institutions" and the "lack of initiative, consistency, and political will within the Government and the Parliament" (HRWG 2012) are the two main reasons why Indonesia had not implemented the ratification. I argue that the four following reasons explain Yudhoyono's passivity regarding the ratification.

First, Yudhoyono did not prioritize human rights standards and institutions in general. After the RANHAM expired in 2009, it took him two years to adopt a follow-up plan and the RANHAM for 2011–2014 envisaged the accession to the ICC for the year 2013 (A/HRC/WG.6/13/IDN/1 2012, 3, 5). His government also regularly disdained its reporting requirements to UN Human Rights bodies and did not respond to requests of UN Rapporteurs to examine, inter alia, enforced disappearances and extrajudicial executions (A/61/855 2007; International Commission of Jurists 2011). Moreover, Yudhoyono terminated the post of human rights adviser in Indonesia, which the OHCHR set up in 2007 to support UN agencies in including human rights to their projects and to strengthen national human rights institutions (A/HRC/WG.6/1/IDN/2 2008, 6).

Second, Yudhoyono was wary of the concept of universal jurisdiction. According to Indonesia, "The application of such jurisdiction in an effort to combat impunity should also respect the principle of the sovereign equality of States" (A/C.6/64/SR.13 2009). Moreover, every state should have "the right [...] to determine whether its own national law conformed to its international legal obligations" (A/C.6/66/SR.13 2011). The suspicions of universal jurisdiction were certainly not eased by an incident around Yudhoyono's planned state visit to the Netherlands in 2010. A few days before the visit, a separatist group in South Maluku filed civil complaints to The Hague's district court, charging Yudhoyono with human rights abuses and calling for his arrest. Yudhoyono heard of the complaint just before his plane was taking off and told reporters: "For Indonesia, for me, if this lawsuit is held while I'm visiting, that concerns our self-respect as a nation, it concerns our honor as a nation" (Simons 2010; see also BBC 2012; Woods 2011). Yudhoyono canceled the trip although the Dutch government assured that he would enjoy immunity in the Netherlands.

Third, the government has not internalized the mandate of the ICC (Aritonang 2012; Hamid 2011), as the Chairman of the National Human Rights Commission (Komnas-HAM), Kasim, said in 2009:

> "most misleading perception about the ICC is the idea that it would take over all human rights violation cases. That is absolutely incorrect," he said, adding that this perception has led to the idea that the ICC would damage Indonesia's image as an independent and respected state. (The Jakarta Post 2009d)

Intriguingly, this statement resembles with Yudhoyono's statement at the airport in October 2010 in that Indonesia puts great emphasis on its honor and respect.

Lastly, and most importantly, the fear of losing state sovereignty shaped Yudhoyono's policy on the ICC. Habibie's Minister of Justice and Human Rights, Muladi (the head of Indonesia's delegation in the Rome conference and a supporter of the ratification) identifies "the presumption of the primacy position of ICC over national courts, anxiety over a possible threat to national sovereignty, poor information and a lack of preparation within the national legal system" (Muladi 2011) as hindrances for the ratification. The government was concerned that after ratification Indonesian legal system would have to yield to the Rome Statute:

> The concept of "inability" and "unwillingness" should not serve easily as a pretext to provide continuous preference to ICC intervention. The principle [of complementarity] is one of the corner stones of the architecture of the Rome Statute. We believe that effective implementation of this principle would increase the universality of the Rome Statute. (Wirana 2010)

Similar state sovereignty-oriented statements are found in other venues that consider national versus international law. For instance, regarding the prosecution of human rights, Indonesia stated that "giving States the responsibility to investigate and prosecute perpetrators of human rights violation would help solidify adherence to the principle of the rule of law" (GA/11357 2013).

Despite these aspects, Yudhoyono made promises to accede to the ICC. In 2013, when a delegation of Indonesian government officials and NGOs activists visited the ICC in The Hague, the Presidential Adviser said that Indonesia would join the ICC soon and one month later Yudhoyono allegedly sent a letter to the ICC-ASP, informing that Indonesia was committed to the ratification (Rully 2012; Saragih and Aritonang 2013; Saragih 2013a, b). Around the same time, the Deputy Head of the President's Unit for Development Monitoring published a positive op-ed about the ICC in the Jakarta Post, the biggest English newspaper of Indonesia (Santosa 2013). These moves either indicate that Yudhoyono was making empty promises or that he was not the one who stalled the ratification.

8.2.3 Ministries' Differing Agendas on the ICC

According to Art. 10 of the Law No. 24/2000 on Treaties, Indonesia's accession to the Rome Statute requires new legislation, because the ICC concerns human rights, limits the sovereign rights of Indonesia, and forms new legal norms. Regarding the accession to the ICC, the central government institutions are the Komnas-HAM, the MLHR, and the Ministry of Foreign Affairs (MFA). According to the RANHAM of 2004, the Komnas-HAM first studies the accession to international human rights instruments, the MLHR prepares the legislation and a memorandum on political and legal aspects of the ratification, then the Executive submits the treaty to the Parliament's deliberation, and, upon the Parliament's approval, the MFA considers political aspects of the ratification. Finally, the President ratifies the treaty.

The Komnas-HAM has been enthusiastic about the accession to the ICC. In its position paper on the ratification, it noted in a normative fashion

> that the Rome Statute is not merely an instrument of international criminal law to suppress and prevent the most serious crimes affecting the international community as a whole, but it is also an international legal instruments that protects human rights and upholds the principles of human rights. (Komnas-HAM 2009)

Although the Government or the Parliament did not follow up the report, the Komnas-HAM has continued to advocate for accession to the Rome Statute (HRWG 2012; Komnas-HAM 2007, 2011). However, the Komnas-HAM is not a very powerful institution (ICICC 2012c, 6; Miller 2009, 109) and with the MLHR and the MFA, the ICC has more persuasive supporters. What is curious about these two institutions is the fact that they react to the matter of ratification only when external actors, such as the EU, NGOs, or the ICC, push them to do so.

At the MLHR, the Director of the Department for Human Rights Protection, Harkrisnowo, has been positive about the ratification. In 2006 and 2007, respectively, she underlined the importance of joining the ICC in conferences organized by NGOs, and when Indonesia was the target country of the CICC's ratification campaign in 2007, her colleague reported that the government was strengthening regional human rights legislation for the implementation of the Rome Statute (CICC 2007b; Khalik 2007b; Hermawan 2009a; CICC 2009; IKOHI 2007). However, when the ratification should have followed in few months, Harkrisnowo told that there were other treaties to ratify, but the draft bill would hopefully be submitted to the Parliament in 2008 (Maulia 2008; U.S. Embassy 2008). After the 2008 deadline had passed, Harkrisnowo reported that the drafting of the bill had been completed, but the memorandum was still being drafted (The Jakarta Post 2009a; PGA 2009a; The Jakarta Post 2009e). However, in 2009 Harkrisnowo told the MLHR was not considering the ratification of the Rome Statute, but of the Optional Protocol to the Convention on the Rights of the Child (Hermawan 2009b). Since 2012, the MLHR has revised the law on human rights courts, reviewed the ratification documents, and arranged a permanent working group on the ratification (ICICC 2012c, 8). The activities intensified after civil servants' visit to the ICC in 2013, led by Deputy Minister of Law and Human Rights, Indrayana, who wanted to know whether "crimes committed in the past, but with tendencies to repeat, such as enforced disappearance, [are] still subject to the ICC's scrutiny, particularly if it is requested?" (Saragih 2013a, b). The visit was according to Indrayana a step toward ratification (Saragih and Aritonang 2013).

Regarding the MFA, Wirayuda, Minister of Foreign Affairs during Megawati and the first term of Yudhoyono, told in 2004 that Indonesia wants to wait and see how the ICC will develop (Xinhua 2004). Three years later, he acknowledged the ICC as the only way to prevent impunity for state officials guilty of massive human rights abuses (Khalik 2007a). In 2007, during the CICC's ratification campaign, an MFA official told that the ministry had discussed the ratification with, among others, the TNI and the Attorney General's Office and "It's clear that we'll ratify the statute with support from the parliament, which we've gained. It will deter future crimes on human rights and lessen impunity" (Hotland 2007). To honor ICC Prosecutor Moreno Ocampo's visit to Jakarta in 2008, the MFA organized a meeting on the accession to the Rome Statute (Mugiyanto 2008, 23) and a MFA spokesperson told that the ratification "is just a matter of time" (Hermawan 2009a). Wirayuda's successor Natalegawa was not as enthusiastic about the ICC. In June 2009, still serving as the UN Ambassador, he stated: "The ratification of the Rome Statute is no panacea to abolish impunity, and the fact Indonesia has yet to ratify the treaty does not cause any disadvantages to the country [...]" (Hermawan 2009b). Yet, in 2011, when the MFA, MLHR, and the Department of Defense (DOD) discussed the ratification, only the DOD and some legal scholars were of the opinion that it is not urgent (ICICC 2012c, 6). Until today, draft legislation for the ratification has not been submitted to the Parliament, because the memorandum and draft bill are still under review. As Natalegawa put it in 2013: "We should not be hasty as it [ICC] would have future impacts. [...] the government needs to build a common understanding among a number of ministries [...]" (Sufa 2013; ICICC 2012c, 3, 5–6).

Under Suharto's regime, military officers occupied most key political positions, had allocated seats in the Parliament and it "was widely recognised throughout Indonesia that no one could run the state without the tacit approval and assistance of the TNI" (Kingsbury 2003, 67; see also Schwarz 1999, 3). Although the TNI was removed from political power by 2004, many influential military figures and the Golkar party, which was one of Suharto's tools of power and dominated by the military, have remained visible in the political life of Indonesia (Tomsa 2008, 72ff.). While officially, the DOD is senior to the TNI in political matters, such as the ratification of the Rome Statute, in practice the TNI reports directly to the President. Accordingly, both the DOD and the TNI can together or separately influence the President and create hindrances for the ratification (Sebastian 2011, 13–14; HRW 2010; ICICC 2012c).

The policy of the DOD on the ICC has been ambivalent. According to the US Embassy in Jakarta, the Minister of Defense, Sudarsono, supported the ratification of the Rome Statute in 2008 and his successor, Yusgiantoro, stated in 2011 that the DOD will adhere to the Government position, if it decides to join the ICC (U.S. Embassy 2008; ICICC 2012c, 5–6). However, by May 2013 Yusgiantoro told that he would oppose the ratification (ICTJ 2013; Aritonang 2013b) and it seems that the reason for this change of mind was the TNI. In March 2013, around the same time as the MLHR delegation visited the ICC, Yudhoyono met with TNI generals and the meeting was suspected to have to do with the visit. In May 2013, it was reported that people close to TNI generals had been lobbying the DOD to stall the ratification and this might well explain Yusgiantoro's new position on the ratification (Lumanow 2013; Aritonang 2013a; Saragih 2013c).

The TNI together with the police forces opposes ratification, due to the fear that some of its generals would end up in front of the ICC for current or past human rights abuses (The Jakarta Post 2009a; Aritonang 2012; HRWG 2012). Such figure is for instance General Wiranto, who was found guilty for command responsibility for crimes against humanity committed in East Timor, but ran for the Presidency in the 2004 elections and for the Vice Presidency in the 2009 elections (UN News Centre 2004; ICTJ and KontraS 2011, 57–58; Kingsbury 2003, 68–69). The former Chair of the Komnas-HAM confirms that the military has negatively influenced Indonesia's position on the ICC:

> Marzuki Darusman, the executive director of the Human Right Resource Center for ASEAN, said [...] that the military's fears about the ramifications of adopting the convention had stopped the House of Representatives from deliberating the convention. 'They are yet to understand that the Rome Statute will only be applicable for actions in the future after a party signs it, not for human rights violations in the past,' [...] Marzuki cited that in 2008 the government had planned to ratify the

> statute. 'However, there have been difficulties since the military's concerns that the court will hold a trial over violations in the past was transferred to the Defense Ministry. Then, there was a debate within the government' [...]. (The Jakarta Post 2011)

Another influential TNI figure is General Widjojo, who in 2011 took a stance on the ICC by stating: "the legal process in the ICC is vulnerable to political intervention. 'That's why Indonesia needs more time to ratify the Rome Statute'" (Nababan and Meliala 2011; see also Taufiqurrahman 2007; Khalik 2007c). Considering that Widjojo worked as Yudhoyono advisor in 2011, who himself is a former TNI General and has appointed his relatives and close allies to high positions in the Army, one could suggest that the TNI's policy plays a key role in the ratification (Crouch 2010, 152; Parlina 2011; CICC 2011)

8.2.4 The Not-So-Transparent Legislative

Before the MFA can submit the Rome Statute for the President's ratification, the Indonesian House of Representatives (DPR) needs to support the ratification. According to newspaper sources, deliberations on the Rome Statute in the DPR have been stalled since 2004 and the Jakarta Post puts the blame on the resistance of "certain fractions" (The Jakarta Post 2009c; Lumanow 2013). Even if there are deliberations on the issue, finding out what is going on in the DPR is not easy, as Tomsa elaborates:

> transparency in the DPR is dreadfully low and important decisions are often made behind firmly closed doors [...] In fact, the key discussions in the legislature are rarely held in the actual special committees [...], but in small informal working committees [...] that are usually headed by the leaders of the parties' parliamentary fractions. (Tomsa 2008, 77)

However, regarding the ratification of the Rome Statute, two "formal" Commissions are central: Commission I on Foreign Affairs and Security and Commission III on Law and Human Rights, which is also in charge of the implementation of the RANHAM (PGA 2009b). Moreover, the two most vocal ICC supporters among the parliamentarians have been both members of the Commission I, represent the Golkar party, and have previously served as Attorney Generals: Sambuaga, chair of

Commission I and the Indonesian PGA, and Darusman, the former chair of the Komnas-HAM (Robinson and Hadiz 2004, 113; PGA 2006; Tomsa 2008, 2, 58, 82, 95).

In 2007, Darusman and Sambuaga organized a meeting on the ICC at the DPR, where parliamentarians and civil servants agreed to follow the RANHAM-plan and join the ICC by 2008. After the meeting, Commission I started to urge the government to submit the accession bill to the DPR (CICC 2007b; Khalik 2007a; CICC 2008a, b). However, according to the US Embassy, by September 2008 the MLHR had not coordinated much with the DPR on the ratification, although the DPR prioritized the matter over other bills. This

> suggests that the DPR intends to give it high priority. DPR legislation typically passes with a broad multiparty consensus. So far, there has been very little public comment on the principle of ICC accession, so it is difficult to tell how easy it will be to reach consensus. That said, if the government pushes, the DPR will probably get on board without too much problem. (U.S. Embassy 2008)

In 2009, DPR's Commissions I and III and the Legislative Council hosted another conference in the framework of the PGA. According to parliamentarians of major parties, there were no obstacles for the accession to the ICC and the ratification bill should be adopted by June 2009. The parliamentarians noted that there had been no clarity about the accession process for two years and called the government to speed up the process (The Jakarta Post 2009a; PGA 2009a). Sambuaga said that Indonesia has "nothing to lose and all to gain" (PGA 2009a) and the chair of the Commission III stated that his commission "is united in support of the ICC and may be able to approve the Accession to the ICC Statute in a few hours' session, provided that the relevant Bill is promptly submitted to its attention by the Government" (PGA 2009b). The deputy chair of the Commission III even envisioned the establishment of a committee for the implementation of the Rome Statute after the ratification (PGA 2009b; The Jakarta Post 2009a).

However, the government did not submit the Rome Statute to the DPR's deliberation before the end of the legislative period in 2009 (The Jakarta Post 2009d). In March 2011, the Deputy Chair of Commission III, Syamsuddin (Golkar Party), reiterated the DPR's commitment to the ratification (PGA 2011), but by December 2011, he had changed his mind: "He explained that Indonesia has a law on a human rights court, despite its imperfections, and it is better to improve it than to ratify the Rome Statute" (Nababan and Meliala 2011). In general, the legislative that was elected for the years 2009 and 2014 held more dissenting opinions than its predecessor. In 2013, a representative of the Prosperous Justice Party suspected that the "ratification could be utilized by certain parties to politically assassinate certain senior political figures" (Saragih and Aritonang 2013; Aritonang 2013b) and the Great Indonesia Movement Party stated that it would reject the ratification (Lumanow 2013). However, shortly after these statements, it was reported that the problem lies not with legislators and that senior Parliamentarians were calling for an immediate ratification (Saragih and Aritonang 2013; Sihaloho 2013; Aritonang 2013a). Thus, finding out what goes on in the DPR is challenging.

8.2.5 History of Human Rights Violations

With the support of the USA, Suharto invaded Portugal's colony East Timor in 1975 and East Timor became "the worst manifestation of Indonesia's authoritarian, brutal, and corrupt rule under the Suharto-led New Order government" (Kingsbury 2009, 7; Burr 2001). In August 1999, after the fall of Suharto, 78% of East Timorese voted for independence over autonomy, which had been suggested by President Habibie. The referendum was followed by a wave of violence, as pro-autonomy militias, supported by the TNI and Indonesian police forces, destroyed much of the country's infrastructure, forced 400,000 people to leave their homes, and massacred more than 1000 civilians (ICG 2001a, 2002b; Martin 2001, 94–95; A/54/660 1999). The international audience was outraged. Clinton withdrew all military aid from Indonesia, the EU raised an arms embargo, the UNSC authorized a multinational force to restore peace and security and demanded that all responsible for the violence should be brought to justice (Martin 2001, 103, 109, 112; S/RES/1264 1999; Burr 2001).

After the Komnas-HAM and a UN Commission of Inquiry found that Indonesian military and police forces had been involved in crimes against humanity (Commission to Investigate Human Rights Violations in East Timor 2000; A/54/726 2000), Habibie issued a regulation on human rights courts, which the Parliament, however, did not ratify (ICG 2001a, 13). To avoid an international tribunal, the newly elected

President Wahid assured that the government would fully cooperate with national investigations (A/54/726 2000). However, the promises were mostly about saving Indonesia's face. For many Indonesians, the accused had fought against an international treachery to deprive part of Indonesia's territory and the government wanted to "avoid the international harassment likely to follow a failure to hold accused accountable through Indonesian judicial processes. The 'national interest' in avoiding 'pariah status' is an important factor in MPR [Congress of Indonesia] calculations" (ICG 2001a, 19; Agus 2010, 151; Linton 2006, 20).

Megawati had not hidden her regret over losing East Timor (Miller 2009, 105), but as President she set up a tribunal in Jakarta and in the following two years, twenty defendants were indicted for individual or command responsibility for crimes against humanity. However, all the indicted were acquitted despite the fear that the Jakarta tribunal could be perceived as a show trial: "If [gross human rights violations] are not handled in a serious and genuine way, we fear that the [ICC] will take them on, an eventuality that we must prevent" (ICG 2002b, 8; Agus 2010, 152). While an ICC prosecution was out of question, because the Rome Statute's jurisdiction started not earlier than in July 2002, fears about a negative international response were well founded. In 2005, according to a UN Commission of Experts,

> the prosecutions before the Ad Hoc Court were manifestly inadequate, primarily owing to a lack of commitment on the part of the prosecution, as well as to the lack of expertise, experience and training in the subject-matter, deficient investigations and inadequate presentation of inculpatory material at trial. (S/2005/458 2005, 5–6)

According to EU, USA, and NGOs, the court failed to deliver justice: It was not able to credibly investigate the crimes or prosecute the defendants, and its verdicts and findings were inconsistent (11928/03 (Presse 232) 2003; BBC 2004; Wald 2006, 333; Cohen 2003). In 2006, the UN Secretary-General recommended further examination of the cases (S/2006/580 2006). Accordingly, Indonesia and East Timor established a joint Truth and Friendship Commission, which did not recommend amnesties for the perpetrators, but whose result was a disappointment: "both governments were using the process as an excuse to close the door to further action and provide protection to perpetrators in the name of reconciliation" (ICTJ and KontraS 2011, 27; CTF Indonesia–Timor-Leste

2008, xii–xiv, xvii–xix). Had the Rome Statute had jurisdiction in 1999, there might have been grounds to declare Indonesia as unwilling to prosecute grave human rights violations.

In addition to East Timor, the Government of Indonesia battles with a multitude of human rights issues. Regarding terrorism and internal conflicts, Islamist groupings have fought for the establishment of an Islamic state in different parts of Indonesia for decades. Jihadi attacks include assassinations and bombings of embassies, public and religious buildings, tourist hotels, and nightclubs (ICG 2005a, 2011a; ICTJ and KontraS 2011, 2–3). The conflicts between the TNI and independence movements in Aceh and West Papua have been particularly violent. In Aceh, thousands of civilians lost their lives as a separatist guerilla Free Aceh Movement fought to gain Aceh independence. The conflict continued until August 2005, when a peace agreement was signed (Miller 2009; ICG 2002a, 1, 4; 2005b, 1). In West Papua, insurgency groups sporadically fight guerilla war against the TNI, which in turn has committed atrocities against civilians (ICG 2011c, 2012). Indonesia has enacted laws that provide for local Truth and Reconciliation Commissions for Aceh and Papua, but only the TRC for Aceh has so far been established (ICTJ and KontraS 2011, 31; KontraS 2016). Hypothetically, it is not completely impossible that the ICC could start an investigation, for instance, in West Papua.

Indonesia's account of prosecuting human rights violations of the Suharto era is weak as well. In 2004, Law No. 27/2004 constituted a Truth and Reconciliation Commission to resolve past human rights violations and establish national peace and unity. The law has been criticized as "a mockery of justice [...]. That a victim must first forgive the perpetrator, and by doing so, effectively grant them prosecutory immunity before being able to claim compensation is farcical" (AHRC 2006). Because the law provides for amnesty, the Constitutional Court declared it unconstitutional and unbinding in 2006 (006/PUU-IV/2006 2006). A new law has been under preparation for years (A/HRC/WG.6/13/IDN/3 2012).

The criminal justice system of Indonesia is unwilling to deal with more recent human rights violations too (European Union 2004a, 106). The Komnas-HAM as the only governmental institution has investigated major human rights cases, but the Attorney General's Office, which is responsible for the prosecutions, ignores its reports and blocks the follow-up of investigations (Komnas-HAM 2007; CAT/C/IDN/CO/2

2008; ICTJ and KontraS 2011, 3). The Attorney General is appointed by the President, which may compromise his independence. Accordingly, Yudhoyono's second Attorney General Arief confirmed that human rights cases have been stalled due to political influence (Lutfia 2011; Amnesty International 2001). Moreover, human rights violations committed by the security forces against civilians are tried in non-transparent military courts, which usually pass low sentences or acquit the perpetrators (AHRC 2010). Paradoxically, Indonesia is concerned about the politicization of the ICC, while its own human rights prosecutions are corrupted (European Union 2004a, 106; EEAS 2010a, 160).

8.3 Unsuccessful Attempts to Influence Indonesia

8.3.1 Indonesian Foreign Policy Tradition: Go to Hell with Your Aid!

Indonesia gained independence from the Dutch colonial rule in 1949. However, President Sukarno started to tighten his authoritarian grip in 1957 by introducing a system of "Guided Democracy" that reduced the power of political parties in favor of the TNI, the Communist Party (PKI), and himself (Jones 2001, 32). During the Cold War, Indonesia was one of the only countries in which the USA and the USSR openly battled over influence through military and economic aid. Instead of aligning with either one, Sukarno wanted to create an Asian counterweight (Simpson 2008, 251; Taylor 1965, 212). As Vice President Hatta put it: "Our policy is independent and active—independent because Indonesia does not wish to align herself with either of the opposition blocs [...]; active because it actively carries out a peaceful policy as a loyal member of the United Nations" (Hatta 1958, 480). Considering the independency, the Western powers were perceived as exploiting imperialists, whose aid had strings attached. Thus, Sukarno together with the Indian Prime Minister Nehru and the Egyptian President Nasser was the mastermind behind the NAM, which was established to oppose "colonialist domination" (NAM 2001; Taylor 1965, 208). Thinking of the idea of an active foreign policy, Sukarno started to rally against the new federation of Malaysia in 1963, which he perceived as Britain's colonialism. As Western powers tried to end the conflict by tying economic aid to the termination of the confrontation, Sukarno told the USA to "Go to hell with your aid" (Jones 2001, 263–4; Taylor 1965, 213).

When Malaysia got a seat in the UNSC, Sukarno withdrew Indonesia's membership of the UN (S/6157 1965)—so far the only time a country has terminated its UN membership. The UN membership was resumed in 1966 (S/7498 1966), but in the meantime a military coup had forced Sukarno to transfer powers to right-wing General Suharto. The coup was followed by a purge of the PKI that was assisted by the USA (Vickers 2005, 41–42; Simpson 2008, 2, 178, 185ff.). Although Suharto maintained the illusion of non-alignment, the government was dependent on aid and investments from Japan and the USA (Simpson 2008, 250; Vickers 2005, 166). Thus, Indonesia's economy boomed until the Asian financial crisis of 1997 hit it unexpectedly hard due to rising external debt and slowing exports (The World Bank 1998, 11). As protests against Suharto started to spread, he appointed Vice President Habibie as the President (ICG 1999, 2). The financial crisis also potentially shaped the USA and the EU's future relations towards Indonesia. The USA made IMF assistance conditional on the implementation of massive structural reforms, which devastated Indonesia's economy (Bresnan 1999, 93ff.; IMF 2003, 13ff.). While bilateral trade and investment between the USA and Indonesia declined, EU trade and investments remained stable during the time when they were most needed (Eurostat 2010; U.S. Department of Commerce 2012).

Over decades, the direction of Indonesia's foreign policy has not changed significantly. In terms of diplomatic cooperation, Indonesia emphasizes the importance of ASEAN countries, other neighbors, East Asia, and it "puts a premium on its relations with the United States and the European Union, both of which are major economic partners" (Public Diplomacy Directorate 2003; Embassy of The Republic of Indonesia 2008). Even some discord with Malaysia has remained. Based upon an agreement of 1997, Indonesia and Malaysia brought a dispute over two islands to the ICJ, which Indonesia bitterly lost and which still might negatively influence its stance towards international courts (ICJ 1998, 2002). Intriguingly, a lot of emphasis is placed on reputation and bilateral relations. For instance, in 2003 the MFA decided to "Restore Indonesia's international image; [...] as well as promote international cooperation that helps build and maintain world peace" (Public Diplomacy Directorate 2003).

During his visit to the USA in 2008, President Yudhoyono described the twenty-first century as one of soft power and globalization and Indonesia's international approach as an "'all direction foreign policy' where we have 'a thousand friends and zero enemy'" (Yudhoyono 2008). The objective to maintain friendly relations in all directions does not provide firm ground for international commitments, such as the USA and EU campaigns on the ICC, because if Indonesia would align with one, it would anger the other one. In general, it seems that the decision to join the ICC would not result from US or EU policies: "Neither the academic memorandum nor the bill itself would address U.S. or other third-country positions regarding the ICC, Harkrisnowo stated. The impact of Indonesia's accession on its relations with other countries was a separate issue that the Department of Foreign Affairs (DEPLU) was already considering but that would not play a major role in the accession" (U.S. Embassy 2008).

8.3.2 *Indonesia and the BIA Campaign of the Bush Administration*

Throughout Suharto's rule, the USA and Indonesia were close allies. However, due to a massacre of protestors in Dili in 1991, the USA suspended its military training in the country, and during the East Timor crisis, Clinton stalled all military cooperation (ICG 2002c). Starting in 2005, the Bush Administration gradually resumed military cooperation and waived Clinton's arms embargo. Before 2005, the US Congress had made military aid to Indonesia conditional on credible prosecution of human rights violations (The White House 2005; H.R. 2673 2003 s. 587 (a); H.R. 4818 2004 s. 572. (a)), and in 2006, it also noted that the US military aid and arms exports are only available, if:

> the Indonesian Government is prosecuting and punishing [...] members of the Armed Forces who have been credibly alleged to have committed gross violations of human rights; [...] the Armed Forces are cooperating with civilian judicial authorities and with international efforts to resolve cases of gross violations of human rights in East Timor and elsewhere [...]. (H.R. 3057 2005 s. 599F. (a))

This Act also mentioned that the above conditions could be waived, if doing so is in the US national interest. Hence, military relations were resumed in the name of national interest, and in 2005, US military aid jumped to USD 7.6 million compared to USD 600,000 in 2004. While Indonesia's geopolitical position and the war on terror were the most important incentives to resume military cooperation (U.S. Department of State 2006; USAID 2007), China's interest in the country motivated the Bush Administration too. Moreover, the Indonesian and East-Timorese TFC might have eased the decision or, the other way around, the US policy to tie aid to post-conflict justice might have influenced the establishment of the TFC (S/2005/458 2005, 7–8).

As with all other countries, the Bush Administration lobbied Indonesia to sign a Bilateral Immunity Agreement (BIA), but Indonesia never signed one. Yet, seemingly at least Megawati considered signing a BIA, because her Administration contacted the Cambodian government regarding the details of its BIA (U.S. Embassy 2003). When the BIA campaign had been running for a year, high officials of the Bush Administration started to pressure their Indonesian counterparts intensively. In March 2004, Bolton visited Jakarta and tried to convince Foreign Minister Wirajuda to sign a BIA. After the meeting, Wirajuda asked

> what will happen if any Indonesian citizens are brought before the ICC, will the U.S. do the same or not?,' Hassan said. [...] considering the fact that key nations like China, Russia, Japan and India have signed neither the Rome Treaty nor Article 98 Agreements with the U.S. 'Why should we be in a hurry to sign an Article 98 agreement with the U.S.?' (Anjaiah 2004; Xinhua 2004)

In 2006, the Secretary of State Rice was about to visit Indonesia and a BIA was supposed to be on the agenda of her meeting with Yudhoyono:

> We want Indonesia to sign an Article 98 waiver [...] Underline your support for an Article 98 agreement, noting the personal commitment that POTUS made and you implemented to make normal military relations possible, and explain that such an agreement would benefit both parties and assist during discussions with and within Congress this year on military relations with Indonesia. (U.S. Embassy 2006e)

Rice confirmed that she had brought up the issue with Indonesian officials. According to the Associated Press, Yudhoyono had requested USD 7 million of military aid from Rice, which could be compromised if Jakarta refuses to sign a BIA (Associated Press 2006).

The cable briefing Rice for her visit is not the only one that brings up the possibility that signing a BIA would benefit Indonesia in terms of military aid. In 2006, US Assistant Secretary of State Hillen met with Defense Minister Juwono, and while discussing military aid and arms sales, Hillen "stressed the importance of describing to Congress bilateral activities and accomplishments. Conclusion of an Article 98 Agreement [...] would signal progress in the relationship" (U.S. Embassy 2006a). Hillen visited Juwono later in 2006 and brought up the issue again (U.S. Embassy 2006h), as did the Pacific Command Admiral Fallon in his meetings with Juwono and TNI Chief Suyanto (U.S. Embassy 2006c, d). A cable briefing Secretary of Defense Rumsfeld for his Jakarta visit in 2006 advises him to underline "support for an Article 98 agreement and explain that such an agreement would benefit both sides and assist during discussions with and within Congress this year on military relations with Indonesia" (U.S. Embassy 2006g).

In addition to Yudhoyono and the DOD, the Bush Administration also approached the MFA. During bilateral political-military talks in 2006, Hillen brought up the issue with the Director for North and Central America in the MFA, Purwanto, who

> explained that having just embraced democracy, the Indonesian government must reflect the positions of all stakeholders—and some oppose conclusion of an agreement that could facilitate impunity for human rights abuses. Further, because Indonesia is not a party to the Rome Statute, it need not consider a non-surrender arrangement. (U.S. Embassy 2006b)

Intriguingly, Purwanto refers to other stakeholders' (most probably the local public's opposition) as the main reason for unwillingness to sign the agreement. It might also be possible that local NGOs or even the EU as an important donor country influenced this statement. The MFA made a similar statement two months later, when Assistant Secretary of Defense Rodman discussed with MFA Secretary-General Cotan. Cotan told that Indonesia questioned the necessity of a BIA, because it was not an ICC State Party. He emphasized the fact that the government would need the support of the DPR for signing one and that it was hard to deal with the DPR's Commission for Foreign Affairs (U.S. Embassy 2006f). Although Indonesian government seemed staunch with its decision, the Bush Administration did not give up. In June 2007, Assistant Secretary of State Mull asked Cotan about Indonesia's potential accession to the ICC and noted that there were "restrictions" from the US side to ICC States Parties (U.S. Embassy 2007).

Over the years, Indonesia reasoned its unwillingness to sign a BIA with the fact that it was not party to the Rome Statute, and therefore, there were no grounds to such an agreement (Anjaiah 2004; Xinhua 2004; U.S. Embassy 2006b, f). Also, as the cable briefing Rice for her Jakarta visit notes: "Indonesia's historical non-aligned orientation and jealous safeguarding of national sovereignty have made it cautious in entering into bilateral agreements" (U.S. Embassy 2006e). Moreover, although Yudhoyono was interested in military and economic cooperation, there is a lot of anti-Americanism among the Indonesian public and parliamentarians, who do not want Indonesia to follow pro-Western policies (Pepinsky 2010; Murphy 2012). Considering the Obama effect that positively influenced some countries decision to join the ICC, apart from the adoption of the national RANHAM in 2011, there were less positive signs of Indonesia's accession to the ICC during the first term of the Obama than during the Bush Administration, although Obama had a better relationship with Yudhoyono than Bush did (King 2011, 303).

8.3.3 *Falling on Deaf Ears: The European Union's Campaign for the ICC*

The EU is a significant trade partner to Indonesia and EU institutions, and EUMS are the second largest donors of development aid after Japan (OECD 2012). Of the EU member states, France, the Netherlands, the UK, and Germany have the strongest economic ties and the UK and France are extensively involved in arms sales to Indonesia (European Union 2000, 27; 2012a, 12). In the last twenty years, the EU has been interested in developing closer ties with Indonesia, because it is a key player in the Asia-Pacific region and in the Muslim world (COM (2000) 50 final 2000; European Union 2004b, 2012a, 9). However, development aid and bilateral trade have not transferred into political influence at least if Indonesians are asked. They rank the USA and other Asian countries as key strategic partners while the EU is primarily perceived as a trade partner that plays a role in low politics (Luhulima et al. 2009, 122; Chaban 2011, 23). However, according to the EU, its importance in policy and security issues is growing as its soft power image balances China's rise in the region (European Commission 2007, 13). In terms of security policy, the Aceh Monitoring Mission to support the peace process in Aceh between 2005 and 2006 probably influenced positively the EU's standing and it was also important for the EU as the first EU/ESDP-led mission in Asia (EU Council Secretariat 2006).

Over the years, the EU has been concerned over Indonesia's human rights situation, including the death penalty, arbitrary detentions, extra-judicial killings, forced disappearances, torture, harassment of activists, and the culture of impunity, and has pushed it to investigate human rights violations effectively and transparently (European Union 1999; 11928/03 (Presse 232) 2003; European Union 2012a, 34). The EU's persuasion for the ICC started in 2003 at the latest, when the Commission proposed to revitalize EU-ASEAN relations, including the accession to the Rome Statute. The EU Council greeted the initiative and in January 2004 called on Southeast Asian countries to join the ICC (5518/04 (Presse 25) 2004; COM (2003) 399 final 2003, 15). As predicted by the normative binding argument, the first official reference to the EU's promotion of the ICC in Indonesia came around the same time as the Bush Administration intensified its BIA campaign. The EU held a diplomatic *démarche* to promote the Rome Statute at some point between July 2005 and July 2006 (European Union 2006, 5, 39), and in January 2006, the head of the Indonesian Legal Aid Institute stated that "Should Indonesia sign a NSA, Indonesia's bilateral relations with the European Union will be threatened" (BBC 2006). In March 2006, the Associated Press noted that Indonesia "has been under pressure to rapidly ratify the [Rome] accord" (Associated Press 2006).

Considering issue-linkages, the EU and Indonesia negotiated a Partnership and Cooperation Agreement (PCA) between 2005 and 2007, which entered into force in 2014 as the first of its kind between the EU and an ASEAN state (15945/09 (Presse 332) 2009; 140501/01 2014). In addition to economic cooperation, environment, and security, an essential element of the agreement is its human rights clause, which ties the agreement to a good human rights account, allows the EU to revise it if Indonesia seriously, and continuously violates human rights and which launched a dialogue on human rights (EEAS 2010a, 160–61). Like all other PCAs, this one also included an ICC clause. The preamble reaffirms both parties' commitment to the Rome Statute and according to Art. 4, Indonesia and the EU will cooperate on the implementation of the RANHAM, including the ratification of the Rome Statute. Moreover, the Commission's explanatory memorandum on the agreement notes "Indonesia has also agreed to a clause committing itself to accede to the Rome Statute of the International Criminal Court"

(COM (2009) 492 final 2009). I have not found sources that would indicate that there were problems with the negotiations on the ICC clause as with the Philippines and Thailand.

In addition to the PCA, the EU-Indonesia Strategy Paper, which set the agenda for EU development aid for Indonesia for the years 2007–2013, defined the implementation of the RANHAM as one of its objectives. Along the lines of the normative binding argument, the Paper mentions Indonesian NGOs, which the EU plans to include in its human rights programs together with cooperation with the government (European Commission 2007, 25). The EEAS reported that the ICC was formally discussed with the Indonesian government in 2008, a month before the RANHAM deadline for the ratification expired (EEAS 2010a, 161), but despite the persuasion, the EU had to note that Indonesia did not meet the RANHAM target (EEAS 2010b, 36; European Parliament 2010). Nevertheless, in 2010 the EU recapped its support for the ICC and welcomed Indonesia's commitment to accede the Rome Statute (European Union 2010).

Since 2010, the EU and Indonesia have discussed the ICC mainly in the framework of the annual human rights dialogue and it seems that the EU has not put as much effort into the ratification campaign in Indonesia as in many other countries. For instance, none of the Blue Books on EU–Indonesia development cooperation mention the ICC, and there are no references to diplomatic *démarches* since 2009 (European Union 2011, 2012c; EEAS 2011, 2012a). This rather phlegmatic approach could be explained by Indonesia's strategic significance. The EU might not want to push it on every issue, but concentrates instead on improving the relationship in general. The fact that Indonesia strongly emphasizes state sovereignty might also contribute to the EU's lack of willingness to invest in the ratification campaign too, because even if the EU would push harder on the issue, the response would probably not change.

8.4 Socialization and Non-Ratification

8.4.1 Different Strands of Persuasion

The academic field in Indonesia is split on the issue of the ICC. The most vocal supporter of the court among legal scholars is Muladi, who has served as Habibie's Minister of Justice and Human Rights, the head of Indonesia's delegation to the Rome conference, and as law professor at Diponegoro University. Moreover, Constitutional Court Justices Mahfud and Mochtar support the ratification, and according to Mochtar, the Rome Statute does not violate the Constitution or the criminal law in Indonesia (Muladi 2011; Nababan and Meliala 2011; ICICC 2012c, 7–8). To the contrary, Professor Juwana of the University of Indonesia, among many other legal scholars, publicly opposes the ICC. According to Juwana, the Darfur case showed that the ICC trumps the principle of state sovereignty and creates double standards for developing and developed countries. Moreover, with the law on human rights courts, Indonesia has demonstrated its ability to prosecute grave human rights violations and there is no need for the ICC (Juwana 2009; Nababan and Meliala 2011). In general, many hold the opinion that a foreign institution should not interfere in the domestic judiciary and Indonesia should reform its own legal system before the ratification (Pangaribuan 2012).

Indonesian NGOs supporting the ICC are organized under Indonesian Civil Society Coalition for the International Criminal Court (ICICC), which was established fairly late compared to many other countries, in 2006 (ICICC 2012a). In addition to the ICICC and the CICC, the International Center for Transitional Justice and the PGA actively promote the ICC and the EU has directly funded NGO projects on international justice and the ICC (European Union 2012b; Delegation of the European Union 2008). The persuasion has taken two main forms: information sharing and organizing of conferences.

ICICC members have prepared an academic paper on the ratification, drafted a ratification bill, and published a book on the importance of the Rome Statute (Hamid and Pangaribuan 2012; IKOHI 2008b; ICICC 2012b). Indonesia has been the target of the CICC's ratification campaign in May 2007, June 2008 and 2009, and July 2011 and 2012 (CICC 2012) and ICC supporters encourage the government to accede the court by bringing to the fore the advantages of the ICC. The arguments are mainly rational, based upon the complementarity of the Rome Statute and the fact that the ICC does not threaten state sovereignty, but may protect Indonesians from grave human rights abuses. In reflectivist manner, they emphasize that Indonesia would lift its international image by joining the ICC (Hamid 2011; Hamid and Pangaribuan 2012; Mugiyanto 2009, 2011; Yudhawiranata 2005).

Regarding conferences, Switzerland, Canada, Norway, and NGOs organized a number of meetings around the time that the ratification was supposed to follow in 2008 (CICC 2007a; Anjaiah 2008; Norway 2008; IKOHI 2008b; PGA 2009a, b). At a diplomatic briefing on the ICC in Jakarta, the Swiss Ambassador said:

> It is my firm opinion that the ICC needs Indonesia on board. [...] Indonesia has now an opportunity to set a landmark example for its region. Political commitment as well as firm action is needed. Among other means, advocacy will certainly remain essential and in addition to NGOs, media may also have an important role to play [...] in fostering understanding within society, supporting thereby the work of the Government and of the Parliament. (IKOHI 2008a)

These events triggered government reactions on the issue, not least because government officials were often invited as speakers. Yet, Yudhoyono did not engage the civil society in the ratification process as the Komnas-HAM noted at Indonesia's 2012 UPR: "the consultation process between the Government and stakeholders was more temporary (just before a report's submission) rather than continuous and long term" (A/HRC/WG.6/13/IDN/3 2012, 2). At the same UPR, Indonesia accepted several countries' recommendations to accede to the Rome Statute, but did not act upon them (A/HRC/21/7 2012).

The ICC itself has also made efforts to move Indonesia toward joining it. In 2004 and 2013, Indonesian delegations visited The Hague and ICC officials have tried to convince the delegates that the court has no universal jurisdiction (Razak 2004). In 2008, ICC Prosecutor Moreno Ocampo met with Foreign Minister Wirajuda and Defense Minister Sudarsono (ICC-ASP/7/25 2008, 10–11) and one year later, ICC President Song arrived in Jakarta. When Song was asked the purpose of his visit, he answered:

> I think this country is the most important, the most influential one in the international community. I am taking this opportunity to find out why you missed your target on ratifying the Rome Statute by the end of last year and to find out if there is anything we can do to perhaps help your government speed up the ratification of the Rome Statute. (Song 2009)

After the year 2009, efforts to persuade Yudhoyono into joining the ICC decreased. In 2011, the ICICC and Paramadina University organized a regional meeting for Asian countries on the ICC, where it was said that "the ratification was included [...] in the 2010–2014 [RANHAM] but there is no guarantee that the government will ratify unless there is strong pressure for them to do it" (CICC 2011, 10). Whether NGOs, other states, or the ICC will ever be persuasive enough to convince Indonesia about the ICC remains to be seen.

8.4.2 Regional and International Reflections

Two regional aspects potentially impact Indonesia's decision to join the ICC. The positive aspect is that by so doing it would profile itself as a trendsetter among Asian countries, which are underrepresented at the ICC. If it wishes so, Indonesia as the most influential ASEAN state has the potential to attract other states to follow its example and regarding regional efforts to strengthen human rights protection, it has already shown such tendencies. In addition to Malaysia, the Philippines, and Thailand, it has a national human rights commission (Komnas-HAM) and since 2007, the four national commissions worked on establishing an ASEAN human rights mechanism that is envisaged in Art. 14 of the ASEAN Charter of 2008 (Abbas 2012). The latest development in furthering human rights cooperation in the region is the ASEAN Human Rights Declaration of November 2012. The declaration mentions international institutions as partners of cooperation, but the promotion and protection of human rights are primarily the responsibility of nation-states and achieved in accordance with the ASEAN Charter that heavily emphasizes state sovereignty, territorial integrity, and non-interference.

The second aspect—the ASEAN affection for state sovereignty and territorial integrity and the fact that many Asian-Pacific countries are wary of human rights mechanisms—poses an obstacle for Indonesia's positive engagement with the ICC for three reasons. First, since Asia is underrepresented in the ICC, Indonesia does not stand out if it does not join the court. Second, Indonesia's regional dependence network plays a role in the non-ratification, as Asian "leaders also worry that their friends and colleagues may be the subject of a trial too, [...] So non-ratification is a way of avoiding such an eventuality" (Macan-Markar 2003). Third, the fact that Asian countries perceive human rights as a Western and specifically a European project might discourage Indonesia from attracting other states to follow it (European Commission 2002, 28). As Kivimäki points out, in contrast to regional integration, ASEAN states pursue cooperation through independence, sovereignty, and non-inference in each other's internal affairs (Kivimäki 2012). As such, Indonesia's approach to the ICC is not exceptional in the region. To conclude, the ASEAN mind-set is wary of international law, it does not easily compromise state sovereignty in favor of the ICC nor does it speak for successful norm diffusion or offer good perspectives for normative binding attempts.

In the international arena, the outlook is also twofold. In the eyes of the ICC States Parties, the ratification would raise Indonesia's international profile, as professor Juwana speculates: "The reason Indonesia sought to ratify the ICC Statute in 2004 might have been to help improve its image internationally, with respect to human rights" (Juwana 2009). Considering such profile setting, it might not have been a coincidence that the RANHAM for the years 2004–2008 was adopted around the same time as Indonesia started its successful campaign for a non-permanent seat in the UNSC. However, Indonesia seems to follow those states that do not support the ICC. The Ministry of Home Affairs stated in 2002 that Indonesia joins the ICC after its States Parties have implemented the Rome Statute and noted that the USA, China, and Russia have joined the ICC (The Jakarta Post 2002). Wirajuda also mentioned the non-ratification of key nations, such as China, Russia, and India, while discussing the BIAs and the ratification in 2004 (Anjaiah 2004).

While Indonesia might prefer to follow those key nations that have not joined the ICC, the development of its policy on the Darfur crisis and its reaction to the indictment of the Sudanese President al-Bashir show that it ultimately pursues its own, economic, interests. Before the ICC had indicted al-Bashir, Indonesia as non-permanent member at the UNSC emphasized that there is no peace without justice and that all perpetrators in Darfur must be brought to justice. Moreover, Indonesia believed "that Sudan's sovereignty must always be respected, but that sovereignty also comes with rights and responsibilities. [...] It is our long-held view that once the Security Council refers a case to the ICC it should be obliged to respect the Court's independence and allow its legal processes to take their due course" (S/PV.5905 2008, 12; See also S/PV.5789 2007, 13). After al-Bashir had been indicted, however, Indonesia aligned with the African Union (AU) and the Arab League calling for deferral of the investigations for the sake of the peace process, assuring that Sudan will follow the principle of complementarity and defending al-Bashir as a legitimately elected head of state (S/PV.5947 2008, 10; S/PV.6028 2008, 14; Budianto 2009).

The reasons behind Indonesia's reaction to al-Bashir's indictment are twofold. On the one hand, Indonesia was concerned about the security of its blue helmets at the AU-UN's operation in Darfur (UNAMID 2012). On the other hand, money plays a big role in the picture. In 2008, the bilateral trade between Indonesia and Sudan increased to USD 780 million (compared to the previous year's USD 240 million) mainly because of a business deal between Indonesia's state-owned oil company Pertamina and the Sudanese government (Roughneen 2009; Embassy of the Republic of Indonesia 2011). Interestingly, the Indonesian Parliament also engaged in boosting the bilateral relations. In 2009, a delegation composed of members of the DPR traveled to Khartoum to collect information about the accusations against al-Bashir. The Parliamentarians were not convinced about the ICC's allegations and the Deputy Speaker told the press "that Indonesia could use her international influential role in supporting Sudan against ICC" (BBC 2009; The Jakarta Post 2009b). In 2011, the Vice Chairmen of the Indonesian and Sudanese Parliaments signed a *Joint-Communiqué* addressing economic and political cooperation, which also included a refusal of al-Bashir's indictment (Ministry of Foreign Affairs 2011). A state that supports the ICC would not sign up to such a *Communiqué*.

8.5 Conclusions: Keeping All Doors Open

When it comes to the ratification of the Rome Statute, Indonesia switches its position depending on the framework in which the issue is being handled. When pushed by external actors, such as the NGOs, the EU, or the UN, Indonesia assures its commitment to the ICC, but the ratification process does not proceed. In the domestic sphere, the lack of political will and the resulting deficiency of coordination among government institutions slow down the accession to the Rome Statute. However, it is questionable whether Indonesia has ever intended to join the ICC, although the ratification has arguably been under debate since 1998. In 2012,

> Indonesia emphasized that the duration of the discussion should not be regarded as a sign of weakness or wavering on anyone's part but, on the contrary, as the determination of the Government to ensure that everyone is involved and that there is a sense of ownership in the eventual accession. (A/HRC/21/7 2012, 7)

Yet, misunderstandings over the ICC's retroactivity have not been corrected and, according to the Chair of Komnas-HAM, the issue needs to be clarified for Indonesia to join the court (CICC 2011, 10). To set the record straight about the ICC is not impossible, and since it has not been done, the government's willingness to conduct a public debate on the ICC is questionable.

Regarding external influence, neither the EU nor the USA has enough influence to get Indonesia to ratify the Rome Statute or to sign into a BIA. The process-tracing pointed out that the question why the EU and the USA have failed in their endeavors finds a twofold answer. First, the leverage of Indonesia allows it to play off these two powerful actors. Regarding the issue-linkages offered by the Bush Administration, the lack of US support during the Asian financial crisis and Indonesia's important role in the war on terror likely increased Indonesia's bargaining power vis-à-vis the USA. Considering the issue-linkages offered by the EU, the support of Europe during the Asian financial crisis might have paid off in the negotiations on the PCA, as the EU is likely perceived as a reliable partner Indonesia did not hesitate to sign into the PCA's ICC clause, which, however, seems to be an insincere commitment to gain the benefits of development aid and bilateral trade. Regarding trade relations with the EU, Indonesia revealed its Janus face by refusing to negotiate a Free Trade Agreement with the EU, probably because the agreement would disadvantage its local manufacturers (Adamrah 2011; EEAS 2010b, 6). While the EU's normative binding attempts have triggered Indonesia to react on the ICC, it has not stood by its promises. Thus, when it comes to a relatively powerful, but reluctant state, the concept of normative binding shows permissive, but not sufficient, conditions for the growth of a coalition in support of the ICC. And after all, the question of why Indonesia would ratify the Rome Statute while it is repeatedly accused of being unwilling and unable to prosecute grave human rights abuses, is a legitimate one (Table 8.1).

However, the main reason for Indonesia's hesitation to join the ICC is its non-aligned foreign policy tradition, which does not prioritize international cooperation or alignment with powerful states. President Yudhoyono's "all direction foreign policy" is a modern version of non-alignment, since being friends with countries with differing agendas inevitably leads to a situation, where one cannot keep one's side of all bargains. The Sudan case elaborates how the policy works in practice. While it took Yudhoyono three years to adopt a new RANHAM

Table 8.1 Theoretical findings of the case study on Indonesia

	External influence	*Liberal explanations*	*Reflectivist explanations*
Reinforcing cooperation	***Normative binding*: Weak** Indonesia was not interested in normative binding An ICC clause was negotiated into the EU-Indonesia PCA, but it did not move Indonesia to ratify the Rome Statute Indonesia responds to EU pressure by making formal statements and empty promises. Thus, normative binding attempts have weak influence	***Governmental motivations*: Mixed** No indications that the executive would be interested in lock-in tactics or credible commitments The promises to join the ICC have been insincere The sovereignty-oriented foreign policy tradition provides strong explanation for non-ratification	***Persuasion*: Weak** Indonesia responds to persuasion by making empty promises. Hence, persuasion has an activating influence, but does not serve its purpose ***Diffusion*: No** Considering the poor ratification rate in Asia, regional diffusion is not a tenable explanation for ratification, although it can explain non-ratification
Obstructing cooperation	***US Policy 1998–2009*: No** Despite active attempts, the USA was not able to move Indonesia into signing a BIA	***Political and Legal Costs*: Strong** Past and ongoing conflicts, terrorism, poor human rights account, and strong military have hindered the ratification No major legal obstacles for ratification	

(continued)

Table 8.1 (continued)

	External influence	*Liberal explanations*	*Reflectivist explanations*
Delaying cooperation	***Obama Effect*: No** Since the Obama Administration entered the White House, there has been less indications of Indonesia's willingness to join the ICC	***Political and Legal Process*: Mixed** The executive has been reluctant to ratify, legislative mixed about the issue The government claims, unconvincingly, that legal review of the Rome Statute slows down the ratification No evidence for legal or economic hindrances to the ratification	
Alternate effects	***Dependence networks*: Mixed** The NAM and other state sovereignty-oriented states form Indonesia's political DN Indonesia recognizes that, e.g., China, Russia, and India are not ICC States Parties Economic interests in the case of Sudan may have tightened Indonesia's stance on the ICC The EU and the USA are important partners in economic terms, but have not influenced Indonesia's agenda		***Common Identities*: Mixed** Common identity with state sovereignty-oriented states may explain non-ratification. No indications that Indonesia would share an identity with ICC supporters

and commit to the ratification of the Rome Statute, the commitment occurred at the same time as he aligned behind al-Bashir and against the ICC. It is not far-fetched to find that Yudhoyono maximized the gains of an oil deal and simultaneously tried to bluff ICC supporters by committing to the ratification. Indonesia's response to al-Bashir's indictment manifested that its intentions to join the ICC were insincere. It ended up undermining the jurisdiction of the court, because of economic interests and because the al-Bashir precedent potentially poses a threat to Indonesian officials. At the same time, it signed up to an agreement in which it promises to accede the Rome Statute. To conclude, Indonesia places a great emphasis on its state sovereignty and territorial integrity and acceding the ICC would potentially compromise these foreign policy maxims and its freedom to conduct an interest-oriented foreign policy.

References

UN Documents (references starting with A/..., CAT/..., GA/..., L/..., and S/...) available at documents.un.org or unbisnet.un.org.

006/PUU-IV/2006. 2006. "Constitutional Court Decision on the TRC Law." Constitutional Court of the Republic of Indonesia.

5518/04 (Presse 25). 2004. "Council Conclusions: South East Asia." Council of the European Union.

11928/03 (Presse 232). 2003. "Declaration by the Presidency on Behalf of the European Union on Ad Hoc Human Rights Tribunal for Crimes Committed in East Timor." Council of the European Union.

15945/09 (Presse 332), Council of the European Union. 2009. "Joint Press Statement: Signing of the Partnership and Cooperation Agreement (PCA) at the Ministerial Troika Meeting Opens New Era for Indonesia-EU Relations." Council of the European Union.

140501/01. 2014. "The EU–Indonesia Partnership and Cooperation Agreement Enters into Force." Council of the European Union.

Abbas, Hafid. 2012. "The Long Road to ASEAN Rights Charter." *The Jakarta Post*, May 23.

Adamrah, Mustaqim. 2011. "EU Mulls Individual FTAs for ASEAN." *The Jakarta Post*, March 2.

Agus, Fadillah. 2010. "Human Rights Courts in Indonesia: A Brief Outline." In *Criteria for Prioritizing and Selecting Core International Crimes Cases*, edited by Morten Bergsmo, 2nd ed., 149–56. Oslo: Torkel Opsahl Academic EPublisher and Peace Research Institute.

AHRC. 2006. *Indonesia: The Human Rights Situation in 2006*. Hong Kong: Asian Human Rights Commission.

———. 2010. "Indonesia: The State of Human Rights in 2010—Ongoing Impunity, Military Violence and Challenges for the New AG." Hong Kong: Asian Human Rights Commission.

Amnesty International. 2001. "Amnesty International's Comments on the Law on Human Rights Courts (Law No.26/2000)".

Anjaiah, Veeramalla. 2004. "Indonesia in No Hurry to Sign ICC Accord with U.S." *The Jakarta Post*, March 18.

———. 2008. "Canada Backs RI's Human Rights Efforts." *The Jakarta Post*, July 7.

Aritonang, Margareth S. 2012. "Government Blasted on Rome Statute Delay." *The Jakarta Post*, July 18.

———. 2013a. "Politics Stalls Ratification." *The Jakarta Post*, May 16.

———. 2013b. "Govt Officially Rejects Rome Statute." *The Jakarta Post*, May 21.

ASIA-Pacific Human Rights Information Center. 2002. "Asia Campaign on the Rome Statute Ratification." *Focus, HURights Osaka* 27.

Associated Press. 2006. "Rights Groups Criticize U.S. for Urging Jakarta to Shield Americans from International Court," March 16.

BBC. 2004. "US 'Dismayed' at E Timor Tribunal." *BBC News*, August 10.

———. 2009. "Indonesian Parliamentary Delegation to Visit Sudan," March 17.

———. 2012. "Indonesia Cancels Netherlands Visit over Arrest Threat", October 5, 2012.

Bresnan, John. 1999. "The United States, the IMF, and the Indonesian Financial Crisis." In *The Politics of Post-Suharto Indonesia*, edited by Adam Schwarz and Jonathan Paris, 87–112. New York: Council on Foreign Relations Press.

Budianto, Lilian. 2009. "Indonesia Questions ICC's Decision on Beshir." *The Jakarta Post*, March 7.

Burr, William. 2001. "East Timor Revisited: Ford, Kissinger and the Indonesian Invasion, 1975–76. National Security Archive Electronic Briefing Book No. 62." Washington, DC: The National Security Archive.

CB/MM-Doc.6. 1998. "Draft Declaration on the United Nations Diplomatic Conference of Plenipotentiaries on the Establishment of an International Criminal Court by the Ministerial Meeting of the Coordinating Bureau of the Non-Aligned Movement." Non-Aligned Movement.

Chaban, Natalia. 2011. "Images of the EU as a Social, Environmental and Developmental Actor: Visions from Asia." *EU External Affairs Review* July 2011, 5–23.

CICC. 2005. "Updates on Indonesia." Coalition for the International Criminal Court.

———. 2007a. "Indonesian Government Officials Announce They Will Accede to the RS by 2008. Country Update." Coalition for the International Criminal Court.

———. 2007b. "Global Coalition Calls on Indonesia to Accede to ICC. Says Country Should Follow Through on Commitment to Join Court by 2008." Coalition for the International Criminal Court.

———. 2008a. "Global Coalition Calls on Indonesia to Join ICC: Says Accession Promised for 2008, the Tenth Anniversary Year of Rome Statute." Coalition for the International Criminal Court.

———. 2008b. "Indonesia, Ratify the Rome Statute on ICC." IKOHI: Victim's Place for Solidarity Building in Fighting for Justice: June 2008, June 13.

———. 2009. "Letter to His Excellency Mr. Susilo Bambang Yudhoyono, President of the Republic of Indonesia. Re: Indonesia's Ratification of the Rome Statute of the ICC." Coalition for the International Criminal Court.

———. 2011. "Asia-Pacific Update." Issue 8. New York: Coalition for the International Criminal Court.

———. 2012. "Universal Ratification Campaign, Target Countries." *Coalition for the International Criminal Court.*

Cohen, David. 2003. *Intended to Fail: The Trials Before the Ad Hoc Human Rights Court in Jakarta.* New York: International Center for Transitional Justice.

COM (2000) 50 final. 2000. "Communication from the Commission to the Council and to the European Parliament: 'Developing Closer Relations Between Indonesia and the European Union.'" Commission of the European Communities.

COM (2003) 399 final. 2003. "Communication from the Commission: A New Partnership with South East Asia." Commission of the European Communities.

COM (2009) 492 final, 2009/0133 (ACC). 2009. "Proposal for a Council Decision on the Signing of the Framework Agreement on Comprehensive Partnership and Cooperation Between the European Community and Its Member States, of the One Part, and the Republic of Indonesia, of the Other Part." Commission of the European Communities.

Commission to Investigate Human Rights Violations in East Timor. 2000. "Executive Summary Report on the Investigation of Human Rights Violations in East Timor." East Timor Action Network.

Crouch, Harold A. 2010. *Political Reform in Indonesia After Soeharto.* Singapore: ISEAS Publishing.

CTF Indonesia–Timor-Leste. 2008. "Final Report of the Commission of Truth and Friendship (CTF) Indonesia—Timor-Leste".

Delegation of the European Union, Indonesia. 2008. "European Instrument for Democracy and Human Rights (EIDHR): EU Aid in Furthering Democracy and Human Rights in Indonesia." Jakarta.

EEAS. 2010a. "Human Rights and Democracy in the World. Report on EU Action July 2008 to December 2009." Brussels: European External Action Service.

———. 2010b. "Indonesia Mid-Term Review 2011–2013." Brussels: European Union External Action.

———. 2011. "EU Annual Report on Human Rights and Democracy in the World in 2010." Brussels: European External Action Service.

———. 2012a. "Human Rights and Democracy in the World. Report on EU Action 2011." Brussels: European Union External Action.

———. 2012b. "Indonesia & The EU: Political & Economic Relations." Brussels: European Union External Action.

Embassy of the Republic of Indonesia. 2011. "RI Optimistic South Sudan Referendum to Remain Peaceful." Washington, DC.

Embassy of The Republic of Indonesia, Washington, DC. 2008. "Indonesia's Foreign Policy/The Principles of the Foreign Policy".

EU Council Secretariat. 2006. "Background: EU Monitoring Mission in Aceh (Indonesia) September 2005–December 2006." ACEH/07. Brussels: Council of the European Union.

European Commission. 2002. "Report of the Conference Held in Brussels 28 and 29 January 2002 and Follow-Up." Brussels.

———. 2007. "Indonesia–European Community Strategy Paper 2007–2013." Brussels.

European Parliament. 2010. "Draft Assessment of the Indonesia Strategy Paper Mid-Term Review 2007–2013." D009672-02-EN-00. Brussels: Directorate-General for External Policies of the Union.

European Union. 1999. *European Union Annual Reports on Human Rights 1999–2006*. Brussels: Council of the European Union.

———. 2000. "European Union Annual Report on Human Rights 2000." Brussels: Council of the European Union.

———. 2004a. "EU Annual Report on Human Rights 2004." Brussels: Council of the European Union.

———. 2004b. "The European Union and Indonesia: European Union Development Co-operation in Indonesia".

———. 2006. "EU Annual Report on Human Rights 2006." Luxembourg: Council of the European Union.

———. 2010. "The Joint Statement of The First Indonesia–European Union Human Rights Dialogue." Jakarta.

———. 2011. "Summary Records: EU–Indonesia Human Rights Dialogue." Brussels.

———. 2012a. "Blue Book 2012: EU–Indonesia Development Cooperation 2010/2011." Jakarta: Delegation of the European Union to Indonesia, Brunei Darussalam and ASEAN.

———. 2012b. "Project Fiche: Strengthening Civil Society Capacity to Promote Accountability for Gross Human Rights Violations." Jakarta: Delegation of the European Union to Indonesia.

———. 2012c. "Indonesia–European Union Human Rights Dialogue: Joint Statement." Jakarta.

Eurostat. 2010. "External and Intra-EU Trade—Statistical Yearbook, Data 1958–2009." European Commission.

Hamid, Usman. 2011. "Why Indonesia, Asia Must Ratify the Rome Statute." *The Jakarta Post*, November 15.

Hamid, Usman, and Aristo Pangaribuan. 2012. "Achieving Universal Humanism and Global Justice." *The Jakarta Post*, April 3.

Hatta, Mohammad. 1958. Indonesia Between the Power Blocks. *Foreign Affairs* 36 (3): 480–90.

Hermawan, Ary. 2009a. "RI Committed to Ratifying ICC, but Doubt Remains." *The Jakarta Post*, May 4.

———. 2009b. "ICC Ratification No Panacea to End Impunity: Marty." *The Jakarta Post*, June 12.

Hotland, Tony. 2007. "Ratifying ICC to 'Deter Rights Crimes.'" *The Jakarta Post*, May 10.

H.R. 2673. 2003. "Consolidated Appropriations Act, 2004." Washington, DC: House of Representatives, Congress of the United States of America.

H.R. 3057. 2005. "Consolidated Appropriations Act, 2006." Washington, DC: House of Representatives, Congress of the United States of America.

H.R. 4818. 2004. "Consolidated Appropriations Act, 2005." Washington, DC: House of Representatives, Congress of the United States of America.

HRW. 2010. *Letter to US Department of Defense Regarding US Military Assistance to Indonesia*. New York: Human Rights Watch.

HRWG. 2012. "Universal Periodic Review on Indonesia: Submission to Indonesia for 1st Session of 2nd Cycle UPR 2012. Indonesian NGO Coalition for International Human Rights Advocacy." Human Rights Working Group.

Huikuri, Salla. 2017. Empty Promises: Indonesia's Non-Ratification of the Rome Statute of the International Criminal Court. *The Pacific Review* 30 (1): 74–92.

ICC-ASP/7/25. 2008. "Report on the Activities of the Court." International Criminal Court.

ICG. 1999. "Indonesia's Shaky Transition." Indonesia Report N° 1. Jakarta: International Crisis Group.

———. 2001a. "Indonesia: Impunity Versus Accountability for Gross Human Rights Violations." Asia Report N° 12. Jakarta: International Crisis Group.

———. 2001b. "Indonesia's Presidential Crisis." Asia Briefing Paper. Jakarta: International Crisis Group.
———. 2002a. "Aceh: A Slim Chance for Peace." Asia Briefing Paper. Jakarta: International Crisis Group.
———. 2002b. "Indonesia: Implications of the Timor Trials." Briefing Paper. Jakarta: International Crisis Group.
———. 2002c. "Resuming U.S.–Indonesia Military Ties." Asia Briefing Paper. Jakarta: International Crisis Group.
———. 2003. "Indonesia Backgrounder: A Guide to the 2004 Elections." Asia Report N°71. Jakarta: International Crisis Group.
———. 2005a. "Recycling Militants in Indonesia: Darul Islam and the Australian Embassy Bombing." Asia Report N°92. Singapore: International Crisis Group.
———. 2005b. "Aceh: A New Chance for Peace." Asia Briefing N°40. Jakarta: International Crisis Group.
———. 2011a. "Indonesian Jihadism: Small Groups, Big Plans." Asia Report N°204. Jakarta: International Crisis Group.
———. 2011b. "Indonesia's Presidential Crisis: The Second Round." Indonesia Briefing Paper. Jakarta: International Crisis Group.
———. 2011c. "Indonesia: Hope and Hard Reality in Papua." Asia Briefing N°126. Jakarta: International Crisis Group.
———. 2012. "Indonesia: Dynamics of Violence in Papua." Asia Report N°232. Jakarta: International Crisis Group.
ICICC. 2012a. "Profile: Indonesian Civil Society Coalition for the International Criminal Court." *Indonesian Civil Society Coalition For the International Criminal Court.*
———. 2012b. "Draft: Naskah Akademis Dan Rancangan Undang-Undang Tentang Pengesahan Rome Statute of the International Criminal Court 1998 (Statuta Roma Tentang Mahkamah Pidana Internasional 1998)." Jakarta: Indonesian Civil Society Coalition for the International Criminal Court.
———. 2012c. "Progress Report: Indonesia Efforts to Ratify the 1998 Rome Statute of the International Criminal Court." Jakarta: Indonesian Civil Society Coalition for the International Criminal Court.
ICJ. 1998. "Indonesia and Malaysia Jointly Bring Dispute Over Islands to the International Court of Justice." Press Release 1998/35. The Hague: International Court of Justice.
———. 2002. "Sovereignty over Pulau Ligitan and Pulau Sipadan (Indonesia/Malaysia), Judgment, I.C.J. Reports 2002, P. 625." The Hague: International Court of Justice.
ICTJ. 2013. "Indonesia Officially Rejects Rome Statute." *International Center for Transitional Justice*, May 22.

ICTJ and KontraS. 2011. *Derailed: Transitional Justice in Indonesia Since the Fall of Soeharto*. New York: International Center for Transitional Justice and KontraS.

IKOHI. 2007. "IKOHI Fights for the Ratification of ICC by Indonesia." *The Indonesian Association of Families of the Disappeared*, January 6.

———. 2008a. "Swiss Ambassador Speech on ICC Diplomatic Briefing by the Indonesian CICC." *The Indonesian Association of Families of the Disappeared*, July 28.

———. 2008b. "EU Urged to Support Indonesia Ratify ICC." *The Indonesian Association of Families of the Disappeared*, November 21.

IMF. 2003. "The IMF and Recent Capital Account Crises: Indonesia, Korea, Brazil." Evaluation Report. Washington, DC: International Monetary Fund.

International Commission of Jurists. 2011. "International Commission of Jurists (ICJ) Submission to the Universal Periodic Review of Indonesia." 13th Session of the Working Group on the Universal Periodic Review, 21 May to 1 June 2012: UNHRC.

Jones, Matthew. 2001. *Conflict and Confrontation in South East Asia, 1961–1965: Britain, the United States, and the Creation of Malaysia*. Cambridge: Cambridge University Press.

Juwana, Hikmahanto. 2009. "Should RI Ratify ICC Statute?" *The Jakarta Post*, April 2.

Khalik, Abdul. 2007a. "RI to Join Global Criminal Court." *The Jakarta Post*, February 10.

———. 2007b. "Indonesia Urged to Ratify ICC's Rome Statue by 2008." *The Jakarta Post*, July 18.

———. 2007c. "SBY Sends 'Reformist' General to Myanmar." *The Jakarta Post*, October 16.

King, Blair A. 2011. "Government and Politics." In *Indonesia: A Country Study*, edited by William H. Frederick and Robert L. Worden, 6th ed., 229–306. Washington, DC: Library of Congress.

Kingsbury, Damien. 2003. *Power Politics and the Indonesian Military*. London: RoutledgeCurzon.

———. 2009. *East Timor: The Price of Liberty*. New York: Palgrave Macmillan.

Kivimäki, Timo. 2012. Sovereignty, Hegemony, and Peace in Western Europe and in East Asia. *International Relations of the Asia-Pacific* 12 (3): 419–47.

Komnas-HAM. 2007. "Submission with Regard to the UPR Mechanism. Related to Indonesia for the 1st Session Scheduled in April 2008." Jakarta: The Indonesian National Human Rights Commission.

———. 2009. "Information on Activities of Komnas HAM Carried Out During the Period of September 2008–July 2009. Submitted to the 14th Annual Meeting of the Asia Pacific Forum on National Human Rights Institutions.

Amman, Jordan, 3–6 August 2009." Jakarta: The Indonesian National Human Rights Commission.

———. 2011. "Submission to the United Nations Universal Periodic Review. 13th Session of The Working Group on the UPR. Human Rights Council, 2012." Jakarta: The Indonesian National Human Rights Commission.

KontraS. 2016. "Presenting Truth Commission in Aceh: A Challenge to Indonesia to Take a Stand on Truth and Justice." Commission for the Disappeared and Victims of Violence, Jakarta.

Liddle, R. William. 1999. "Indonesia's Unexpected Failure of Leadership." In *The Politics of Post-Suharto Indonesia*, 16–39. New York: Council on Foreign Relations Press.

Linton, Suzannah. 2006. Accounting for Atrocities in Indonesia. *Singapore Year Book of International Law* 10: 1–33.

Luhulima, C.P.F., Edward M.L. Panjaitan, and Anika Widiana. 2009. EU Images in Indonesia. In *The EU Through the Eyes of Asia: Volume II New Cases, New Findings*, ed. Natalia Chaban, Martin Holland, and Peter Ryan, 93–124. Singapore: World Scientific Publishing.

Lumanow, Devi. 2013. "World Criminal Court on Agenda in Indonesia." *Jakarta Globe*, March 21.

Lutfia, Ismira. 2011. "Lack of Political Will Hinders Action on Indonesian Human Rights Abuses: AG." *The Jakarta Globe*, November 16.

Macan-Markar, Marwaan. 2003. "Asia: ICC's Uncertain Future Could Be a Break for Dictators." *IPS-Inter Press Service*, December 17.

Martin, Ian. 2001. *Self-Determination in East Timor: The United Nations, the Ballot, and International Intervention.* Boulder: Lynne Rienner Publishers.

Maulia, Erwida. 2008. "Government Urged to Join Int'l Criminal Court." *The Jakarta Post*, July 11.

Miller, Michelle Ann. 2009. *Rebellion and Reform in Indonesia: Jakarta's Security and Autonomy Polices in Aceh.* New York: Routledge.

Ministry of Foreign Affairs. 2011. "Sudan President Expects RI Establish Institute of Engineering and Agriculture." Republic of Indonesia.

Ministry of Justice and Human Rights. 2011. "Human Rights and Constitutional Mandate." Republic of Indonesia.

Mugiyanto. 2008. "Indonesia's Promise to Ratify in 2008 - Fact or Fiction?" *The Monitor: Journal of the Coalition for the International Criminal Court* 26 (May–October): 23.

———. 2009. "Indonesia Is Ready and Should Ratify the ICC." *The Jakarta Post*, April 10.

———. 2011. "Indonesia Should Ratify the Rome Statute on ICC." *Mugiyanto*, July 7. http://mugiyanto.blogspot.fi/2011/07/indonesia-should-ratify-rome-statute-on.html.

Muladi. 2011. "The Necessity to Ratify the 1998 Rome Statute." *The Jakarta Post*, August 23.

Muladi, Minister of Justice. 1998. "Statement by H.E. Mr. Muladi, Minister for Justice, Head of Delegation of the Republic of Indonesia Before the Plenipotentiaries Conference of the Establishment of the International Criminal Court." Republic of Indonesia.

Murphy, Ann Marie. 2012. Democratization and Indonesian Foreign Policy: Implications for the United States. *Asia Policy* 13: 83–111.

Nababan, Pirhot, and Aurora Meliala. 2011. "Ongoing Debate on Rome Statute Ratification." *Hukum Online English*, December 14.

NAM. 2001. "The Non-Aligned Movement: Description and History".

Newsweek. 1998. "Unexpected Allies," July 20.

Norway, The Official Site in Indonesia. 2008. "Norway Co-Sponsors Human Rights Workshops for TNI Officers." February 21.

OECD. 2012. "Query Wizard for International Development Statistics, ODA from DAC-EU Members, USA, Japan, EU Institutions, and All Donors (incl. International Organizations) in Current USD Millions to Indonesia, 2002–2009." Organization for Economic Co-Operation and Development.

Pangaribuan, Aristo. 2012. "Steps to Achieve Universal Humanism and Justice." *Pemuda Indonesia Progresif*, May 31.

Parlina, Ina. 2011. "Imparsial: Yudhoyono Appointing Brother-In-Law to Restore Power." *The Jakarta Post*, June 30.

Pepinsky, Thomas B. 2010. "Politics, Public Opinion, and the U.S.–Indonesian Comprehensive Partnership." NBR Special Report 25. Seattle: The National Bureau of Asian Research.

PGA. 2006. "List of Participants. PGA 28the Annual Parliamentary Forum on Human Security and IV Consultative Assembly of Parliamentarians on the International Criminal Court, Tokyo." Parliamentarians for Global Action.

———. 2009a. "Working Meeting on ICC in Parliament of Indonesia." Parliamentarians for Global Action.

———. 2009b. "Parliamentarians Urge the Indonesian Government to Transmit As Early As Possible to Parliament the International Criminal Court (ICC) Accession Bill. Indonesia's Accession to the Rome Statute of the ICC Anticipated to Take Place Later in 2009." Parliamentarians for Global Action.

———. 2011. "Second PGA Asia-Pacific Parliamentary Consultation on the Universality of the Rome Statute of the International Criminal Court, Kuala Lumpur." Parliamentarians for Global Action.

Public Diplomacy Directorate, Department of Foreign Affairs. 2003. *Indonesia's Foreign Policy*. Wellington, New Zealand: The Embassy of the Republic of Indonesia.

Razak, Imanuddin. 2004. "ICC, an Alternative to Prosecuting War Criminals?" *The Jakarta Post*, April 1.

Robinson, Richard, and Vedi R. Hadiz. 2004. *Reorganizing Power in Indonesia: The Politics of Oligarchy in an Age of Markets.* London: RoutledgeCurzon.

Roughneen, Simon. 2009. "Indonesia: Obama's New Buddy Keeps Bad Company." *World Politics Review*, March 26.

Rully, Sandra. 2012. "Does International Justice Matter for Indonesia?" *The Jakarta Post*, December 11.

Santosa, Mas Achmad. 2013. "The ICC and the Commitment to Human Rights." *The Jakarta Post*, March 19.

Saragih, Bagus B. T. 2013a. "RI Seeks Help on Criminal Court Approval." *The Jakarta Post*, March 3.

———. 2013b. "Denny to Leave for The Hague for Study on Rome Statute." *The Jakarta Post*, March 4.

———. 2013c. "SBY Suspected of Discussing Rights Abuses with Ex-Generals." *The Jakarta Post*, March 14.

Saragih, Bagus B. T., and Margareth S. Aritonang. 2013. "RI to Ratify Rome Statute." *The Jakarta Post*, March 6.

Schwarz, Adam. 1999. Introduction: The Politics of Post-Suharto Indonesia. In *The Politics of Post-Suharto Indonesia*, ed. Adam Schwarz and Jonathan Paris, 1–15. New York: Council on Foreign Relations Press.

Sebastian, Leonard C. 2011. "Assessing 12-Year Military Reform in Indonesia: Major Strategic Gaps for the Next Stage of Reform." Singapore: S. Rajaratnam School of International Studies Working Paper No. 227.

Sihaloho, Markus Junianto. 2013. "Defense Minister Dodges Question on Blocking ICC Treaty's Ratification." *Jakarta Globe*, May 21.

Simons, Marlise. 2010. "Dutch Court Rejects Demand for Indonesia President's Arrest." *The New York Times*, October 6, 2010, Reprints edition.

Simpson, Bradley R. 2008. *Economists with Guns: Authoritarian Development and U.S.-Indonesian Relations, 1960–1968.* Stanford: Stanford University Press.

Song, Sang-Hyun. 2009. "Ratification of Rome Statute Would Signal Belief in Justice. Excerpt of Imanuddin Razak's and Irawaty Wardany's Discussion with ICC President Song." *The Jakarta Post*, May 4.

Sufa, Ira Guslina. 2013. "Govt Prepares International Criminal Court Ratification." *Tempo.Co*, May 24.

Taufiqurrahman, M. 2007. "Amnesties OK for Timor Leste Rights Violators, Says Body." *The Jakarta Post*, January 17.

Taylor, Alastair M. 1965. Sukarno - First United Nations Drop-Out. *International Journal* 20 (2): 206–13.

Terra Viva. 1998. "India and US Broadsides Threaten Consensus, Raise Prospect of Votes on Nuclear Weapons and Jurisdiction." 24 (July).

The Jakarta Post. 2001. "Ratification of ICC Delayed," October 25.

———. 2002. "RI Defers Signing ICC Statute," November 30.

———. 2009a. "House Cannot Wait for Deliberation of Humanitarian Bill," February 19.

———. 2009b. "Legislators to Visit Sudan Over Al-Bashir Issue," March 12.

———. 2009c. "ICC President Due to Arrive for Talks on Rome Statute," April 28.

———. 2009d. "ICC Asks RI to Join Its Ranks," April 30.

———. 2009e. "Chances Dim for Immediate ICC Ratification," May 5.

———. 2011. "Military's Fears Stalling Rome Statute Ratification: Expert," July 21.

The Washington Times. 1998. "The World Court: Symbolism vs. Reality," August 9.

The White House, Office of the Press Secretary. 2005. "Joint Statement Between the United States of America and the Republic of Indonesia: Remarks by President Bush and Indonesian President Yudhoyono." Washington, DC.

The World Bank. 1998. "Indonesia in Crisis: A Macroeconomic Update." Washington, DC.

Thompson, Eric C. 1999. "Indonesia in Transition: The 1999 Presidential Elections. NBR Briefing, Policy Report No. 9." Seattle: The National Bureau of Asian Research.

Tomsa, Dirk. 2008. *Party Politics and Democratization in Indonesia: Golkar in the Post-Suharto Era*. London: Routledge.

UNAMID. 2012. "UNAMID African Union/United Nations Hybrid Operation in Darfur: Facts and Figures".

UN News Centre. 2004. "Timor-Leste Court Issues Warrant for Former Indonesian Defence Minister—UN." United Nations.

UNTC, United Nations Treaty Collection. 2018. "Status of Treaties: Multilateral Treaties Deposited with the Secretary-General".

USAID. 2007. "U.S. Overseas Loans and Grants. Obligations and Loan Authorizations July 1, 1945–September 30, 2007." CONG-R-0105. Washington, DC: U.S. Agency for International Development.

U.S. Department of Commerce. 2012. "Trade in Goods with Indonesia." United States Census Bureau.

U.S. Department of State. 2006. "U.S.–Indonesia Military Ties Moving Toward Full Normalization; But U.S. Presses for Accountability on Past Human Rights Abuses." Washington, DC: State Department Documents and Publications.

U.S. Embassy, Jakarta. 2006a. "Indonesia: A/S Hillen's Meeting with Defense Minister Juwono." Confidential 06JAKARTA1818. Jakarta: U.S. Department of State, Wikileaks.

———. 2006b. "Indonesia–U.S. Politica-Military Talks." Confidential 06JAKARTA1819. Jakarta: U.S. Department of State, Wikileaks.

———. 2006c. "Admiral Fallon's Meeting with Defense Minister Juwono Sudarsno." Confidential 06JAKARTA2744. Jakarta: U.S. Department of State, Wikileaks.

———. 2006d. "Admiral Fallon's Meeting With New TNI Chief Djoko Suyanto." Confidential 06JAKARTA2914. Jakarta: U.S. Department of State, Wikileaks.

———. 2006e. "Your Visit to Indonesia: Moving Our Renewed Bilateral Relationship Forward." Confidential 06JAKARTA2917. Jakarta: U.S. Department of State, Wikileaks.

———. 2006f. "ASD Rodman's Meeting With Indonesian Foreign Ministry SECGEN." Confidential 06JAKARTA5789. Jakarta: U.S. Department of State, Wikileaks.

———. 2006g. "Scenesetter: Secretary Rumsfeld's Visit to Jakarta." Confidential 06JAKARTA6493. Jakarta: U.S. Department of State, Wikileaks.

———. 2006h. "PM A/S Hillen's Political-Military Talks in Jakarta." Confidential 06JAKARTA13170. Jakarta: U.S. Department of State, Wikileaks.

———. 2007. "A/S Mull Updates Bilateral Political-Military Agenda With Indonesian Officials." Confidential 07JAKARTA1656. Jakarta: U.S. Department of State, Wikileaks.

———. 2008. "ICC—GOI Plans to Accede to Rome Statute in 2008." Confidential 08JAKARTA1753. Jakarta: U.S. Department of State, Wikileaks.

U.S. Embassy, Phnom Penh. 2003. "Ambassador's Meeting With Cambodian Foreign Minister Hor Namhong." Classified 03PHNOMPENH1990. Phnom Penh: U.S. Department of State, Wikileaks.

Vickers, Adrian. 2005. *A History of Modern Indonesia*. Cambridge: Cambridge University Press.

Wald, Patricia M. 2006. International Criminal Courts—A Stormy Adolescence. *Virginia Journal of International Law* 46 (2): 319–46.

Wirana, Mulya. 2010. "Statement by the Head of Indonesian Delegation to the Review Conference of the Rome Statute."

Woods, Genevieve. 2011. "From President to Defendant? Time Is Running Out for SBY to Get His House in Order." *Inside Indonesia*, December 1, 2011.

Xinhua. 2004. "Indonesia Considers to Implement ICC Convention." *Xinhua General News Service*, March 17.

Yudhawiranata, Agung. 2005. "Indonesia's Security Policy." *The Jakarta Post*, July 25.

Yudhoyono, Susilo Bambang. 2008. *Indonesia and America: A 21st Century Partnership*. Washington, DC: USINDO Luncheon.

CHAPTER 9

Conclusion

9.1 Normative Binding and the Institutionalization of the ICC

This book puzzled over the institutionalization of the ICC. As the overall argument suggests, the EU was able to influence the institutionalization of the ICC by using normative binding as a foreign policy strategy. The strategy of normative binding aims at making specific norms universally effectual and takes advantage of the binding virtues of institutions and coalition building tactics. Part II demonstrated that the EU successfully acted as a normative binder during the negotiations on the Rome Statute and that its leadership in the domain of international criminal law derives mainly from its commitment to multilateralism. Arguably, multilateralism and the promotion of international institutions can be translated into legitimacy and credibility, which are central attributes of an actor wishing to gain more leverage in the human rights regime. At least in the field of international criminal law, multilateralism proved to be a more useful vehicle to promote one's own and common interests than unilateralist attempts or exceptionalist behavior.

However, at the outset of the negotiations on the ICC, not all European countries shared the same agenda. The US' exceptionalist and unilateral policies toward the ICC deepened the EU's common policy and enabled the EU to take the lead. The ICC became a joint venture of the EUMS, and it also offered an opportunity to raise the EU's international profile and to build an international coalition in favor of multilateral

S. Huikuri, *The Institutionalization of the International Criminal Court*,
https://doi.org/10.1007/978-3-319-95585-8_9

aspirations. Indeed, the abolition of impunity for gravest human rights violations is a neat framework to expand multilateral ideas outside the borders of the EU—who wants to say that punishing genocide is not moral? Or as former UN General-Secretary Annan put it: "You can demand that those who claim the mantle of global leadership accept the duty of promoting global values. None would deny that punishing war crimes, crimes against humanity and genocide is such a value" (Annan 2010).

Yet, the EU's motivation to promote the ICC was manifold. First, the EU does indeed share the humanitarian values of the ICC and wanted to establish a permanent institution to uphold these standards. Second, the EU statements on the ICC continuously point out the desire to intensify the international rule of law and to institute an international order, based on effective multilateralism and not on unilateral exercise of power. Third, a permanent ICC was also a rational choice as it is a more economic and easily accessible alternative to further ad hoc courts that would remain under the control of the UNSC. Lastly, by building support for the ICC, the EU wanted and was able to check and bind US power through international norms. During the negotiations on the Rome Statute, the EU was successful in its undertaking, which proves that institutionalization is not modified by one powerful country, but several powerful actors.

At the Rome conference, the EU-led coalition of Like-Minded States secured relative institutional independence of the ICC, and after the conference, one hundred countries disregarded the US opposition and ratified the Rome Statute over the following six years. The first evidence of the ICC's normative bindingness was the UNSC referral of the Darfur case to the ICC, which the USA eventually did not oppose. After this referral, the ICC conclusively claimed its place in the international architecture and the USA has recognized its standing too. Regarding the purposes and mandate of the ICC, it does not really matter whether the USA perceives it as purely instrumental as long as it does not sabotage the institution—although the US financial support would not, of course, harm the ICC's work.

9.2 Binders, Outliers, and Stragglers

State commitment to the ICC has repeatedly been investigated by quantitative means. This book opted to address the question by utilizing the method of process-tracing within qualitative case studies. The attempt was to show that the process resulting in the commitment cannot easily be explained with one variable but is an outcome of a cascade of events that can still be reduced to certain explanatory variables. While a small-N case study approach does not allow the making of generalizations, the following attempts to draw some inferences.

Germany's commitment to the ICC is puzzling at first sight, especially if one compares it to the US policy. One might expect that the USA, as founder of the UN system and ad hoc international tribunals, would have chosen to support a cooperational solution for the development of international justice too. Alternatively, Germany as the leading EU country, the fourth largest economy, and a relatively strong military power could have hesitated to commit to the ICC like many other powerful countries, such as the USA, China, Russia, or India. Yet, the USA remained outside the ICC and Germany chose to prefer multilateralism. Arguably, Germany's support for the ICC and common norms in general is the result of the peaceful change that was brought about in the post-Second World War developments, in particular European integration and generational changes. Due to these transformations, Germany has become a binder among other EU countries.

In contrast to Germany, it is fascinating that the American policy toward international criminal law has not significantly changed over the decades. From the negotiations on the Genocide Convention in 1947 to the 2010 Kampala Review Conference of the Rome Statute, the USA has had one guiding light above all: the guarding of state sovereignty. This maxim has often been effectively implemented through US power at the UNSC, but in the case of the ICC its inflexibility became America's pitfall. After some years of strong opposition, the USA had to accept the reality of the court and the Obama Administration adopted a friendly approach to the ICC. However, when the USA chooses to cooperate, the decision follows rational calculations and the general approach to international justice is selective, no matter whether the President is a Democrat or a Republican. As Koh put it in 2012:

> Among other things, supporting global criminal justice serves U.S. national interests by promoting a culture of accountability that can help increase stability and thus decrease the need for far more costly military interventions in the future. We have much to gain from the effective functioning of the rule of law, and the architecture of international criminal justice can play an important part in that effort. [...] So, while the United States will always protect U.S. personnel [...] we have applied a pragmatic, case-by-case approach towards ICC issues. (Koh 2012)

Democratic Presidents undoubtedly have been more accommodating to international criminal law and although Republican administrations hesitate to commit to international rules, they do seem to follow them—when it is in the national interest and as long as there are no good reasons to oppose them. A good example of this kind of rationality is the Bush Administration's justification for the withdrawal of the US signature to the Rome Statute. It was argued that the action was consistent with the Vienna Convention of the Law of the Treaties, a treaty that the USA has not ratified. Hence, certain norms, including the ICC, can be perceived as binding even by those who do not formally recognize them. If the ICC would threaten American citizens or other US interests, then the picture clearly changes.

While Part II allowed to conclude that building a normative binding coalition is a valuable strategy in the establishment of international institutions, Part III did not provide solid evidence of persuasion and positive issue-linkages being strikingly effective tools to induce reluctant states to commit to the ICC. The case study on the Philippines' ratification reveals that the commitment can indeed be a result of overlapping processes and interests. The Philippine ratification started to materialize after the regime change from Arroyo to Aquino, but the ICC President's visit to the country served as a trigger for the process. Moreover, the possibility to have a Filipino judge in an international court explains the exact timing of the ratification. Whereas domestic preferences rationalize the timing of the ratification, the case study supports the hypothesis that exogenous pressure exercised by the USA was the reason behind the delay in the ratification. Although President Arroyo had some reasons to be concerned that the numerous human rights violations committed on her watch would qualify for an ICC prosecution, the close relationship to the USA is a more plausible explanation for her hesitance to ratify the Rome Statute. The impact of the US pressure finds extensive support in core primary documentation. Aquino hardly would have ratified the Rome Statute, if the ratification had resulted in economic sanctions. In turn, supposing that the USA had tolerated the ICC from the beginning, Arroyo might have ratified the Rome Statute, because she signed an implementing legislation for the Rome Statute in 2009. Hence, the case study indicates that external pressure is a plausible explanation for the non-ratification decision.

Although the Filipino policymakers were aware and concerned about the European pressure, neither the EU nor the legislative branch, nor the civil society were able to trigger the ratification through persuasion and issue-linkages. However, the outcome ultimately reflected the EU's interests. While normative binding attempts were not successful in the short term, in the endgame the ICC was attractive enough for the Philippines to join the institution. Although one case study does not allow generalization, it contests the existing endogenous and reflectivist explanations for the ratification of human rights treaties. For instance, due to past human rights abuses and a regime change, the Aquino government had several reasons to signal a credible commitment or to lock-in domestic policies, but such aspirations do not surface. Furthermore, the timing of ratification points out that the commitment, when it occurs, is based on rational calculations and not on the logic of appropriateness. If the constructivist theory would hold, then the Philippines had joined the ICC earlier, like the majority of the ICC States Parties, or not at all, like most other ASEAN states. Lastly, instead of the influence of a dependence network, composed of several countries, the change in one single actor's policy, the USA, works as a causal mechanism in the ratification decision.

With the case of Indonesia, the EU's exogenous pressure did not move the domestic political scene to meet Megawati's and Yudhoyono's promises of ratification nor did the Bush Administration manage to conclude a BIA with the country. However, the process-tracing pointed out that the EU's persuasion did not fall on deaf ears. All statements from the Ministries and the Executive on the ICC resulted from actions and events supported by the EU or the civil society. Moreover, as the international society negatively reacted on the aftermath of the East Timor conflict, Indonesia enacted laws and established human rights courts. Although the actions have proved to be empty promises for justice, Indonesia's reactions show that external pressure, if exercised continuously and properly, may have effect on its policy choices.

What is striking about Indonesia is the rigorousness, with which it follows a state sovereignty-oriented foreign policy tradition. While this practice comes very close to the US example, it leaves less space for humanitarian values and undertakings than the American alternative. This is probably explained by the fact that, unlike the US, Indonesia is not interested in pursuing global leadership nor has it the resources or the credibility to do so. It favors an international order based on territorial integrity; a condition in which states co-exist in their own spheres and every state tries to realize its own preferences. However, due to policy interdependence, Indonesia needs to make concessions, if it wants to reap gains from the current system. This leads to the situation where it makes promises in all directions. Indonesia opposes the ICC, because of lucrative oil deals with Sudan, and at the same time it commits to ratifying the Rome Statute, because the EU provides it with development aid. This is an all direction foreign policy indeed, which, however, might easily drift Indonesia into a situation, where it does not have "a thousand friends and zero enemy," but vice versa.

What does, then, a cross-case analysis tell about the similarities and differences between these four states' policies toward international criminal law? Clearly, Germany has the least in common with the other three countries under examination. Germany is a binder and as such a follower of multilateralism and international norms. Together with other European countries, it acts as a norm entrepreneur in the case of the ICC and as a generator of an order, based on the rule of law. In contrast to the value-laden agenda of Germany, the Philippines is a typical straggler, which does not put much weight on international norms, but utilizes them to serve its preferences. The Philippines main interest is to raise its profile in the international arena and in particular in the domain of human rights. This aspiration is easily realized with actions that deviate from other regional actors' behavior, because ASEAN remains a region of laggards in terms of human rights.

Of all four case studies, the USA and Indonesia have most commonalities, the main common denominator being their high regard for state sovereignty. Due to their foreign policy preferences, it is unlikely that either one would join the ICC anytime soon. Nevertheless, the two significantly differ in terms of their international roles, aspirations, and leverage. In the field of international criminal law, the USA is a declining hegemon that despite the erosion of its power keeps on acting as a hegemon and, later than others, notices that its actions are not always fruitful. While the USA actively engages in the development and management of the system, Indonesia is an outlier. It does not take notice of human rights norms and obligations unless the international society forces it to do so and when it acts on issues, the actions are half-hearted attempts to cache its disregard. Compared to the Philippines, however, Indonesia has more leverage to follow its own path, which explains the failure of the EU and the USA to realize their preferences in the country.

9.3 How to Facilitate State Participation to the ICC?

Why do stragglers, who do not put much weight on the human rights regime, decide to cooperate in the framework of the ICC? And what would inspire outliers like Indonesia to do the same? As already stated above, late ratifications of the Rome Statute are best explained with theories of rational choice: Once the threat of losing economic benefits disperses, the domestic decision to join the ICC is "motivated by a conscious calculation of advantages" (Schelling 1980, 4). As the Philippines ratification shows, these advantages need not have a long-term perspective, and as Indonesia's responsiveness to persuasion illustrates, the commitment is not necessarily sincere. These findings are consistent with the hypothesis of issue-linkages being a useful tool of normative binding, which implies that the pay-offs of actions are important for the stragglers and they are more prone to respond to external pressure and persuasion.

Based on these findings, the side product of the theory testing is the exploration of ways that potentially contribute to further commitments to the ICC. Evidently, there is a plurality of strategies that can be employed to influence the evolution of international institutions; some have been used for decades, including the exercise of hegemonic power, bargaining, and economic incentives. Rather novel approaches include persuasion and normative binding. The case studies point out that traditional economic coercion, as exercised by the Bush Administration, effectively brings immediate results, which however are not long-standing. In contrast, normative binding attempts that combine positive tactics of persuasion and economic inducements are a useful strategy to realize one's preferences over time. Since rules do not become normatively binding overnight, the binder needs to be patient, but, as the case of the ICC indicates, the strategy is rewarding in the long-term perspective.

Normative binding can prove to be a useful tool when creating binding international or regional rules or institutions, such as the Arms Trade Treaty, Tobin Tax, or the Asian Court for Human Rights. However, the case studies point out that for normative binding to be effective, the following practical aspects should be taken into account. First, the engagement of normative binding presupposes credible and legitimate leadership of the binder: The binder needs to set an attractive example that others want to follow. Second, especially those who do not jump on the binder's bandwagon voluntarily are likely inclined to respond to short-term incentives. This, thirdly, has the implication that the binder needs to identify what kind of incentives, pay-offs, and persuasion tactics are likely to be effective in specific cases. This presupposes the study of the object's preferences over time. Lastly, one can start to identify windows of opportunity, during which the responsiveness to binding attempts would be optimal as stragglers are prone to respond to short-term incentives. However, as the case of the Philippines showed, over time the result will likely favor international norms, and therefore, normative binding is a promising way to facilitate ratifications to the Rome Statute and other binding norms.

9.4 The ICC's Implications to International Order

The same year when the ICC was created, March and Olsen wrote:

> Nearly everyone agrees that wars, conquests, and foreign occupations will contribute significantly to the elaboration and modification of the international political order, as they have in the past. And nearly everyone agrees that more peaceful, gradual changes will come about because such changes match the changing interests of powerful political actors and the changing demands of the environment. (March and Olsen 1998, 947–48)

While the ad hoc tribunals for former Yugoslavia and Rwanda reflected the power of the UNSC, the institutionalization of the ICC demonstrates that hegemonic struggles in today's world are not necessarily conducted on battlefields, but at negotiation tables and in the domain of international institutions. Accordingly, the international order and the mechanisms of change have themselves been transformed. Most states refuse to accommodate unilateral policies, and instead, credible leadership needs to acknowledge certain common rules. At the very least, the US power faces increasing checks and balances not only at home, but also in the international domain, leading to a situation where the USA cannot realize its preferences as effortlessly as before. Gradual changes strongly reflect the needs of the environment: The ICC undeniably fills a gap in international jurisdiction and corresponds with the needs of the wider international society to overcome the problems of impunity and selective justice. As a result, changes in the order occur through peaceful means, they are slow, and do not always correspond to the interests of the most powerful states.

International cooperation necessitates treaties to establish institutions and international law. Although treaties are based on state consent and are sometimes proven to be powerful, sometimes they also fail. A sad example of treaty failure is the ongoing violence in Syria, which the international community does not manage to restrain. Yet, a world without regulative institutions is not a desirable option. It would be a world of Hobbesian anarchy, steered by self-help and feeding violence between states. More importantly, a world without common rules would leave people more vulnerable to states' arbitrariness. The key to hindering grave breaches of human rights is to gain more control over the behavior of nation states and that is something the ICC can, for its part, legally provide. Yet, the ICC is no silver bullet. It is not self-driven, has no enforcing authority except through judicial proceedings, and relies on its States Parties' financial and political support. However, there is no doubt about the importance of the ICC. Its institutionalization highlights the fact that the international order has changed: No one who commits grave human rights abuses today can be certain that she will go unpunished. Although the ICC will not stop evil for once and for all, it has the potential to make the world a little more just place.

References

Annan, Kofi. 2010. "Address by H.E. Kofi Annan. Review Conference on the Assembly of States Parties to the Rome Statute of the International Criminal Court." Kampala: Kofi Annan Foundation.

Koh, Harold Hongju. 2012. "International Criminal Justice 5.0: Justice Address 2012 at the Vera Institute of Justice, The Paley Center, New York, NY." U.S. Department of State.

March, James G., and Johan P. Olsen. 1998. "The Institutional Dynamics of International Political Orders." *International Organization* 52 (4): 943–69.

Schelling, Thomas C. 1980. *The Strategy of Conflict*. Cambridge: Harvard University Press.

Index

S. Huikuri, *The Institutionalization of the International Criminal Court*,
https://doi.org/10.1007/978-3-319-95585-8

I

J

The manufacturer's authorised representative in the EU is Springer Nature Customer Service Centre GmbH, Europaplatz 3, 69115 Heidelberg, Germany. If you have any concerns regarding our products, please contact ProductSafety@springernature.com

Printed and bound by CPI Group (UK) Ltd, Croydon, CR0 4YY
30/09/2026
02225653-0012